PAGAN MYSTERIES
IN THE RENAISSANCE

PAGAN MYSTERIES
IN THE RENAISSANCE

BY

EDGAR WIND

Oxford New York Toronto Melbourne

OXFORD UNIVERSITY PRESS

1980

Oxford University Press, Walton Street, Oxford OX2 6DP

OXFORD LONDON GLASGOW
NEW YORK TORONTO MELBOURNE WELLINGTON
KUALA LUMPUR SINGAPORE JAKARTA HONG KONG TOKYO
DELHI BOMBAY CALCUTTA MADRAS KARACHI
NAIROBI DAR ES SALAAM CAPE TOWN

First published by Faber and Faber Limited 1958
Second edition published by Penguin Books in association with Faber and Faber 1967
Revised and reprinted by Faber and Faber 1968
First published as an Oxford University Press paperback 1980

British Library Cataloguing in Publication Data
Wind, Edgar
Pagan mysteries in the Renaissance – New and enlarged ed.
1. Art, Renaissance
2. Paganism in art
3. Symbolism in art
I. Title
704.94'6   N6370
ISBN 0-19-281295-5

Printed in Great Britain by
Cox & Wyman Limited,
Reading

TO
MAURICE BOWRA

CONTENTS

CONTENTS

LIST OF ILLUSTRATIONS

ACKNOWLEDGEMENTS

Alinari (figs. 5, 9, 15, 31, 61, 65), Anderson (figs. 2. 6, 16, 25-30, 32-4, 37, 39, 40, 102), Bibliothèque Nationale (fig. 80), British Museum (fig. 73), Brogi (figs. 97, 100, 101), Earl of Crawford and Balcarres (figs. 44, 45), Eton College (fig. 1), Hessische Treuhandverwaltung des früheren preussischen Kunstgutes (fig. 75), Houghton Library, Harvard University (figs. 7, 8, 54, 55), Library of Congress (figs. 20, 95), Louvre (fig. 59), Metropolitan Museum of Art (figs. 76, 83), Musei Vaticani (fig. 19), National Gallery, London (figs. 43, 46, 47, 49, 60, 63, 74), National Gallery of Art, Washington (fig. 51), Duke of Northumberland (fig. 50), Trinity College, Cambridge (fig. 99), Universitätsbibliothek, Erlangen (fig. 48), Victoria and Albert Museum (fig. 91).

PREFACE

ALTHOUGH the argument of this book remains unchanged from what it was in the first edition eight years ago, some stylistic improvements have been attempted, and the documentation has been increased substantially, both in the textual references and in the illustrations. I owe a great debt to my publishers who, instead of confining their enterprise to a third printing, have agreed to produce a fresh book. As before, the footnotes can be ignored by readers more interested in the text than in its foundations; and the same applies to the appendixes, which are new. Although related to problems set by the text, they are conceived as independent pieces.

In preparing this revised edition I have enjoyed the encouragement and advice of Austin Gill and Colin Hardie. Apart from making important amendments, they had the patience to read the whole book in proof. The flaws that remain are my own fault.

On many subjects a bare list of names can scarcely convey what I owe to conversations with Jean Adhémar, Alfred Alexander, Rosalind Dale-Harris, Herbert Davis, Eduard Fraenkel, Cecil Gould, Raymond Klibansky, Lotte Labowsky, Alessandro Perosa, John Pope-Hennessy, Martin Robertson, Jean Seznec, and John Sparrow.

To M. Pradel, at the Louvre, I am especially indebted for generous help in connexion with fig. 59.

E. W.

Oxford
1 September 1966

THE LANGUAGE OF MYSTERIES

ANY attempt to penetrate the pagan mysteries of the Renaissance should perhaps begin with the admission that the term 'mysteries' has several meanings, and that these already tended to become blurred in antiquity, to the great enrichment and confusion of the subject.[1] For the purpose of this introduction it may be useful to distinguish roughly between three meanings.

The first and original meaning of mysteries, which is exemplified by the festival of Eleusis, is that of a popular ritual of initiation. In it the neophytes were purged of the fear of death and admitted into the company of the blessed, to which they were bound by a vow of silence. But since the sacred rites were administered to a multitude without regard to individual merit,[2] philosophers inclined to look upon them with a certain disdain, which Diogenes expressed with

1. In Greek, the plural μυστήρια was used interchangeably with ὄργια and τελεταί, whereas the singular μυστήριον could mean 'secret' without ritual associations. On the resulting ambiguities, see A. D. Nock, 'Hellenistic Mysteries and Christian Sacraments', *Mnemosyne* V (1952), pp. 177–213; also Wilamowitz, *Der Glaube der Hellenen* II (1932), p. 45 note 4, p. 71 note 1; and the article 'Mysterien' by O. Kern and T. Hopfner in Pauly-Wissowa, *Realencyclopädie* XVI (1935), [col.] 1209–350.

2. The Telesterion at Eleusis held three thousand persons (cf. Nock, op. cit., p. 180; P. Foucart, *Les mystères d'Eleusis*, 1914, p. 351). About ten times as many, if we may trust Herodotus VIII, 65, took part in the Eleusinian procession. Plutarch, *De profectu in virtute* 10, regarded large crowds as typical of mystical ceremonies: '. . . persons who are being initiated into the Mysteries throng together at the outset amid tumult and shouting, and jostle against one another, but when the holy rites are being performed and disclosed the people are immediately attentive in awe and silence . . .' (*Moralia* 81E, tr. F. C. Babbitt). On the absence of intellectual instruction in the mysteries, see Plutarch, *De defectu oraculorum* 22 (*Moralia* 422C): ἐν τελετῇ καὶ μνήσει μηδεμίαν ἀπόδειξιν τοῦ λόγου, a remark confirming the much-discussed fragment 15 (Rose) of Aristotle (tr. Ross, XII, p. 87), which says that the neophytes were not taught but moulded: τοὺς τελουμένους οὐ μαθεῖν τι δεῖν ἀλλὰ παθεῖν. Cf. J. Croissant, *Aristote et les mystères* (1932), pp. 137–88, with further literature; also J. Bidez, 'À propos d'un fragment retrouvé de l'Aristote perdu', *Bulletin de l'académie royale de Belgique*, classe des lettres, XXVIII (1942), pp. 201–30.

characteristic bluntness. 'He was never initiated, they tell us, and replied to someone who once advised him to be initiated: "It is absurd of you, my young friend, to think that any tax-gatherer, if only he be initiated, can share in the rewards of the just in the next world, while Agesilaus and Epaminondas are doomed to lie in the mire."'[3]

Although this combination of truculence and common sense would not have pleased the 'dark' Heraclitus, his judgement of mystical initiations did not differ much from Diogenes': he dismissed them as fit for the vulgar;[4] and a similar attitude is reported also of Anaxagoras, of Socrates, and many others.[5] Plato, however, whose words on the subject were to exceed all these in historical resonance, was far too ironic and circumspect to be satisfied with a simple rejection of mysteries. It is true that he rarely spoke of them without mockery;[6] and in the seventh Letter[7] there is a scathing

3. Julian, *Orationes* VII, 238A (tr. W. C. Wright). The same anecdote in Diogenes Laertius VI, 39.

4. Fragments 14 f. (Diels), cf. also 5, 96.

5. On Socrates see Lucian, *Demonax* 11. Further sources in E. Derenne, *Les procès d'impiété intentés aux philosophes à Athènes* (1930), particularly pp. 64 ff., on Diagoras's disrespect for mysteries; pp. 190 f., on Aristotle and Eleusis. The charge of ἀσέβεια against philosophers, although partly provoked by their aloofness, had several other and deeper causes, among them a nervous concern for social cohesion: see E. R. Dodds, *The Greeks and the Irrational* (1951), pp. 189–95; B. Snell, *Die Entdeckung des Geistes* (1955), pp. 45 f.

6. *Republic* 365A (ὡς δὴ τελετὰς καλοῦσιν) and 366A (αἱ τελεταὶ καὶ οἱ λύσιοι θεοί) correspond almost literally to the disdainful remark of Diogenes quoted above. The scornful reflection on 'sacrificing a mere pig' for the admission to mysteries (*Republic* 378A) refers certainly to Eleusis: cf. Jane Harrison, *Prolegomena to the Study of Greek Religion* (1908), pp. 153 f., with illustration of the sacrificial pig on Eleusinian coins. See furthermore *Euthydemus* 277B, *Gorgias* 497C, *Theaetetus* 155E–156A, *Republic* 560E; also a jest on a *Mysterienformel* in *Symposium* 218B, discussed by A. Dieterich, *Abraxas* (1903), p. 127. These scoffs, which are more numerous, though less famous, than the poetic metaphors in *Symposium* 210–12 and *Phaedrus* 250, would surely be relevant to an interpretation of the latter passages since Plato never abandoned his criticism of religious inspiration, *Meno* 99C–D and *Timaeus* 71D–72B being cool statements of his view. See also *Meno* 97D–98A and *Euthyphro* 11B on the mobile 'images of Daedalus', which are of great value only when 'fastened' since they otherwise 'play truant and run away'; a theme related to *Phaedo* 82B, where the philosopher alone is 'fastened' and therefore safe in the Beyond.

7. Leonardo Bruni, who translated the Letters into Latin, held them in higher esteem than the Dialogues, for the surprisingly pedestrian reason that the style was

remark on the social damage that may result from an uncritical surrender to communal feasts of initiation.[8] Yet instead of disclaiming
for his philosophy any kinship with such rites, Plato declared on the
contrary that philosophy itself was a mystical initiation of another
kind, which achieved for a chosen few by conscious inquiry what
the mysteries supplied to the vulgar by stirring up their emotions.
The cleansing of the soul, the welcoming of death, the power to
enter into communion with the Beyond, the ability to 'rage correctly' (ὀρθῶς μαίνεσθαι),[9] these benefits which Plato recognized
were commonly provided by the mystical initiations were to be
obtained through his philosophy by rational exercise, by a training
in the art of dialectic, whose aim it was to purge the soul of error.[10]

The *mystères cultuels* (which is Festugière's term for the ritual
initiations) were thus replaced by *mystères littéraires*,[11] that is, by a
figurative use of terms and images which were borrowed from
the popular rites but transferred to the intellectual disciplines of
philosophical debate and meditation.[12] In a half-serious, half-playful

---

'procul ab ironia atque figmento' (*Praefatio in traductionem Epistolarum Platonis*, 1427;
see H. Baron's edition of Bruni, *Humanistisch-philosophische Schriften*, 1928, pp. 135 f.),
whereas Pier Candido Decembrio rejected all the Letters as false (ibid., p. 138 note 1).
Ficino ascribed the first and fifth Letters to Dion, but accepted the others as Plato's own
(*Opera*, 1561, pp. 1530–6). To judge by the weight of his commentary, the second
Letter was to him the most important; see also below, page 243. Even if apocryphal
without exception, the Letters remain important documents for the kind of thought
that was ascribed to Plato by early Platonists and likewise by Plotinus, Proclus, and
their Renaissance followers.

8. *Epistles* VII, 333E: μυεῖν καὶ ἐποπτεύειν, both technical terms of initiation, used
here in a derogatory sense. Cf. Wilamowitz, *Platon* I (1920), p. 39 note 1; *Glaube der
Hellenen* II, p. 162; also Kern, 'Mysterien', op. cit., 1254; H. Berve, *Dion* (1957), p. 43.

9. *Phaedrus* 244B; cf. I. M. Linforth, 'Telestic Madness in Plato, Phaedrus 244DB',
University of California Publ. in Class. Philol. XIII (1946), pp. 163–72.

10. See for example *Sophist* 230C ff.: dialectic as catharsis. Perhaps Plato's adoption
of a ritual terminology, besides being a powerful poetic device, was also his way of
giving a new twist to a legal obligation: for the formation of a philosophical school at
Athens required its establishment as a θίασος; see Wilamowitz, *Antigonos von
Karystos* (1881), pp. 263–91, 'Die rechtliche Stellung der Philosophenschulen'; E.
Howald, *Platons Leben* (1923), p. 39; A.-J. Festugière, *Épicure et ses dieux* (1946), p. 32
note.

11. Festugière, *L'idéal religieux des Grecs et l'Évangile* (1932), pp. 116–32.

12. A. Diès, *Autour de Platon* (1927), 'phraséologie des mystères' (I, pp. 97 f.);
'Le mysticisme littéraire – La transposition platonicienne' (II, pp. 438–49). On 'the

appraisal of himself the philosopher took on the attitude of a new hierophant, and addressed his disciples in solemn words which sounded like the noble parody of an initiation: 'And what is purification but the separation of the soul from the body . . . , the habit of the soul gathering and collecting herself into herself on every side . . . ? And what is that which is termed death, but this very separation of the soul from the body? . . . And the true philosophers, and they alone, are ever seeking to release the soul. . . . Then, Simmias, as the true philosophers are ever studying death, to them, of all men, death is the least terrible. . . . And I conceive that the founders of the mysteries had a real meaning, and were not mere triflers when they intimated in a figure long ago that he who passes unsanctified and uninitiated into the world below will lie in a slough, but he who arrives there after initiation and purification will dwell with the gods. For "many", as they say in the mysteries, "are the thyrsus-bearers, but few are the bacchoi" – meaning, as I interpret the word, the true philosophers.'[13]

Introduced thus by Plato with a note of irony, but then thoroughly systematized by Plotinus, the adoption of a ritual terminology to assist and incite the exercise of intelligence[14] proved

---

epoptic part of philosophy' Plutarch (De Iside et Osiride 77; Moralia 382D) echoes Plato, Symposium 210A. For further examples (e.g. Chalcidius, In Timaeum 272) see J. H. Waszink in Mnemosyne XV (1962), p. 454; also below, note 14. According to Diès, 'Plato plays with the sacred formulas' even in his enthusiastic moments, but Werner Jaeger (much like Rohde in his chapter on Plato in Psyche) upholds a solemn interpretation throughout; see 'Aristotle's Verses in Praise of Plato', The Classical Quarterly XXI (1927), pp. 13–17, also Aristotle (1934), pp. 160 f., and the monochrome passages in Paideia.

13. Phaedo 67–9. Cf. the 'philosophical initiation' travestied in Aristophanes' Clouds (250 ff.), where a rule of silence is imposed on the neophytes (140), and the very word μυστήρια applied to Socrates' lessons (143). Although with opposite intentions, Aristophanes and Plato seem here to concur in ascribing to Socrates the provocative habit of borrowing his terms from the mysteries. Such borrowings were not unprecedented in Aristophanes' own poetic diction, as in Frogs 356 ff., γενναίων ὄργια Μουσῶν (pointed out to me by Eduard Fraenkel), where Aristophanes treats poetry as a mystic rite from which the profane are excluded, much as Socrates treats philosophy.

14. For example, Enneads I, vi, 6, where the παλαιὸς λόγος about 'mire' (the same as in Phaedo 69C) is turned into a parable on 'matter' and 'vice'; or Enneads VI, ix, 11, a parallel between the vow of silence in the popular mysteries and the 'ineffable'

exceedingly useful as a fiction, but ended, as such fictions are likely to do, by betraying the late Platonists into a revival of magic. As a pedagogue Plotinus was beguilingly tolerant of what he called 'the lesser spectacles'.[15] Always indulgent to religious needs, he did not dissuade his pupil Amelius from sacrificing to the gods although he declined it for himself: 'The gods must come to me, not I to them',[16] and the *Enneads* close with a withdrawal into the purest solitariness (φυγὴ μόνου πρὸς μόνον). But while Plotinus made it absolutely clear that the mystic philosopher 'is as one who presses onward to the inmost sanctuary, leaving behind him the statues in the outer temple',[17] he always admitted the importance of tangible symbols for those who are still outside and yearn to enter. On one occasion, when his school assembled to celebrate the birthday of Plato, his disciple Porphyry recited an enthusiastic hymn on the ἱερὸς γάμος, the 'sacred marriage', which was a token of divine communion in the popular mysteries; but his performance was not well received by the fastidious audience. 'Porphyry,' they said, 'is off his head.' Plotinus, however, rose to his defence: 'You have shown yourself a poet, a philosopher, and a hierophant.'[18]

In this gracious remark the word 'hierophant' still had a figurative meaning. The performance in question was not a ritual act but a poetic rhapsody, composed *ad hoc* to edify a group of philosophers who were only too ready to debate it. But it is possible that the irreverent critics of the chant had more foresight than Plotinus. If the soul could be induced by a certain kind of poetic hymn to rise to a state of philosophic enthusiasm in which it would commune

---

experience of the philosophical mystic. S. Eitrem, *Orakel und Mysterien am Ausgang der Antike* (1947), pp. 20 f., refers to 'neue Mysterien des Gedankens' produced by the philosophical use of 'Mysterienterminologie'. See also Nock, *Conversion* (1933), p. 182. Extreme instances in Proclus, *In Parmenidem* V, 993 (Cousin²) on τῆς ἐποπτι-κωτάτης μυσταγορίας, also ibid., V, 1037.

15. *Enneads* VI, ix, 11: δεύτερα θεάματα.

16. Porphyry, *Vita Plotini* 10.

17. *Enneads* VI, ix, 11; tr. Dodds, *Select Passages illustrating Neoplatonism* (1923), p. 124.

18. The incident is related by Porphyry himself (*Vita Plotini* 15; see also Bidez *Vie de Porphyre*, 1913, p. 47), but the hymn is unfortunately lost. On the ἱερὸς γάμος and its place in the mysteries, see below, page 156.

with the Beyond, then a similar force might be claimed also for the magical skills of incantation, for the art of invoking sacred names or numbers, of fumigating with sacred herbs, or of casting spells by drawing figures or by manipulating magical tools. All that bewitching hocus-pocus, apparently so incompatible with dialectical exercises, was gradually readmitted as a handmaid of philosophy and soon rose to become her mistress.[19] And the ceremonies performed by these solemn triflers, whom Cumont called 'les disciples infidèles de Plotin',[20] again went under the name of 'mysteries' – *theurgorum mysteria sive potius deliramenta*.[21] Before entering on a discussion of pagan mysteries in the Renaissance, it would seem important therefore to make clear in which of these three senses the term 'mysteries' is to be used: the ritual, the figurative, or the magical.

The question should not be answered dogmatically, because in the literature transmitted to the Renaissance the three phases were already thoroughly mixed.[22] However, it is possible to bring the

19. For this development, see now the appendix on Theurgy in Dodds, *The Greeks and the Irrational*, pp. 283–311; of earlier literature the studies of Bidez, 'Le philosophe Jamblique et son école', *Revue des études grecques* XXXII (1919), pp. 29–40; *Vie de Porphyre*, ch. viii f.; *Vie de l'empereur Julien* (1930), pp. 67–81. Also F. Cumont, 'De Porphyre à la déchéance du paganisme', in *Lux perpetua* (1949), pp. 361–84. On the sources of Porphyry's *Philosophy of Oracles* see Hans Lewy, *Chaldaean Oracles and Theurgy* (1956), pp. 8 ff.

20. ibid., p. 363. The passage corrects Cumont's earlier statement 'Le culte égyptien et le mysticisme de Plotin', *Monuments Piot* XXV (1921–2), pp. 77–92, which does not yet draw a clear distinction between Plotinus and the theurgists.

21. C. A. Lobeck, *Aglaophamus* (1829), p. 115. Cumont, *Lux perpetua*, p. 362, justly warns: 'Lorsque les auteurs nous parlent de "mystères" dont la connaissance aurait été ... transmise aux philosophes néoplatoniciens, ces mystères ne sont pas comparables à ceux de l'ancien paganisme, auxquels participait une assemblée nombreuse d'initiés. ... L'interrogateur ... conversait "seul à seul" avec le dieu qui se présentait à sa vue éblouie.' The *modus operandi* of these séances is discussed in Dodds's appendix on Theurgy, op. cit., pp. 291–9, and by Hans Lewy, *Chaldaean Oracles and Theurgy*, pp. 177–257, 461–71, 487–96. See also Bidez, 'Notes sur les mystères néoplatoniciens', *Revue belge de philologie et d'histoire* VII (1928), pp. 1477–81; 'La liturgie des mystères chez les Néoplatoniciens', *Bulletin de l'académie royale de Belgique*, classe des lettres (1919), pp. 415–30; 'Proclus, Περὶ τῆς ἱερατικῆς τέχνης', in *Mélanges Cumont* (1936), pp. 85 ff.; Hopfner, 'Theurgie', in Pauly–Wissowa VI (1937), 258–70. Essential corrections in P. Boyancé, 'Théurgie et télestique néoplatoniciennes', *Revue de l'histoire des religions* CXLVII (1955), pp. 189–209.

22. See *Testi umanistici su l'ermetismo*, ed. E. Garin, M. Brini, C. Vasoli, C. Zambelli 1955), an annotated selection of texts from Lodovico Lazzarelli, Francesco Giorgio,

problem into focus by observing the attitude that prevailed among the great Renaissance antiquaries, since it is they who were chiefly responsible for reviving the study of the subject. While they differed widely from each other in the degree to which they promoted, tolerated, or resisted a magical or ritual re-enactment of mysteries, they were unanimous in regarding the figurative understanding as basic.[23] Whenever 'the mysteries of the ancients' were invoked by De Bussi, Beroaldo, Perotti, or Landino, not to mention Ficino or Pico della Mirandola, their concern was less with the original mystery cults than with their philosophical adaptation. Good judgement alone did not impose the restriction; it was largely a case of good luck, for it derived from a historical misconception: they assumed that the figurative interpretation was part of the original mysteries. As indefatigable readers of Plutarch, Porphyry, and Proclus, they saw the early mystery cults through the eyes of Platonic philosophers who had already interlarded them with *mystères littéraires*. Thus Plato appeared to them not as a critic or transposer of mysteries, but as the heir and oracle of an ancient wisdom for which a ritual disguise had been invented by the founders of the mysteries themselves. And the philosophical cunning thus imputed to those early sages was ascribed also to the Neoplatonic magicians – *les*

and Agrippa of Nettesheim. On Lazzarelli's dramatic conversion in 1484 by the Hermetic prophet and hierophant Giovanni 'Mercurio' da Correggio, see P. O. Kristeller, *Studies in Renaissance Thought and Letters* (1956), pp. 221–57; also D. P. Walker, *Spiritual and Demonic Magic from Ficino to Campanella* (1958), pp. 64–72. Lazzarelli's poem *De gentilium deorum imaginibus* was written at least thirteen years before his conversion, since one of the two manuscripts in the Vatican Library (Cod. Urb. lat. 716) carries a cancelled dedication to Borso d'Este as duke of Ferrara, a title conferred on Borso in the year of his death, 1471 (see F. Saxl, *Verzeichnis astrologischer und mythologischer illustrierter Handschriften des lateinischen Mittelalters in römischen Bibliotheken*, 1915, pp. 101 f.). The illustrations of this poem are disappointing. With the exception of four, they are copied from the *Tarocchi* engravings (cf. A. M. Hind, *Early Italian Engraving* I, 1938, p. 232).

23. Even Gyraldus, who was sceptical of the neo-Orphic vagaries of Ficino and Pico (see below, page 42 note 30), and gave a sober account of the actual sources available to the Renaissance for reconstructing the ritual of Eleusis (*Historia deorum gentilium*, syntagma xiv: 'De Cerere et Triptolemo', in *Opera omnia* I, 1696, [col.] 429–31), subscribed to the figurative understanding of the mysteries; see also preface to his 'Pythagorae symbolorum interpretatio', *Opera* II, 637 f.

disciples infidèles de Plotin – whose elaborate prescriptions for working charms and spells were regarded as amplifications or disguises,
rather than betrayals, of the Platonic discipline.[24] 'In Porphyry you
will enjoy,' wrote Pico della Mirandola, 'the copiousness of matter
and the multiformity of religion; in Iamblichus you will revere an
occult philosophy and strange foreign mysteries (*barbarorum mysteria*)
... not to mention Proclus, who abounds in Asiatic richness, and
those stemming from him, Hermias, Damascius, Olympiodorus, ...
in all of whom there ever gleams ... "the Divine", which is the
distinctive mark of the Platonists.'[25]

The enjoyment Pico derived from occult authors was vicarious
and poetical; they exercised his imagination in the employment of
outlandish metaphors. It never occurred to him, as it did to less
speculative minds, that the turgid lore of the dialectical magi might
be put to a more nefarious use than amplifying the Platonic *mystères
littéraires*. Black magic, in the sense that it appealed to Agrippa of
Nettesheim, he rejected as a vile superstition.[26] But the comparative

24. cf. P. Boyancé, *Le culte des Muses chez les philosophes grecs* (1937), p. 164 note 1:
'Il s'agit, croyons-nous, moins de mystères propres aux Néoplatoniciens, que d'une
sorte de technique du mystère, qui prétend retrouver dans tous les mystères positifs la
philosophie de Platon.' Whatever the merits of that formula with regard to Iamblichus
or Proclus, it applies to their Renaissance followers.

25. *De hominis dignitate*, ed. E. Garin (1942), pp. 140–2. I have made use of, but not
literally followed, the translation by E. L. Forbes in *The Renaissance Philosophy of Man*,
ed. Cassirer, Kristeller, and Randall (1948), pp. 223–54.

26. On the subject of synastry and horoscopy, which in Agrippa's *De occulta
philosophia* are inseparable from sympathetic magic (see also below, page 215 note 72),
Ficino did not share the intransigent view of Pico, although Pico acknowledged in the
Disputationes adversus astrologiam divinatricem I, i (ed. Garin, p. 60) that their difference
of opinion was not so great as might appear (cf. P. O. Kristeller, *The Philosophy of
Marsilio Ficino*, 1943, pp. 310 ff.). Towards pagan rituals both had an attitude of poetic
detachment. Despite the famous celebration of Plato's birthday with a symposium,
and other ceremonious assemblies in the Florentine Academy (on which see A. Chastel,
Marsile Ficin et l'art, 1954, pp. 10 ff.), Ficino's circle at Careggi was less addicted to
ritual initiations than the circle of Pomponius Laetus in Rome whose members
acquired cryptic names, a custom extended in the sixteenth century to almost all the
academies in existence. The mystifying effect of this practice, occasionally heightened
by a defiant tone, may have contributed to Paul II's suspicions of the Roman Academy,
which he mistook for a conspiratorial society (V. Zabughin, *Giulio Pomponio Leto* I,
1909, pp. 38–189; Gregorovius, *Geschichte der Stadt Rom im Mittelalter* XIII, vi, 4). It
is but a refinement of the same error to picture the academies of the Renaissance like

study of sacred images and incantations, and the extraction from them of a philosophic wisdom, of which the hidden sense remained the same through all its verbal transformations, seemed to him eminently worthy of a follower of Plato and Plotinus, because both had persistently stressed the basic lesson: that even though language is deceptive and remains 'unserious' (as Plato explained in the *Phaedrus* and the Seventh Letter),[27] it is the only instrument available for a serious philosophical discipline. 'He that would speak exactly,' wrote Plotinus, 'must not name it [the ultimate One] by this name or by that; we can but circle, as it were, about its circumference, seeking to interpret in speech our experience of it, now shooting near the mark, and again disappointed of our aim by reason of the antinomies we find in it. The greatest antinomy arises in this, that our understanding of it is ... by a presence higher than all knowing. . . . Hence the word of the Master [Plato], that it overpasses speech and writing. And yet we speak and write, seeking to forward the pilgrim upon his journey thither. . . .'[28]

In attempting to mark the disparity between verbal instrument and mystical object, Pico made his own language sound at once provocative and evasive, as if to veil were implicitly to reveal the sacred fire in an abundance of dense and acrid smoke. The sources of the contrived and 'conceited' style of Pico, and of the brusque oratory he developed in it, have not, to my knowledge, been succinctly traced. His persuasive power as a mystagogue certainly owed less to the judicial manner of the Schoolmen, whom he ostensibly

---

Rosicrucian conventicles, as G. F. Hartlaub inclines to do, 'Giorgione und der Mythos der Akademien', *Repertorium für Kunstwissenschaft* XLVIII (1927), pp. 233–57, a restatement of *Giorgiones Geheimnis* (1925). On the other hand, the notorious case of Lodovico Lazzarelli, who called himself *Enoch* after his Hermetic conversion (see above, page 7 note 22), shows how easily an erudite poet laureate, who consorted with the Roman and Neapolitan academies, could succumb to the spell of necromancy.

27. *Phaedrus* 275–8; *Epistles* VII, 344C. Ficino recognized the connexion between the two passages. 'Confirmantur eadem in Epistolis,' he wrote in his commentary on the *Phaedrus*, *Opera* (1561), p. 1386.

28. *Enneads* VI, ix, 3–4; tr. Dodds, *Select Passages*, p. 57. On concealment as an essential feature of Truth, cf. Boyancé, *Le culte des Muses*, pp. 162 f. with further Neoplatonic references.

imitated in the *Conclusiones*,[29] than to the parabolic fervour and tenebrosity he had found in the late-antique Platonists and the early-Christian Fathers.[30] In his book *Saint Augustin et la fin de la culture antique*, Marrou gave an excellent description of the odd blandishments of their secretive style: 'L'obscurité de l'expression, le mystère qui entoure l'idée ainsi dissimulée, est pour celle-ci le plus bel ornement, une cause puissante d'attrait. . . . *Vela faciunt honorem secreti.*'[31] And Festugière remarked on the same subject: 'Cette notion de mystère, d'obscurité, est un complément de celle d'autorité. Plus une vérité est cachée, secrète, plus elle a de force.'[32] Although these remarks refer to late-antique writing, they could be taken for descriptions of a neo-barbaric fashion in Renaissance diction. 'Learning on its revival,' to quote David Hume, 'was attired in the same unnatural garb which it wore at the time of its decay among the Greeks and Romans.' The Platonic revival, in particular, was suffused with that 'Asiatic richness' which Pico enjoyed so abundantly in Proclus. His first essay in the philosophy of myths was deliberately couched in exotic language. 'If I am not mistaken,' he wrote proudly to a friend, 'it will be intelligible only to a few, for it is filled with many mysteries from the secret philosophy of the ancients.'[33]

29. '. . . in quibus recitandis non Romanae linguae nitorem, sed celebratissimorum Parisiensium disputatorum dicendi genus est imitatus.' *Opera* (Basle 1557), p. 63. His eloquent defence of the 'barbaric' style, in a letter to Ermolao Barbaro, ibid., pp. 351–8, has been re-edited by Garin, *Filosofi italiani del Quattrocento* (1942), pp. 428–45, and translated by Q. Breen in *Journal of the History of Ideas* XIII (1952), pp. 384–412. With deliberate paradox the letter is composed in an elegant style and should warn us against mistaking Pico (as in A. Dulles, *Princeps Concordiae*, 1941) for a thoroughgoing scholastic.

30. On patristic sources of Renaissance Platonism, see E. Garin, 'La "dignitas hominis" e la letteratura patristica', *La Rinascita* I, iv (1938), pp. 102–46; P. O. Kristeller, 'Augustine and the Early Renaissance', *The Review of Religion* VIII (1944), pp. 339–58; E. Wind, 'The Revival of Origen', in *Studies in Art and Literature for Belle da Costa Greene* (1954), pp. 412–24; also 'Maccabean Histories in the Sistine Ceiling', in *Italian Renaissance Studies*, ed. E. F. Jacob (1960), pp. 324 ff.; 'Typology in the Sistine Ceiling', *The Art Bulletin* XXXIII (1951), p. 45, with reference to the Patristic Renaissance.

31. (1938), pp. 488 ff.   32. *Revue des études grecques* LII (1939), p. 236.

33. L. Dorez, 'Lettres inédites de Jean Pic de la Mirandole', *Giornale storico della letteratura italiana* XXV (1895), pp. 357 f., referring to Pico's commentary on Benivieni's *Canzona d'amore*.

It would be a mistake to belittle this cryptic pomp as mere youthful affectation: for Pico adhered to it in all his writings, and these were regarded by his contemporaries as models of how to adumbrate an ineffable revelation through speech. To Pico it would have seemed both frivolous and illogical to discuss mysteries in plain language. He knew that mysteries require an initiation: *Hinc appellata mysteria: nec mysteria quae non occulta.*[34] But secrecy was not only part of their definition; it contributed also to the respect they inspired. The fact that these sublime revelations were not easily accessible seemed to heighten their authority. And yet, if their authority was to be felt, it was not sufficient to keep the mysteries hidden; they must also be known to exist. Hence Pico contrived, when he wrote about mysteries, a style of elliptical vulgarization which enabled him to hint at the secrets that he professed to withhold: *si secretiorum aliquid mysteriorum fas est vel sub aenigmate in publicum proferre.*[35] The proper manner for an official mystagogue, he suggested, was to speak in riddles, in words that are 'published and not published', *editos esse et non editos.*[36] The phrase recalls the verbal juggling of Apuleius when he described his experience as a neophyte in the rites of Isis: 'Behold, I have conveyed to you what you must not know although you have heard it', *ecce tibi rettuli quae, quamvis audita, ignores tamen necesse est.*[37]

A consummate Renaissance master and critic of the art of cryptic expression was the Ferrarese humanist Celio Calcagnini, whose reflections on the use and abuse of mysteries deliberately alternated between attack and defence. 'You believe,' he wrote to his nephew, 'that mysteries cease to be mysteries when they are promulgated. ... But I hold the opposite view. ... You think that treasures should be buried? That is the opinion of avaricious men. ... For what is the use of hidden music? ... Mysteries are always mysteries, so long as they are not conveyed to profane ears.'[38] Yet the last

34. *Heptaplus*, prooemium, ed. Garin, p. 172.

35. *De hominis dignitate*, ed. Garin, p. 130.

36. ibid., p. 156. See also below, page 13 note 42, page 190 note 37, page 236 note 1.

37. *Metamorphoses* XI, 23.

38. Celio Calcagnini, *Opera aliquot* (1544), p. 27. On the uselessness of 'hidden music', cf. Erasmus, *Adagia*, s.v. *occultae musices nullus respectus*.

reservation, that mysteries must be protected from the vulgar, merely restated the initial problem. Calcagnini was aware that 'published mysteries' would be a contradiction in terms, but the withholding of knowledge seemed to him vain and ignoble. An essay entitled *Descriptio silentii* contains his shrewd solution of the dilemma.[39] Although the essay was inspired by an image of Harpocrates[40] and ostensibly composed in praise of silence, he managed nevertheless to pour forth in it a veritable catalogue of arcana,[41] which he concluded by praising the virtues of speech: 'For it is as Hesiod said: speech is man's best treasure.' But, he added, the treasure must not be wasted: a 'prudent man' should always 'observe the proper alternation between speech and silence'. The verbal ciphers and hieroglyphs, however, with which Calçagnini adorned his argument, show him admitting still a third possibility – the prudence of speaking in riddles. By a judicious use of enigmatic words and images it was possible, he thought, to combine speech with silence: and that was the language of the mysteries. 'All those who are wise in divine matters,' wrote Dionysius the Areopagite, 'and are inter-

39. Calcagnini, *Opera*, pp. 491–4.

40. On Harpocrates as a god of mystical silence see Politian, *Miscellanea* I, lxxxiii; Gyraldus, op. cit., syntagma i (*Opera* I, 57 f.); Valeriano, *Hieroglyphica* (1575), fol. 261ʳ; and again Calcagnini, 'De profectu', *Opera*, p. 333 (after Plutarch, *De Iside et Osiride* 68, *Moralia* 378C). His typical gesture of lifting a forefinger to his lips – *quique premit vocem digitoque silentia suadet* (Ovid, *Metamorphoses* IX, 692) – was transferred by Achille Bocchi, *Symbolicae quaestiones* (1574), no. lxiv, from Harpocrates to Hermes the mystagogue (our fig. 23) who guides the souls from outward appearances back to the inward One: *Silentio deum cole – Monas manet in se*; cf. Ficino, *In Mercurium Trismegistum* xiii: 'Mercurii . . . de impositione silentii', *Opera*, pp. 1854 ff.; referring to *Poimandres* XIII, 16, 22, cf. *Corpus Hermeticum*, ed. Nock–Festugière II (1945), pp. 207, 209. For a good-natured joke on Harpocrates with his characteristic gesture, see Alciati, *Emblemata* (1542), no. 3: 'In silentium'. Valeriano, however, was serious in his belief (*Hieroglyphica* XLIX, fol. 363ᵛ, s.v. 'Pietas', after Plutarch, *De Iside et Osiride* 75, *Moralia* 381B) that the Egyptians worshipped the crocodile as a token of divine silence because that animal had no tongue (*elinguis*). Calcagnini, *Encomium pulicis*, jocosely praised the flea for that virtue: 'silentium servat, quale ne Pythagorici quidem.' On Pythagoras as *magister silentii* see below, page 53 note 4.

41. Notable among these is the figure of the Roman goddess of silence, Angerona, who makes the same gesture as Harpocrates (see Pliny, *Natural History* III, v; Macrobius, *Saturnalia* I, x; III, ix, 4). Her fame in the Renaissance is shown by the frequency with which she is cited (Calcagnini, *Opera*, pp. 333, 401, 492, 568; Cartari, *Imagini*, s.v. 'Angerona'; Valeriano, *Hieroglyphica* XXXVI, s.v. 'Silentium'; Gyraldus, *Opera*

preters of the mystical revelations prefer incongruous symbols for holy things, so that divine things may not be easily accessible.'[42]

Had the cult of the incongruous produced nothing but monsters, it would have only a limited, anthropological interest. We could then be content to survey the *Hieroglyphica* of Pierio Valeriano, and marvel at the ingenious piety of the author in evading the divine splendour he professes to worship.[43] But in great Renaissance works of art, which often draw on the same sources as Valeriano, the splendour shines out through the disguise, and gives to the veil itself a peculiar beauty. Egidio da Viterbo, the celebrated Augustinian preacher who extolled the pagan mysteries as models of elegance in religion,[44] emphatically stressed, in an attempt to translate for his

---

I, 56 f., s.v. 'Angerona et Tacita') and by the remarkably numerous casts of a bronze statuette, pseudo-archaic in style and perhaps purporting to reproduce an ancient image (W. Bode, *The Italian Bronze Statuettes of the Renaissance* I, 1908, p. 37, note to pl. 93; L. Planiscig, *Die Bronzeplastiken, Kunsthistorisches Museum in Wien*, 1924, p. 19, nos. 25 f.). A drawing by Francia of Angerona with her forefinger raised to her lips (Ashmolean Museum, Oxford, Italian Schools no. 10) may refer to a commission Francia received from Isabella d'Este for her Camerino (cf. Wind, *Bellini's Feast of the Gods*, 1948, p. 24): her celebrated emblem of silence, a musical notation confined to rests (*pause*), is preserved on ceilings of the Palazzo Ducale, Mantua.

42. *De coelesti hierarchia* II, 5. The same argument in Julian, *Orationes* V, 170A–C; VII, 222C. Plutarch, *De Pythiae oraculis* 21 (*Moralia* 404D), quotes Heraclitus (= fr. B93, Diels) on the Delphic prophecies of Apollo: οὔτε λέγει οὔτε κρύπτει ἀλλὰ σημαίνει, 'he neither tells nor conceals but gives a sign'.

43. In the dedication to Duke Cosimo de' Medici: 'In nova vero lege novoque instrumento cum Assertor noster ait, "Aperiam in parabolis os meum, et in aenigmate antiqua loquar", quid aliud sibi voluit, quam "hieroglyphice sermonem faciam, et allegorice vetusta rerum proferam monumenta"?' *Hieroglyphica* (1575), preface, fol. 4ᵛ.

44. cf. Calcagnini, *Opera*, p. 101, praising Egidio's literary genius *ad eruenda totius vetustatis arcana*; also Valeriano, *Hieroglyphica*, fols. 123ʳ, 300ʳ, 322 ff. He inspired Sannazaro to write *De partu Virginis* and occasioned Pontano's dialogue *Aegidius*. In a letter to Bembo, Sadoleto refers to him as 'quem ego et tu saepe soliti sumus in sermonibus nostris clarissimum huius seculi tamquam obscurascentis lumen appellare' (*Epistolae* XVII, xx; *Opera omnia* II, 1738, pp. 165 f.). On Egidio's circle at Sant' Agostino in Rome, cf. below, page 187. See also F. Fiorentino, *Il risorgimento filosofico nel Quattrocento* (1885), pp. 251–74; G. Signorelli, *Il cardinale Egidio da Viterbo* (1929); G. Toffanin, *Giovanni Pontano fra l'uomo e la natura* (1938), pp. 15–35; Garin, *Filosofi italiani*, pp. 532 f.; Wind, *Michelangelo's Prophets and Sibyls* (1966), pp. 82 f.; also 'The Revival of Origen', op. cit., pp. 416 ff. with further literature in note 20. A useful

Renaissance audience Dionysius's praise of incongruity, the beauty achieved by mystical adumbration: 'As Dionysius says, the divine ray cannot reach us unless it is covered with poetic veils.'[45]

It has been observed that in a great work of art the depth always comes to the surface, and that it is only because of their irresistible oratory that great works survive the capriciousness of time. 'Dans le grand naufrage du temps,' says Gide, 'c'est par la peau que les chefs-d'œuvre flottent. ... Sans l'inégalable beauté de sa prose, qui s'intéresserait encore à Bossuet?' Our interest in Renaissance mysteries might indeed be slight, were it not for the splendour of their expression in Renaissance art. But the fact that seemingly remote ideas shine forth through a surface of unmistakable radiance is perhaps a sufficient reason for pursuing them into their hidden depth. For when ideas are so forcefully expressed in art, it is unlikely that their importance will be confined to art alone.

Although the chief aim of this book will be to elucidate a number of great Renaissance works of art, I shall not hesitate to pursue philosophical arguments on their own terms, and in whatever detail they may require. The question to what extent any Renaissance painter, even one so renowned for his intellect as Botticelli or Raphael, would have cared to master a philosophical system is perhaps less awkward to answer than it might seem: for we must not confuse our own labour in reconstructing their knowledge with their relatively effortless way of acquiring some of it by oral instruction. Calcagnini, who knew him well, remarked that it was Raphael's greatest pleasure in life 'to be taught and to teach', *doceri ac docere*.[46] But if the Renaissance painter could thus avail himself of a royal road to knowledge through learned dialogue, by what method can his knowledge now be reconstructed historically?

---

summary in F. X. Martin, 'The Problem of Giles of Viterbo: a historiographical survey', *Augustiniana* IX (1959), pp. 357–79; X (1960), pp. 43–60, to which must now be added F. Secret, *Les kabbalistes chrétiens de la Renaissance* (1964), pp. 106–26: 'Le cardinal Gilles de Viterbe'.

45. *In librum primum Sententiarum commentationes ad mentem Platonis*, Cod. Vat. lat. 6325, fols. 13 f. An edition by Eugenio Massa of this important work is in preparation.

46. Letter to Jacob Ziegler, *Opera*, p. 101.

The process of recapturing the substance of past conversations is necessarily more complicated than the conversations themselves. A historian tracing the echo of our own debates might justly infer from the common use of such words as microbe or molecule that scientific discovery had moulded our imagination; but he would be much mistaken if he assumed that a proper use of these words would always be attended by a complete technical mastery of the underlying theory. Yet, supposing the meaning of the words were lost, and a historian were trying to recover it, surely he would have to recognize that the key to the colloquial usage is in the scientific, and that his only chance of recapturing the first is to acquaint himself with the second. The same rule applies to an iconographer trying to reconstruct the lost argument of a Renaissance painting. He must learn more about Renaissance arguments than the painter needed to know; and this is not, as has been claimed, a self-contradiction, but the plain outcome of the undeniable fact that we no longer enjoy the advantages of Renaissance conversation. We must make up for it through reading and inference. Iconography is always, as Focillon observed with regret, *un détour*, an unavoidably round-about approach to art. Its reward, in the study of Renaissance mysteries, is that it may help to remove the veil of obscurity which not only distance in time (although in itself sufficient for that purpose) but a deliberate obliqueness in the use of metaphor has spread over some of the greatest Renaissance paintings. They were designed for initiates; hence they require an initiation.

Aesthetically speaking, there can be no doubt that the presence of unresolved residues of meaning is an obstacle to the enjoyment of art. However great the visual satisfaction produced by a painting, it cannot reach a perfect state so long as the spectator is plagued by a suspicion that there is more in the painting than meets the eye. In literature, the same sort of embarrassment may be caused by Spenser's, Chapman's, or even Shakespeare's verse in a reader who has been advised to surrender himself to the music of the poetry without worrying whether he understands every line or not. But it is doubtful how long that attitude, however justified as a preliminary approach, can be sustained without flattening the aesthetic enjoyment.[47]

I hope therefore I shall not be misunderstood as favouring the doctrine of mysteries I am about to expound. The axiom proposed by Pico della Mirandola, that for mysteries to be deep they must be obscure, seems to me as untrue as the pernicious axiom of Burke that 'a clear idea is another name for a little idea'. But there is no evading the fact, however unpleasant, that a great art did flourish on that impure soil. In studying the subject I shall strive for clarity, an objectionable aim from the point of view of the Renaissance mystagogues themselves. Yet the understanding of these disturbing phenomena is not furthered by succumbing to them, any more than by ignoring their existence. As Donne observed, disguise is one of the great forces of revelation: 'For as well the Pillar of *Cloud*, as that of *Fire*, did the Office of directing.'

47. In recent years, esoteric studies of Donne, Herbert, Blake, and Yeats have raised the question of their poetic utility. While it is certain that readers repelled by recondite meanings are likely to miss some magnificent poetic metaphors, on the other hand those addicted to esoteric studies may lose sight of the poetry altogether. But the danger of these studies does not lessen their importance. In each instance their relevance is a question of poetic tact; that is, it cannot be settled in the abstract, but depends on that altogether indefinable but unmistakable sense of pitch which distinguishes a pertinent from a rambling interpretation. But this is not meant to discourage the ramblers.

CHAPTER I

POETIC THEOLOGY

PICO DELLA MIRANDOLA planned to write a book on the secret
nature of pagan myths which was to bear the title *Poetica theologia.*
'It was the opinion of the ancient theologians,' he said in his Commentary on Benivieni's *Canzona d'amore*, 'that divine subjects and
the secret Mysteries must not be rashly divulged. . . . That is why the
Egyptians had sculptures of sphinxes in all their temples, to indicate
that divine knowledge, if committed to writing at all, must be
covered with enigmatic veils and poetic dissimulation. . . . How that
was done . . . by Latin and Greek poets we shall explain in the book
of our Poetic Theology.'[1]

Although the book has not survived (assuming that it was written), the method employed by Pico, as well as some of his conclusions, can be inferred from his other works.[2] He held that pagan
religions, without exception, had used a 'hieroglyphic' imagery;
that they had concealed their revelations in myths and fables which
were designed to distract the attention of the multitude, and so
protect the divine secrets from profanation: 'showing only the
crust of the mysteries to the vulgar, while reserving the marrow of
the true sense for higher and more perfect spirits.'[3] As an example
Pico quoted the Orphic Hymns; for he supposed that Orpheus had
concealed in them a religious revelation which he wished to be

1. *Commento*, lib. III, cap. xi, stanza 9 (ed. Garin, pp. 580 f.). See also *De hominis dignitate*,
ed. Garin, p. 156; *Heptaplus*, prooemium, ibid., p. 172. The remark about the sphinxes
is not Pico's invention but derives from Plutarch, *De Iside et Osiride* 9 (*Moralia* 354C).
It recurs in Valeriano, *Hieroglyphica* VI, fol. 48ᵛ: 'arcana tegenda'; also in Francesco
Giorgio, *De harmonia mundi totius* (1525) I, ii, 8: 'Cur antiqui studuerint abscondere
dogmata, quae tradebant sub metaphoris et aenigmatibus.'

2. Besides the *Commento*, see *Heptaplus*, *De hominis dignitate*, *Apologia*, and the mythological sections of the *Nongentae conclusiones*.

3. *Commento* III, xi, 9 (ed. Garin, p. 580).

17

understood only by a small sect of initiates: 'In the manner of the ancient theologians, Orpheus interwove the mysteries of his doctrines with the texture of fables and covered them with a poetic veil, in order that anyone reading his hymns would think them to contain nothing but the sheerest tales and trifles.'[4] But having studied Plato, Plotinus, and Proclus with care, Pico felt certain that these philosophers had been initiated into the mysteries of Orpheus,[5] and he proposed with their help to penetrate the arcana of the Orphic Hymns.

In praising the wisdom of such religious disguises, Pico claimed that the pagan tradition had a virtue in common with the Bible: there were Hebrew mysteries as well as pagan. The book of Exodus, for example, recorded that on two occasions Moses had spent forty days on Mount Sinai for the purpose of receiving the tablets of the Law.[6] Since it would be absurd to suppose that in each of these instances God needed forty days to hand Moses two tablets inscribed with ten commandments and accompanied by a series of liturgical rules, it was evident that God had conversed with Moses on further matters, and had told him innumerable divine secrets that were not

4. *De hominis dignitate* (ed. Garin, p.162). The phrasing recalls Iamblichus, *De vita pythagorica* xxiii, 104 f.

5. The relevant passages have been collected by O. Kern, *Orphicorum fragmenta* (1922), Index ii. He lists 34 passages in Plato, 4 in Plotinus, and well over 200 in Proclus. A lost work ascribed by Suidas to both Syrianus and Proclus dealt with 'the symphony of Orpheus, Pythagoras, and Plato'. Cf. Rohde, *Psyche* II (1903), pp. 415 f., whose remarkably sane and fresh observations on the subject are still well worth consulting. A useful compilation in F. Weber, *Platonische Notizen über Orpheus* (1899), less confident than F. M. Cornford, 'Plato and Orpheus', *Classical Review* XVII (1903), pp. 433–45, and less destructive than H. W. Thomas, 'Ἐπέκεινα (1938). For the present state of the problem, see Dodds, *The Greeks and the Irrational*, pp. 147–9, and 168–72, a critical middle course between the extreme scepticism of I. M. Linforth, *The Arts of Orpheus* (1941), and the over-confidence of K. Ziegler, 'Orphische Dichtung', in Pauly–Wissowa XVIII (1942), 1321–417, or now of R. Böhme, *Orpheus: Das Alter des Kitharoden* (1953). The thesis carried farthest by Boyancé, op. cit., pp. 21–31, 89, etc., that what is said about, and against, Orphic τελεταί in Plato refers wholly or in part to the Eleusinian mysteries, is still open to dispute (cf. Dodds, op. cit., pp. 222, 234 note 82, on *Republic* 363C – *Laws* 907B), despite Wilamowitz, *Glaube der Hellenen* II, pp. 58 f. and 162: 'So schätzt er die eleusinischen Mysterien ein.' See also above, page 2 note 6.

6. Exodus xxiv, 18: first visit of forty days. Exodus xxxiv, 28: second visit of forty days.

to be written down.[7] These were transmitted among the rabbis by an oral tradition known as Cabbala (in which the theory of the *sephiroth* and the 'absconded God' resembled the Neoplatonic 'emanations' and the 'One beyond Being').[8] In relation to the written law of the Old Testament, the Cabbala was thought by Pico to hold the same position as Orphic secrets held in relation to pagan myths. The biblical text was the crust, the Cabbala the marrow. The law was given to the many, but its spiritual understanding to only a few. With an unanswerable oratorical gesture Pico pointed to 'the tailors, cooks, butchers, shepherds, servants, maids, to all of whom the written law was given. Would these have been able to carry the burden of the entire Mosaic or divine understanding? Moses, however, on the height of the mountain, comparable to that mountain on which the Lord often spoke to his Disciples, was so illumined by the rays of the divine sun that his whole face shone in a miraculous manner; but because the people with their dim and owlish eyes could not bear the light, he addressed them with his face veiled.'[9]

And the same device, Pico observed, was also used by Christ. 'Jesus Christ, *imago substantiae Dei*, did not write the gospel but preached it.'[10] To the common people he spoke in parables, but to a few disciples he explained more directly the mysteries of the kingdom of heaven.[11] 'Origen wrote that Jesus Christ revealed many mysteries to his disciples which they did not wish to put down in

7. See 2 (= Vulgate 4) Esdras xiv, 4–6: 'And I . . . brought him up to the mount of Sinai, where I held him by me a long season, . . . and shewed him the secrets of the times, and the end; and commanded him, saying, These words shalt thou declare, and these shalt thou hide' (. . . *et ostendi ei temporum secreta et finem, et praecepi ei dicens: Haec in palam facies verba, et haec abscondes*).

8. cf. Pico, *De hominis dignitate*, ed. Garin, pp. 154 ff., repeated in *Apologia*, *Opera*, pp. 122 f.: 'Scribunt non modo celebres Hebraeorum doctores, sed ex nostris quoque Esdras, Hilarius, et Origenes, Mosem non legem modo, quam quinque exaratam libris posteris reliquit, sed secretiorem quoque et veram legis enarrationem in monte divinitus accepisse . . . dicta est Cabala', etc.

9. *Heptaplus*, prooemium (ed. Garin, p. 174). An impressive veiled figure holding a sphinx represents the mystical understanding of the Scripture in Poussin's frontispiece to the Bible (1642); reproduced in G. Wildenstein, *Les graveurs de Poussin au XVIIᵉ siècle* (1957), p. 224, no. 169.

10. *Heptaplus*, loc. cit.   11. Matthew xiii, 10 f.

writing, but communicated only by word of mouth to those whom they regarded as worthy.'[12] And Pico added that this was 'confirmed by Dionysius the Areopagite', that is by the Athenian disciple of St Paul (Acts xvii, 34) to whom a series of mystical Neoplatonic writings, apparently composed in the fifth century A.D., were piously ascribed by their anonymous author. Dionysius was assumed to have received his mystical initiation directly from St Paul, again in a secret and purely oral manner; but like the late Cabbalists and the Platonic heirs of Orpheus, he – or the late scribe whom he inspired – committed the laudable indiscretion of entrusting the revelation to paper. Without so remarkably universal a breach of etiquette, it might have been difficult for the Renaissance to revive the Orphic, Mosaic, and Pauline secrets.[13]

In comparing the mysteries to each other, Pico discovered between them an unsuspected affinity. In outward dogma, reconciliation would not seem possible between the pagan, Hebrew, and Christian theologies, each committed to a different revelation; but if the nature of the pagan gods were understood in the mystical sense of the Orphic Platonists, and the nature of the Mosaic Law in the hidden sense of the Cabbala, and if the nature of Christian Grace were unfolded in the fullness of the secrets which St Paul had revealed to Dionysius the Areopagite, it would be found that these theologies differed not at all in substance but only in name.[14] A

12. *Commento* III, xi, 9 (ed. Garin, p. 580); also *De hominis dignitate* (ed. Garin, p. 156).

13. A simple summary of this triple concordance in Cod. Vat. lat. 5808, fol. 2ʳ, by Egidio da Viterbo, published in *Scechina et Libellus de litteris hebraicis*, ed. F. Secret, (1959), pp. 23 f.: 'Sane divinae res quae legi possunt, secantur in partes tres: quaedam gentes: quaedam prophetae veteres: quaedam novae legis scriptores prodidere. Gentium theologiam Plato post Orpheos, Museos, Linos ... colligere ... laborat. Dionysius novam, Platonis exemplo motus, sed Pauli oraculis eruditus, ... contemplatur. Pars tertia superest, Prophetarum veterum. ... Soli qui per chabala ... traditionem quasi per manus accipere, magna vi librorum aggressi id sunt: sicut Picus nobis primus innuit. ...' In naming Orpheus, Musaeus, and Linus as the earliest theological poets among the Gentiles, Egidio follows Augustine, *Civitas Dei* XVIII, xxxvii (cf. also XVIII, xiv) where these three are allowed (presumably on the authority of Diodorus III, lxvii and IV, xxv) to antedate the canonical prophets of the Bible.

14. 'These books [of the Cabbala] I procured at no small expense, and read them with the greatest attention and indefatigable labours. In them I found – God is my

philosophy of tolerance was accordingly worked out in the form of a hidden concordance which seemed to confirm the statement of St Augustine: 'The thing itself (*res ipsa*), which is now called the Christian religion, was with the ancients (*erat apud antiquos*), and it was with the human race from its beginning to the time when Christ appeared in the flesh: from when on the true religion, which already existed, began to be called the Christian.'[15] Cabbalistic thought and pagan imagery might therefore, according to Pico's conclusions, become new handmaidens of Christian theology, and should be used by the theologian to his own advantage. From the Cabbalists he might acquire an additional finesse of biblical learning which would reveal a concealed depth in the use of Hebrew letters, while the pagans would teach him how to express the mysteries in an incomparably rich and poetical form.

An element of doctrine was thus imparted to classical myths, and an element of poetry to canonical doctrines. The Scripture itself, in Pico's opinion, was like an external deposit, a crust which tended to harden unduly; but the apocryphal tradition was a deep well from which the faith in the canon might be refreshed and nourished. His relentless attack on rigidities of any kind, whether in theologians, grammarians, or astrologers, gave to his apparently abstruse speculations an anti-dogmatic force and freshness. *A myth gets its animation from a mystery.* With that postulate he confounded the catechizers

---

witness – not so much of the Jewish as the Christian religion. Here was the mystery of the Trinity, here the incarnation of the Word, here the divinity of the Messiah ... the same as we daily read in Paul and Dionysius, in Jerome and Augustine. On those matters which pertain to philosophy you would think you were hearing Pythagoras and Plato, whose theories are so akin to the Christian faith that our Augustine gave infinite thanks to God because the books of the Platonists had come into his hands.' *De hominis dignitate*, ed. Garin, p. 160. See also J. L. Blau, *The Christian Interpretation of the Cabala in the Renaissance* (1944), p. 25, but the statement on p. 29 that there is no explicit Cabbala in the *Heptaplus* must be due to an oversight (cf. p. 378 in Garin's edition). For further corrections see F. Secret, *Le Zôhar chez les kabbalistes chrétiens de la Renaissance* (1964), pp. 9 ff.; also *Les kabbalistes chrétiens de la Renaissance*, which includes a full account of Pico's cabbalistic teachers (pp. 24–37).

15. *Retractationes* I, xiii. In preaching on the Areopagus, St Paul himself had referred to the religious evidence in pagan poets, Acts xvii, 28: 'For in him we live, and move, and have our being; as certain also of your own poets have said.'

who, 'on hearing a speech delivered from a rostrum, believe the rostrum produces the speech'.[16]

For the secret affinity which Pico so ingeniously discovered between pagan and biblical revelations, the historical cause is depressingly simple. Whether neo-Orphic, Cabbalistic, or pseudo-Dionysian, the sources adduced by Pico were all late-antique, if not medieval. Apart from bearing the common stamp of their time, they owe a common debt to the metaphysics of Plato. The claim that in these late Neoplatonic speculations there was a vestige of an ancient mystery religion, older than Homer and Hesiod, was a theory which it would be difficult either to prove or refute, because a purely oral transmission, if it existed, could of course not be traced or tested with documents. Pico was aware that only at a late period were the mysteries recorded in script.[17] The pagan revival to which he adhered was therefore less a 'revival of the classics' than a recrudescence of that ugly thing which has been called 'late-antique syncretism'.[18] His defence of literary barbarism, in a letter addressed to Ermolao Barbaro,[19] shows him ready to sacrifice a polished style to the suggestiveness of a more rugged diction. He persistently claimed, as several romantic scholars have claimed since, that in the recondite and often monstrous decomposition which the classical heritage suffered in the Hellenistic age the genuine and permanent foundations of the classical achievement are laid bare.[20]

16. Compare Plutarch, *De Iside et Osiride* 66 (*Moralia* 377E).

17. See his explanation in the case of the Cabbala, *De hominis dignitate*, ed. Garin, p. 158; *Apologia, Opera*, p. 123: Esdras was the first to alter the rule, for fear that the oral tradition might be interrupted and lost in 'a period of exiles, persecutions, flights, and captivities' (cf. 2 Esdras xiv, 16–48). Similar reasons could undoubtedly explain why the supposedly ancient Egyptian wisdom of Hermes Trismegistus was recorded in Greek; why the preservation of the Chaldean Oracles in Greek did not invalidate their ascription to Zoroaster; or why the writer named Dionysius the Areopagite was so prompt in disclosing his revelations through books.

18. E. Anagnine, *G. Pico della Mirandola: Sincretismo religioso-filosofico*, 1937.

19. *Opera*, p. 354. See above, page 10 note 29.

20. That was one of the assumptions in Friedrich Creuzer's *Symbolik*, first published 1810–12, which also recur in Nietzsche and Usener, and in some of Jane Harrison's reflections. A fair summary of Creuzer's system in O. Gruppe, *Geschichte der klassischen Mythologie und Religionsgeschichte* (1921), pp. 131 f., with special emphasis on the doctrine 'that whoever starts from the Olympian gods of Homer, fails to touch the

Though Pico used the method of mystical reduction for a more radical purpose than Ficino, there can be little doubt that he had it from his teacher. To understand a classical author 'deeply', Ficino would always turn to a Hellenistic commentary. Even Plato, to whose translation and exposition the major part of his life was devoted, he read with the eyes of Plotinus,[21] in whom he discovered 'an inspiration no less noble but occasionally more profound (*in Plotino autem flatum ... non minus augustum, nonnumquam ferme profundiorem*)'.[22] His commentary on Plato's *Symposium* was largely derived, as he himself admitted, from the sixth book of the first *Ennead*;[23] and in preparing his readers for the study of Plotinus he paraphrased the relation of this profounder Platonist to Plato by alluding to the descent of the Holy Ghost during the baptism of

---

primeval sources of religious life among the Greeks' (p. 132). 'Since he [Creuzer] found similar thoughts among the Neoplatonists, the fallacious inference was inevitable that they had preserved the oldest Greek religion, ... which was only superficially overlaid by poetry. For this supposition he thought there was also direct evidence in the Orphic fragments: for although he conceded, on the authority of Herodotus, that their ancient date could not be upheld, he yet assumed with the Neoplatonists that the doctrines preserved in them were *uralt* (*Symbolik* III, pp. 155 ff.), and interpreted them, as they did themselves, by reading into them Neoplatonic doctrines.' On the question of going back beyond Homer, Creuzer's autobiography, *Aus dem Leben eines alten Professors* (1848), pp. 113 ff., quotes two remarkable letters from Goethe and Jacobs. Both, in conceding that Homer does not represent the primitive stage of Greek religion, regretted the absence of definable limits in Creuzer's search for primitive roots. 'Geht's nun aber gar noch weiter, ... aus dem hellenischen Gott-Menschenkreise nach allen Regionen der Erde, um das Ähnliche dort aufzuweisen in Worten und Bildern, hier die Frost-Riesen, dort die Feuer-Brahmen, so wird es uns gar zu weh, und wir flüchten wieder nach Ionien. ...' (Goethe). In his *Antisymbolik* (1824), J. H. Voss protested more rudely against Creuzer's 'bombastisch boppelnden Wogenschwall asiatischer Beredsamkeit' (pp. 12 f.). Creuzer's philosophical ally, Schelling, produced a comparable effect on Jacob Burckhardt, who had attended some of his lectures in Berlin: 'Schelling is a gnostic. ... I thought that any moment some monstrous Asiatic god would waddle in on twelve legs and raise twelve arms in order to take off six hats from his six heads' (W. Kaegi, *Jacob Burckhardt* I, 1947, p. 467, from a letter to Gottfried Kinkel, 13 June 1842).

21. '... Platonem ipsum sub Plotini persona loquentem vos audituros ...', *Opera*, p. 1548.

22. ibid.

23. *In* [Plotini] *librum de pulchritudine*, ibid., p. 1574: 'nam de his in Convivio de Amore latius disputamus'.

Christ (Luke iii, 22): 'And you may think that Plato himself spoke thus to Plotinus: "Thou art my beloved son; in thee I am well pleased."'[24] To make Plato appear as God the Father giving his blessing to Plotinus as God the Son is to remove Plato to the in-human heights of the Almighty, from which Plotinus descends as a philosophical redeemer, a Christ of the Platonic mysteries. That Ficino sensed no blasphemy in the metaphor shows to what extent Christian and Platonic sources of revelation were regarded as con-cordant and interchangeable.[25]

The notorious ease with which the Renaissance transferred a Christian figure of speech to a pagan subject, or gave pagan features to a Christian theme, has generally been interpreted as a sign of the profound secularization of Renaissance culture. If a Madonna or a Magdalen could be made to resemble a Venus, or if Sannazaro could write his *De partu Virginis* in the form of a polished Virgilian epic, Christian piety had patently given way to a taste for the pagan and profane. Before accepting so simple a judgement, it is perhaps useful to remember that hybridization works both ways. In Sannazaro's poem, the Virgilian tone has acquired a twist of mystical ardour which is unmistakably Christian; and Renaissance art produced many images of Venus which resemble a Madonna or a Magdalen. An extreme instance is the *Hypnerotomachia*, in which Venus is pictured as a *mater dolorosa*, nourishing her infant son with tears:

Non lac, saeve puer, lachrymas sed sugis amaras.[26]

24. *Opera*, p. 1548.

25. In Lazzarelli's dialogue *Crater Hermetis*, for instance, the Hermetic vase becomes interchangeable with the Christian chalice; in fact, this text originally bore the title *Calix Christi et Crater Hermetis* (cf. M. Brini in *Testi umanistici su l'ermetismo*, op. cit., pp. 52 ff.). Perhaps the boldest example is Pico's identification of Christ with 'Porus, son of Counsel' in Plato's *Symposium* (see below, Appendix 9, pages 276–81), illus-trated by the enigmatic inscription on a medallic portrait of Christ by Giovanni dal Cavino (our fig. 92). See also *De hominis dignitate* (ed. Garin, pp. 112–24), where the three phases of angelic ecstasy defined by Dionysius the Areopagite as *purgari – illuminari – perfici* (*De coelesti hierarchia* VII, iii), and supposedly experienced by St Paul himself when he was 'caught up to the third heaven' (cf. 2 Cor. xii, 2), are found to agree with the three inscriptions on Apollo's temple at Delphi (μηδὲν ἄγαν – γνῶθι σεαυτόν – εἶ) as quoted by Plutarch, *De εἶ apud Delphos* 2 (*Moralia* 385D).

26. *Hypnerotomachia Poliphili* (1499), fol. z vii[v].

Unquestionably, once the transference of types became a universal practice, it was applied without much thought by inferior artists. It would be absurd, therefore, to look for a mystery behind every hybrid image of the Renaissance. In principle, however, the artistic habit of exploring and playing with these oscillations was sanctioned by a theory of concordance which discovered a sacred mystery in pagan beauty, conceiving it to be a poetic medium through which the divine splendour had been transmitted: 'As Dionysius says, the divine ray cannot reach us unless it is covered with poetic veils.'[27]

How completely the veils could occasionally disguise the profundity of a thought they were designed to 'circumfuse' is shown by the image of the three Graces on Pico della Mirandola's medal (fig. 10). Since Pico praised the cunning of Orpheus because one might think his Hymns 'contained nothing but the sheerest tales and trifles', it is perhaps gratifying that Pico's own symbol was described as a trifle by Sir George Hill. In the opinion of this unrivalled connoisseur of Renaissance medals, 'the three Graces on the reverse, named Beauty, Love, and Pleasure, hardly do justice to the noble ideals of the philosopher'.[28] Yet when we have examined the ideas of the philosopher more closely, and inquire into the meaning of the inscription, we shall find that the figures illustrate a well-defined Neoplatonic argument, a proposition of such crucial importance to one particular phase of Pico's thought that the medal can be dated almost to the year. But before attempting to decipher the medal, it will be necessary to trace a few traditional ideas, chiefly of Stoic origin, which entered into what the Renaissance called 'the mystery of the Graces'.

27. Egidio da Viterbo, as quoted above, page 14 note 45.
28. G. F. Hill, *A Guide to the Exhibition of Medals of the Renaissance in the British Museum* (1923), p. 30. A like judgement in Julius Friedlaender, 'Die italienischen Schaumünzen des fünfzehnten Jahrhunderts', *Jahrbuch der preussischen Kunstsammlungen* II (1881), p. 251, no. 45: 'Dies ist der berühmte Philosoph, "der Phönix der Geister". Die Kehrseite passt nicht für ihn.'

CHAPTER II

SENECA'S GRACES

A REMARKABLY devious theory of grace was occasioned by the placid image of the *Three Graces* (fig. 9).[1] Perhaps no other group from antiquity has so persistently engaged the allegorical imagination, or served so well to conceal and preserve, as in an innocuous-looking vessel, some perilous alchemy of the mind. Certain commonplaces of Stoic morality might not have been so long condoned, nor some of the extravagances of Neoplatonism so willingly accepted, had they not both been sustained by the three Graces:

> *Vain wisdom all and false philosophy,*
> *Yet with a pleasing sorcery could charm . . .*

If allegory were only what it is reputed to be – an artifice by which a set of ideas are attached, one by one, to a set of images[2] – it would

1. This Pompeian fresco, unknown of course to the Renaissance, and a group recently uncovered in Cyrene (*Notiziario archeologico* II, 1916, pp. 51–60) are the clearest surviving examples of an ancient type which must have been familiar to the Quattrocento, since it was copied (as observed by E. Schmidt, 'Übertragung gemalter Figuren in Rundplastik', in *Festschrift Paul Arndt*, 1925, pp. 102 f.) in two Florentine medals (our figs. 10 and 13). These show the central figure in a stiff posture, with legs tightly joined, unlike the famous group in Siena, whose freer posture recurs in Raphael's painting of the Graces (our fig. 61). Hill's suggestion (*A Corpus of Italian Medals*, 1930, no. 1021) that the antique group copied by the medallist was 'not, apparently, the Sienese version, but possibly that which was once in the possession of Prospero Colonna', overlooks the testimony of Fra Giocondo that the two are one: 'Erant olim in domo R^mi Car^lis de Columna cum subscriptis versibus. Nunc vero sunt in R^mi Car^lis Senensis sine infrascriptis carminibus', R. Lanciani, *Storia degli scavi di Roma* (1902), p. 114, also p. 82. On the *Silloge Giocondiana* in the Vatican (Cod. Reg. 2064) and at Chatsworth, see ibid., p. 96. The epigram, which locates the group in Casa Colonna ('Sunt nudae Charites . . .', *Corp. inscr. lat.* VI⁵, no. 3*b), continued to be quoted long after the group had left for Siena, for example by Cartari at the conclusion of his *Imagini* (1556), p. 565. A fragment of an ancient relief in Pisa, reproduced in E. Tea, 'Le fonti delle Grazie di Raffaello', *L'arte* XVII (1914), pp. 41–8, fig. 4, is closer to the medals than the Sienese group, but not as close as the Pompeian fresco. Another relief, now lost, was in the Podocataro Collection in Rome (see below, page 28 note 5). 2. Croce, *Breviario di estetica* (1958), p. 29.

be difficult to account for its nefarious use. Since there is little demand
for repeating the simple, and no advantage in doubling the complicated, an image designed to duplicate a thought should be either
superfluous or distracting. But persuasive allegory does not duplicate.
If a thought is intricate and difficult to follow, it needs to be fastened
to a transparent image from which it may derive a borrowed simplicity. On the other hand, if an idea is plain there is an advantage
in tracing it through a rich design which may help to disguise its
bareness. Allegory is therefore a sophistic device, and it was used
with cunning by Plato. It releases a counterplay of imagination and
thought by which each becomes an irritant to the other, and both
may grow through the irksome contact:

> Machinery just meant
> To give thy soul its bent.

If the process seems absurd, it may be the more, not the less, useful
for that; for we remember the absurd more easily than the normal,[3]
and the monster often precedes the god. As in the study of rituals,
it is an almost unfailing rule that those allegories which seem the
most ridiculous at first may prove in the end to be the most vital;
of this *The Graces* are a perfect instance. The easy symmetry of the
group, relieved by the sideward turn of the middle figure, should
have saved it, one might think, from moral vagaries. But its very

3. A basic rule of the *ars memorativa*, anticipated in the Ciceronian *Rhetorica ad
Herennium* III, xxii, and fully illustrated in the mnemonic images collected by L.
Volkmann, 'Ars memorativa', *Jahrbuch der kunsthistorischen Sammlungen in Wien* III
(1929), pp. 111–200. Constructive absurdity is also at the root of that supposedly
rational use of allegory by which an idea or image which has become objectionable is
'saved' through a figurative interpretation. The spiritual way of 'saving' an objectionable passage is to turn it upside down. St Gregory, *Moralia* III, xxviii, 55, extracted
from the story of David and Bathsheba a prophetic allegory which rendered David
innocent and Uriah culpable: 'Ille, per vitae culpam, in prophetia signat innocentiam;
et iste, per vitae innocentiam in prophetia exprimit culpam.' And he was satisfied that
this ingenious inversion followed the logic of biblical prefiguration: 'sic in facto rem
approbat, ut ei in mysterio contradicat' (*Patr. lat.* LXXV, 626 f.). It is not difficult to
recognize the same form of cunning in Neoplatonic allegories of Mars and Venus (see
below, pages 86 ff.), or of Saturn eating his children (page 135 note 22). Plotinus went
so far as to claim that, according to the 'mystical wisdom of the ancient sages' (οἱ πάλαι
σοφοὶ μυστικῶς ἐν τελεταῖς), the phallic symbols on terminal statues of Hermes
suggest that all generation derives from the mind (*Enneads* III, vi, 19).

transparency made the design a suitable target. Although supposedly very unnatural, allegory is like nature in that it abhors a vacuum.

When Chrysippus composed a treatise on liberality, on how to be gracious in the offering, accepting, and returning of benefits, he tried to render his precepts memorable by attaching them to the Graces. As his book is lost, we would know little of the advantage he took of these patient figures, had not Seneca, despite his own advice that 'these ineptitudes should be left to the poets', gone to the trouble of collecting them. 'Why the Graces are three, why they are sisters, why they interlace their hands', all that is explained in De beneficiis by the triple rhythm of generosity, which consists of giving, accepting, and returning. As gratias agere means 'to return thanks', the three phases must be interlocked in a dance as are the Graces (ille consertis manibus in se redeuntium chorus); for 'the order of the benefit requires that it be given away by the hand but return to the giver', and although 'there is a higher dignity in the one that gives', the circle must never be interrupted.[4]

A further moral was added by Servius, which, to judge by the frequency with which it was repeated – for example, by Fulgentius, Boccaccio, Perotti, and Spenser – must have been regarded as singularly apt: 'That one of them is pictured from the back while the two others face us is because for one benefit issuing from us two are supposed to return.'[5] When 'Calidore sees the Graces

4. De beneficiis I, iii. Besides quoting Chrysippus directly, Seneca made use also of extracts from Chrysippus in a work, now lost, by Hecaton, which H. Gomoll (Der stoische Philosoph Hekaton, 1933, pp. 72 ff.) believes to have been a treatise περὶ χαρίτων.

5. Servius, In Vergilii Aeneidem I, 720. Since a few quotations from this text were recently mistaken for an original invention by Beroaldus the Elder (Journal of the Warburg and Courtauld Institutes XIII, p. 169), this famous Servius passage is cited here in full: 'ideo autem nudae sunt, quod gratiae sine fuco esse debent, ideo conexae quia insolubiles esse gratias decet: Horatius "segnesque nodum solvere Gratiae". Quod vero una aversa pingitur, duae nos respicientes, haec ratio est, quia profecta a nobis gratia duplex solet reverti.' Characteristic quotations in Fulgentius, Mythologiae II, iv; Scriptores rerum mythicarum latini tres (Bode) II, 36; III, 11, 2; Boccaccio, Genealogia deorum V, xxxv; Niccolò Perotti, Cornucopiae (1489), fol. 121ᵛ, and (1499), p. 213; Ripa, Iconologia, s.v. 'Gratie'; Spenser, Faerie Queene VI, x, 24. An instructive case is Antonius Laelius Podager's copy of Jacobus Mazochius, Epigrammata antiquae urbis (1521), Cod. Vat. lat. 8492, fol. 105ᵛ. While rigorously correcting the inscriptions and illustrations in Mazochius, the owner inserted the moralization from Servius under a woodcut representing the nude group of the three Graces in the collection Podocataro:

daunce' (*Faerie Queene* VI, x, 24), their choreography illustrates
Servius:

> *And eeke themselues so in their daunce they bore,*
> *That two of them still forward seem'd to bee,*
> *But one still towards shew'd her selfe afore;*
> *That good should from us goe, then come in greater store.*[6]

The Gloss of the *Shepheardes Calender* gives a useful summary of
Seneca's and Servius's arguments combined, and by now adorned
with the names of Theodontius and Boccaccio:[7]

The Graces ... otherwise called Charites, that is thanks. Whom the
Poetes feyned to be the Goddesses of al bountie and comeliness, which therefore (as sayth Theodontius) they make three, to wete, that men first ought
to be gracious and bountiful to others freely, then to receive benefits at
other mens hands curteously, and thirdly to requite them thankfully: which
are three sundry Actions in liberalitye. And Boccace saith, that they be painted naked (as they were indeede on the tombe of C. Iulius Caesar), the one
having her back toward us, and her face fromwarde, as proceeding from

---

'Gratiae nudae finguntur, quia sine fuco esse gratiae debent. Ideo autem conexae quia
insolubiles esse oportet. Quod vero una aversa pingitur, duae nos respiciunt, est quia
profecta a nobis gratia duplex solet reverti. Ser.' On Ludovico Podocataro and his
collection, see Lanciani, op. cit., p. 204; also *Corp. inscr. lat.* VI[1], no. 548, which says
that the group was a relief (*tabula marmorea*). For the character of Antonius Laelius, see
E. Pèrcopo, 'Di Anton Lelio Romano e di alcune Pasquinate contro Leon X', *Giornale
storico della letteratura italiana* XXVIII (1896), pp. 45–91.

6. In the second line, the word 'forward', which appears in Spenser's own edition
of 1596, and also in that of 1609, was changed by later editors into 'froward', although
this is incompatible with the moral of the last line and with the gloss on *April* in the
Shepheardes Calender, quoted below. The Variorum Edition of the *Faerie Queene*
(Baltimore 1938) gives the original reading in the textual appendix (Book VI, pp. 466,
475) but retains the later emendation in the main text. On Spenser's sources see the
excellent study by D. T. Starnes, 'Spenser and the Graces', *Philological Quarterly* XXI
(1942), pp. 268–82. However, the specific conclusion drawn on p. 281 from the unique
use of 'froward' = 'fromward' ('nowhere else in Spenser') does not hold if 'froward'
is a mis-editing of 'forward'.

7. On the mysterious Theodontius, a Campanian mythographer of uncertain date
(*saec.* ix–xi), see J. Seznec, *La survivance des dieux antiques* (1940), p. 189; also the recent
edition of the *Genealogia deorum* by V. Romano (1951), pp. 889 f., where 215 quotations
from Theodontius are listed.

us: the other two toward us, noting double thanke to be due to us for the benefit we have done.[8]

Although so casually juxtaposed in this fluent Gloss, the two views deriving from Seneca and Servius are not quite easy to reconcile. Seneca distinguished 'three sundry actions in liberality' (giving, receiving, and returning), but Servius allowed for only two (giving and returning), the second being enacted by a pair of figures. Like Seneca he pictured the Graces as interlaced (*conexae, quia insolubiles esse gratias decet*), but without insisting that they join their hands in a complete circle. Instead of a revolving series, *ille consertis manibus in se redeuntium chorus*, he saw them as an antithetical group: *una aversa pingitur, duae nos respicientes*.

As Chrysippus wrote in the third century B.C., and Seneca copied his observations, it is not surprising that the image described by Seneca should be of a considerably older type than that pictured by Servius (fourth century A.D.). Servius knew the Roman group which we ourselves regard as typical: a triad of naked figures in symmetrical postures (fig. 9); and he also gave a reason for their nakedness: 'ideo autem nudae sunt, quod gratiae sine fuco esse debent' (they are naked because Graces must be free of deceit). From a passage in Pausanias it appears, however, that the representation of the Graces in that form was a relatively late invention. Writing in the second century A.D., he observed that in his own day the Graces were represented as nudes, but that he had not been able to find out which artist had introduced the innovation.[9] Seneca still imagined

8. *Aprill*, 109 ff. On the sources of the gloss see W. P. Mustard, 'E. K.'s Note on the Graces', *Modern Language Notes* XLV (1930), pp. 168 f.; D. T. Starnes, 'E. K.'s Classical Allusions Reconsidered', *Studies in Philology* XXXIX (1942), pp. 143–59. What is meant by the 'tomb of Caesar' is doubtful, since Caesar's ashes were supposed to be enclosed in the sphere on the top of the Vatican obelisk (cf. Hülsen, *La Roma antica di Ciriaco d'Ancona. Disegni inediti del secolo XV*, 1907, p. 32), which could hardly be confused with a sarcophagus showing the Graces.

9. Pausanias IX, xxxv, 6 f. On the emergence of the new type, and its further history, cf. W. Deonna, 'Le groupe des trois Grâces nues et sa descendance', *Revue archéologique* XXXI (1930), pp. 274–332; also J. Six, 'La danse des Grâces nues', *Revue archéologique* XX (1924), pp. 287–91, with references to Callimachus and Euphorion, on which see now R. Pfeiffer, *Callimachus* I (1949), pp. 14 (fr. 7⁹) and 317 (fr. 384⁴⁴). The latter fragment is of particular interest because, being among the earliest literary

them as clothed: '. . . and nothing in them [i.e. benefits] should be bound or restricted. That is why they are clad in ungirdled garments, and these are transparent because benefits should be seen.'[10]

Although the earlier group, with the figures clothed, has survived in several examples,[11] and was known to the Renaissance,[12] it never became as popular as the naked and symmetrical triad[13] which, once rediscovered, was quickly accepted as the classical formula.[14] Since the argument of Servius matches this group whereas Seneca's does not, one would expect Seneca henceforth to be overshadowed by Servius in the iconography of the Graces, but exactly the

references to 'naked Graces', it plays on the idea that they should be dressed: οὐκέτι γυμνάς. Horace also knows both types: *Carmina* III, xix, and IV, vii, describe the Graces as nudes, but in I, xxx, they wear loose garments ('et solutis Gratiae zonis').

10. *De beneficiis* I, iii, 5. Nude Graces appear behind a transparent veil in a fourteenth-century manuscript in the British Museum (Royal MS 6 E ix, fol. 24ᵛ, *c.* 1340; illustrated in K. Clark, *The Nude*, 1960, p. 21 fig. 18). The motif survives in the frontispiece of a sixteenth-century *Carmen eucharisticum* by Jules Le Blanc addressed to Pope Sixtus V, Rome 1587 (*Mostra del libro illustrato romano del Cinquecento*, Biblioteca Angelica, Rome, 1950, no. 95, plate xv).

11. E. Paribeni, 'Ninfe, Charites e Muse su rilievi neoattici', *Bollettino d'arte* XXXVI (1951), p. 108, figs. 4 f., replicas of 'Socrates's Graces'; cf. C. Picard, *Manuel d'archéologie grecque* II (1939), pp. 41 f., 90 f.; S. Gsell in Daremberg-Saglio, *Dictionnaire des antiquités grecques et romaines* II, ii (1896), s.v. 'Gratiae', p. 1666.

12. *Hypnerotomachia Poliphili*, fols. n viiiᵛ–o iᵛ. In the Codex Pighianus (Staatsbibliothek, Berlin, MS lat., libr. pict. A, 61, fol. 320) the clothed group bears the inscription 'Gratiae Horatii saltantes'. O. Jahn, 'Die Zeichnungen antiker Monumente im Codex Pighianus', *Berichte der königl. sächsischen Gesellschaft der Wissenschaften* XX (1868), p. 186, no. 49, refers the inscription to Horace I, iv, whereas A. Warburg, *Die Erneuerung der heidnischen Antike* (1932), p. 28, suggests Horace I, xxx. The same codex reproduces also the naked group, fols. 5 and 7; cf. Jahn, op. cit., pp. 177 f., nos. 18 f.

13. cf. Warburg, op. cit., p. 29 note 3 (a list of Renaissance quotations including Jacopo Bellini and Filarete); A. Frey-Sallmann, *Aus dem Nachleben antiker Göttergestalten* (1931), pp. 78 ff.; A. von Salis, *Antike und Renaissance* (1947), pp. 153 ff., 259.

14. Its only rival was the plastic group of the Hecate-type which, showing the Graces *dos-à-dos* and with hands interlocked, became the model for Pilon's group in the Louvre. See again *Hypnerotomachia*, fol. f iᵛ; further examples in Deonna, op. cit., pp. 318 f. In several Renaissance books (for example Cartari, *Imagini di dei degli antichi*, 1556, p. 534, but already in a Mainz print of 1492, illustrated in Seznec, op. cit., fig. 95) the Hecate-type is reproduced in a frontal perspective which likens it to the familiar triad of Servius: *una aversa pingitur, duae nos respicientes*. On the religious association of Hecate with the Graces, see C. Robert, 'De Gratiis Atticis', *Commentationes philologicae in honorem Theodori Mommsen* (1877), p. 147; also O. Jahn's important digression on the Graces in *Die Entführung der Europa auf antiken Kunstwerken* (1870), pp. 32–44, particularly p. 37.

opposite occurred. Whether it was the greater weight of the Stoic's authority, or the superior moral of his argument, or the sheer accident that Alberti had recommended Seneca's text to the attention of painters before the classical group was rediscovered,[15] it appears that Seneca retained so strong a hold over the imagination that a friction resulted between the literary and the pictorial memory. As his arguments were read into the antithetical group, for which they had not been intended, they produced visual deformations of a curious kind. In the *Hieroglyphica* of Pierio Valeriano, for example, the designer, while obviously acquainted with the naked group, refashioned it after a late-medieval type which showed the first Grace from the back, the second full face, and the third in profile (fig. 17).[16] The adoption of this bastard version, as the accompanying text of the *Hieroglyphica* shows, was inspired by a desire to match and amplify Seneca's argument: for after quoting from *De beneficiis* that the three Graces signify the three phases of liberality, the author continued as follows:

That is what Seneca says. We believe, however, that we should also not pass by in silence that one Grace is pictured with averted and hidden face in order to indicate that he who gives a present must do it without ostentation. ... The other Grace shows her face openly because he who receives a benefit should publicly show and declare it; and the third Grace shows one side of her face and hides the other, thus signifying that in the returning of benefits we should hide the restitution but exhibit the benefit obtained.[17]

15. *De pictura* III.

16. For the same variation of posture in the three Graces see a French illumination attributed to Robinet Testart (Commentary on *Les échecs amoureux*, Bibliothèque Nationale, Paris, MS fr. 143, fol. 36ᵛ), with text mistakenly describing these three figures as the nine Muses (fols. 37 ff.), perhaps because they appear in the company of Apollo. This type belongs to a tradition known to the Renaissance from Macrobius, *Saturnalia* I, xvii, 13 and Pausanias IX, xxxv, 3 (cf. Perotti, *Cornucopiae*, 1513, col. 990; also Gafurius, *De harmonia musicorum instrumentorum*, 1518, fol. 94ʳ: 'dextro insuper Apollinis lateri Graeci ipsi tres iuvenculas fingere soliti sunt quas Charites seu gratias vocant'), and recently traced back by Pfeiffer to an epigram by Callimachus (fr. 114) addressed to an archaic statue of the Delian Apollo ('The Image of the Delian Apollo and Apolline Ethics', *Journal of the Warburg and Courtauld Institutes* XV, 1952, pp. 20-32). In another illustration of the same French manuscript (fol. 104ᵛ) the Graces recur as attendants of Venus, and here their roles and postures are discussed at length (fols. 108 ff.).

17. Pierio Valeriano, *Hieroglyphica*, fol. 434ᵛ (appendix by Celio Agostino Curione).

It would be hardly worth dwelling on such a pedantic elaboration, did it not supply the key to Correggio's splendid painting of the Graces in the Camera di San Paolo at Parma (fig. 16). That he imparted a whirling motion to the static symmetry of an ancient group has been ascribed, on purely formal grounds, to a stray effect of the *Laocoon*. Be that as it may, in designing the fresco of the Graces, Correggio's imagination was not diverted at a tangent but remained centred in Seneca's idea of liberality. By representing one Grace straight from the front, another straight from the back, and the third moving sideways, he characterized the last as the 'returning' Grace, while the 'giving' and the 'receiving' Graces are frontally juxtaposed. In strict conformity to the Stoic idea, the giving Grace appears as the most majestic ('there is a higher dignity in the one that gives'), the receiving Grace as more humble and dependent, and the returning Grace as deliberate. Turning her face frontward, she balances the receptive Grace on the left by fully exhibiting the benefit obtained; and thus she restores the symmetry of the classical triad.

While the image appears like a free and spirited rendering of the ancient group by an imaginative painter who wished to remind us of his classical model without copying it too literally, every deviation from the model is dictated by a scrupulous regard for allegorical accuracy that has heightened the eloquence of expression. In contrast to the original design, in which all the figures were facing outward (fig. 9), Correggio's group is dominated by a centripetal movement: for 'the order of the benefit requires that it . . . return to the giver'; and although the hands of the figures again do not touch, and the group retains its antithetical character, the arms are so artfully entwined that the effect is exactly that of a circular dance as described by Seneca: *ille consertis manibus in se redeuntium chorus*. A forerunner of the Baroque in so many other respects, Correggio reveals here again an affinity with Rubens who was, as his portrait-group of Lipsius and his friends as disciples of Seneca may remind us,[18] a professed Stoic, and often painted Seneca's Graces.[19]

18. Palazzo Pitti, Florence.   19. Examples in the Prado and in the Uffizi.

In view of the slightness of the theme, its persistent attraction for great artists would seem to call for an explanation. But it is not unusual for a seemingly trivial subject, which would be the undoing of any minor master, to tempt the great magicians to try their hand at it because it tests their skill in transfiguration. It is perhaps worth recalling in this context that Goethe, who was not a Stoic but much attached to the Graces, turned Seneca's moral into rhymes of a wonderful freshness and felicity; and since these German Graces adorn a Renaissance pageant (*Faust* II, Act I), an excuse is offered for quoting them here:

> *Anmut bringen wir ins Leben;*
> *Leget Anmut in das Geben.*

> *Leget Anmut ins Empfangen,*
> *Lieblich ist's den Wunsch erlangen.*

> *Und in stiller Tage Schranken*
> *Höchst anmutig sei das Danken.*

Grace in giving, accepting, and returning – 'three sundry actions in liberality' – could not be remembered with more grace and precision.

And yet, the more we are struck with the ubiquity of Seneca's Graces, the more we are left with a final doubt. 'Stoic Liberality' is an intelligible concept, but 'Stoic Graces' sound like a contradiction in terms. How could a Stoic think of such a pleasing image? Did not Seneca wish, in an incidental clause, he could 'leave these ineptitudes to the poets'? While there is no question that the Renaissance learned about the Graces from Seneca, and that Seneca borrowed the image from Chrysippus, it may be important to remember that among the lost works by Epicurus listed in the *Lives* of Diogenes Laertius, there is one with the title *De beneficiis et gratia* (Περὶ δώρων καὶ χάριτος);[20] and since Diogenes Laertius further records that 'Carneades called Chrysippus the literary parasite of Epicurus because he wrote on every subject that Epicurus had treated before him',[21] one may well wonder whether Chrysippus's argument

20. Diogenes Laertius X, 28.   21. ibid. X, 26.

34

about the Graces, which was so faithfully repeated by Seneca, was
not first prompted by his emulation of Epicurus. A trace of an
Epicurean argument on the Graces is preserved in Plutarch's
Moralia,[22] which is quoted here from the Renaissance translation of
Xylander:

At vero Epicurus ... beneficium dare non modo pulchrius sed etiam
iucundius esse ait quam accipere. Nihil enim tam est ferax gaudii atque
gratia (χαρᾶς γὰρ οὐδὲν οὕτω γόνιμόν ἐστιν ὡς χάρις); et sapuit qui Gratiis
nomina imposuit, Aglaiae, Euphrosynes, et Thaliae ...[23]

The fame of this passage in the Renaissance is attested by an antiquarian eclectic, Caelius Rhodiginus, who opened his *Antiquae
lectiones* with it.[24] Perhaps it is not too far-fetched to surmise that in
collating Seneca with Plutarch and Diogenes Laertius a Renaissance
humanist might easily have reached the same conclusion as Gas-
sendi,[25] or as the author of a nineteenth-century treatise entitled *De
Seneca Epicureo*:[26] namely, that Seneca had preserved for posterity
some of the gracious features of his enemy Epicurus.[27] 'Miramur
Stoicum Senecam,' wrote Usener in the preface to his edition of the
Epicurean fragments, 'quod philosophi adversarii de cupiditatibus,
de fortuna, de morte sententias tam studiose tractat'[28] – to which
might be added *et sententiam de gratia*.

22. *Cum principibus philosophandum esse* 3 (*Moralia* 778E).

23. Venice 1572, p. 279; cf. Usener, *Epicurea* (1887), fr. 544.

24. Basle 1517, fol. α-3ʳ. The use of an Epicurean phrase at the head of a learned
compendium expressed the author's faith in the pleasure and utility of learning;
compare the title of Giorgio Valla's encyclopedia, *De expetendis et fugiendis rebus*
(1501), which is a Ciceronian translation, taken from *De finibus* I, xiv, of Epicurus's title
Περὶ αἱρέσεων καὶ φυγῶν (Diogenes Laertius X, 27).

25. *De vita et moribus Epicuri* II, vi (*Opera* V, 1658, p. 190).

26. O. Weissenfels (1886), cited by Usener, op. cit., p. lvii note 1.

27. As Garin has since shown (see *Epicurea in memoriam Hectoris Bignone*, 1959, p.
231), this conclusion was in fact drawn by Landino, who said of Epicurus: 'è molto
e in molti luoghi lodato da Seneca filosofo gravissimo'. The same also in Benvenuto
da Imola (ibid., p. 221 note 5): 'Nam Seneca moralis multum commendat eum, et
saepe allegat eius sententias pulchras.'

28. *Epicurea*, p. lvii. See also Thomas Moore, 'A Vision of Philosophy', *Epistles,
Odes and other Poems* (1806), p. 297 note 1: 'Even ... the rigid Seneca has bestowed
such commendations on Epicurus that if only those passages of his works were preserved to us, we could not, I think, hesitate in pronouncing him an Epicurean.'

CHAPTER III

THE MEDAL OF PICO DELLA MIRANDOLA

WHILE the triad of the Graces signified liberality to the Stoics, for the Neoplatonists it was a symbol of love, inviting celestial meditations. Since the Graces were described and pictured as attendants of Venus, it seemed reasonable to infer that they unfold her attributes: for it was an axiom of Platonic Theology that every god exerts his power in a triadic rhythm. 'He that understands profoundly and clearly,' wrote Pico della Mirandola in his *Conclusiones*, 'how the unity of Venus is unfolded in the trinity of the Graces, and the unity of Necessity in the trinity of the Fates, and the unity of Saturn in the trinity of Jupiter, Neptune, and Pluto, knows the proper way of proceeding in Orphic theology.'[1]

In this riddling sentence the words 'Orphic theology' refer to the *Theologia Platonica* as expounded by Iamblichus and Proclus. 'All theology among the Greeks,' wrote Proclus, 'is sprung from the mystical doctrine of Orpheus. First Pythagoras was taught the holy rites concerning the gods by Aglaophamus; next Plato took over the whole lore concerning these matters from the Pythagorean and Orphic writings.'[2] Marsilio Ficino, who chose to conclude that legendary list with his own name,[3] explicitly referred to Orpheus as

1. *Conclusiones . . . de modo intelligendi hymnos Orphei*, no. 8.
2. Proclus, *In Platonis theologiam* I, vi, ed. A. Portus (1618), p. 13 = Kern, *Orphicorum fragmenta*, p. 77, no. 250. See also Linforth, *The Arts of Orpheus*, p. 252, for the translation quoted above. A curious monument to Orphic initiation is described by Pausanias IX, xxx, 4: he saw on the Helicon a statue of Orpheus, with a figure of *Telete* at his side.
3. Letter to Cavalcanti, *Opera*, p. 634. The genealogy Orpheus–Aglaophamus–Pythagoras–Plato reappears in the prefaces to Ficino's commentaries on Plotinus (ibid., p. 1537) and Hermes Trismegistus (ibid., p. 1836). The ancient sources are criticized in Lobeck, *Aglaophamus*, p. 723; for Ficinian Orphica, ibid., pp. 956 ff.; recently D. P. Walker, 'Orpheus the Theologian and Renaissance Platonists', *Journal of the Warburg and Courtauld Institutes* XVI (1953), pp. 100, 105; '*Prisca theologia* in France', ibid. XVII (1954), pp. 243–51.

cuius theologiam secutus est Plato.[4] And the tradition was stressed also by Pico della Mirandola. 'It is written by Iamblichus,' he said, 'that Pythagoras took the Orphic Theology as a model after which he patterned and shaped his own philosophy. And for that reason alone are the sayings of Pythagoras called sacred, that they are derived from the Orphic initiations, from which flowed, as from a fountain-head, the secret doctrine of numbers and whatever was great and sublime in Greek philosophy.'[5] If Pico went so far as to substitute 'Orphic' for 'Pythagorean' and 'Platonic', it was because he held, not unlike Thomas Taylor in the eighteenth century,[6] that the theology transmitted from the Pythagoreans to Plato was poetically foreshadowed in the Orphic Hymns, and that their sequence and imagery could be completely explained as a mystical expression, suitably veiled, of the theorems recorded by Proclus.[7]

To expound the system in all its ramifications, Pico required several hundred *Conclusiones*, each about as cryptic as the one just quoted. Fortunately we need not traverse the entire range of his or Ficino's philosophical mythology to understand the role assigned in it to the Graces. All we must remember is that the bounty bestowed by the gods upon lower beings was conceived by the Neoplatonists as a kind of overflowing (*emanatio*), which produced a vivifying rapture or conversion (called by Ficino *conversio, raptio,* or *vivificatio*) whereby the lower beings were drawn back to heaven and rejoined the gods (*remeatio*).[8] The munificence of the gods having thus been

4. *In Philebum Platonis* I, xi (*Opera*, p. 1216).

5. *De hominis dignitate*, ed. Garin, pp. 160 ff.; after Iamblichus, *De vita pythagorica* xxviii, 145-7, 151.

6. *The Mystical Initiations; or Hymns of Orpheus translated from the original Greek with a Preliminary Dissertation on the Life and Theology of Orpheus*, 1787.

7. Hence in Pico's *Nongentae conclusiones* some of the fifty-five *Conclusiones secundum Proclum* can serve as a commentary on the *Conclusiones de modo intelligendi hymnos Orphei*. No. 24 of the first group, for example, explains no. 8 in the second.

8. Ficino, *In Plotinum* I, iii (*Opera*, p. 1559): 'de trinitate producente, convertente, perficiente.' A profusion of synonyms for the same sequence in *De amore* II, i–ii (ibid., pp. 1323 f.): 'creat–rapit–perficit', 'incipit–transit–desinit', 'effluit–refluit–profluit', etc., all of them describing a triadic cycle which 'returns to the source from which it flowed': *in idem, unde manavit, iterum remeat*. In his commentaries on the *Timaeus* (ibid., p. 1440) and on Plato's second Letter (ibid., p. 1531) Ficino associates the cycle with a triad of causes: *causa efficiens, causa exemplaris,* and *causa finalis* – a terminology

unfolded in the triple rhythm of *emanatio*, *raptio*, and *remeatio*, it was possible to recognize in this sequence the divine model of what Seneca had defined as the circle of grace: giving, accepting, and returning.[9]

If we further consider that all communion between mortals and gods was established, according to Plato, through the mediation of Love, it becomes clear why in Ficino's and Pico's system the entire Greek pantheon began to revolve around Venus and Amor. All the parts of the splendid machine (*machinae membra*), Ficino wrote, 'are fastened to each other by a kind of mutual charity, so that it may justly be said that love is the perpetual knot and link of the universe: *amor nodus perpetuus et copula mundi*'.[10] Although Venus remained one deity among others, and as such the bestower only of particular gifts, she defined, as it were, the universal system of exchange by which divine gifts are graciously circulated. The image of the Graces, linked by the knot of mutual charity (*segnesque nodum solvere Gratiae*),[11] supplied a perfect figure to illustrate the dialectical

---

borrowed from Proclus, *In Timaeum* IC–D (Diehl), and used by Ficino as a philosophical link between Orphic and Christian speculations: *Theologia Platonica* XVIII, i (*Opera*, p. 397); *Orphica comparatio solis ad Deum* (ibid., p. 826); *In Epistolas divi Pauli* vii (ibid., p. 437). On the historical origins of these 'three causes' see below, page 243 note 9; also pages 242 ff. on Ficino's attempt to vindicate them as a vestige of the Holy Trinity, supposedly hidden in a verbal cipher that was thought to have been wrought by Plato himself (*Epistolae* II, 312E).

9. Neither Ficino's nor Pico's triadic arguments agree literally with the authentic Neoplatonism of Porphyry, Iamblichus, or Proclus because both incline to read an 'outgoing' tendency into the first phase, perhaps because they think, in a Judeo-Christian way, of the first cause primarily as creator. As a result, 'procession from the cause' appears to them as the first phase, 'rapture by the cause' as the second, and 'return to the cause' as the third; and since 'rapture by the cause' is already a phase of reversal (ἐπιστροφή), and as such comparable to what Proclus calls ὄρεξις (cf. *Elements of Theology*, prop. 31: πρὸς ὃ δὲ πρῶτον ἡ ὄρεξις, πρὸς τοῦτο ἡ ἐπιστροφή), Pico is quite consistent in distinguishing within a triad the 'two reverting' phases from the 'one proceeding' (*Commento* II, xv; ed. Garin II, xvii, p. 509). But in Proclus, *Elements of Theology*, prop. 35 (ed. Dodds, 1933, pp. 38 f.), the sequence reads: (1) inherence in the cause, (2) procession from the cause, (3) reversion to the cause; and that is the original Neoplatonic scheme. It is obvious that the latter could not be assimilated to the argument of the three Graces, the use of which by Ficino and Pico is further proof of a bias in their reading of Neoplatonic texts.

10. *De amore* III, iii.   11. Horace, *Carmina* III, xxi, 22.

rhythm of Ficino's universe. His villa at Careggi, the seat of the Platonic academy, seemed to him predestined by its very name to become *Charitum ager*, the soil of the Graces: 'Quid enim gratius quam in Charegio, hoc est, gratiarum agro, una cum Cosmo gratiarum patre versari?'[12] Perhaps because Plato had advised Xenocrates that he should 'sacrifice to the Graces',[13] Ficino worshipped them as an exemplary triad, the archetype on which all the other triads of Neoplatonism appeared to be modelled. No matter whether he was discussing the logical triad of *species–numerus–modus*, or the theological triad of Mercury–Apollo–Venus, or the moral triad of *Veritas–Concordia–Pulchritudo* – since every one of these groups was governed by the law of procession, rapture, and return, Ficino did not hesitate to compare all of them in turn to the Graces, calling them 'quasi Gratiae tres se invicem complectentes', or 'quasi Gratiae tres inter se concordes atque conjunctae', or 'tamquam Venus tribus stipata Gratiis', etc.[14] Apparently he felt none of the scruples that might have beset a less confident dialectician. It is obvious, for example, that if the three Graces were subordinated to Venus in a strictly logical sense, the triad Mercury–Apollo–Venus could not be coextensive with that of the Graces. Ficino was fully

---

12. *Epistolarium* I, *Opera*, p. 608.

13. Diogenes Laertius IV, 6, repeatedly quoted in Ficino's Letters (*Opera*, pp. 721, 765). The Graces were associated with Plato on two further occasions: Speusippus's gift of a group of the Graces to Plato's Museion in the Academy (Diogenes Laertius IV, 1), and the tradition, presumably apocryphal, that the sculptor Socrates who made the group of the Graces for the Acropolis was identical with the philosopher (ibid. II, 19; also Pausanias I, xxii, 8; IX, xxxv, 7: 'Socrates, the son of Sophroniscus'). It is of this group that Pausanias says (IX, xxxv, 3): 'by their side are celebrated mysteries which must not be divulged to the many'.

14. *Opera*, pp. 1561, 536, 1559, etc. Even the spiritual organs of 'eye, ear, and mind', which Ficino distinguished from the bodily senses of touch, smell, and taste, he identified (*De amore* I, iv and V, ii) with the three Graces: 'Atque haec tres illae gratiae sunt, de quibus sic Orpheus', etc. An echo of the same argument in Lorenzo de' Medici, *L'altercazione* II, 16–18: 'ecco in un punto sente, intende e mira / l'occhio, la mente nobile e l'orecchio / chi suona, sua dottrina e la sua lira'. In a letter on the theme 'Sola illa gratia non senescit quae a rebus non senescentibus oritur' (*Opera*, p. 828), Ficino managed to extract a combination of *splendor*, *laetitia*, and *viriditas* (which correspond to the names given to the three Graces in the Orphic Hymns LX, 3, translated by Ficino, *De amore* V, ii) from an elegy of Tibullus (I, iv, 37): *solis aeterna est Phoebo Bacchoque iuventus* (Phoebus = *splendor*; Bacchus = *laetitia*; Iuventus = *viriditas*).

aware of this question but did not consider it a difficulty because, in the Neoplatonic system, the structure of the whole is repeated in every part. Any smaller or subordinate unit can serve as an image or mirror of the larger, like Leibniz's *miroirs vivants de l'univers*.[15] On one occasion, having identified the three Graces with *animus–corpus–fortuna*,[16] Ficino proceeded, in the very same sentence, to distinguish within the sphere of *animus* between the three Graces of *sapientia, eloquentia,* and *probitas*.[17] However objectionable as logic, Ficino's circular regressions conformed to a principle which Proclus had defined in the *Elements of Theology* (Proposition 67) as ὅλον ἐν τῷ μέρει, that is, 'whole in the part';[18] and from it Proclus himself had drawn the kind of lesson that Ficino applied so persistently: 'Whichever among these you assume, it is the same with the others, because all of them are in each other, and are rooted in the One.'[19]

Pico restated the principle in his *Conclusiones . . . secundum Proclum*, no. 17: 'Granting . . . that the divine hierarchies are distinct, it must yet be understood that all are contained in all according to

15. Leibniz was anticipated by Gemistus Pletho, *Laws* III, xv (ed. C. Alexandre, 1858, p. 92), who compared the Neoplatonic unfolding of the One into Many to the effect of multiple mirror images, τῇ διὰ πλειόνων ἐνόπτρων εἰδωλοποιίᾳ. The figure derives from Plotinus, *Enneads* IV, iii, 11 f.; Bréhier sees it also in *Enneads* VI, vi, 4: 'image d'origine platonicienne et que Leibniz a reprise' (*Ennéades*, 1954, VI², p. 8); cf. also Dodds's commentary on Proclus, *Elements of Theology*, p. 254; J. Trouillard, 'La monadologie de Proclus', *Revue philosophique de Louvain* LVII (1959), pp. 309–20.

16. cf. Plato, *Epistles* VIII, 355B.

17. *Opera*, p. 890, a letter about Pico, addressed to Salviati and Benivieni. Ficino complicated matters further by equating the three Graces here also with Phoebus–Mercury–Jupiter, associating Phoebus with *animus* as such, Mercury with *animus* employing *corpus*, and Jupiter with *fortuna* guided by *consilium* (a conjunction illustrated in a medal of Andrea Gritti, inscribed DEI OPT MAX OPE, cf. below, page 261), thus obtaining *sapientia–eloquentia–probitas* which, though explicitly qualified as attributes of *animus*, are again equated with Phoebus–Mercury–Jupiter and thus identified with the three Graces. It is obvious that the involutions are deliberate and jocose; they form part of a mystifying epistolary style which is meant to amuse the recipients, who would recognize, for example, in the equation of Jupiter with *consilium* a famous mystery about divine names on which Pico, in particular, had paradoxical things to say (see below, pages 276 ff.).

18. *Elements of Theology*, ed. Dodds, p. 64, prop. 67.

19. *In Parmenidem* VI (Cousin² 1050, 9 ff.); cf. Thomas Taylor, *The Six Books of Proclus on the Theology of Plato* (1816), pp. xxv f.

their particular modes.'[20] In the *Heptaplus*, a triadic account of the biblical Creation was expanded by Pico according to the same scheme: 'Quidquid in omnibus simul est mundis, id et in singulis continetur, neque est aliquis unus ex eis, in quo non omnia sint quae sunt in singulis.'[21] A single triad, however limited in range, could therefore serve as a cipher for the universe, because the divine trinity had left its traces on every part of the creation. 'Divinam trinitatem in rebus cunctis agnosces,' wrote Ficino;[22] and Pico repeated the same idea in a more precise formulation: 'Est trinitatis divinae in creatura multiplex vestigium.'[23] The phrasing recalled a passage in St Augustine which it was easy to transfer to the *Charites* or Graces: 'Tria in Charitate, velut vestigium Trinitatis.'[24]

*

The doctrine of the 'vestiges of the Trinity' belonged to the mysterious revelations which Christians and pagans were believed to have in common. Augustine had phrased the doctrine with perfect clarity: 'Oportet ... ut Creatorem ... Trinitatem intelligamus, cuius in

20. 'Licet, ut tradit Theologia, distinctae sint divinae hierarchiae, intelligendum est tamen omnia in omnibus esse modo suo.' See Proclus, *Elements of Theology*, prop. 103: πάντα ἐν πᾶσιν, οἰκείως δὲ ἐν ἑκάστῳ (= *In Timaeum* 3D and 147B), with Dodds's commentary, p. 254; also L. J. Rosán, *The Philosophy of Proclus* (1949), p. 96.

21. Second preface to *Heptaplus* (ed. Garin, p. 188): 'Quam Anaxagorae credo fuisse opinionem ... explicatam deinde a Pythagoricis et Platonicis.' For the reference to Anaxagoras (= Diels, fr. 4, 6, 11 f., etc. after Simplicius) see also Cusanus, *De docta ignorantia* II, v, where the principle 'all is in all' is shown to entail its opposite, namely, that no two things can be exactly equal. The argument resembles Leibniz's attempt to derive the *principium individuationis* from the law of sufficient reason. An interesting expansion of 'all is in all' is in Leonardo da Vinci's Notebooks, headed 'Anasagora', *Codice Atlantico* fol. 385ᵛ, cf. J. P. Richter, *The Literary Works of Leonardo da Vinci* II (1939), no. 1473. Egidio da Viterbo boldly accused Anaxagoras of having appropriated this principle from the Cabbala (*Scechina*, ed. cit., II, p. 84): 'mysterium hinc usurpatum ab Anaxagora: omnia in omnibus'. Giordano Bruno, *Eroici furori* (Introduction), explained jestingly that it is possible to change anything into anything else: 'come tutto essere in tutto disse il profondo Anassagora'. In *De la causa, principio et uno* (v) his formulation recalls Proclus (cf. preceding note): 'tutto essere in tutto, ma non totalmente et omnimodamente in ciascuno'.

22. *Opera*, p. 701.

23. Preface to *Heptaplus* VI (ed. Garin, p. 308).

24. *De Trinitate* VIII, x, 14.

creatura, quomodo dignum est, apparet vestigium.'[25] Ficino found the same thought among the Pythagoreans and Platonists: 'The Trinity ', he wrote in *De amore*, that is, in his commentary on Plato's *Symposium*,[26] 'was regarded by the Pythagorean philosophers as the measure of all things; the reason being, I surmise, that God governs things by threes, and that the things themselves also are determined by threes.[27] Hence that saying of Virgil's: *numero deus impare gaudet*.[28] For the supreme maker first creates things, then seizes them, and thirdly perfects them (*primo singula creat, secundo rapit,*[29] *tertio perficit*). Thus they first flow from that perennial fountain as they are born, then they flow back to it as they seek to revert to their origin, and finally they are perfected after they have returned to their beginning. This was divined by Orpheus when he called Jupiter the beginning, the middle, and the end of the universe:[30] the beginning

25. *De Trinitate* VI, x, 12. The doctrine is systematically developed in Books IX–XV. Augustine's concept of *vestigium* derives from the Greek ἴχνος, as used, for example, by Plotinus (*Enneads* V, viii, 13). On Plato's cosmological use of ἴχνη, for traces of the original four elements in their chaotic mixture (*Timaeus* 53B), translated by Chalcidius as *elementorum vestigia*, see J. H. Waszink in *Mnemosyne* XV (1962), p. 455.

26. II, i (*Opera*, p. 1323).

27. cf. Aristotle, *De caelo* I, 268A (tr. Ross): 'For, as the Pythagoreans say, the world and all that is in it is determined by the number three. . . . And so . . . we make further use of the number three in the worship of the Gods.' In the fifteenth-century battle between Aristotelians and Platonists (cf. Bessarion, *In calumniatorem Platonis* II, v) the passage suited both sides: the Aristotelians because it came from Aristotle, the Platonists because he credited the Pythagoreans. For a more detailed account of the Pythagorean triad (τριοειδές = τέλειον), see Porphyry, *Vita Pythagorae* 51.

28. *Eclogae* VIII, 75 (cf. Servius *ad loc.*: 'iuxta Pythagoreos . . .')

29. The verb *rapere*, so frequently used by Ficino to indicate the divine seizure which starts off the Platonic reversion (ἐπιστροφή), is a literal translation of ἁρπάζειν, which Proclus used in the same sense, *In Parmenidem* V (ed. Cousin², 1033, 27). It also occurs in a verse from the Chaldean Oracles (ed. Patricius, 1591, fol. 8ʳ) cited and translated by Ficino, *Theologia Platonica* III, i (*Opera*, p. 117): ἥρπασεν = *rapuit*. The most famous instance is of course 2 Corinthians xii, 2–4. A complete definition in Agrippa of Nettesheim, *De occulta philosophia* (1533), p. 316: 'Raptus est abstractio et alienatio et illustratio animae a deo proveniens, per quem deus animam, a superis delapsam ad infera, rursus ab inferis retrahit ad supera.'

30. The relevant verses (= Kern, *Orphicorum fragmenta*, nos. 21a, 168; cf. quotations in Ficino, *Epistolae* xi, *Opera*, p. 934; Francesco Giorgio, *De harmonia mundi* I, viii, 2) are cited by Gyraldus in his *Syntagma* on Jupiter (*Opera* I, 75 f.), where he severely questions their authenticity. As a critique of the Platonic vagaries about Orpheus, coming from an author closely associated with Gianfrancesco Pico della Mirandola,

because he creates, the middle because he draws his creatures back to himself, the end because he perfects them as they return.'[31]

In the course of discussing how 'God governs things by threes', Ficino introduced the triad Pulchritudo–Amor–Voluptas, which is inscribed on Pico's medal (fig. 10).[32] Although verbal triads abound in Pico's own writings, this particular sequence does not, so far as I know, occur in them.[33] Since it does, however, occur literally in Ficino's *De amore* II, ii, where he traces the circle of divine love through three phases, the inscription clearly derives from him, which will prove important for dating the medal. As explained by Ficino, the first phase issues from God as a kind of beacon, the second enters into the world which it moves to rapture, and the third returns to its maker in a state of joy:

> Circulus ... prout in Deo incipit et allicit, *pulchritudo*: prout in mundum transiens ipsum rapit, *amor*; prout in auctorem remeans ipsi suum opus coniungit, *voluptas. Amor igitur in voluptatem a pulchritudine desinit.*[34]

The last sentence – 'Amor starts from Pulchritudo and ends in Voluptas' – corresponds to the group on the medal exactly. The converting power of Amor is illustrated by the Grace in the centre who, represented from the back, looks towards Voluptas on her

---

the passage is important: 'Citantur porro et alii versus his consimiles a Proclo, aliisque Platonicis, quos curiositatis gratia ascribam: nam plerisque mecum sentientibus, quid de huiusmodi Orphicis statuendum, parum adhuc liquet: praesertim cum neque Aristoteli, nec M. Ciceroni satis notus fuisse Orpheus videatur, ut qui de eo ambigue statuant.' Gyraldus's sceptical view of the Orphic poems, *quae fere dubia sunt omnia et incerta* (*De historia poetarum* ii, op. cit. II, 76), may explain his complete omission of the theories of Ficino and Pico from his account of the Orphic Hymns. His distrust of Ficino's philology was sharply expressed in his *Pythagorae symbolorum interpretatio* (ibid. II, 673) on the occasion of a Pythagorean symbol he had found listed in Ficino (cf. *Opera*, p. 1979) but nowhere else: 'This is either a symbol, or a riddle, or both, or perhaps neither, since only Marsilio Ficino has reported it among the symbols of Pythagoras.'

31. For further details on 'pagan vestiges of the Trinity', see Appendix 2, pages 241–55.

32. Hill, *A Corpus of Italian Medals*, no. 998.

33. Concerning his only explicit statement on the Graces (*Commento* II, xv; ed. Garin II, xvii), see below, page 67.

34. Italics mine.

right and stretches out her arm in her direction. Her left hand rests, as if for support, on the shoulder of Pulchritudo from whom she turns.

A curious effect, a slight change of focus, is produced by imposing on the classical group the action defined by the inscription: for the latter requires a dynamic shift of emphasis not quite in keeping with the static symmetry of the figures. However, since Amor and Voluptas turn their heads to the right while Pulchritudo faces to the left, it was possible to divide the group asymmetrically, $\overleftarrow{a} \mid \overrightarrow{b}\, c$, and thus to read into it the Neoplatonic triad of procession, conversion, and return.

*

Historically, the asymmetrical reading of the group was not so much of an artifice as might be suspected: it had an impressive medieval pedigree;[35] and while originally transmitted without benefit of monuments (cf. fig. 18), it proved so forceful that it outlived the archaeological discoveries of the Renaissance. The fastidious care with which Pico's medal reproduced the symmetry of the rediscovered group did not prevent the use of an inscription which was visually *retardataire*; and that curious disparity between verbal reading and visual fact, which ought to have strained the allegorical understanding, continued for several centuries undisturbed. In Ripa's *Iconologia*, for example, the Graces 'which may be seen sculptured in marble

---

35. cf. Petrarch, *Africa* III, 216 ff. Mythographical illustrations in Warburg, op. cit., figs. 112 f. The commentary of *Les échecs amoureux* (MS cit., fols. 108ʳ–110ᵛ, with illustration fol. 104ᵛ) stresses the asymmetrical grouping: '. . . troys iouvencelles nues, dont les deux regardoyent la tierce et aussi la déesse [Venus], et la tierce au contraire ne les regardoit pas, ains leur tournoit le dos. . . .' The two 'reverting' Graces are here represented as facing the goddess, while the averted Grace is the 'outgoing' one. This reading of the group, which recurs in illustrated MSS of the *Ovide moralisé* and seems to derive from Pierre Bersuire [Berchorius], *Reductorium morale* XV (cf. Warburg, op. cit., p. 640), is not, as has been suggested, a mere corruption of the Servius tradition but good trinitarian logic, the rules of which were familiar to both the author and the illuminator of the commentary: 'car les subtils philosophes et saiges ne veulent pas si plainement parler aucunnesfois'. The three Graces in Gafurius (fig. 20) belong to the same tradition: the figure on the left is the 'outgoing' Grace, the two on the right are 'returning'. Cf. also *Tarocchi*, our fig. 18.

in several places in Rome'[36] are still described as an asymmetrical group;[37] and as late as 1716, an illustrated guidebook to the Villa Borghese shows the group of the Graces, now in the Louvre, in a perspective distortion by which the two figures on the right, associated in the text with the 'twofold return' of gifts, stand out as a pair.[38] Even the neo-classic Graces on Appiani's monument in the Brera (1821) retain an asymmetrical design.[39] It can thus be shown that the medieval division of the figures was not unusual with artists and authors who were fully acquainted with the classical type: although not all of them had, like Pico, a Neoplatonic motive for focusing on the asymmetry.

Nevertheless, if we go back to the Stoic prescriptions for the giving, receiving, and returning of benefits, it may seem strange that the enraptured Grace, who receives the benefit, should now be the one who turns her back; but that is not without sense if we consider that the Platonic conversion or rapture consists in turning away from the world in which we are, so as to rejoin the spirit beckoning from the Beyond. In one of the *stucchi* in Raphael's *Logge*, the three Graces (fig. 19) look like an illustration of *De beneficiis* in the form recommended by Pierio Valeriano: one Grace is seen full-face, another straight from the back, and the third in profile; yet, although they resemble Correggio's group (fig. 16), the triad they enact is Neoplatonic. The open, inviting gesture of the Grace on the left characterizes her as the 'offering' Grace, while the Grace turning her back is clearly the 'enraptured' or 'converted' one; and the Grace in profile is 'returning'. *Emanatio, raptio,* and

36. '... che se ne veggono anco scolpite in marmo in più luoghi di Roma' (s.v. 'Gratie').

37. Ripa's description of the naked group as asymmetrical ('una hà la faccia volta in là da banda sinistra; l'altre due dalla destra guardano verso noi') has been followed to the letter by Leonhard Kern in a group of the Graces discovered by E. von Ybl, 'Leonhard Kerns bisher unbekanntes Meisterwerk im Museum der schönen Künste zu Budapest', *Jahrbuch der preussischen Kunstsammlungen* XLVII (1927), pp. 53–7. Unaware of its literary origins, the author ascribes the asymmetrical grouping to 'Einfluss des Frühbarockstils des 17. Jahrhunderts'.

38. Andreas Brigentius, *Villa Burghesia* (1716), pp. 82 f. Illustration and argument derive from Domenico Montelatici, *Villa Borghese* (1700), pp. 298 ff.

39. Andrea Appiani, the founder of the Brera, was a neo-classic painter known as *il pittore delle Grazie*. The monument is by Thorvaldsen.

remeatio have rarely been illustrated in a clearer or more engaging sequence, although the Neoplatonic triad appears as Stoicism recast.[40]

If now we return to the classical group on Pico's medal, we shall find that the ancient description of the Graces by Servius – *una aversa pingitur, duae nos respicientes* – has acquired a metaphysical meaning which seems to reverse the old moral. Instead of issuing from us to the world, the first benefit (*Pulchritudo*) descends from the Beyond to us, and it is only right, therefore, that the enraptured Grace (*Amor*) 'turns back' from us to the Beyond (*Voluptas*). At the same time, the impulse to read the group symmetrically was reinforced by Neoplatonism, because the middle term in a dialectical triad, while separating the extremes, has also the function of keeping them together: a $\overrightarrow{b}\overleftarrow{c}$. As the Grace Amor is seen from the back, she may still be understood in the sense of Servius as the 'outgoing' Grace: turning towards the Beyond, she is doubly rewarded by the other Graces, who grant Pulchritudo and Voluptas 'in return' for the offering of Amor.

The function assigned here to Amor, of mediator between Pulchritudo and Voluptas, corresponds exactly to the definition of Love first given by Plato in the *Symposium*, and then adopted by all the Platonists: 'Love is Desire aroused by Beauty.'[41] Desire alone, without Beauty as its source, would not be Love but animal passion; while Beauty alone, unrelated to passion, would be an abstract entity which does not arouse Love. Only by the vivifying rapture of Amor do the contraries of Pulchritudo and Voluptas become

40. Executed by Giovanni da Udine, the Graces in the *Logge* were unmistakably designed by Raphael. The central figure, in particular, should be compared with Fischel, *Raphaels Zeichnungen* VI (1925), no. 269. It is interesting to observe, incidentally, that Correggio's stoical Graces (fig. 16) have not remained untouched by Neoplatonism. While liberality *emanates* from the Grace in the centre and properly *remeates* with the returning Grace, the Grace on the left, who 'receives' the benefit, is in a state of *raptio* – a trait compatible with Seneca although it is not prescribed by him.

41. Ficino, *De amore* I, iv: 'Cum amorem dicimus, pulchritudinis desiderium intelligite. Haec enim apud omnes philosophos amoris definitio est.' Pico, *Commento* II, viii (ed. Garin II, x): 'essendo amore appetito di bellezza'. Derived, of course (cf. ibid. II, ii), from *Symposium* 200A ff.: 'e così nel *Convivio* da Platone è diffinito amore: desiderio di bellezza'.

united: 'Contradictoria coincidunt in natura uniali.'[42] But to achieve the perfect union of contraries, Love must face the Beyond; for as long as Love remains attached to the finite world, Passion and Beauty will continue to clash. In the *Docta ignorantia* Cusanus explained that a circle and a straight line are incompatibles as long as they remain finite, but coincide when infinite.[43] In the same way do Beauty and Pleasure coincide if they are projected into the Beyond, that is, if they become transcendent Graces united by the rapture of Love.

Although Voluptas is the ultimate term of the triad and represents the goal at which Amor aims, the middle term is indispensable to unite the two extremes. 'The mean term,' wrote Proclus, 'reaching out towards both the extremes, links the whole together with itself as mediator; it . . . implants in all a common character and mutual nexus – for in this sense also givers and receivers constitute a single complete order, in that they converge upon the mean term as on a centre.'[44] With all its insistence on a supernatural orientation, this philosophy produced a theory of balance, in which Aristotle's prudence, his ethics of the 'golden mean', was reconciled with the Platonic enthusiasm of Proclus. Both authors had designated the vital 'mean' by the same Greek term, μεσότης.

In the *Shepheardes Calender*, Spenser expressed the union of balance and transcendence, which he knew from his study of Italian Neoplatonists, by juxtaposing two seemingly incompatible mottoes: *in medio virtus – in summo felicitas*.[45] For an explanation the Gloss referred to 'the saying of olde Philosophers, that vertue dwelleth in the middest . . . with continuance of the same Philosophers opinion,

---

42. Pico, *Conclusiones paradoxae numero LXXI*, no. 15.

43. *De docta ignorantia* I, xiii: 'De passionibus lineae maximae et infinitae' (ed. Hoffmann–Klibansky, 1932, pp. 25 f.). See also Ficino's equation of *voluntas* and *voluptas*: 'Appetitus atque laetitia duo quidem in nobis sunt . . . circa finitum bonum, sed penes bonum infinitum voluntas omnis est ipsa voluptas' (*Opera*, p. 881).

44. *Elements of Theology*, ed. Dodds, p. 131, prop. 148. See also his commentary, p. 277.

45. *Shepheardes Calender, Iulye*. For the study of Italian philosophy by Spenser and Harvey, cf. *Three proper and wittie familiar Letters*, etc. (1580), in which Harvey quotes at length from Gianfrancesco Pico della Mirandola, whom he confuses, however, with Giovanni Pico, pp. 24 ff.

that albeit all bountye dwelleth in mediocritie, yet perfect felicitye dwelleth in supremacie'.[46] Pico explained the connexion of 'mediocrity' with 'supremacy' by man's affinity and distance to God: 'There is this diversity between God and man, that God contains in himself all things because he is their source, whereas man contains all things because he is their centre.' *Est autem haec diversitas inter Deum et hominem, quod Deus in se omnia continet uti omnium principium, homo autem in se omnia continet uti omnium medium.*[47] The aim of Ficino's doctrine of divine love was to teach man to feel his affinity with God, and thereby become aware of his own centre. With the shrewdness of an experienced physician, he conceived of transcendence as an integrating force, and a source of temporal well-being. Only by looking towards the Beyond as the true goal of ecstasy can man become balanced in the present. Balance depends upon ecstasy.

The pleasurable and gracious note of this dialectic distinguishes the original Florentine Platonism from the more sombre tones it acquired later, for example in Michelangelo. It is one of the amiable traits in Ficino's character that he began his literary career as an Epicurean. Although he claimed to have burned these youthful essays,[48] and even stoutly denied their authorship when he was teasingly reminded of them by Politian,[49] he always retained, even while posing as a Platonic high priest, an air of tolerant worldly benevolence which he could hardly claim to have acquired from Plato. A picture of the smiling Democritus, defying the tears of Heraclitus, continued to decorate his study,[50] and reminded him and

46. The phrasing recalls Aristotle, *Nicomachean Ethics* II, vi, 1107A (μεσότης-ἀκρότης), although in this passage Aristotle does not speak of felicity, but only of virtue.

47. *Heptaplus* V, vi (ed. Garin, p. 302).

48. Letter to Martinus Uranius (*Opera*, p. 933). See also *Supplementum Ficinianum* I, ed. Kristeller (1937), p. cxlii; II, pp. 81–4.

49. Letter to Politian (*Opera*, p. 618).

50. *Opera*, pp. 636–8: 'neque stulti amplius erimus neque miseri, sed sapientes iam atque beati'. In *Theologia Platonica* XIII, ii, Democritus and Heraclitus are listed together with Plotinus (*Opera*, p. 286). On the praise of Democritus by Platonists of the Renaissance, in particular Cristoforo Landino, see Wind, 'The Christian Democritus', *Journal of the Warburg Institute* I (1937), pp. 180 f. Although the painting mentioned by Ficino has not survived, a considerable modern literature has grown around it (A. della Torre, *Storia dell'accademia platonica di Firenze*, 1902, pp. 639 f.; Kristeller, *The Philosophy of Marsilio Ficino*, p. 294), and no less than three conflicting attributions

his visitors that εὐθυμία (cheerfulness) was a quality becoming a philosopher.[51] Among his early compilations was one with the title *De voluptate*,[52] which clearly foreshadowed his later attempts to redefine the nature of Pleasure with such care that it could become the highest good of a Platonist.[53] In an *Apologus de voluptate*, for example, he invented a fable by which to explain why Pleasure, originally residing on earth, was transferred to heaven where she is

---

have been proposed for this *chef-d'œuvre inconnu*. O. Brendel assigns it to Alberti (*Gnomon* XIII, 1937, p. 171), E. H. Gombrich to Botticelli (*Warburg Journal* VIII, p. 58), Chastel to Pollaiuolo (*Marsile Ficin et l'art*, p. 70 note 16). Equally questionable are the claims that because it antedates Bramante's painting of the same subject in the Brera, Ficino's picture must have been an iconographical innovation. The parable of Democritus and Heraclitus was already used for clerical instruction in the fourteenth century (Ridewall, in *Fulgentius metaforalis*, ed. H. Liebeschütz, 1926, pp. 76 f.), exemplifying *vanitas mundi*, and there is no reason to assume that an image made popular by such widely read ancient texts as Seneca, *De ira* II, x, 5, and *De tranquillitate animi* XV, 2, Juvenal, *Saturae* X, 28 ff., Lucian, *De sacrificiis* 15, *Anthologia graeca* IX, 148 (cf. Alciati's translation and illustration in *Emblemata*, 1542, no. 96), was newly invented for or by Ficino, or that Democritus and Heraclitus were, apart from the bust of Plato, the only philosophers portrayed in the hall of the Florentine Academy. Equipped as a library ('nostra haec sive academia sive bibliotheca', Ficino, *Opera* I, p. 859), it probably had, as was customary in Renaissance libraries, a series of philosophers' portraits placed above the panelling. The term *gymnasium*, which Ficino uses in referring to the location of the painting, is a Ciceronian synonym for *academia*: 'Platonis ... academia, quod est alterum gymnasium' (*Academicae quaestiones* I, iv, 17); 'nobilissimum orbis terrarum gymnasium' (*Epistolae ad familiares* IV, xii). Cf. Diogenes Laertius III, 7. An entertaining digression *de imaginibus philosophorum in veterum gymnasiis* by Pietro Crinito, *De honesta disciplina* I, xi (ed. C. Angeleri, 1955, pp. 73 f.), quotes a typical series of philosophers' portraits from Sidonius Apollinaris, *Epistolae* IX, ix, 14, among them 'Heraclitus fletu oculis clausis, Democritus risu labris apertis'.

51. cf. *Supplementum Ficinianum* I, p. 83, on Democritus' ideal of *euthymia* and its adoption by Epicurus. Like the Florentine academicians, those in Milan cherished the image of Democritus and Heraclitus, but without giving the palm to Democritus. Bramante's painting in the Brera should be compared with a long poem in *terza rima* by Antonio Fregoso, *Riso de Democrito et pianto de Heraclito* (1506), where Heraclitus has the last word. The poem was cited by Bramante's pupil Cesare Cesariano in his commentary on Vitruvius, *De architectura* II, ii (1521), fol. 34ʳ. In a painting by a follower of Leonardo da Vinci (reproduced in F. Malaguzzi Valeri, *La corte di Lodovico il Moro* II, 1915, p. 636, fig. 689), Leonardo's features are given to Heraclitus.

52. Completed in 1457. *Opera*, pp. 986–1012. The book begins with Plato and ends with Democritus.

53. *Theologia Platonica* XIV, vii: 'Quod animus summam expetit opulentiam et volu[p]tatem' (*Opera*, pp. 315 ff.). Also *In Plotinum* VI, vii, 30 (*Opera*, p. 1792). On religious affinities between Epicurus and Plato, see recently Festugière, *Épicure et ses dieux*, p. 95: '... cette religion d'Épicure s'apparente à celle de Platon'.

still to be found, while her place on earth is occupied by a deceptive double.[54] Distrust of the false *Voluptas*, however, should not deceive us into believing that knowledge is a higher good than pleasure. The fruition of knowledge is in pleasure, and therefore pleasure and joy, in a philosophical lover, are superior to inquiry and vision. This hedonistic conclusion, so unexpected by the common standards of Platonism,[55] was firmly asserted by Ficino in his *Epistola de felicitate*, an important little treatise addressed to Lorenzo de' Medici, who translated Ficino's lesson into the verses of *L'altercazione*. 'Amanti convenit,' wrote Ficino, 'ut re amata fruatur et gaudeat, is enim est finis amoris; inquirenti autem ut videat. Gaudium igitur in homine felice superat visionem.'[56] In the contest between cognition and enjoyment, which was so fully developed in *L'altercazione*, the palm was again given to enjoyment, which remained the *summum bonum*:

> *E come più nostra natura offende*
> *dolersi che ignorar, pel suo contrario*
> *il gaudio per più ben che 'l veder prende.*

> *Non è giudicio buon dal nostro vario,*
> *che questo gaudio sia l'ultimo bene, . . .*

> *Così gaudio per sé disia il core,*
> *e pel gaudio ogni cosa, ed a quel corre,*
> *sì come a sommo bene, il nostro amore.*[57]

To stress divine joy as the highest good Ficino concluded the tenth book of his *Epistolarium* with the *Apologi de voluptate*. In dedicating

54. *Opera*, p. 924. The argument resembles Porphyry, *Vita Pythagorae* 39: διττὴν εἶναι διαφορὰν ἡδονῶν.

55. See below, page 70.

56. *Opera*, p. 663, *Quid est felicitas*: 'It behoves the lover to find fruition and joy in the beloved: for that is the goal of love; whereas vision behoves an inquirer. In a blessed man, vision is therefore vanquished by joy.' See also Ficino's definition of *decora voluptas* (ibid., p. 1574) and *honesta voluptas* (p. 999). Platina's use of the title *Honesta voluptas* for a cookery book seems not to have diminished its prestige among Platonists, who also disregarded Cicero, *Academicae quaestiones* IV, xlv: 'Tu, cum honestas in voluptate contemnenda consistat, honestatem cum voluptate, tanquam hominem cum belua, copulabis?'

57. *Altercazione* V, 31–42: 'And as our nature is more offended by pain than by ignorance, conversely it holds joy to be a higher good than vision', etc.

them to Martinus Uranius, he playfully used the name Uranius to characterize the final *voluptas* as celestial: 'Cum vero amor nihil desideret aliud quam voluptatem, merito decimus hic liber, consecratus amori, finem in voluptaté facit. Voluptate, inquam, Urania, id est, coelesti, quandoquidem haec Uranio dedicatur.'[58]

This is the *Voluptas* on Pico's medal – the final joy at which *Amor* aims, while the initial vision is aroused by *Pulchritudo*. If *Amor* turns from Pulchritudo to Voluptas, it is because Love must turn from Vision to Joy. Joy as the highest good, and a gift superior to the intellect, was defended by Pico with his usual vigour: 'Intelligentiam enim voluptas consequitur, qua nulla maior, qua nulla verior, nulla est permanentior.'[59] Distinguishing in the *Commento* between *virtù cognoscente* and *virtù appetitiva*, he left no doubt that the first comes to fruition in the second: 'la quale quel che la cognoscente iudica essere buono, ama ed abbraccia ...'[60] His insistence on the appetitive act as an act of the will (*appetitio sive voluntas*), without which the cognitive act would be incomplete,[61] imparted to his theory of *voluptas* an energetic force which he occasionally veiled, in what he called his Parisian manner, by an excessive use of scholastic diction.[62] Yet in one of the cryptic *Conclusiones ... in doctrinam Platonis* (no. 6) he expressed his mystical hedonism in an unforgettable paradox:

Love is said by Orpheus to be without eyes because he is above the intellect (*Ideo amor ab Orpheo sine oculis dicitur, quia est supra intellectum*).[63]

58. *Opera*, p. 921. Biographical facts on Martinus Uranius (alias Martin Prenninger) in Klibansky, *The Continuity of the Platonic Tradition* (1939), pp. 43–5.

59. *Heptaplus* V, i (ed. Garin, p. 292).

60. *Commento* II, iii (corrected in ed. Garin II, v, p. 491).

61. *De ente et uno* v (ed. Garin, p. 408): 'cognitio ... imperfecta est, quia cognitio tantum est et non est appetitio'.

62. It is not easy, for example, to realize that the following two *Conclusiones* are identical with the argument put into verse in *L'altercazione*: 'Tenendo communem viam theologorum quod felicitas sit in intellectu vel in voluntate, dico duas conclusiones, quarum prima est haec: Quod intellectus ad felicitatem non perveniret nisi esset actus voluntatis, qui in hoc est ipso actu intellectus potior. Secunda conclusio est haec: Licet actus intellectus formaliter felicitatis attingat objecti essentiam, tamen quod actus suus circa illum actus sit felicitatis, formaliter habet ab actu voluntatis' (*Conclusiones in theologia numero XXIX*, nos. 24 and 25).

63. *Opera*, p. 96.

The tradition that saw in the blind Cupid a symbol of unenlightened animal passion, inferior to the intellect, could not have been more forcefully challenged and reversed.

So important was this paradox in setting the tone of neo-Orphic thought and imagery in the Renaissance, and in causing debates between Ficino and Pico, that it is worth inquiring a little more closely into its sources and developments. With regard to the supremacy of blind love, we shall find at the outset a complete agreement between Ficino and Pico, and at the end a sharp divergence; which will bring us back to Pico's medal, and help us to establish its date.

CHAPTER IV

ORPHEUS IN PRAISE OF BLIND LOVE

THE traditional complaints against Blind Cupid are too well known to require rehearsal, particularly since they have been reviewed and summarized in a masterly essay by Erwin Panofsky.[1] The author inferred from his survey, perhaps too readily, that any positive evaluation of Love would necessarily have to reject his blindness. 'As could be expected,' he wrote, 'the Renaissance spokesmen of Neoplatonic theories refuted the belief that Love was blind as emphatically as the medieval champions of poetic Love, and used the figure of Blind Cupid, if at all, as a contrast to set off their own exalted conception.'[2] But the rule admits of some rather notable exceptions. That the supreme form of Neoplatonic love is blind was plainly asserted not only, as we have seen, by Marsilio Ficino, by Pico della Mirandola, by Lorenzo de' Medici, but the idea was expanded to inordinate lengths in the *Eroici furori* by Giordano Bruno, who distinguished no less than nine kinds of amorous blindness.[3] The ninth and highest of these is the sacred blindness produced by the immediate presence of the deity: 'wherefore the most profound and divine theologians say that God is better honoured and loved by silence than by words, and better seen by closing the eyes to images than by opening them: and therefore the negative theology of Pythagoras and Dionysius is so celebrated and placed above the demonstrative theology of Aristotle and the Scholastics'.[4]

1. 'Blind Cupid', *Studies in Iconology* (1939), pp. 95–128.   2. ibid., p. 125.

3. *Eroici furori* II, iv: 'la ragione de' nove ciechi, li quali apportano nove principi e cause particolari di sua cecità, ben che tutti convegnano in una causa generale d'un comun furore'.

4. The inclusion of Pythagoras among the 'negative theologians' is explained by his fame as 'master of silence' (ἐχεμυθία): 'ab eis edoctus Pythagoras silentii factus est magister' (Pico, *Heptaplus*, prooemium, ed. Garin, p. 172; see also Calcagnini, *Opera*, pp. 333, 492; Gyraldus, *Opera* I, 57; II, 671 f.). Originally conceived as a preliminary discipline (cf. Gellius, *Noctes Atticae* I, ix; Diogenes Laertius VIII, 10; also Iamblichus, *De vita pythagorica* xvi, 68; xvii, 72; xxxi, 188), Pythagorean silence became for the

In one respect, Pico's conclusion that Love is blind 'because he is above the intellect' was indeed far from revolutionary. Among Renaissance theologians it was almost a commonplace to say that the highest mysteries transcend the understanding and must be apprehended through a state of darkness in which the distinctions of logic vanish. The 'negative theology' of Dionysius the Areopagite had developed the argument in ecstatic language; and by the dialectical skill of Nicolaus Cusanus 'the portentous power of the negative' had been refined as a 'learned ignorance'.[5] One did not need to turn to Pico's *Conclusiones* to learn of this particular principle. Any Platonist knew it as 'the One beyond Being', to which Plato had pointed in the *Parmenides*;[6] any Cabbalist knew it as 'the concealed God' (*Ensoph*).[7] And all agreed with the Areopagite that the ineffable power of the One could be described only by contradictory attributes, that is by negating those traits which would render it finite and thereby accessible to the intellect. In another part of the *Conclusiones* Pico himself had already stated the principle in strictly philosophical terms: 'Contradictoria coincidunt in natura uniali.'[8] And in this form, so closely reminiscent of the Areopagite and of Cusanus,[9] the proposition did not yet contain any 'Orphic 'secret.

Neoplatonists the final consummation of wisdom (Iamblichus, ibid. xxxii, 226 f.), ultimate truth being ineffable. On two epigrams from the Greek Anthology (XVI, 325 f.), picturing Pythagoras in the attitude of silence, see Lessing, *Anmerkungen über das Epigramm* (*Schriften*, ed. Lachmann–Muncker, XI, 1895, pp. 230 ff.), with Lessing's contraction of the whole argument to an epigram of one line: 'Warum dies Bild nicht spricht? Es ist Pythagoras.' A more elaborate poem by Raphael's friend Andrea Navagero, *De Pythagorae simulacro*, which Lessing found wordy, was inspired, I think, by the silent Pythagoras in *The School of Athens* (generally misnamed 'Heraclitus'): '... Dignum aliquid certe volvit: sic fronte severa est: / sic in se magno pectore totus abit. / Posset et ille altos animi depromere sensus: / sed, veteri obstrictus religione, silet.'

5. *De docta ignorantia* I, xxvi: 'De theologia negativa.'

6. Klibansky, 'Plato's *Parmenides* in the Middle Ages and the Renaissance', *Mediaeval and Renaissance Studies* I (1943), pp. 281–330; *Plato latinus* III (1953): 'Parmenides usque ad finem primae hypothesis ... Procli commentarium in Parmenidem, pars ultima'.

7. Blau, op. cit., pp. 9, 12, etc.   8. *Conclusiones paradoxae numero LXXI*, no. 15.

9. cf. Dionysius Areopagita, *De coelesti hierarchia* II, v: 'Since negations (ἀποφάσεις) are true in divine things, but affirmations (καταφάσεις) incongruous, it is appropriate to the darkness of the arcana to expound them through contradictories.' On 'Cusanus in Italy', see below, Appendix 1, pages 239 f.

It was only by association with the image of Blind Love, as the power 'above the intellect', that Pico's argument acquired an unexpected 'Orphic' twist: unexpected, because the blind Eros was known as a wanton god, a demon befuddling man's intelligence by arousing his animal appetites. The common *voluptas*, which gratified these desires, was known as blind pleasure unguided by the counsels of reason, and hence deceptive, corrupting, and short-lived. How could the god responsible for these delusions be transformed into a force superior to reason, a guide to delights that are secure?

The use of the same word *voluptas* to designate the most primitive and also the most exalted forms of pleasure was common among Epicureans, and it was recommended by Lorenzo Valla.[10] In any Neoplatonic argument it would seem like a pointless equivocation, since the pleasures assigned to heaven and earth would have to be kept strictly apart. But it is significant that they were not. Plotinus himself repeatedly advised his disciples to model their expectation of spiritual joy on what they knew of the delusive joys of the senses: 'And those to whom the Heaven-passion is unknown may make guess at it by the passions of earth. Knowing what it is to win what most one loves, let them reflect that here our love is . . . a wooing of shadows that pass and change, because . . . our true beloved is elsewhere, who is ours to enjoy . . . by true possession. . . .'[11]

In the joys of mystical exaltation the principle of Pleasure, or man's appetitive impulse, is vindicated against the encroachments of Stoics, and of the more priggish among the Christian moralists. As Ficino was never tired of repeating, the trouble about the pleasures of the senses is not that they are pleasures but that they do not last. It is their transitory, not their enjoyable nature which needs to be amended; and for that purpose the intellect is indispensable. But while the intellect raises us above pleasant delusions, it still detains us below the enjoyment of the real. In reducing the confusions of the senses to reason, the intellect clarifies but it also contracts: for it

10. *De voluptate* III, ix. For the Epicurean tradition in antiquity, see Boyancé, *Lucrèce et l'épicurisme* (1963), pp. 65 ff.

11. *Enneads* VI, ix, 9; tr. Dodds.

55

clarifies by setting limits; and to transcend these limits we require a new and more lasting confusion, which is supplied by the blindness of love. Intellect excludes contradictions; love embraces them. This was why Lorenzo de' Medici observed in *L'altercazione* that his nature contracted whenever he tried to comprehend God through the understanding, but expanded when he approached him through love.[12]

With Pico, the doctrine took on a darker hue; for it was, above all, the blindness in ultimate love that attracted his imagination. 'Let us enter,' he wrote, 'into the light of ignorance and, blinded by the darkness of the divine splendour, exclaim with the prophet: I fainted in thy halls, O Lord!'[13] That Pico expressed the supreme ecstasy by a quotation from David, Psalms lxxxiii, 3 (Vulgate), was a piece of virtuosity: for although he could point out that God was said by David to have 'placed his dwelling in darkness' (Psalms xvii, 12: *et posuit tenebras latibulum suum*), the more tangible and obvious biblical parallel was of course to be found in the Epistles of Paul. The mystery of joy above understanding, whether called Neoplatonic or Orphic in its pagan form, seemed to reveal the same experience of love as St Paul described in the Letter to the Ephesians (iii, 19). With so impressive a biblical concordance to sustain it, it is not surprising that the Orphic mystery of Blind Love was generously divulged by Renaissance humanists. In the famous handbook by Agrippa of Nettesheim, *De occulta philosophia*, Pico's conclusion was literally repeated with the marginal heading *Cur Amor caecus* (why Amor is blind): 'Ideoque amorem Orpheus sine oculis describit, quia est supra intellectum.'[14]

*

In defining the blindness of supreme love as Orphic, Pico relied on a Platonic text: he remembered an allusion to Orpheus in Proclus's *Commentary on the Timaeus* (33c). In explaining the creation of the

12. *Altercazione* IV, 104 f. (= Ficino, *Opera*, p. 663). On the equivalence of 'will' and 'love' in Ficino, and their gradual elevation over the intellect, see Kristeller, 'Volontà e amor divino in Marsilio Ficino', *Giornale critico della filosofia italiana* XIX (1938), pp. 185–214, resumed in *The Philosophy of Marsilio Ficino*, pp. 269–76.

13. *De ente et uno* v, ed. Garin, p. 414.

14. *De occulta philosophia* (1533) III, xlix, p. 316.

world, Plato had written that an all-embracing body would not require eyes to see, or ears to hear, since all things would be within it, and none outside. Proclus inferred from this statement that the highest mysteries must be seen without eyes and heard without ears, and he claimed that Orpheus meant to refer to that secret when he 'said Love to be eyeless' (καὶ γὰρ ἐκεῖνον ἀνόμματον Ἔρωτά φησιν ἔχειν Ὀρφεύς). And he also cited the relevant Orphic verse:

ποιμαίνων πραπίδεσσιν ἀνόμματον ὠκὺν ἔρωτα.

This line from a lost Orphic poem – 'in his breast guarding eyeless swift love' – is a fragment known only in Neoplatonic quotations,[15] but to Neoplatonists it must have been a very familiar text. Proclus alone cited it in three places, of which the second was again in the *Commentary on the Timaeus* (39E), while the third occurred in the *Commentary on Alcibiades I* (103A), of which Ficino made a Latin selection: *Excerpta Marsilii Ficini ex graecis Procli commentariis in Alcibiadem Platonis primum*.[16] In these excerpts by Ficino the decisive passage, on the blind Amor, completely agrees with Pico's *Conclusio*:

... he [Amor] unites the intelligible intellect (*intelligibilem intellectum*) to the first and secret beauty by a certain life which is better than intelligence (*per vitam quandam intelligentia meliorem*). The theologian of the Greeks himself [Orpheus] therefore calls this Amor blind (*itaque Graecorum ipse Theologus caecum illum appellat amorem*). ... And Plato also seems to me to have found that god in Orpheus, where he is called both Love and a great demon ...[17]

15. Kern, *Orphicorum fragmenta*, p. 155, fr. 82.

16. *Opera*, pp. 1908-28. In a publication by Aldus of 1497, these extracts from Proclus were combined in one volume with Ficino's *De voluptate*, his translation of Iamblichus, *De mysteriis*, and other texts referring to the pagan mysteries. A. A. Renouard, *Annales de l'imprimerie des Alde* (1834), no. 14.

17. *Opera*, pp. 1911 f. The superiority of blindness to sight is also stressed in Ficino's commentary on Dionysius the Areopagite (*Opera*, p. 1066): 'Lumen namque divinum, re qualibet cognoscenda superius, attingi non potest nisi per actum cognitione quavis excelsiorem, ideoque *oculos non habentem*' (italics mine). Love 'without eyes' (*sine oculis* or *oculos non habens*),· and thus downright 'blind' (*caecus*) rather than 'blindfolded', does not lend itself easily to illustration, but does occur in *Les échecs amoureux*. MS cit., fol. 104ᵛ, where Amor, described in the text as *aveugle*, is pictured not with his eyes bandaged, but with vacant, dead eyes, minutely rendered.

As if to perfect the demonstration, the word μυούμενοι ('being initiated') in *Phaedrus* 250c was derived by Proclus and Hermias from μύειν ('to close the eyes'): '... for to close the eyes in initiation,' Hermias explained in his commentary on the *Phaedrus*, 'is no longer to receive by sense those divine mysteries, but with the pure soul itself'.[18] And Proclus also wrote of 'giving ourselves up to the divine light, and closing the eyes of the soul, after this manner to become established in the unknown and occult unity of beings'.[19] There is a mocking echo of the mystic phraseology in Shakespeare:

> *Love looks not with the eyes, but with the mind;*
> *And therefore is wing'd Cupid painted blind.*
>
> [*A Midsummer Night's Dream*, I, 1]

In Greek, the same can be read in Olympiodorus:

ἀνόμματος γὰρ ὁ Ἔρως ὡς τῷ νῷ ὁρῶν καὶ ἀκούων.[20]

Coleridge remembered the argument (perhaps from Shakespeare as well as from the Neoplatonists) in the verses called *Reason for Love's Blindness:*

> *I have heard of reasons manifold*
> *Why Love must needs be blind,*
> *But this the best of all I hold –*
> *His eyes are in his mind.*

'And of this,' wrote Pico, 'there is a good proof in the fact that many who were rapt to the vision of spiritual beauty were by the same cause blinded (*accecati*) in their corporal eyes.'[21] In elaborating the theme he referred to the blindness of Tiresias, Homer, and St Paul. Beroaldus's *Commentary on Apuleius* reinforced the same lesson by a quotation from *Symposium* 219A: 'For Plato writes in the

18. *In Platonis Phaedrum* (ed. P. Couvreur, 1901, p. 178, under 250B); cf. Taylor, *Proclus on the Theology of Plato* I, p. 242 note 1. A copy of Hermias's *Commentary on the Phaedrus* is among Lorenzo de' Medici's manuscripts in the Laurenziana, Plut. 86, 4. Ficino's translation into Latin, mentioned in his correspondence (*Opera*, p. 899), is preserved in Cod. Vat. lat. 5953, fols. 134–316; cf. Kristeller, *Supplementum Ficinianum* I, p. cxlvi.

19. *In Theologiam Platonis* I, xxv; ed. Portus, p. 61; tr. Taylor, I, p. 79.

20. Olympiodorus, *Commentary on the First Alcibiades of Plato* 103A, ed. L. G. Westerink, 1956.

21. *Commento*, ed. Garin, p. 529.

Symposium that the eyes of the mind begin to see clearly when the eyes of the body begin to fail.'[22] When Psyche succumbs, in the story of Apuleius, to the desire to see Amor with her eyes, she learns that this causes the god to vanish; and it is only after she has atoned for her curiosity, and produced the vessel of beauty from the realm of death, that she is allowed to rejoin the transcendent Amor, by whom she conceives 'a daughter whom we call Voluptas', *quam Voluptatem nominamus* (Apuleius VI, 24).[23] Beroaldus's reading of Apuleius is sustained by an important passage in Plotinus about 'pictures and fables' of Amor and Psyche:

That the Good is Yonder, appears by the love which is the soul's natural companion (ὁ ἔρως ὁ τῆς ψυχῆς ὁ σύμφυτος), so that both in pictures and in fables Eros and the Psyche make a pair. Because she is of God's race, yet other than God, she cannot but love God. Whilst she is Yonder she knows the Heaven-passion. . . . But when she enters into generation . . ., then she likes better another and a less enduring love. . . . Yet learning afterwards to hate the wanton dealings of this place, she journeys again to her father's house, when she has purified herself of earthly contacts, and abides in well-being (εὐπαθεῖ).[24]

To expound the theory of divine Voluptas, there was no want of Neoplatonic witnesses. Besides 'Orpheus', Apuleius, Hermias, and

22. Apuleius, *Opera . . . cum Philippi Beroaldi . . . commentariis* (Lyon 1587), p. 4. Conversely, *Phaedo* 81C–D describes how souls plagued 'with the fear of the invisible and the Beyond' (φόβῳ τοῦ ἀιδοῦς τε καὶ ˮΑιδου, cf. *Cratylus* 403A–404A) become cloyed with sight and 'dragged down' into the visible (τὸ ὁρατόν). As Amor warns Psyche in Apuleius V, 11: 'quos [vultus], ut tibi saepe praedixi, non videbis, si videris'. Contrary to Reitzenstein, *Das Märchen von Amor und Psyche bei Apuleius* (1912), pp. 19, 25, 74 ff., these references to the Beyond in Apuleius, as recognized, among many others, by G. Heinrici, 'Zur Geschichte der Psyche, eine religionsgeschichtliche Skizze', *Preussische Jahrbücher* XC (1897), pp. 390–417, are quite sufficient to account for the sepulchral use of the myth; cf. recently Cumont, *Recherches sur le symbolisme funéraire des Romains* (1942), p. 319 note 8. On Amor as a god of death, see below, pages 152 ff.

23. Beroaldus's commentary on Apuleius VI, 24 (ed. cit., fol. 79v) refers to *voluptas* as *qua summum bonum clarissimi philosophorum metiuntur*.

24. *Enneads* VI, ix, 9, tr. Dodds. This iconographic passage in Plotinus, which seems to have escaped Cumont, is a formidable witness against the attempt made by Wilamowitz, *Glaube der Hellenen* II, p. 365, and supported by Nock, 'Sarcophagi and Symbolism', *American Journal of Archeology* L (1946), p. 148, to dissociate the theme of Eros and Psyche from the Platonic tradition and funerary symbolism.

Proclus, there was the *De mysteriis* of Iamblichus, translated by Ficino, in which 'the way to felicity' (*via ad felicitatem*) ends in a joyous union with the god: *tunc opifici totam copulat animam*.[25] There were the 'Celestial Hierarchies' of Dionysius the Areopagite, in which the seraphs, who are closest to the deity, burn with a love that is above knowledge.[26] There was Plutarch *On the* εἰ *at Delphi*, in which Pico discerned the same consummation of ecstasy which the Cabbalists called *binsica* (*mors osculi*),[27] etc. Yet none of these texts enjoyed quite the same veneration as a curiously painstaking description by Plotinus of mystical hilarity in *Enneads* VI, vii, 34–6. These soberly corybantic chapters, which left a profound impression not only on Ficino and Pico, but before them on Hermias, Proclus, and Dionysius,[28] have recently been acclaimed by M. Émile Bréhier as 'la description la plus complète qui soit chez Plotin de l'attitude mystique'.[29] It may suffice to quote from them one central passage, with Ficino's translation, or paraphrase, added in Latin:

And it may be said therefore that the mind has two powers. ... The one is the vision of the sober mind (*sanae mentis visio*), the other is the mind in a state of love (*ipsa mens amans*): for when it loses its reason by becoming drunk with nectar (*quando enim insanit nectare penitus ebria*), then it enters into a state of love, diffusing itself wholly into delight (*se ipsam in affectionem suavitatemque beatam saturitate diffundens*): and it is better for it to rage thus than to remain aloof from that drunkenness.[30]

25. Iamblichus, *De mysteriis*, ed. Ficino (Aldus 1497), fols. e viiiᵛ–f iʳ; Ficino, *Opera*, p. 1908.

26. Pico, *De hominis dignitate*, ed. Garin, pp. 110 ff. 'Dionysio interprete'. See also Ficino, *In Dionysium Areopagitam*: 'Bonum est super essentiam et intellectum', *Opera*, p. 1015; 'quomodo fruamur bono perfectius quam simpliciter intelligendo', p. 1016; 'quomodo fruamur Deo per modum quendam intellectu praestantiorem', p. 1019; also p. 1025, etc.

27. *De hominis dignitate*, ed. Garin, p. 124; *Commento*, ibid., p. 558.

28. See Hans Lewy, *Sobria ebrietas, Untersuchungen zur Geschichte der antiken Mystik* (1929), pp. 103 f.; H. Koch, *Pseudo-Dionysius Areopagita in seinen Beziehungen zum Neuplatonismus und Mysterienwesen* (1900), pp. 141, 249 f.; H. F. Müller, *Dionysios. Proklos. Plotinos*. (1918), pp. 97 ff.

29. Plotinus, ed. Bréhier (1954), notes to *Enneads* VI, vii, 34–6. Also Bréhier, *La Philosophie de Plotin* (1928), pp. 155–8: ecstasy as 'sentiment de présence'.

30. *Enneads* VI, vii, 35.

Ficino's feeling about the profusion of delight may be judged by his rendering the single noun εὐπάθεια by an over-abundant compound of three words: *affectio suavitasque beata.*

On the evidence of the *Republic* (363C–D) it would be difficult to claim (although Ficino attempted it in his commentary on the passage) that Plato looked with favour on the banquet of the blessed, 'where they have the saints lying on couches at a feast, everlastingly drunk', because 'their idea seems to be that an immortality of drunkenness is the highest meed of virtue'.[31] But in the *Phaedrus*, the classical text on divine madness, Plato himself happened to mention 'nectar' as one of the supernatural nourishments of the soul (247E); and that sufficed for Proclus and Hermias and their Renaissance followers to presume that Plotinus's 'drunkenness with nectar' was the same as the 'divine madness' in the *Phaedrus*, particularly as Plato, too, had there asserted that 'madness is superior to a sane mind, for the one is only of human, but the other of divine origin' (244D).

Plotinus compared the divine ecstasy to 'the passions of lovers' (*amantium passiones*) because 'they do not love as long as they remain preoccupied with a visible image (*circa figuram oculis manifestam*); but when their soul ... becomes inwardly possessed by an invisible force, then they begin to love (*amor protinus oritur*)'.[32] The lesson that vision is less perfect than delight is here conveyed in terms which so clearly anticipate Ficino's *De felicitate*, Lorenzo's *L'altercazione*, and Pico's *Conclusiones* that there can be no doubt they were all three inspired by this section of the *Enneads*, which Ficino thus summarized in his commentary on Plotinus: 'Since the good is far superior to the intellect, and its fruition is hence not correctly named intelligence, it appears that it should also not be called cognition: for it is more natural and more desirable than cognition.' *Cum bonum sit longe superius intellectu, et idcirco fruitio eius non recte dicatur intelligentia, videtur neque cognitio nominanda. Est enim naturalior et optabilior quam cognitio.*[33]

31. It is curious to observe Ficino twisting Plato's clearly derogatory passage into a positive argument on divine *voluptas*, *Opera*, p. 1399. See also below, page 278.

32. *Enneads* VI, vii, 33.

33. Ficino, *Opera*, p. 1793, referring to *Enneads* VI, vii, 36. Cf. also Plotinus's own phrasing in *Enneads* VI, ix, 4, κατὰ παρουσίαν ἐπιστήμης κρείττονα and ἀποστῆναι δεῖ

In Ficino's preface to the *Mystical Theology* of Dionysius the Areopagite, the name Dionysius offered the occasion for describing as Bacchic the approach to God through a negation of the intellect.[34] The prayer in which Ficino asked to be inspired by the Bacchic ecstasy was almost literally borrowed from Plotinus: and yet it was addressed in the last line to the Christian trinity: *eadem prorsus oratione trinitas obsecranda.* 'The spirit of the god Dionysus,' Ficino explained, 'was believed by the ancient theologians and Platonists to be the ecstasy and abandon of disencumbered minds, when partly by innate love, partly at the instigation of the god, they transgress the natural limits of intelligence and are miraculously transformed into the beloved god himself: where, inebriated by a certain new draught of nectar and by an immeasurable joy, they rage, as it were, in a bacchic frenzy (*ubi novo quodam nectaris haustu, et inexistimabili gaudio velut ebrie, ut ita dixerim, debacchantur*). In the drunkenness of this Dionysiac wine our Dionysius expresses his exultation. He pours forth enigmas, he sings in dithyrambs. . . . To penetrate the profundity of his meanings . . . to imitate his quasi-Orphic manner of speech (*quasi Orphicum dicendi characterem*) . . ., we too require the divine fury. And by the same prayer let us implore the Trinity that the light which God infused into Dionysius, in answer to his pious wish that he might penetrate the mysteries of the prophets and the apostles, that the same may also be infused into us, who make a similar supplication. . . .'

*

In carrying his Orphic paradox to its logical conclusion, Pico developed a mystical radicalism which Ficino was not prepared to

καὶ ἐπιστήμης καὶ ἐπιστητῶν. And again the metaphor of the *passio amatoria*, οἷον ἐρωτικὸν πάθημα. For the supreme blindness of love, cf. also *Enneads* VI, vii, 35, θεός, καὶ οὗτος οὐ κατ' ὄψιν φανείς, and for the identification of *beatitudo* with inherent *voluptas*, Ficino's commentary on *Enneads* VI, vii, 30: 'Actus eiusmodi beatitudo est; etiamsi nulla huic voluptas exterior adjungatur, neque tamen ipse est voluptatis expers. Ipsa enim expedita actionis integritas atque summitas est voluptas.'

34. *Opera*, p. 1013. The same use in Pico, *Heptaplus* III, v (ed. Garin, p. 260): 'Vide quam haec Dionysiacis mysteriis apte conveniant', where 'Dionysiaca mysteria' means the mysteries of Dionysius the Areopagite.

accept. Both agreed that the highest form of love is blind, but while for Ficino it was the blindness of joy (*gaudium*), Pico's enthusiasm entailed a doctrine of mystical self-annihilation. In order to ascend to 'the cloud in which God resides' (*caligo quam Deus inhabitat*),[35] Pico believed that man must surrender himself utterly to a state of unknowing, and approach the divine secret in the blindness of self-destruction. This supreme form of love, he argued, is distinguished from friendship in that it is not returned; for it would be absurd to assume that the love of a mortal for God were of the same kind as the love extended by God to a mortal. 'In friendship, reciprocity is always necessary, as Plato says in many places; that is, one friend must love the other in the same way and by the same power as he is loved by him. . . .'[36] But to extend reciprocity to God is impossible. 'Amor de quo in Symposio loquitur Plato, in Deo nullo modo esse potest.'[37] That Ficino did not distinguish between these two forms of affection was to Pico a sign of 'utter confusion' (*confundendo in tutto*). Not recognizing that divine love was the supreme expression of a discord, and should be inspired by a deep sense of the disproportion between mortal and god, Ficino had supposed that they were commensurable, and that divine love could be pictured as a supreme form of friendship, through which all human friendships were divinely sustained. 'Thus there are not only two friends,' wrote Ficino, 'but necessarily always three, two of them men and one God.'[38]

For Ficino the world was 'full' of a god who transcends it: *Iovis omnia plena*. He therefore worshipped God simultaneously both beyond and within the creation. While Pico accepted Ficino's doctrine in principle,[39] he derived from it, in the *Heptaplus*, two divergent forms of felicity: 'natural felicity' (*naturalis felicitas*), which may be reached by uncovering the traces of God in oneself; and 'supreme felicity' (*summa felicitas*), which is achieved by losing

35. *De ente et uno* v (ed. Garin, p. 412).

36. *Commento* II, ii (ed. Garin, p. 488).

37. *Conclusiones secundum propriam opinionem . . . in doctrinam Platonis*, no. 22.

38. 'Ideo non duo quidem soli, sed tres necessario amici sunt semper, duo videlicet homines, unusque Deus' (*Opera*, p. 634).

39. *Heptaplus* VII, prooemium; ed. Garin, p. 328.

oneself in God. It is important to observe that, as he grew more independent of Ficino, he inclined to play out these two forms against
each other: 'The former,' he warned in the *Heptaplus*, 'is . . . rather
the shadow of felicity than felicity itself (*umbra potius felicitatis
quam vera felicitas*) inasmuch as the creature in which God is traced
. . . is but a tenuous shadow (*tenuis umbra*) of . . . divine goodness.
Furthermore, things are restored by that pursuit to themselves
rather than to God; the aim is not that they should return to their
origin but merely that they should not fall off from themselves (*ne
a seipsis discedant*).'[40] On this point Pico made a distinction which
threatened to undermine Ficino's system. Ficino always held the
two ways to be one, because he believed that only by reverting to
God do men achieve 'not falling off from themselves'. Since transcendence was the restorer of immanent virtue, man should find,
not merely lose, himself in God.

But Pico suspected Ficino's optimism of a Narcissus-like self-love
through God. Ficino had inadvertently recommended, under the
title *Quomodo Deus amandus*, that for the sake of our self-perfection
'we should so appear to venerate things in God that we would
embrace ourselves before others, and by loving God appear to have
loved ourselves'.[41] But however poorly argued,[42] Ficino's idea of an
amiable God, who sustains friendships among men by entering into
them and endowing them with an ideal perfection, is perhaps the
more Grecian in spirit; and it also recalls the poetic *Sternenfreund-*

40. *Heptaplus* VII, p. 332. See also p. 338: 'Ad hanc felicitatem [i.e. summae felicitatis
gradum] religio nos promovet . . ., quemadmodum ad naturalem duce utimur philosophia.'

41. *De amore* VI, xix. Giulio della Torre's two medals (Hill, nos. 570 f.), both
inscribed ME IPSUM HONESTE AMO, seem inspired by Ficino's words. Giulio is represented 'embracing himself': the naked image shows him in the image of God, the
cloaked image in his doctor's gown, both making the same gesture, but in reverse.
On the 'philosophy of clothes' involved in this distinction, see below, page 143.

42. In his Commentary on Dionysius the Areopagite, for example (*Opera*, p. 1070),
Ficino defined self-love as a primary attribute of God, from which human self-love is
a natural derivative. Our egotism thus becomes an imitation of God: 'Ex hoc primo
amore [quo se ipsum Deus amat], ex quo accenduntur omnes, factum est, ut unumquod-
que quodammodo prius se ipsum quam caetera diligat.' See also *Theologia Platonica*
XIV, viii: 'Quod colimus nos ipsos ac Deum' (*Opera*, pp. 317 f.). Pico, *Heptaplus* VI,
prooemium, ed. Garin, p. 310 ('universae caritatis ordo'), may have been designed as an
improvement of Ficino's argument.

schaft[43] as well as St Augustine's idea of 'friendship in God';[44] whereas an Averroistic note may be detected in Pico's refusal to conceive of 'ultimate peace in God' and 'all-embracing friendship' (*unanimis amicitia*) as anything but human self-effacement: 'qua omnes animi in una mente, quae est super omnem mentem, *non concordent* adeo, sed ineffabili quodam modo unum penitus evadant'.[45] On this point, as on so many others, Pico's quarrel with Ficino was clearly related to his Paduan training and sympathies.[46]

As the acumen and youthful intransigence of Pico detected many more flaws in Ficino's system, the celebrated harmony between master and pupil was of a remarkably short duration. The tension ended in an open breach when the *mirandus iuvenis* publicly offended his master by the hostile tone and content of *De ente et uno*. 'Oh that the admirable youth,' complained Ficino, 'had carefully considered

43. Ficino's *Epistolarium* shows that he made a cult of synastry, by which the harmony or 'identity' between two friends is ascribed to a star which they have in common. Cf. F. Boll, 'Synastria', *Socrates* V (1917), p. 458; F. Boll and C. Bezold, *Sternglaube und Sterndeutung* (1926), p. 113.

44. *Confessiones* IV, ix, 14.

45. *De hominis dignitate*, ed. Garin, p. 118 (italics mine).

46. On Pico's Averroism, see Garin, *Giovanni Pico della Mirandola* (1937), pp. 12 ff., 22, 26 f., 205 ff.; Anagnine, op. cit., pp. 8–13; Cassirer in *Journal of the History of Ideas* III (1942), pp. 134 ff., 335. While Pico's definition of *summa felicitas* as the ultimate extinction of the self in God would be difficult to reconcile with the Christian eschatology, his attempt to reduce the self-perfection of man on earth to a mere shadow felicity resembles Savonarola's preachings. Whether he ever succumbed to Savonarola in the same degree as his nephew Gianfrancesco has been doubted by Garin (op. cit., pp. 9 f., 43 ff.) and R. Ridolfi (*Vita di Girolamo Savonarola* I, 1952, p. 147; II, p. 133 note 11: documentary evidence from Savonarola's friend, Fra Giovanni Sinibaldi), whereas Festugière ('Studia Mirandulana', *Archives d'histoire doctrinale et littéraire du moyen âge* VII, 1932, pp. 144 ff.) supports the traditional view. The problem is complicated by the fact that Gianfrancesco is a biased witness on this question. From Pico, *De ente et uno* v (ed. Garin, p. 414), 'Defeci in atriis tuis, Domine', it would appear that he never abandoned his view of *summa felicitas* as personal 'extinction in God', and that alone would exclude a strict adherence to Savonarola's theology. See also his Orphic–Cabbalistic conclusion no. 15: 'Idem est nox apud Orpheum, et Ensoph in Cabala', which means 'Night and God are one.' He introduced, however, a number of concessions and safeguards in the *Conclusiones in Averroem* no. 4, *in Porphyrium* no. 12, *in doctrinam Platonis* no. 36, and *Conclusiones paradoxae* no. 69: 'quod tamen non assertive sed probabiliter dictum est'. His strictly philosophical opinion is unmistakably stated in *Commento* I, iii (ed. Garin, pp. 464 f.), concerning the plurality or uniqueness of the angelic mind. He subscribed to the latter opinion as being 'più filosofica e più conforme ad Aristotele e Platone e da tutti e' Peripatetici e migliori Platonici seguitata'.

these propositions and arguments before venturing forth with such confidence against his teacher, and declaring himself so firmly against the opinion of all the Platonists.'[47] The first unmistakable signs of the estrangement occur in the original version of the *Commento*, which was composed in 1486, that is three years after Pico's arrival in Florence. Here Pico interspersed his own observations on the Platonic theology with such remarks as 'not as Marsilio thinks', 'greatly do I wonder (*mi maraviglio*) how Marsilio can hold', 'a matter on which Marsilio should have greatly guarded himself from erring because on it depends the entire subject, and he that errs on this one point necessarily deviates in all the other parts not a little from the truth', winding up with an unqualified condemnation of Ficino's *De amore*:

Puoi dunque considerare, lettore, quanti errori . . . commetta el nostro Marsilio confundendo in tutto, . . . e pervertendo ciò che d'amore parla. . . . In ogni parte di questo trattato abbia commesso in ogni materia errori, come io credo nel processo chiaramente manifestare.[48]

As these remarks are directed against the very book from which the inscription on Pico's medal was taken, it is reasonable to infer that the medal must have been made before the autumn of 1486, which appears to be the date when the *Commento* was composed.[49] The medal would belong therefore to the first years of Pico's settlement in Florence (which began in the winter of 1483), when he still considered the *De amore*, as did all the loyal disciples of Ficino, the bible of the Platonic revival. Allowing for a certain period on either side, which was needed for acquiring Ficino's view and for relinquishing it, the date of the medal can be reasonably fixed as 1484-5.

These observations also help to solve another problem which might disturb a careful reader of Pico. In Pico's *Commento* the argument about the Graces does not correspond to the Graces on Pico's

47. *In Parmenidem* xlix (*Opera*, p. 1164).

48. *Commento*, ed. Garin, pp. 559, 466, 499, 488. These passages were omitted from the edition of Buonaccorsi (1519), on which all subsequent editions, except Garin's, are based. Cf. Garin, pp. 16 f.

49. For the date, see ibid., p. 11, with letters addressed by Pico to Andrea Corneo, 15 October 1486, when the treatise neared completion (*paulo mox*), and to Domenico Benivieni, 10 November 1486, when it was finished (*egimus*).

medal. Instead of Pulchritudo–Amor–Voluptas they represent Pulchritudo–Intellectus–Voluntas.[50] The triad again forms, as is clear from Pico's text, a Neoplatonic cycle of procession, conversion, and return. Pulchritudo emanates from the Beyond while Intellectus and Voluntas revert to it. Pico therefore pictured the last two Graces as turning away ('col volto in là'), as if 'returning from us to the gods', and the first Grace as facing us ('col volto inverso noi'), 'proceeding and not returning'. In other words, he retained the asymmetrical division of the classical group, a | b c, which was also prescribed by the legend on his medal, the orientation of the Graces being defined by the posture of their heads rather than their bodies.[51] It would be an error therefore to claim, as has occasionally been done, that in this passage Pico imagined the classical group turned around. He read it exactly as it would have to be read on his own medal to produce the sequence Pulchritudo–Amor–Voluptas, except that he replaced Amor and Voluptas by Intellectus and Voluntas. As a result, he produced a more sober, restricted triad, depriving the third Grace (Voluntas) of the fulfilment of joy (Voluptas), and reducing the second Grace to an *amor intellectualis*, that is, a desire of understanding. The difference was one of degree, Ficino himself having explained that Voluntas becomes Voluptas when it expands from the finite to the infinite: 'penes bonum infinitum voluntas omnis est ipsa voluptas'.[52]

With the deliberate reduction of Voluptas to Voluntas, and of Amor to Intellectus, Pico withdrew the triad of the Graces from that ultimate ecstasy in which, as he claimed against Ficino, the triad would altogether vanish into the One. Ficino sustained the gentler view that union with the ultimate need not always entail extinction. 'It is possible,' he wrote in his commentary on Plotinus, 'to achieve

50. *Commento* II, xv (ed. Garin II, xvii, p. 509): 'Bellezza–Intelletto–Voluntà.'

51. See above, page 44. The names of the Graces listed by Pico as *Viridità, Splendore,* and *Letizia* were again made to fit the argument. *Viridità* represents the permanent imperishable freshness of Beauty ('lo essere verde non è altro che permanere e durare') which shines forth from the Beyond, whereas the two powers of the soul which revert to the Beyond are represented by *Splendore* (= 'illumination of the intellect') and *Letizia* (= 'motivation of the will').

52. *Opera*, p. 881. See also p. 108, on the relation of *voluntas* (= *inclinatio mentis ad bonum*) to *voluptas* (= *quies voluntatis in bono*).

this not only after the present life but also while we are living (*etiam in hac vita*).'⁵³ And Plotinus himself seemed to supply the proof. He had experienced these extreme states occasionally,⁵⁴ and without detriment to his sober vision, and he did not hesitate to speak of them as reflected or copied in more familiar states of love: μίμησις δὲ τούτου καὶ οἱ ἐνταῦθα ἐρασταὶ καὶ ἐρώμενοι συγκρῖναι θέλοντες. In Ficino's rendering: 'Id enim apud nos imitari solent amantes et amati mutuo redamantes, qui conflari nituntur in unum.'⁵⁵

The frequent allusions to the passions of lovers, by which Plotinus paraphrased the mystical ecstasy, encouraged Ficino in his belief that *voluptas* should be reclassified as a noble passion. Here again his Neoplatonism is marked by a curiously anti-ascetic strain: for however insistent he was in explaining the agreement of his philosophy with the Christian creed, he tried to infuse into Christian morals a kind of neo-pagan joy, for which the *passio amatoria* served as a model. It is in the positive revaluation of an impulse which Christian asceticism tended to scorn that Ficino revealed himself as a neo-pagan thinker. So much has been written in recent years on the continuation of the Middle Ages into the Renaissance, and of medieval modes of thought in Renaissance Platonism, that we are apt to underestimate the decisive 'transvaluation of values' which Ficino and some of his Florentine friends achieved in the theory of morals. A noble form of irascibility, for instance, remained a contradiction in terms as long as *ira* was classed irrevocably as a deadly sin.⁵⁶ Yet under the influence of Seneca's *De ira*, although the medieval classification continued, a 'noble rage' was separated from the common vice and defended as a virtue by Florentine humanists, in particular

---

53. *Opera*, p. 1793 (referring to *Enneads* VI, vii, 34).

54. Four times, according to Porphyry, *Vita Plotini* 23.

55. *Enneads* VI, vii, 34. The same comparison in *Asclepius* 21 (*Corpus Hermeticum*, ed. Nock–Festugière II, pp. 321 ff.), annotated by Ficino, *Opera*, pp. 1864 f. ('In Mercurii Trismegisti Asclepium' viii).

56. In order to explain Psalms iv, 5 [Vulgate]: 'irascimini et nolite peccare', St Gregory (*Moralia* V, xlv, 82 f.; *Patr. lat.* LXXV, 726 f.) and St Bernard (*Sermones*, *Patr. lat.* CLXXXIII, 487) found themselves forced to postulate a deliberate anger which 'does not burst forth', but comes when called – in other words, an anger which is no anger. And even to that St Gregory added a *cavendum*: 'Cavendum ne ira menti ex zelo commotae dominetur.'

by Bruni, Palmieri, Politian, and Landino.[57] By a similar transmutation the vice of sloth, the horrid *acedia*, was distilled into noble
melancholy: for although *acedia* remained a deadly sin, an Aristotelian refinement of the affliction became the privilege of inspired
men.[58] It is with these Renaissance vindications of melancholy and
rage as noble passions that the cult of a noble *voluptas* should be compared.[59] Like *acedia* and *ira*, the vice of *luxuria* continued to be classed
as a deadly sin, and the vulgar *voluptas*, that is incontinence, was
pictured in her image. And yet, on the authority of Plotinus, sustained in this instance by Epicurus, a noble *voluptas* was introduced
as the *summum bonum* of Neoplatonists.[60]

57. A characteristic example is Politian's *De ira* (*Opera* II, 1519, fols. 54ᵛ f.), a short
note on the education of children. He distinguishes within *ira* between a vicious *rancor*
(μῆνις, κότος), the sign of an illiberal spirit, and a generous *excandescentia* (θυμός),
which should be encouraged because it is the opposite of stupor. Yet he regards *iracun-
dia* as their common source and describes them as *duo diversi inter se affectus ab uno quasi
capite et fonte emanantes*. On the revaluation of anger by political thinkers, cf. H. Baron,
'La rinascità dell'etica statale romana nell'umanesimo fiorentino del Quattrocento',
Civiltà moderna VII (1935), p. 38; D. Cantimori, 'Rhetoric and Politics in Italian
Humanism', *Journal of the Warburg Institute* I (1937), p. 92. A theological justification
was attempted by Pico, *Heptaplus* IV, v (ed. Garin, p. 282), in connexion with God's
blessing of the animals: 'Be fruitful, and multiply.' He argued that anger, pride, con-
cupiscence, and other animal passions, far from being inherently evil, become evil only
through abuse, being intrinsically divine endowments adjusted to man's particular
state. 'We should feel anger, but within measure; and revenge is often a work of
justice, and each must protect his own dignity, nor are honours to be spurned which
are obtained by honest means.' This passage, in one of Pico's last theological writings,
is so contrary to Savonarola's praise of self-mortification that it seems to justify the
doubts expressed by Garin and Ridolfi concerning the extent of Pico's conversion by
Savonarola (see above page 65 note 46).

58. *Problemata* XXX, i; cf. Panofsky, *Albrecht Dürer* I (1943), pp. 156-71; Panofsky-
Saxl, *Dürers Kupferstich 'Melencolia I'* (1923); Klibansky-Panofsky-Saxl, *Saturn and
Melancholy* (1964), pp. 241 ff. Of earlier literature see the basic work of K. Gichlow,
'Dürers Stich "Melencolia I" und der maximilianische Humanistenkreis', in Supple-
ment to *Die graphischen Künste* XXVI (1903), pp. 29-41; XXVII (1904), pp. 6-18, 57-78.

59. See recently Garin, *L'umanesimo italiano* (1952), pp. 64-8: 'Il mondo delle pas-
sioni e il valore del piacere.'

60. Ficino conceded (*In Philebum* I, xxxvii, *Opera*, p. 1252) that the definition of
voluptas as the highest good would be difficult to reconcile with a literal reading of
Plato, but he found support for it in *Phaedrus* 247E by an allegorical reading of the
passage on ambrosia and nectar. Cf. *Epistola de felicitate*, *Opera*, p. 663; *De voluptate*,
ibid., p. 987. His occasional attempt to escape the dilemma by postulating a coincidence
of pleasure and intellect in God (*Theologia Platonica* X, viii, *Opera*, p. 237; also *Epistolarium* II, ibid., p. 693) did little to resolve the duality, conflict, and subordination

Some sixty years ago the hedonistic element in Ficino was clearly observed by F. Gabotto in an article 'L'epicureismo di Marsilio Ficino',[61] a sequel to his studies in Renaissance Epicureanism;[62] but not only did his analysis fail at the time to impress, disturb, or reform the conventional view of the Platonic revival – even today, after D. C. Allen has newly demonstrated 'The Rehabilitation of Epicurus and his Theory of Pleasure in the Early Renaissance',[63] the Epicurean element in Renaissance Platonism seems to cause consternation, embarrassment, and disbelief.[64] The author of a recent article, 'The Defence of Pleasure in More's Utopia', is so perplexed by More's definition of pleasure as the supreme good that he tries to reduce the argument to a rhetorical showpiece, a provocative *declamatio* designed to challenge rather than persuade.[65] Yet anyone reading Book II of the *Utopia* without prejudice will discover that More not only means exactly what he says, but that he says exactly the same as Ficino and Pico: 'Therefore the matter diligently weighed and considered, thus they [the Utopians] think that all our actions, and in them the virtues themselves, be referred at the last to pleasure, as their end and felicity.' In his famous colloquy *The Epicurean* Erasmus remarked that 'if they are Epicureans that live pleasantly, none are more truly Epicureans than those that live holily and religiously',[66] implying that Christianity should be a guide to the most pleasant life both in this world and in the next. The Reverend E. Johnson, who edited Bailey's translation of the

---

between *intellectus* and *voluptas* in man. On the whole he retained the position of Plotinus (*Enneads* VI, vii, 25–30 ff.) who starts from the problem posed by the 'mixture' of *intellectus* and *voluptas* in the *Philebus* (τάχα ἂν αἰσθόμενος ταύτης τῆς ἀπορίας, in Ficino's translation: *fortasse ambiguitatem eiusmodi sentiens*), and then resolves it by the theory of supreme, unmixed *voluptas*, which transcends the intellect altogether.

61. *Rivista di filosofia scientifica* X (1891), pp. 428–42.
62. ibid. VIII (1889), pp. 552–63; 651–72; 730–9.
63. *Studies in Philology* XLI (1944), pp. 1–5.
64. A marked exception is of course Kristeller, *The Philosophy of Marsilio Ficino*, pp. 296 f.
65. E. L. Surtz, in *Studies in Philology* XLVI (1949), pp. 99–112. In another article, 'Epicurus in Utopia', *ELH* XVI (1949), pp. 89–103, the same author extends his paradoxical interpretation also to Erasmus's colloquy *The Epicurean*.
66. *The Colloquies of Desiderius Erasmus*, tr. N. Bailey, III (1900), p. 260.

Colloquies with notes, remarked very justly that Erasmus's observations on Pleasure anticipate Montaigne's: 'Whatever they may say, in virtue itself the ultimate aim of our effort is enjoyment [*volupté*]. It pleases me to knock this word, which is so distasteful to them, about their ears; and if it signifies some supreme joy and exceeding contentment, it is more due to the assistance of virtue than to any other assistance.'[67]

The Stoic assumption that pleasure must be deficient in virtue, and virtue deficient in pleasure, never gained much credence among Renaissance Neoplatonists. Granted that the pursuit of virtue may at times be unpleasant, and the pursuit of pleasure at times lead to vice, it would be in either case, Ficino argued, only a limited virtue and a limited pleasure which would be attended by such negative effects. The more comprehensive the virtues and the pleasures become, the more largely they are bound to overlap; and when a pleasure or virtue becomes all-embracing – that is, when they reach a perfection achieved only in states of ecstasy – then goodness becomes indistinguishable from bliss. In illustrating the motto: *cum virtute alma consentit vera voluptas*, Bocchi pictured Minerva and Venus embracing each other while they crown the drunken Silenus (fig. 56).[68]

*

67. Montaigne, *Essais* I, xix (ed. 1595) = I, xx (MS de Bordeaux); cf. *Colloquies of Erasmus*, ed. cit. III, p. 314.

68. Achille Bocchi, *Symbolicae quaestiones* (1574), no. x. Although the first edition appeared as late as 1555, the book preserves some of the symbolism of the middle and late Quattrocento, as seen clearly in Symbolon no. cxlvii (ed. 1574), which copies verbatim, for the benefit of Bocchi's son, a table of hieroglyphs from the *Hypnerotomachia*, 1499, fol. cʳ. It is not surprising therefore to find Bocchi useful in resolving problems of the Quattrocento. Like Valeriano and Gyraldus, who were his friends, he was imbued with the spirit of fifteenth-century hieroglyphics, transmitted to this group of sixteenth-century authors by Valeriano's uncle and teacher, Fra Urbano, who lived from 1440 to 1524. Although most of their books appeared late in print, they differ from Ripa's and Cartari's iconologies by being originally conceived for a recondite circle, and not as manuals for popular use. In fact, some of the incongruities in Valeriano and Gyraldus result from the insertion of early writings into encyclopedic compendia whose style they do not fit. In Gyraldus's *Syntagmata*, the chapters on Bacchus and the Muses show these vestiges very clearly; but the most interesting case is Book XXXIII of Valeriano's *Hieroglyphica*, which incorporates the remnants of an independent Dialogue, with Fra Urbano as chief speaker. It is possible that this piece

71

If the literature on the Graces has helped to define the nature of the breach between Ficino and Pico, it also informs us about the harmony which prevailed between them at first. In a letter entitled *De tribus gratiis et concordia*, which seems to antedate their quarrel,[69] Ficino made a good-humoured attempt to define the philosophical eminence of his pupil by applying to him his own favourite image. The occasion for this was offered by Pico's title, Count of Concordia. It was part of Ficino's epistolary style to embellish the names of his friends with puns – puns of an oracular or diagnostic jocularity, as if the nature of the man could be extracted from his name (quite possibly a mannerism adopted from Plato). If Mirandola gave rise to *mirandus iuvenis*, Concordia did not fail to recall the concord of the Graces. Now the Latin word for count being *comes*, which means follower, the *comes Concordiae* was to all appearances a 'follower of the Graces'. But Ficino knew that he was more than that. By his sense of concord Pico was able to reconcile the most divergent philosophers: Platonists and Aristotelians, Christians and Jews, Latins and Greeks, all dropped their quarrels in his presence to reveal an unexpected harmony. Clearly, this supposed follower of the Graces was their leader; for they followed him wherever he went. And as the Latin word for leader is *dux*, which also means duke,

---

preserves the form in which Valeriano had originally hoped to cast the *Hieroglyphica*, before he was engulfed by lexicography. Although cruelly disjointed by its adaptation to the sectional headings of the book, the Dialogue is not an unworthy pendant to Valeriano's *De infelicitate literatorum*, of a later date, which ends with a eulogy of Fra Urbano. A further link with the Quattrocento was Bocchi's close association with Alberto Pio, prince of Carpi (on which see G. M. Mazzuchelli, *Scrittori d'Italia*, 1758, pp. 1389–92), who, like Gyraldus's patron, Gianfrancesco Pico, was a nephew and literary executor of Giovanni Pico della Mirandola. On Bocchi's friendship with Valeriano see the dedication of Book VII of Valeriano's *Hieroglyphica*. A less favourable opinion of Bocchi's character is given below, page 99 note 6.

69. Addressed to Salviati and Benivieni, *Opera*, p. 890. The letter bears no date. It was included by Ficino in a group of letters of 1488, but to judge by its content, it must antedate Pico's conflict with the Church, which began in 1487. Ficino's description of Pico as a genius of peace, introducing harmony and concord wherever he went, could hardly have been written during the period in which Pico was indicted for heresy, pursued and arrested because of his obstinacy, and returned to Florence as a virtual prisoner, in the friendly custody of Lorenzo. The indictment was not revoked until 1493, one year before Pico's death.

Ficino promoted Pico *honoris causa* from a count to a duke of Concordia.

All this was a joke, and rather laboured. But in Florence literary jokes had a serious aspect. They were a way of attaching a label. Since the Graces appear on Pico's medal with an inscription taken from Ficino, it is very likely, in view of Ficino's letter, that it was he who fastened the emblem on Pico. And there is further evidence that, in this period of his life, Pico not only accepted the emblem with grace, but made of it the playful use prescribed by the rites of Florentine Platonism.

Like troubadours, the Platonic lovers were expected to choose an ideal lady, to whom they could address amorous courtesies in emblematic language. The lady would return the honour by accepting the emblem of her Platonic suitor, and adapting it to her own use. Given the custom,[70] it can hardly be an accident that the medal of Giovanna degli Albizzi, the wife of the gifted Lorenzo Tornabuoni to whom Politian refers in a letter to Pico as 'non discipulus modo sed et alumnus',[71] shows the image of the three Graces in a design (figs. 12, 13) which is cast from the same model as Pico's medal[72] and bears an inscription that answers his. Instead of PULCHRITUDO–AMOR–VOLUPTAS, it reads CASTITAS–PULCHRITUDO–AMOR. The shift of emphasis introduces a cooler tone which reflects the mood of the admired woman. Amor, originally in the centre, is now on the right; Pulchritudo, which was on the left, has moved to the centre; Castitas, not previously recorded, has entered on the left; and Voluptas has vanished altogether. In the place of a Platonic definition of Love: 'Love is Passion aroused by Beauty', a motto suitable for a man, we now have a Platonic definition of Beauty: 'Beauty is Love combined with Chastity', which is the answer of a woman. Again the Grace in the centre unites the opposites: for in

---

70. cf. Warburg, 'Delle imprese amorose', op. cit., pp. 79–88; also pp. 331–9.

71. *Epistolae* XII, vii, in *Opera*, ed. cit. I, fol. 100ᵛ. He also dedicated the *Ambra* to him, *Epistolae* X, xi, ibid., fol. 90ʳ.

72. Hill, no. 1021, cf. no. 998: 'from same model'. The date of the obverse, which represents Giovanna as married (1486), need not be the date of the first use of the reverse. She may well have used the image of the three Graces both before and after her marriage.

Pulchritudo the contraries of Castitas and Amor coincide. But like the Grace of Amor on Pico's medal, Pulchritudo now also achieves a conversion. As Love there turned from Beauty towards Pleasure, so Beauty now turns from Chastity towards Love.

In these elaborate games of disinterested courtship, which culminated in tournaments and masques, the dialectical language of Neoplatonism acquired a playful, chivalrous accent. But although the terms of the 'mysteries of Plato' were eminently suited to sustain the formal pleasures of hide-and-seek, the worldly use made of the mysteries did not detract from the reverence in which they were held, but merely proved their vitality. Just as it was customary in the exchange of sonnets to reverse the argument while retaining the rhymes,[73] so the exchange of emblems made it obligatory to retain the image but reverse its meaning.[74] On both sides of the argument

---

73. This game of poetical retorts (*tenzoni*) whose French origins date back to the twelfth century (cf. A. Jeanroy, *La poésie lyrique des Troubadours* II, 1934, pp. 246 ff.: 'tenson, partimen, coblas'; also *Recueil général des jeux-partis français*, ed. A. Långfors, A. Jeanroy, L. Brandin, 1926) was fully naturalized in Italy by the time of Dante and Petrarch (S. Santangelo, *Le tenzoni poetiche nella letteratura italiana delle origini*, 1928). To play it with fastidious regularity became the duty even of casual Petrarchists. Among Michelangelo's sonnets, for example, the famous verses on the vanity of his art (*Giunto è già 'l corso della vita mia*, ed. Girardi, 1960, no. 285) were answered by Vasari in 'a sonnet of corresponding rhymes' (*Vite*, ed. Milanesi, VII, 1881, p. 246). Lodovico Beccadelli replied to *Le favole del mondo m'hanno tolto* (Girardi, no. 288) with *Con passo infermo et bianca falda al volto* (ibid., p. 455). By the same token Michelangelo's sonnet on the Crucifixion, *Non fur men lieti che turbati e tristi* (Girardi, no. 298), must be an answer to Vittoria Colonna's *Rime sacre* no. 67, which dates Michelangelo's poem earlier than Girardi suggests (p. 469). The most celebrated of these reversals was Michelangelo's reply to Giovanni Strozzi's epigram on the *Night* (Vasari, loc. cit., p. 197; Girardi, no. 247).

74. The custom was parodied by Pietro Aretino. His emblem VERITAS ODIUM PARIT (cf. Cicero, *De amicitia* xxiv, 89; Terence, *Andria* I, i, 41), best shown in the medal ascribed to Leone Leoni (National Gallery of Art, Washington, no. A1164.427A, formerly Gustave Dreyfus Collection), reverses the design of Federigo Gonzaga's medal, GLORIAM AFFERTE DOMINO (Hill, nos. 267 f., ascribed to Giambattista Cavalli). The medal signed A.V. (Alessandro Vittoria?), with the notorious inscription PRINCIPI TRIBUTATI DAI POPOLI IL SERVO LORO TRIBUTANO (placed by Sir Thomas Browne in his *Museum clausum*), parodies a famous medal of Paul III by Alessandro Cesati: OMNES REGES SERVIENT EI. Unmatched was Politian's virtuosity in loading a simple phrase or image with contentious matter. An emblem that he designed for the young Piero de' Medici, suggesting that flames burn more fiercely in fresh wood: IN VIRIDI TENERAS EXURIT FLAMMA MEDULLAS (illustrated in

it was considered elegant to introduce ideas that were sanctioned by a fixed tradition. Hence the names chosen for the Graces by Giovanna degli Albizzi were, no less than those on Pico's medal, adopted rather than invented for the purpose. In the engraving of the *Tarocchi*, for example, which antedates these medals by about twenty years, the three Graces, still unaware of their obligation to assume a classical posture (fig. 18), are characterized by three attributes – a loin cloth, a flower, and a flame – which signify Castitas, Pulchritudo, and Amor.[75]

Giovanna degli Albizzi was not satisfied, however, with only one emblem for the reverse of her medal. As an alternative to the three Graces she employed a surprisingly martial and vigorous design (fig. 14). This shows a huntress carrying bow and arrow, wearing a winged crown on her head and heavy boots on her feet, and standing on a small cloud which covers the sun, but allows its rays to be seen around it. The inscription is a verse from the *Aeneid* in which Venus appears disguised as a nymph of Diana, the goddess of love as a devotee of chastity:

Virginis os habitumque gerens et virginis arma.[76]

As in a musical modulation, the theme of the three Graces, CASTITAS-PULCHRITUDO-AMOR, has been restated in a different key. The union of Chastity and Love through the mediation of Beauty is now expressed by one hybrid figure in which the two opposing goddesses, Diana and Venus, are merged into one.[77]

Paolo Giovio, *Dialogo dell'imprese militari et amorose*, 1574, p. 49), conceals three literary allusions: (1) to Petrarch's *Canzoniere* II, iii, 10 f., where exactly the contrary is said: 'arso tanto più quanto son men verde legno'; (2) to Virgil, *Aeneid* IV, 66–8: 'Est mollis flamma medullas . . . uritur infelix Dido'; (3) to Ficino's idea, disapproved by Politian, of transferring these verses to an elderly lover, *De amore* VII, ix: 'senioris viscera'.

75. Detail from Hind, *Early Italian Engraving*, pl. 362: 'Venus.'

76. I, 315.

77. Being a single figure, this image may have been designed for Giovanna as a companion piece to the single figure of Mercury on her husband's medal (Hill, no. 1068), although Mercury would of course also be in place as leader of the Graces (cf. Warburg, op. cit., pp. 39, 320). Hill's attempt to date Lorenzo Tornabuoni's

An exact parallel to the two emblems of Giovanna is to be found in the medals of Maria Poliziana, who is believed to have been the sister of Politian.[78] She, too, used two alternative designs, one of them martial, the other amiable.[79] In the amiable version the three Graces reappear, with the inscription CONCORDIA, while the martial design shows a single energetic figure of CONSTANTIA (figs. 69, 70). Normally, Constantia would hold a lance and lean on a column (fig. 72),[80] and the present figure repeats that well-known posture. But the lance is replaced by an arrow of love which she swings in a defiant bellicose manner, and the column on which she leans is formed by a bundle of arrows, the traditional symbol of Concordia. The visibly fierce, unassailable Constantia is therefore a concealed Concordia; like a closed fist withholding an open palm. Or, to borrow the terminology of Cusanus, Constantia is represented as an 'infolded' Concordia – Concordia as an 'unfolded' Constantia[81] (a terminology which fits also the Albizzi medal: Venus-Virgo unfolded in the Graces, the Graces infolded in Venus-Virgo).

medal by the sword of Mercury, in which he sees an allusion to Lorenzo's execution, is untenable because a 'sword-bearing Mercury' is a medieval and Renaissance commonplace, derived from his byname *Argeiphontes*: 'onde posero alle volte ancora une scimitarra in mano alla sua statoa' (Cartari, *Imagini*, s.v. 'Mercurio'); 'falcatum gladium habens, id est Harpen' (Gyraldus, *Opera* I, 298); '*Harpedophorum* Mercurium etiam appellatum legimus, ab Harpe falce, qua Argum mactasse ferunt: de Harpe Ovidius, Hyginus, alii' (ibid., 303).

78. Very little is known about her: see I. del Lungo, *Florentia* (1897), pp. 54ff.; Hill, 'Notes on Italian Medals xxiv, 1: Maria Poliziana', *Burlington Magazine* XXXI (1917), p. 99; J. Hill Cotton, 'Iconografia di Angelo Poliziano', *Rinascimento* II (1951), pp. 264 ff. To call her Politian's wife (Gombrich in *Warburg Journal* VIII, p. 35 note 4) is to ignore that Politian had taken holy orders.

79. Hill, nos. 1003, 1005. A third medal, no. 1004, has no design but a punning inscription which harps on the verb *carpere*, perhaps alluding to one of the princes of Carpi.

80. ibid., no. 758.

81. Costanza Bentivoglio, who married Antonio Pico della Mirandola and thence became countess of Concordia, combined *Constantia* and *Concordia* in her name; and since the only known reverse of her medal (Hill, no. 997) shows an image of *Constantia* cast after the same model as our fig. 72, one cannot but wonder whether it was not from her that Maria Poliziana adopted the Constantia–Concordia imagery. Their medals are of the same size; and as Hill has pointed out in many other instances, the combination of obverse and reverse that has come down to us is not always the original one.

Unquestionably, the most authoritative of these composite figures was the Venus-Virgo from the *Aeneid*. In her the Renaissance Platonists thought they had found a fine poetical confirmation for their doctrine of the union of Chastity and Love. While it is doubtful whether Virgil intended the image to convey any mystery of that kind, they expanded it into a semi-chaste, semi-voluptuous cult of Venus, in which her double nature could be refined to the highest points of either reverence or frivolity or both.[82] A popular ornament on Florentine marriage *cassoni*,[83] the emblem acquired a new courtly twist in France and England, where its potentialities were developed more fully than in Italy itself. The imagery of Diane de Poitiers, for example, in which her role as the king's mistress is unblushingly celebrated, would seem to contradict her part as Diana, were it not that Diana is here a Venus in disguise, at times in fact so little disguised that she appears actually as Venus. In a characteristic portrait of her attributed to François Clouet,[84] the mythological 'bath of Diana' is transformed into a *toilette de Vénus*, with all the appurtenances of the goddess of love, including a background-scene directly quoted from Titian's *Venus of Urbino*.

In view of the Italian sources of Elizabethan imagery, perhaps the question is not unjustified whether the worship of Queen Elizabeth as Diana was not also a cult of Venus in disguise. Among the portraits of the queen by Isaac Oliver there is one that bears, in the engraving of Crispin van de Passe, an inscription which unmistakably refers to the verse in Virgil:

Virginis os habitumque geris, divina virago.[85]

82. Warburg's concept of a 'plastische Ausgleichsformel', which he developed in his essay on Francesco Sassetti (op. cit., pp. 151, 158, 364 f.), grew out of his early interest in the appearance of the Venus-Virgo (ibid., pp. 30 f., with additional notes pp. 312–16).

83. P. Schubring, *Cassoni* (1923), plates 48 ff. Examples in the Yale University Art Gallery; Kestner Museum, Hanover; etc.

84. Worcester (Mass.) Art Museum. The decorations of the Fountain Room in the Château d'Anet, the titles of which are listed in F. A. Yates, *The French Academies of the Sixteenth Century* (1947), p. 135 note 5, were also designed in pairs of opposites – Sobriety and Inebriation, Love extinguished and Love returned, Virginity tested and protected, Narcissus opposed to Hermaphroditus, etc.

85. Hind, *Engraving in England in the Sixteenth and Seventeenth Centuries* I (1952), p. 282, no. 1; pl. 141.

A similar allusion occurs again in Spenser, where the combination of 'Thenots Embleme: *O quam te memorem virgo?*' and 'Hobbinolls Embleme: *O dea certe*' is thus explained in the Gloss: 'This Poesye is taken out of Virgile,[86] and there of him used in the person of Aeneas. to his mother Venus, appearing to him in likenesse of one of Dianaes damosells. . . . To which similitude of divinitie Hobbinoll comparing the excelency of Eliza . . .' etc.[87]

But to return to the virago on the Albizzi medal: the idea that Chastity is a weapon of Venus, arousing the passions it professes to restrain, lends a particular significance to the bow and arrow which the figure triumphantly displays (fig. 14). These are unquestionably the weapons of Diana – *virginis arma*, as Virgil says. But they are also the weapons of Cupid. In their operation the two implements reveal between themselves what Plato called ἁρμονία τόξου (literally, 'the harmony of the bow'), which he said Heraclitus had defined as 'the One united by disunion'.[88] While the arrow flies and hits blindly like passion,[89] the bow, held steadily in its place, is used with a seeing eye; and because its strength resides in its tension, it is a symbol of restraint. A bow without arrow, and an arrow without bow, are clearly of no possible use; but combined they impart energy to each other, and illustrate that 'harmony in discord' which Pico defined as the essence of Pulchritudo: '. . . la contrarietà unita, e la discordia concorde, il che si può per vera definizione assignare di essa bellezza, cioè che non sia altro che una amica inimicizia e una concorde discordia.'[90]

In the mysterious allegory by Titian in the Borghese Gallery, which represents an initiation into Love (fig. 15), bow and arrow are carried by two separate figures. The one bringing the bow resembles

---

86. *Aeneid* I, 327 f.

87. *Shepheardes Calender, Aprill.* Cf. also *Faerie Queene* IV Proem, 4, in which Elizabeth is celebrated as 'the Queene of love'.

88. *Symposium* 187A.

89. On the symbol of the 'blind arrow', see Pico's description of *desiderio naturale, Commento* II, ii (ed. Garin II, iv, p. 490): '. . . al fin suo dirizate come la sagitta del sagittario al suo bersaglio, el quale non è dalla sagitta cognosciuto, ma da colui che con occhio . . . verso quello la muove'. The same image in Ficino, *Theologia Platonica* XIV, viii (*Opera*, p. 318), also XIV, i (ibid., p. 306).

90. *Commento* II, vi (ed. Garin II, viii, p. 495).

the chaste huntress Diana, while her companion, who holds the arrows, is a passionate figure partly nude. They present their gifts to a crowned Venus attended by two cupids, one blind, the other seeing. As bow and arrow belong together, so the perfect Venus combines passion and perspicacity. While she listens to the advice of the seeing cupid, she herself puts a blinding band over the eyes of his restive brother so that he may bring knowledge to fruition in joy. 'Nature has decreed,' according to Pico, 'that to every cognitive virtue be joined an appetitive virtue', and he adds that the 'appetitive virtue as such is blind and does not know' (*virtù appetitiva ... per sè è cieca e non conosce*).[91] Yet it is the state of appetitive 'unknowing', a state of *docta ignorantia*, for which knowledge aims and in which it finds its fulfilment: 'Love is said by Orpheus to be without eyes because he is above the intellect.' Or in the words of Ficino: 'Amanti convenit ut re amata fruatur et gaudeat ... inquirenti autem ut videat. ... Gaudium igitur in homine felice superat visionem.' In the verses of Lorenzo de' Medici, the same theme was further developed as an 'altercation' between 'Sight' (*veder*) and 'Joy' (*goder*), between perceptive meditation and voluptuous pleasure, in which pleasure was proved to be higher and more profound than meditation:

> *A chi cerca veder, veder conviensi;*
> *ma all'amante della cosa che ama*
> *goder sempre e fruir piacere immensi.*[92]

And he repeatedly argues to the conclusion that 'sight' is only a preliminary to 'joy':

> *Render ragion possiamo a chi richiede*
> *a che fin noi cerchiam, ch'è per fruire*
> *quel ben che nostra mente prima vede.*[93]

Thus the inquiring spirit, while retaining an advisory role, must in the end give way to the impulsiveness of passion because 'the soul by love acquires more divine goodness than it does by knowledge'.[94] In the *Dream of Poliphilus* the supremacy of joyous desire is

91. *Commento* II, iii (ed. Garin II, v, pp. 491 f.). 92. *Altercazione* IV, 139 ff.
93. ibid. V, 19 ff.   94. ibid. IV, 104 f.

illustrated by the victory of the hero's emotional over his reasonable self. At the gate of the ultimate mystery, to which he has been led by the two guides Logistike and Thelemia, he is suddenly abandoned by Logistike and entrusts himself to Thelemia alone.[95] It is consistent with the ancillary part of Logistike that in the composition of Titian's painting the deliberating Cupid and the Diana-like nymph are in a marginal position, while the foreground and the more central place are assigned to the blindfolded Cupid and the nymph holding the arrows. The action of the chief figure sustains this conclusion. She herself blindfolds the Cupid in her lap.[96]

It is unfortunate that the painting, which ought to be called *The Blinding of Amor*, has acquired in fairly recent years the misleading title *The Education of Amor*. This designates an entirely different scene (painted, for example, by Correggio)[97] in which Amor is taught by Mercury how to read, in its turn a very popular subject in the Renaissance because it represents the love of learning. While a painting of that subject would demonstrate the nature and growth of intellectual love (*amor intellectualis*), Titian's picture shows, on the contrary, how intellectual love is not an end in itself but must find its fruition in passion (*voluptas*). In the seventeenth century the picture went under a title more clearly inappropriate to the characters portrayed but less misleading. It was listed by Ridolfi as *The Graces*.[98] However wrong, this older title retains a vestige of the truth, for the picture does illustrate a mystical initiation for which the three Graces had served as a figure.

95. *Hypnerotomachia*, fol. i ii[r] – not, incidentally, a Venetian idiosyncrasy, but common to all writers on mysteries (cf. above, pages 58 ff.; also page 1 note 2).

96. Panofsky's attempt to interpret the painting on the theory that the blindfolded Cupid represents a frivolous and inferior form of love from which the main figure advisedly withdraws leads to the hardly tenable description that 'she has already stopped blindfolding him' (*Studies in Iconology*, p. 166). The position of her fingers rather suggests the reverse: they are tying, not loosening, the 'knot of love'. I notice that in the recent guides to the Galleria Borghese by Aldo de Rinaldis (1935) and Paola della Pergola (1952) the scene is correctly described as 'Venus blindfolding Amor' (*Venere che benda Amore*).   97. National Gallery, London.

98. Ridolfi, *Le maraviglie dell'arte*, ed. Hadeln, I (1914), p. 197: 'le Gratie con Cupidine ed alcune pastorelle'. Clearly one of Ridolfi's confusions, but which seems to rest on an anterior tradition. According to Pergola, *The Borghese Gallery*, p. 58, the painting is 'called the "Three Graces" in the ancient inventories of the Gallery'.

CHAPTER V

VIRTUE RECONCILED WITH PLEASURE

AMONG the most engaging paintings by the young Raphael is the little picture of the *Dream of Scipio* (fig. 60), now in the National Gallery, which was presumably painted for a young Scipione Borghese.[1] The young hero lies at the foot of a laurel tree,[2] apparently dreaming of his fame. Two women approach him. The sterner one presents him with a sword and a book, the more gracious offers a flower. These three attributes – book, sword, and flower – signify the three powers in the soul of man: intelligence, strength, and sensibility, or (as Plato called them) mind, courage, and desire. In the Platonic scheme of the 'tripartite life', two gifts, the intellectual and moral, are of the spirit while the third gift (the flower) is of the senses. Together they constitute a complete man, but as they mingle in different proportions they produce different characters and dispositions: 'The philosophers,' wrote Fulgentius in copying out Plutarch, who in his turn restated a view of Plato, 'have decided that the life of humanity consists of three parts, of which the first is

---

1. Panofsky, *Hercules am Scheidewege* (1930), pp. 76 ff.; R. Eisler, *Revue archéologique* XXXII (1930), pp. 134 f. Although not mentioned by these authors, it was surely Macrobius's commentary on Cicero's *Somnium Scipionis* that suggested the idea of a 'dreaming Scipio', a subject genuinely antique and Neoplatonic (cf. Boyancé, *Études sur le songe de Scipion*, 1936, pp. 121–46, 173 ff.), and not created *ad hoc* by Raphael's adaptation of a 'dreaming Hercules' from a Northern woodcut illustrating Sebastian Brant (Panofsky, op. cit., p. 79). On a marble relief in the Louvre, conceived as an ideal portrait of Scipio (our fig. 59), see Bode, *Studien über Leonardo da Vinci* (1921), pp. 30 f., where the design is ascribed to Leonardo, the stone work to Francesco di Simone, a pupil of Desiderio, working in Verrochio's atelier.

2. 'Lauri residens iuvenis viridante sub umbra' (Silius Italicus, *Punica* XV, 18). The derivation of the episode from the Choice of Hercules (Xenophon, *Memorabilia* II, i, after Prodicus) remained a favourite topic among eighteenth-century antiquaries: for example, Joseph Spence, *Polymetis* (1747), p. 142, who added an execrable poem of his own on The Choice of Hercules, twenty-seven stanzas long (pp. 155–62). Panofsky (op. cit., p. 38 note 1) cites G. A. Cubaeus, *Xenophontis Hercules Prodicius et Silii Italici Scipio* (1797), and T. C. Schmid, *De virtute Prodicia et Siliana* (1812).

called theoretical, the second practical, the third pleasurable: which in Latin are named *contemplativa, activa,* and *voluptaria.*'³

In the *Dream of Scipio* by Macrobius, which ends with a discourse on *tripartita philosophia,* the hero is warned against the voluptuous life and urged to pursue the active and contemplative virtues – *perfectionis geminae praecepta.*⁴ The 'precepts of twofold perfection' are impressed upon him also in Raphael's picture, but not to the exclusion of Pleasure. While he is offered the sword and the book with which to pursue the arduous path of virtue, suggested in the background by the steep rock and the spire rising above it, he is also offered the pleasing flower: the landscape on the right is a friendly valley. His posture suggests that he inclines towards virtue, but the flower is also part of his dream; and in that he follows the morality of Ficino, for whom the *triplex vita* was a persistent subject of meditation. 'No reasonable being doubts,' he wrote to Lorenzo de' Medici,⁵ 'that there are three kinds of life: the contemplative, the active, and the pleasurable (*contemplativa, activa, voluptuosa*). And three roads to felicity have been chosen by men: wisdom, power, and pleasure (*sapientia, potentia, voluptas*).' To pursue any one of them at the expense of the others is, according to Ficino, wrong, or even blasphemous. Paris chose pleasure, Hercules heroic virtue, and Socrates chose wisdom rather than pleasure. All three were punished by the deities they had spurned, and their lives ended in disaster. 'Our Lorenzo, however, instructed by the oracle of Apollo, has neglected none of the gods. He saw the three [that is, the three goddesses who had appeared to Paris], and all three he adored according to their merits; whence he received wisdom from Pallas, power from Juno, and from Venus grace and poetry and music.' To compliment a prince on his universality by comparing his judgement to that of Paris became a fixed formula of Renaissance euphuism. In Lyly's *Euphues and his England* (1580), Peele's *Arraignment of Paris* (1584), Sabie's *Pans Pipe* (1595), to name only a few,⁶ the same compliment

3. Fulgentius, *Mythologiae* II, 1: 'De iudicio Paridis.' Cf. Plutarch, *De liberis educandis* 10 (*Moralia* 8A), which repeats Plato, *Republic* 441, 580D ff.

4. *In Somnium Scipionis* II, xvii, 183.

5. *Opera,* pp. 919 f. See also *Supplementum Ficinianum* I, pp. 80–6: 'De triplici vita et fine triplici.'　6. cf. E. C. Wilson, *England's Eliza* (1939), pp. 136, 147 f., 239 note.

was addressed to Queen Elizabeth. It was carried to extremes in an allegorical portrait at Hampton Court in which the Queen puts the three goddesses to shame because, as the inscription asserts, she combines in herself the gifts which they possess only separately.[7] The flattery is more subdued in Raphael's *Scipio*. He humbly dreams of the gifts he is to receive. No doubt, he will accept them all three, but prudently divided in the proportion of 2 : 1.

It is significant commentary on the painting that it had *The Three Graces* (fig. 61), now in Chantilly, as a companion piece. The two pictures are of the same size, and since they both came from the Borghese Collection, and are inscribed with consecutive numbers, there can be no doubt that they form a pair;[8] and they were still together in the collection of Sir Thomas Lawrence.[9] But they must not be imagined as a diptych, which is excluded by their square shape, and also by the change of scale in the figures. It is more likely that they were placed back to back, as they are in our illustrations, the two parts being related to each other like the obverse and reverse of a medal.

Although the three Graces in the picture look indistinguishable, they are characterized very lightly by a certain difference of attributes. Castitas wears a loin-cloth, and has no jewels around her neck. Voluptas, on the opposite side, is distinguished by a long necklace with a sizeable jewel. The Grace in the centre is more modest. The chain hanging from her hair is shorter than the necklace of her neighbour, and also the jewel attached to it is smaller. Not quite so abstemious as Chastity, nor so liberally adorned as Pleasure, Beauty holds the balance between them, being chaste and pleasurable in one. She touches Chastity's shoulder as she turns towards Pleasure;

7. C. H. Collins Baker, *Catalogue of the Pictures at Hampton Court* (1929), p. 47, no. 635 (*Inv.* 301); R. C. Strong, *Portraits of Queen Elizabeth I* (1963), p. 79, no. 81. The Latin distichs and the early date (1569) recall the Queen's visits to Cambridge (1564) and to Oxford (1566), which occasioned volumes of complimentary verses 'in Greek and Latin, Hebrew, Caldee, and English' (Wilson, op. cit., pp. 70, 72). One of the Latin poems, by Henry Bust, welcoming Elizabeth to Oxford (31 August 1566), is quoted in J. D. Reeves, 'The Judgment of Paris as a device of Tudor Flattery', *Notes and Queries* CXCIX (1954), p. 8.

8. Panofsky, op. cit., pp. 142 f.

9. J. A. Crowe and G. B. Cavalcaselle, *Raphael* I (1882), pp. 202 note, 209 note.

and so subtle is the distribution of weights that, although the group retains its classical symmetry, the emphasis is decidedly on the right. Two apples are here offered, as against one;[10] and the two little chains also add their weight. Only one foot of the left figure is freely visible, so that her counter-movement has little support. And the landscape in the background sustains the asymmetrical action, the expanse of water flowing freely towards the right while it stops short behind the figure of Chastity. All these features combine to convey the same moral: Beauty inclines Chastity towards Love. The proportion of 2:1 is weighted on the side of Pleasure.

The golden apples in the hands of the Graces characterize them as the servants of Venus; for it is to her that the golden apples are sacred, and she is occasionally described as holding them herself: 'Mala aurea tria ferebat.'[11] In Politian's vision of the garden of Venus, the fruits it bears are *pomi d'oro*.[12] As attributes of the Graces, apples are not so unusual as has been claimed.[13] Cartari and Gyraldus

10. There is an interesting *pentimento* in the painting. The central Grace originally held no apple but touched the shoulders of the two other Graces. The alteration stresses the asymmetry.

11. Gyraldus, *Opera* I, 387; also Cartari, *Imagini*, s.v. 'Venere': 'con tre pomi d'oro in una mano'. The three apples which Hercules got from the Hesperides were also 'mala aurea Veneri consecrata' (*Libellus de deorum imaginibus* xxii, MS Vat. Reg. lat. 1290, fol. 6ʳ), but the suggestion that because of these Herculean apples Raphael's picture of the Graces should be associated with the Hesperides is surely unfounded, particularly if the figure on the obverse is Scipio and not Hercules. In the Venus fresco of the Palazzo Schifanoia the Graces hold four apples, not three: which would also seem to rule out any necessary association of these apples with Hercules or the Hesperides. The golden apples of Atalanta were again apples of Venus, so described by Alciati, *Emblemata*, no. 61.

12. *Giostra* I, xciv, 2. On apples as general attributes of Venus, see Pierio Valeriano, *Hieroglyphica*, fols. 394 ff., 'De malo', with a long excursus on the ball game of apples, after Philostratus, *Imagines* I, 6. On lovers throwing apples, see also two epigrams ascribed to Plato (Diogenes Laertius III, 32; *Anthologia graeca* V, 79 f.) and a charming verse by Virgil (*Eclogae* III, 64 f.). In one of the so-called Otto prints (Hind, *Early Italian Engraving*, pl. 139) the lovers are equipped with a large basket filled with apples which they throw at each other (our fig. 64).

13. 'Die goldenen Kugeln auf unserem Gemälde ... freilich ein Unikum', Salis, *Antike und Renaissance*, p. 154. The idea that the Graces might be imagined as playing ball goes back as far as Chrysippus. Seneca, *De beneficiis* II, xvii, 3 (also II, xxxii, 1): 'Volo Chrysippi nostri uti similitudine de pilae lusu.' Hence Ripa, *Iconologia*, s.v. 'Gratie':'perciò Crisippo assimigliava quelli che danno e ricevono il benefitio, a quelli che giuocano alla palla. ...'The same image in Plutarch, *De genio Socratis* 13 (*Moralia*

described the Graces as *nexis manibus poma gestantes*,[14] and as they are supposed to unfold the unity of Venus, it is not unreasonable for them to hold her fruit.

In offering these gifts of love, the Graces counterbalance the demands of Scipio's heroic dream. Instead of two gifts of the spirit and one of the senses, they bring two delectable gifts and one of restraint. While the hero is advised to adopt a rule of action by which he subordinates his pleasure to his duties, he is here invited to soften those severities and allow virtue to come to fruition in joy. The discipline of Scipio is only one side of the picture; the other is his affectionate liberality. *Virtus* and *Amor* belong together:

> For what is noble should be sweet.
> [Ben Jonson, *Pleasure Reconciled to Virtue*]

*

The combination of a martial spirit with amiability, which is the moral of Raphael's *Scipio and the Graces*, was so essential and natural to the Renaissance code of chivalry that it would seem unnecessary to assign to it any hidden roots in an antiquarian study of mysteries. Nor was the double life led by the average courtier, that of a warrior and of a lover, so novel as to require philosophers to propose it. Yet when it came to sanctioning these two lives, and to explaining their relation to each other, philosophers and antiquaries were much in demand; and as might be expected, they made the most of the opportunity to season glorification with paradox.

The ancient 'mystery' upon which they seized was the unlawful

---

582F), tr. Xylander, p. 485: 'Nam si pulchrum est amicis benefacere, non est turpe ab amicis beneficium accipere. Gratia enim non minus accipiente quam dante opus habet, ab utrisque perficitur ad pulchritudinem. Qui vero non accipit, tanquam pilam recte obiectam dedecorat, decidentem frustra.' On the ex-libris of Johannes Cuspinianus, which derives from a Cranach portrait now in the Reinhart Collection, Winterthur (cf. H. A. von Kleehoven, 'Cranachs Bildnisse des Dr Cuspinian und seiner Frau', *Jahrbuch der preussischen Kunstsammlungen* XLVIII, 1927, p. 231, fig. 1), the Graces, inscribed DO-ACCIPIO-REFERO, are represented in the act of playing ball (our fig. 62).

14. The phrase in the Latin version of Cartari (1687, p. 219) is the same as in Gyraldus, loc. cit. I, 387. On the ancient concept of Graces as fruit-bearing deities, see Carl Robert, 'De Gratiis Atticis', op. cit., p. 148; Jahn, *Die Entführung der Europa*, pp. 37–43.

union of Mars and Venus, from which issued a daughter named
Harmony. Born from the god of strife and the goddess of love, she
inherits the contrary characters of her parents: *Harmonia est discordia
concors*.[15] But her illegitimate birth, far from being a blemish, was
taken for a sign of mystical glory, according to a rule set forth very
clearly in Leone Ebreo's *Dialoghi d'amore*. In discussing the love and
procreation of the gods as metaphors for universal forces in nature,
he explained that 'when this union of the two parents occurs
regularly in nature, it is called marriage by the poets, and the
partners are called husband and wife; but when the union is an
extraordinary one, it is styled amorous or adulterous, and the parents
who bring forth are styled lovers.'[16]

In reflecting on the extraordinary nature of Harmony, which
became the core of his theory of beauty, Pico della Mirandola
delved rather deeply into Plutarch's theory of Mars and Venus. 'It
is well known,' wrote Plutarch in the essay *De Iside et Osiride*, 'that,
in the fables of the Greeks, Harmony was born from the union of
Venus and Mars: of whom the latter is fierce and contentious, the
former generous and pleasing. And see how philosophers have
agreed with this. Heraclitus openly called war the father, king and
master of all things, and declared that Homer, in wishing that discord
would vanish from the councils of gods and men, had secretly
blasphemed against the origin of all things because they are born
from strife and adversity. . . . Empedocles calls the force effective of

15. cf. Gafurius, *De harmonia musicorum instrumentorum*, frontispiece, also fols. 2ᵛ,
97ʳ. Among ancient sources see Horace, *Epistulae* I, xii, 19; Ovid, *Metamorphoses* I,
433; Lucan, *Pharsalia* I, 98; and above all Plutarch as quoted below, page 87. Gafurius
alternates between the classical formula *concordia discors* and its inversion, *discordia
concors* (for which see Manilius, *Astronomica* I, 142; Augustine, *Epistolae* XVI, 4).

16. Leone Ebreo, *Dialoghi d'amore*, ed. S. Caramella (1929), p. 108; tr. F. Friedeberg-
Seeley and J. H. Barnes (1937), p. 122. On the humorous illustration of the doctrine in
the *Parnassus* by Mantegna see Wind, *Bellini's Feast of the Gods*, pp. 9–20; with further
notes on Homeric laughter in 'Mantegna's Parnassus', *Art Bulletin* XXXI (1949), pp.
224–31. It is interesting that Plato's censure of the laughter of the gods did not deter
Proclus from reading a cosmogonic mystery into it, which he found foreshadowed in
the *Timaeus*, the *Republic*, and the *Parmenides*. The relevant passages are cited by Koch,
Pseudo-Dionysius Areopagita, pp. 253 f.; for their interpretation see Lobeck, *Aglaophamus*, pp. 891 f.; Dieterich, *Abraxas*, p. 28; also K. Preisendanz, *Die griechischen
Zauberpapyri* II (1931), pp. 95 ff., 110 ff.

good by the name of love and friendship ... and the destructive force he calls pernicious strife. ... The Pythagoreans attach several names to each of these forces. ... But Plato, concealing and fore-shadowing his opinion in many places, calls the first of these contrary principles the Same, and the second the Other. ... For mixed is the origin of this world, and its frame composed of contrarious powers. ...'[17]

And in *De Homero*, included by Xylander in Plutarch's *Moralia*, we read again: 'This is what the fable of Mars and Venus suggests, of whom the latter corresponds to Empedoclean friendship, the former to Empedoclean strife. ... And with this agrees what is transmitted by other poets, that Harmony was born from the union of Mars and Venus: for when the contraries, high and deep, are tempered by a certain proportion, a marvellous consonance arises between them.'[18]

In Plato's *Sophist* (242D–E) the doctrine of contraries uniting in concord is ascribed to 'the Ionian and Sicilian muses' – according to Simplicius (also Schleiermacher and Diels)[19] an ironic reference to Heraclitus and Empedocles: Plato makes these 'muses' say 'that being is one and many, and is held together by enmity and friendship ... ; peace and unity sometimes prevailing under the sway of Aphrodite, and then again plurality and war, by reason of a principle of strife'.[20] Plotinus, who mentioned Heraclitus and Empedocles by

17. *De Iside et Osiride* 48 (*Moralia* 370D–371A).

18. *Moralia*, tr. Xylander, p. 25. Calcagnini paraphrased the passage in 'De concordia', *Opera*, p. 414: '... quod in citharis maxime agnoscitur, ut ex dissonis fiat concentus. Sic enim prudenter veteres Harmoniam ex Marte et Venere genitam existimarunt, quod gravis et acuta seorsum opponi videantur: quom vero una componantur, incredibilem suavitatem auribus reddant.' Another example in Codrus Urceus, *Orationes seu sermones* (1502), fol. G iᵛ: 'Fabula etiam quam de Venere et Marte coniunctis scripsit Homerus, amicitiam Empedoclis significat, quando vero dissolvuntur contentionem ... unde ex Veneris et Martis coitu fingitur nata harmonia .... Hoc est quod ex contrariis sonis, gravibus scilicet et acutis simul proportione mixtis, nascitur consonantia.'

19. Simplicius, *In Aristotelis Physicorum libros*, ed. H. Diels (1882), p. 50; see also Diels, *Die Fragmente der Vorsokratiker* I (1934), p. 288, no. 29; Schleiermacher, *Platons Werke* II, ii (1857), p. 94.

20. See also *Republic* 545D–E: 'Shall we, after the manner of Homer, pray the Muses to tell us how discord first arose?' On Love and Strife in the Judgement of Paris, see below, Appendix 7, pages 270 f.

name,[21] treated the doctrine with more solemnity: 'How are enchantments produced? ... through the natural concord of like principles and contrariety of unlike. ... The true magic is the Love contained within the universe, and the Hate likewise. This is the original enchanter and master of potions. ... In all the universe there is but one general harmony though it be formed of contraries.'[22]

It is clear that Pico had such passages in mind when, writing 'On the general nature of Beauty',[23] he defined beauty as a 'composite' and inherently 'contrarious' principle, without fearing the heresies that it might entail. His account may be said to go to the root of the matter, and despite its prolixity, it must be quoted at length:[24]

And for this reason no simple thing can be beautiful. From which it follows that there is no beauty in God because beauty includes in it a certain imperfection, that is, it must be composed in a certain manner: which in no way applies to the first cause. ... But below it [the first cause] begins beauty because there begins contrariety, without which there would be no creation but only God. Nor do contrariety and discord between various elements suffice to constitute a creature, but by due proportion the contrariety must become united and the discord made concordant; and this may be offered as the true definition of Beauty, namely, that it is nothing else than an amicable enmity and a concordant discord. For this reason did Heraclitus say that war and contention are the father and master[25] of all

21. *Enneads* IV, viii, 1 ff.   22. ibid. IV, iv, 40 f. (tr. Dodds).

23. *Commento* II, vi (ed. Garin II, viii, pp. 495 f.).

24. The argument which follows is difficult to reconcile with *Enneads* I, vi, where Plotinus insists on the phenomenon of simple beauty, and with *Enneads* V, viii, and VI, vii, 33, where 'intelligible beauty' is defined as pure and without parts. See also Ficino, *Opera*, pp. 1792 f. Apparently Pico felt certain, to the point of Platonic heterodoxy, that if the One is assumed to be above Beauty (*Enneads* VI, ix, 11), it follows that Beauty must depend on composition. As in the case of intelligence and will, it suited his radicalism to stress the inapplicability of beauty to the supreme One more ruthlessly than Ficino, who had also treated of God's 'intelligence' in positive terms *Theologia Platonica* II, ix f., *Opera*, pp. 103 ff.), which Pico tended to ridicule. In *Commento* I, i (ed. Garin, p. 462) he reflected with amusement that 'a great Platonist' had felt disturbed because Plotinus seemed to deny intelligence to the supreme One – apparently a quarrel over *Enneads* VI, vii, 37.

25. The Italian text, which gives the word *genetrice*, is clearly faulty at this point, since Pico was transcribing Heraclitus fr. 53. Possibly a word like *governatore* for βασιλεύς was shortened in the first draft and then wrongly expanded by a copyist.

things, and, concerning Homer, that he who curses strife may be said to have
blasphemed against nature. But Empedocles spoke more perfectly when he
introduced discord not by itself but together with concord as the origin of
all things, understanding by discord the variety of elements of which they
are composed, and by concord their union; and therefore he said that only in
God is there no discord because in him there is no union of diverse elements,
but his unity is simple, without any composition. And since in the con-
stitution of created things it is necessary that the union overcomes the strife
(otherwise the thing would perish because its elements would fall apart) –
for this reason is it said by the poets that Venus loves Mars, because Beauty,
which we call Venus, cannot subsist without contrariety; and that Venus
tames and mitigates Mars, because the tempering power restrains and overcomes the strife and hate which persist between the contrary elements.
Similarly, according to the ancient astrologers, whose opinion Plato and
Aristotle follow, and according to the writings of Abenazra the Spaniard
and also of Moses, Venus was placed in the centre of heaven next to Mars,
because she must tame his impulse which is by nature destructive and corrupting, just as Jupiter offsets the malice of Saturn. And if Mars were always
subordinated to Venus, that is, the contrariety of the component elements
to their due proportion, nothing would ever perish.

The many and famous Renaissance idylls (figs. 74-6) in which
the victorious Venus, having subdued the fearful Mars by love, is
seen playing with his armour, or allowing her cupids and infant
satyrs to play with it, all celebrate this peaceable hope: that Love is
more powerful than Strife;[26] that the god of war is inferior in
strength to the goddess of grace and amiability. In Cossa's fresco
of the *Triumph of Venus*, in the Palazzo Schifanoia (fig. 77), the
vanquished Mars not only kneels before her but is actually chained
to her throne as a prisoner. The fetter of love, an amiable reminiscence of the more sinister chain contrived through the cunning of
Vulcan, is reduced in Veronese's allegory of Mars and Venus (fig. 76)
to a knot tied by a winged cupid.[27] But in the idylls of the same

26. Compare Lucretius's famous invocation of Venus against Mars, *De rerum
natura* I, 30-41. Also *Symposium* 196D, Mars 'the captive and Love is the lord, for love,
the love of Aphrodite, masters him . . . and the master is stronger than the servant.'

27. The allegory is very involved. While Mars bends down in adoration and
submission, his *fortezza* is characterized as a restraining *virtù* because it is he who holds
up the garment of chastity that covers Venus; while she, by touching her breast from

subject painted by Botticelli and Piero di Cosimo (figs. 74 f.) no chain or ribbon is required to demonstrate the bondage of Mars. Venus has put his fierceness to sleep. While Cossa's fresco of her triumph belongs to an astrological cycle and should be interpreted accordingly, any thought of 'sextile and trine aspects', which have occasionally been read into the paintings by Botticelli and Piero, would destroy their peculiar poetry. Since the planet Mars always retains, even when dominated by the planet Venus, a certain degree of boldness and bellicose fervour – a point clearly brought out by Ficino in *De amore* V, viii, and not neglected by Cossa – the reduction of Mars to a sleeping loving swain, surrounded by *amoretti* playing at war, is, with all due allowance for the wide influence of horoscopy, emphatically *not* an astrological image.[28]

Botticelli has added a further touch of bucolic raillery by transforming the cupids into infant satyrs who sneak impishly into the armour surrendered by Mars. His formidable weapons are reduced to toys.[29] Only the wasps that buzz round the head of the sleeper

which milk flows, reveals *castità* as transformed into *carità* (a motive reminiscent of the *Caritas Romana*). The restraints of Love imposed by a noble *fortezza* are playfully imitated on the right by a cupid using the sword of Mars to restrain the horse, which is already bound by its bridle. In a curious painting by Veronese in Turin (Gualino Collection) the lovers turn in surprise towards the apparition of a horse's head whose bridle is held by Cupid. On the bridling of horses to signify the chastening of animal passion, see *Sacred and Profane Love* as discussed below, page 145.

28. Cast as a stucco relief, the figures of Venus awake and Mars asleep, surrounded by a swarm of playing cupids, frame a Renaissance mirror, reproduced in John Pope-Hennessy, *Catalogue of Italian Sculpture in the Victoria and Albert Museum* (1964), no. 129, fig. 151. The frame is set in an emblematic ring bearing the famous device of 'diamond with foliage' (not confined to the Medici family, but used by the Este and others as well; cf. Hill, nos. 103, 120, 365). Applied to a mirror, it designates the owner as a woman both amiable and adamant, *Venus semper invicta*. One of the putti crowns Venus with a wreath, another rides a goose (a watchful as well as amorous bird: see Valeriano, *Hieroglyphica*, fols. 174ᵛ, 175ʳ). On the side of the vanquished Mars they are taming a dragon.

29. Cupids playing with the armour of Mars are common in ancient reliefs and epigrams which celebrate the triumphs of Amor, for example *Anthologia graeca* XVI, 214 f. (Loeb Library V, p. 287, with illustration). In Lucian's *Herodotus*, cupids playing with martial weapons are introduced into Aëtion's painting of Alexander and Roxana; but instead of suggesting a triumph of love over war, their symbolic function is here the reverse: Lucian says that they signify Alexander's abiding 'love of war'.

are a reminder of his pugnacious spirit: 'quod per vespam . . .
pugnacitatem et infestum adversos hostes ingenium ostendebant'.[30]
As a marginal comment on the scene, the wasps should not be underrated: for although Venus 'tames and mitigates' the contentiousness
of Mars, she also 'loves Mars because Beauty, which we call Venus,
cannot subsist without contrariety'; and thus a union of sweetness and
sting remains implicit in the *discordia concors* of Mars and Venus.[31]

The discordant element becomes more prominent when, instead
of putting Mars to sleep, Venus adopts the martial weapons for
her own. Dressed in armour (ὅπλα Κυθήρης), the *Venus victrix* or
Venus armata signifies the warfare of love:[32] she is a compound of
attraction and rejection, fostering her gracious aims by cruel methods.

30. Valeriano, *Hieroglyphica*, fol. 31ᵛ, s.v. 'Pugnacitas'; also fol. 189ᵛ: 'De vespa',
with illustration inscribed *pugnacitas*.

31. In Alciati, *Emblemata*, no. 89, the amorous motto *dulce et amarum* is illustrated
by the pseudo-Theocritean idyll (no. xix) of Cupid stung by bees while tasting honey,
a subject which Melanchthon, Cranach, and Hans Sachs found singularly attractive
(R. Förster, *Das Erbe der Antike*, 1911, pp. 6 f.). Sting and sweetness are also combined
in a pair of humorous paintings by Piero di Cosimo representing *Silenus stung by Wasps*
as a sequel to *Bacchus's Discovery of Honey* (after Ovid, *Fasti* III, 735–60, cf. Panofsky,
Studies in Iconology, pp. 59–63). Since these pictures were painted for a Vespucci, Gombrich was surely right in suspecting (*Journal of the Warburg and Courtauld Institutes* VIII,
p. 49) that because of the *vespae* in their coat-of-arms, the Vespucci favoured paintings
with wasps, and that Botticelli's *Mars and Venus* may have been one of them. But it is
characteristic of Renaissance 'inventions' that the heraldic subject would not be introduced flatly for its own sake, but as motivated by the theme of the painting.

32. The mythographical sources listed in Gyraldus, *Opera* I, 394 ('Venus armata')
and I, 399 ('Venus victrix'); Cartari, *Imagini* (1571), pp. 544 ff. On the ancient image
and its revival see L. Curtius, 'Zum Antikenstudium Tizians', *Archiv für Kultur-
geschichte* XXVIII (1938), p. 236. In giving the armed Venus a shield with a Gorgoneion,
more usually associated with Minerva or Mars (cf. the shield of Mars in Marcantonio
Raimondi's engraving, Bartsch no. 345; or the shield of Minerva, Bartsch no. 337),
Agostino Veneziano did not invent a new conflation of attributes for the *Venus victrix*
(R. Wittkower, 'Transformations of Minerva in Renaissance Imagery', *Journal of the
Warburg Institute* II, 1939, p. 202, pl. 38a) but followed ancient precedent: see D. le
Lasseur, *Les déesses armées* (1919), p. 187, on a black-figured amphora in the British
Museum (B. 254) inscribed 'Aphrodite' and depicting her with aegis; likewise an
ancient gem formerly in the Berlin antiquarium (no. 11362), illustrated in Furtwängler,
Die antiken Gemmen III (1900), pp. 336 f., figs. 183 f. The cuirass placed at the feet of
Venus in a drawing ascribed to Marco Zoppo (our fig. 73), again far from representing
'the corselet of Minerva' (Wittkower, loc. cit.), belongs to the martial equipment of
the *Venus victrix*, on whose armour, employed in the warfare of love, see *Anthologia
graeca* XVI, 173: ὅπλα Κυθήρης.

Like the 'bitter-sweet' pun of *amare–amaro*, to which Bembo devoted a whole book of the *Asolani*,[33] the threatening equation of *amare–armare* became indispensable to lovesick sonneteers. Michel-angelo employed it for his *cavalier armato*,[34] and the ridiculous Armado recalled it in *Love's Labour's Lost*. Even Virgil's Diana-like Venus (fig. 14) – *virginis os habitumque gerens et virginis arma* – is but a variant of the *Venus armata*: a bellicose Venus who has donned the weapons that normally belong to her opponent – either Diana, Minerva, or Mars.

But again, while appearing armed, Venus may give to the armour a peaceable motive. The martial Venus may stand for the strength that comes from love, for the fortitude that is inspired by charity,[35] or – in the reverse – for a sweetness derived from strength: *de forti dulcedo*.[36] In a poetical self-portrait by Navagero, *De imagine sui armata*, she introduces the rueful patriotism of a poet who accepts his martial calling with regret:

> *Quid magis adversum bello est bellique tumultu*
> *Quam Venus? ad teneros aptior illa jocos.*
> *Et tamen armatam hanc magni pinxere Lacones,*
> *Imbellique data est bellica parma Deae . . .*
> *Sic quoque, non quod sim pugna versatus in ulla,*
> *Haec humeris pictor induit arma meis.*
> *Verum, hoc quod bello, hoc patriae quod tempore iniquo,*
> *Ferre vel imbellem quemlibet arma decet.*[37]

33. Book I is a plaintive declamation, with Petrarchan interludes, against *amore amaro* (cf. Plautus, *Trinummus* 260: 'Amor amara dat'; Petrarch, *Trionfi* I, i, 76 f.)

34. *Rime*, ed. Girardi, no. 98 (= ed. Frey, no. 76).

35. Raphael's allegory of *Fortezza–Carità* in the Stanza della Segnatura (on which see Wind, 'Platonic Justice designed by Raphael', *Journal of the Warburg Institute* I, 1937, pp. 69 f.) was fittingly compared by O. Fischel, *Raphael* (1948), p. 91, to the martial heroines of love in Ariosto, and he referred to Catarina Sforza as a historical embodi-ment of the type.

36. *Aenigma Sampsonis* (Judges xiv, 14) discussed by Gyraldus, 'Aenigmata', *Opera* II, 621 f., with reference to a coin of Alfonso d'Este inscribed DE FORTI DULCEDO and showing bees nesting in a helmet, *Corpus nummorum italicorum* X (1927), pl. xxx, 23. The same image in Alciati, no. 45, with the motto EX BELLO PAX.

37. Andreas Naugerius, *Orationes duae carminaque nonnulla* (Venice 1530), fol. 38ʳ; cf. *Opera omnia*, ed. Vulpius (1718), pp. 218 f.

Thus, in response to the perilous hour, the heroic warrior disguises his softness by a display of steel, and compares himself, although he is a man, with the ambiguous figure of the *Venus armata*.

No doubt, the incongruity of the simile was a deliberate device in Navagero.[38] He intended to perplex and surprise the beholder, and also perhaps to remind him that the martial Venus, originally a Spartan deity, was for Roman poets and orators a cryptic figure on which, Quintilian says, they exercised their wit: 'cur armata apud Lacedaemonios Venus'.[39] But side by side with the jocose tradition, which was inherited from the Greek epigrammatists, the Romans retained towards the armed Venus an attitude of religious respect. The ancestral goddess of the Julian house, she appears on gems and coins of Caesar and Augustus, as a martial figure of Roman peace, of victorious generosity relying on her strength.[40] Humanist poets preferred on the whole (even in so ponderous a cycle as *Die geharnschte Venus*, included in Lessing's *Allotria*[41]) to glorify her seductive cunning. Amidst an abundance of spirited pedantries, of which Politian's witty epigram *In Venerem armatam* is perhaps the most ingenious,[42] she was allowed to drop the heroic style, presiding instead over scenes of domestic good humour which celebrate the inescapable triumphs of love, *omnia vincit amor*. Curiously decked

---

38. cf. the androgynous portrait of Francis I (fig. 80), discussed below, page 214.

39. *Institutio oratoria* II, iv, 26. The variety of answers may be gathered from *Anthologia graeca* XVI, 171–7; also IX, 321, which advises Venus to disarm, and IX, 320, a palinode like Stesichorus's *Helen*: 'It is not true. . . .' Ausonius, *Epigrammata* 64, a verbal combat between the armed Venus and Minerva, is a translation of *Anthologia graeca* XVI, 174. Plutarch referred to the Spartan Venus in *De Fortuna Romanorum* 4 (*Moralia* 317F): 'Even as the Spartans say that Aphrodite, as she crossed the Eurotas, put aside her mirrors and ornaments and her magic girdle, and took a spear and shield, adorning herself to please Lycurgus, even so Fortuna . . . when she was approaching the Palatine and crossing the Tiber . . . took off her wings, stepped out of her sandals, and abandoned her untrustworthy and unstable globe.'

40. Furtwängler, *Die antiken Gemmen* III, p. 304, illustrated ibid. I, pl. xxxvii, 30; xliv, 77 f.; lxiv, 65. H. Mattingly, *Coins of the Roman Empire in the British Museum* I (1923), pp. cxxiii, 98 f., nos. 599 ff.; II (1930), p. xlii. See also Winckelmann, *Description des pierres gravées du feu Baron de Stosch* (1760), p. 118, no. 564: 'Jules César la portait ainsi gravée sur son cachet.' The Rev. T. M. Parker drew my attention to Rutilius Namatianus, *De reditu suo* I, 67–70, in praise of the union of Mars and Venus.

41. cf. Lessing, *Schriften*, ed. Lachmann–Muncker, XVI, p. 451; XVIII, p. 321.

42. *Opera* II, fol. 102ᵛ.

out in martial trophies, like Omphale when she made Hercules attend to the spindle while she usurped his club and lion's skin, she may look slightly encumbered by her outfit (fig. 73);[43] but since she has conquered the rudest god by her wiles, a touch of bizarrerie is not unbecoming to the *victrix* in this unequal battle.

In comparing the pictures of the martial Venus with Navagero's self-portrait as an amiable warrior, we find that the roles of Mars and Venus, which would normally be divided between man and woman, both recur within man and woman as such. The principle of the 'whole in the part' entails this rather baffling conclusion: that Venus is not only joined to Mars, but that his nature is an essential part of her own, and *vice versa*. True fierceness is thus conceived as potentially amiable, and true amiability as potentially fierce. In the perfect lover they coincide because he – or she – is the perfect warrior. But whenever their 'infolded' perfection is 'unfolded', the argument requires two opposing images which, by contrasting the martial with the amiable spirit, reveal their transcendent unity (fig. 79).[44]

It is curious to observe, and not irrelevant, that while these equations of fierce virtue and pliant love were playfully developed on Florentine medals in the pagan idiom of poetic theology (figs. 14, 69), the medals designed for Savonarola expressed a similar contrast

43. Campbell Dodgson, *A Book of Drawings formerly ascribed to Mantegna* (1923) p. 25; now attributed to Marco Zoppo, cf. A. E. Popham and P. Pouncey, *Italian Drawings in the British Museum* (1950), no. 260. On the iconography see above, page 91 note 32.

44. Hill, no. 858, medal of Rodrigo de Bivar, inscribed QUORUM OPUS ADEST. Since the obverse shows the portrait of Rodrigo alone, the inscription and image of the reverse refer to the valour and grace combined in his person. Hill's assumption that the presence of Venus refers to Rodrigo's 'matrimonial prospects' in Rome is iconographically inconclusive. Nor should the employment of an Italian medallist by the Spanish prince be cited in support of that hypothesis, since his Spanish castle La Calahorra, in a remote corner of the Sierra Nevada, was rebuilt by him in the Italian style with the help of Italian workmen, and trimmed in Carrara marble specially imported. See Carl Justi, 'Die Einführung der Renaissance in Granada', *Miscellaneen aus drei Jahrhunderten spanischen Kunstlebens*, I (1908), pp. 218–23. Although much of the marble has been plundered, mythological and emblematic reliefs still adorn the window-frames of the splendid court, offering a natural parallel to the Italian workmanship of the medal. Justi calls the building 'the earliest monument of pure Italian workmanship in this realm'.

in images that were inspired by his prophetic visions: GLADIUS DOMINI SUPER TERRAM CITO ET VELOCITER, SPIRITUS DOMINI SUPER TERRAM COPIOSE ET ABUNDANTER (fig. 87).[45] The wrathful symbol of the God of vengeance whose sword or dagger hovers over the earth is not only contrasted in this medal with the burning love of the winged dove rising to heaven, but these are the contrary aspects of one deity: the God of vengeance is the God of love. His justice is mercy, His anger pity; His punishment itself is sent as a blessing because it purges the soul of sin. The famous conversions performed by Savonarola were helped by an inherent affinity of thought between pagan and Christian mysticism. The same tensions, conflicts, and contradictions which have so often been ascribed to the incompatibility between Renaissance paganism and Christianity prevailed actually within each of the rival attitudes; and this made communication between them so easy. The pagan courtier who thought of himself as inspired by a Venus–Diana or a Venus–Mars was quite accustomed to translate his ideal of action into a pair of Christian virtues: *carità* united with *fortezza*. For he would recall the divine identity of wrath and love which is the secret of the Bible. 'There is,' as we may remember from Pico,[46] 'this diversity between God and man, that God contains in himself all things because he is their source, whereas man contains all things because he is their centre.' In the centre the opposites are held in balance, but in the source they coincide. In so far as man therefore approaches his own perfection, he distantly imitates the deity. Balance is but an echo of divine transcendence.

The wise Federigo da Montefeltro who, as a successful *condottiere*, delighted in cultivating the arts of peace, expressed his faith in harmonious balance through the discordant symbol of a cannon-ball, which he placed under the protection of the thundering Jupiter. On his medal (fig. 71) the three stars in the sky form a constellation of Jupiter between Mars and Venus, and their symmetry is repeated in the group of emblems below; the sword and cuirass belonging to

---

45. Hill, no. 1080. Inscription and image derive from a visionary dream recorded by Savonarola in his *Compendium revelationum* (1514, fol. 5).

46. See above, page 48.

Mars, the whisk-broom and myrtle to Venus, while the ball in the centre is dedicated to *Jupiter tonans*, whose flying eagle carries the unusual still-life on its wings.[47] Although the balance looks safe, it is not solid: for the slightest dip of the eagle's wings would set the cannon-ball rolling. The inscription says, however, that Venus 'touches' the threatening Jupiter, who enables her to counter-balance Mars. Yet contrary to other triumphs of Venus (figs. 74–7),[48] the design suggests that her complete dominion over Mars might also set the cannon-ball rolling. The supreme god alone is the guardian of equity, the source and arbiter of the *discordia concors*, of which Mars and Venus are the component parts.

47. Hill, no. 304. Although it is known, and explicitly stated by Hill, that Federigo da Montefeltro used the emblem of a bombshell in other instances, the cannon-ball in the medal has not been recognized as such, despite the reference to *Jupiter tonans* in the inscription. Giehlow, who identified all the other emblems in the design, assumed that the sphere must refer to Jupiter but interpreted it as a symbol of the earth, 'Die Hieroglyphenkunde des Humanismus in der Allegorie der Renaissance', *Jahrbuch der kunsthistorischen Sammlungen in Wien* XXXII (1915), p. 37. In a later medal, clearly posthumous (Hill, no. 1118), the globe is flanked by cornucopiae and surmounted by a triumphant eagle, while winged putti carry the whole affair on a shield. The allusion to the cannon-ball has been dropped. In its stead the design recalls Ficino's pun *Urbinas–Orbinas* (*Opera*, p. 1294).

48. In an engraving by Marcantonio Raimondi (Bartsch no. 345), which might have the title *Discordia concors*, Mars chides Venus for her amiable tricks. Having taken off his armour and laid it down at her feet (a clear sign that he is under her domination), he still hopes by admonition to forestall the sequel to his surrender: for it is evident that, pushed by Cupid, Venus will play the part of a goddess of Peace by putting her flaming torch to the trophies of war (cf. Hill, pl. 201, no. 872 bis). The contrived wit of Marcantonio's engraving is in the manner of Alexandrian epigrams: In consorting with Venus the apprehensive Mars tries to save his armour from her fire.

CHAPTER VI

'RIPENESS IS ALL'

THE theory that 'transcendence' is a source of 'balance' because it reveals the coincidence of opposites in the supreme One is a doctrine of such extreme dialectical nicety that it may seem strange it should ever have succeeded in firing the artistic and practical imagination of the Renaissance. Granting that artists, poets, princes, and merchants conversed with philosophers and could acquire from them a general knowledge of metaphysics without having to master its technical detail; granting furthermore that this particular doctrine has, by virtue of being a paradox, a striking quality easy to remember; and granting finally that it often takes less time to grasp an enigma which is bound up in a knot than to follow a straight argument of indefinite length: there still remains a certain suspicion, which it would not be right to dismiss, that the subject is too esoteric for the wide success it apparently enjoyed.

But in making a broad appeal without losing its depth, the doctrine profited by its own theory of translatability. The mystical scale as such allowed for so many levels of understanding, the principle of 'the whole in the part' permitted so many kinds of foreshadowings and foreshortenings that the speculative phases of the argument could remain hidden in the clouds, and yet be accurately 'mirrored' in a practical adage. Mystical Platonism thus fulfilled the prerequisite of any philosophy fashionable in its day: it combined the obscure with the familiar. But to secure this junction, a magic word is always needed, a felicitous phrase sufficiently compact to be quickly grasped and easily repeated, and at the same time sufficiently wide and mysterious to suggest a comprehensive philosophy of life. Characteristically, the indispensable word was found by the humanists in an ancient grammarian.

Among the rambling manuals of grammar and morals, into which the humanists liked to dip, none was more admired than the *Attic*

Nights by Aulus Gellius,[1] the model of Politian's *Miscellanea*. In a chapter on the adverb *mature*, in which he discussed at some length what is meant by 'ripening', Gellius had introduced a motto of the emperor Augustus which recommended a combination of speed with patience, of daring abandon with prudent restraint.[2] As Erasmus explained in the *Adagia*,[3] σπεῦδε βραδέως or *festina lente* ('make haste slowly') became the most widely cherished Renaissance maxim; and those who chose it as a device made a sport of expressing the same idea by an unlimited variety of images. A dolphin around an anchor (fig. 52), a tortoise carrying a sail, a dolphin tied to a tortoise, a sail attached to a column, a butterfly on a crab, a falcon holding the weights of a clock in its beak, a remora twisting around an arrow, an eagle and a lamb, a blindfolded lynx,[4] – these and

1. H. Baron, 'Aulus Gellius in the Renaissance and a Manuscript from the School of Guarino', *Studies in Philology* XLVIII (1951), pp. 107–25.

2. Aulus Gellius, *Noctes Atticae* X, xi; also Macrobius, *Saturnalia* VI, viii. On Augustus's motto see Suetonius, *De vita Caesarum* II, xxv, 4, where the proverbial phrase σπεῦδε βραδέως is followed by a Greek verse, justly suspected by Erasmus (*Adagia*, s.v. 'festina lente') of being a tetrameter taken from a classical drama: it occurs in Euripides, *Phoenissae* 599. However, contrary to Erasmus's guess, the word στρατηλάτης, on which Suetonius ends his quotation, belongs to the verse, whereas σπεῦδε βραδέως does not.

3. The article on *festina lente*, which appeared for the first time in the Aldine edition of 1508 (*Chil.* II, *cent.* i, no. 1), grew larger with every new edition of the *Adagia*, in its final version filling six folio pages, greeted by Claude Mignault as a magnificent flood: 'in quod uberrimum copiosae orationis quasi fluvium congessit' (Commentary on Alciati's *Emblemata*, s.v. 'maturandum'); see also Perotti, *Cornucopiae*, s.v. 'festinatio'; Valeriano, op. cit., fol. 195ᵛ, s.v. 'maturitas'. For historical accounts cf. L. Dorez, 'Études Aldines', *Revue des bibliothèques* VI (1896), pp. 143–60, 237 f.; L. Volkmann, *Bilderschriften der Renaissance* (1923), p. 72.

4. Listed in the same order as above, these emblems were used, among others, by the following: (1) Aldo Manuzio, after a coin of Titus; (2) Duke Cosimo I de' Medici; (3) Girolamo Gualdo; (4) Lionello d'Este; (5) Jacopo Strada, after a coin of Augustus; (6) Cardinal Ippolito d'Este; (7) Andrea Alciati, after Erasmus (*Adagia*, s.v. *festina lente*); (8) Pietro Pomponazzi; (9) Lionello and Francesco d'Este. The inscription DUPLEX GLORIA on Pomponazzi's medal (fig. 88), which shows the pride of the eagle combined with the humility of the lamb, alludes to his use of 'two-fold truth', so often mistaken for a subterfuge, although it actually reveals a cautious daring in pursuing philosophy and theology as contradictories. Like Thomas Browne in *Religio medici* I, vi, Pomponazzi assumed that the two disciplines would sustain each other because (not although) they rely on opposite types of evidence. How conscientiously the method was applied by his disciples is shown by the correspondence of Johannes Genesius Sepulveda, *Epistolarium* V, lxxviii (*Opera omnia*, 1602, pp. 234 f.).

innumerable other emblematic combinations were adopted to signify the rule of life that ripeness is achieved by a growth of strength in which quickness and steadiness are equally developed.

As ceremonious 'Advice to a Governor', the lesson reappears on a medal of Altobello Averoldo, governor of Bologna (fig. 57), with the inscription MATURA CELERITAS,[5] the image having been invented for him by Achille Bocchi, who also used it – no doubt with permission – for his own medal.[6] As he explained in his book *Symbolicae quaestiones* (our fig. 58),[7] the philosopher addressing the governor holds a spur attached to a bridle (*duris calcaria iuncta lupatis*), while in the background an elderly sage admonishes a youth carrying a horn of plenty. A man who could thus display his vitality with caution was called a *puer senex* or *paedogeron*, that is, a 'hoary youth'.[8] To illustrate that composite virtue, the medal of Galeotto

---

5. National Gallery of Art, Washington, no. A1208.470A, formerly Gustave Dreyfus Collection.

6. *Museum Mazzuchellianum* I (1761), pl. lxix, 5 f.; A. Armand, *Les médailleurs italiens* II (1883), p. 219, no. 30. As shown by Bocchi's biography (cf. Mazzuchelli, *Scrittori d'Italia*, pp. 1389 ff.; also above, page 72 note 68), this industrious pedagogue and adviser was something of a busybody. Besides being knighted and created Count Palatine for his skill in the management of public affairs, he was granted special powers to confer doctor's degrees, to legitimize bastards, to certify armorial bearings, to appoint notaries. For a satirical epigram, *In Achillem Bocchium*, see Niccolò d'Arco, *Numeri* (1762), p. 267.

7. op. cit., no. lxxxii: 'Bocchiani symbolum numismatis.'

8. For the combination of *puer* and *senex* in one hieroglyph, uniting Infancy and Old Age, Calcagnini used the expression *paedogeron* (*Opera*, p. 20). He first employed the term, with the explanation *id est puer senex*, in his translation of Plutarch's *De Iside et Osiride* (ibid., p. 237), which Panofsky mistakenly describes as 'never published and apparently lost' (*Dürer* II, no. 84). It appeared under the title *De rebus Aegyptiacis* in Calcagnini's *Opera*, published by Froben in 1544, incidentally the only edition of his collected works. A manuscript is preserved in the Biblioteca Estense in Modena (MS Campori App. no. 292: *De rebus Aegyptiacis*). Admired by Erasmus for his erudition and eloquence (*Epistolae*, ed. Allen, nos. 1576, 1587, 2869), Calcagnini was a pioneer in the exploration of Plutarch's ill-preserved treatise, which Eduard Norden still regarded as 'one of the most difficult in the Greek language' (*Die Geburt des Kindes*, 1924, p. 98). Panofsky's surmise that, in using the term *paedogeron*, Calcagnini was 'misunderstanding both Plutarch's grammar and meaning', whereas Pirckheimer would have been 'quite capable of translating him correctly', assumes in both these authors a knowledge of the Teubner edition, in which this mutilated passage (363F) has been emended by an extensive interpolation. Wyttenbach's edition of 1796

Ferreo Orsini (fig. 89) shows the wind-blown sail of Fortuna (Youth) attached to the serpent of Prudentia (Old Age), with the motto DUMQUE SENEX PUER.[9]

The ability to let things mature was thus to exert, like a double-faced Janus, the gift of watchful energy. One should always follow Aristotle's Good Counsel: deliberate slowly, but then act very fast.[10] However shocking to a less flexible sense of morals, Machiavelli's parable of the lion and the fox, his advice that one quick act of cruelty propitiously applied might dispense with the wasteful cruelties of a precarious reign,[11] could neither surprise nor offend his Italian contemporaries who had learned, on the excellent authority of the Bible, to be shrewd as serpents and mild as doves.[12] Elasticity of conduct was a Renaissance ideal and, what is more, a Renaissance

(*Moralia* II, ii, p. 491) still records the corrupt διογέρων (first printed in the Aldine edition of 1509, p. 402, and now restored to δ' ὁ γέρων, with a large lacuna filled in front). It may be inferred that in Calcagnini's manuscript this bothersome compound was emended into παιδογέρων which links up directly with the preceding words (γινόμενοι καὶ ἀπογινόμενοι, παιδογέρων). Calcagnini was probably not the inventor of this reading, since he transmitted it to his nephew without further comment (*Opera*, p. 20, cf. Giehlow, 'Die Hieroglyphenkunde des Humanismus', op. cit., p. 169). As the term was believed to be Plutarch's, it is more than likely that H. Tietze and E. Tietze-Conrat were right in suggesting (*Burlington Magazine* LXX, 1937, pp. 81 f.) that Dürer's *Bearded Child* in the Louvre is a *paedogeron* or *puer senex* conceived as a hieroglyphic image. Like the triple-headed monsters in which Youth and Old Age counterbalance each other (see below, pages 260 f.), this hoary infant would again signify Good Counsel or Prudence, that is, practical wisdom.

9. Hill (no. 1166) reads the inscription as 'puer dumque senex', and suggests that 'dumque' is a mistake for 'denique', but this would produce a thought that bears no relation to the image. On the ancient and medieval history of *puer senex* see E. R. Curtius, *Europäische Literatur und lateinisches Mittelalter* (1954), pp. 108–15; also *Gesammelte Aufsätze zur romanischen Philologie* (1960), pp. 12 f.

10. *Nicomachean Ethics* VI, ix, 1142B: εὐβουλία. A seventeenth-century allegory of Good Counsel, published by L. Freund, *Journal of the Warburg Institute* II (1938), pp. 81 f., pl. 17a, represents a conjunction of Youth and Old Age, united under the sign of Serapis, on which see below, Appendix 4, pages 259 ff.

11. *The Prince* xvii and xviii.

12. In the device of the printing house of Froben, described in the *Adagia*, s.v. *festina lente*, the Christian maxim of Matthew x, 16 is illustrated by a pagan image: a Mercury-staff (traditional symbol of *concordia*) on which a dove perches between the serpents. See H. W. Davies, *Devices of the Early Printers* (1935), pp. 652 ff.

habit, a strategy of life sustained and sanctioned by the classical motto *festina lente*.[13] Perhaps it is not surprising that emblematic designs were invented *ad libitum* to symbolize 'slow haste' in the abstract. But was it possible to express it visibly in a human action? Could it be rendered as a pictorial scene?

'An endeavour to concentrate in a single subject those various powers, which, rising from different points, naturally move in different directions', was regarded by Sir Joshua Reynolds as unprofessional in a painter. 'Art has its boundaries, though imagination has none.' The expression of a 'mixed passion' was 'not to be attempted'.[14] But Renaissance artists rarely feared to attempt what the eighteenth century pronounced impossible. In a fresco designed in the style of Mantegna (fig. 53), a swift, winged-footed figure of Chance, her eyes covered by her forelock, incites a youth to grasp her quickly as she passes before him on a rolling sphere.[15] Behind the youth a steady, quiet figure of Wisdom restrains his eager steps. She stands on a solid block: 'for as the ancients depicted Chance on a

13. Over-confident is Gombrich's proposition: 'No sane person believed that *festina lente* embodied a very profound truth' ('Icones Symbolicae', *Journal of the Warburg and Courtauld Institutes* XI, 1948, p. 173). Aristotle, Gellius, and Erasmus were surely sane. And a maxim which attracted the acid intelligence of Pomponazzi (not to mention the evidence of both Suetonius and Gellius that Augustus favoured it) is not likely to be either simple-minded or shallow. The dolphin combined with an anchor, incidentally, appeared in antiquity on coins of Titus, not of Augustus, as Gombrich states, but this error is of good standing since it occurs, as Mlle Antoinette Huon has pointed out to me, even in Rabelais.

14. Fifth Discourse.

15. Unquestionably, Warburg was correct in observing (op. cit. I, p. 151 note) that in representing Chance not with a flying forelock but with a forelock that covers her face (*crine tegis faciem*), and with wings attached to her feet (*talaria habes*), the painter remembered Ausonius's description of an *Occasio*, supposedly by Phidias, in *Epigrammata* 33 (on which see Politian, *Miscellanea* I, xlix, who gives a meticulous analysis of Ausonius's sources: 'Phidias' was originally 'Lysippus'). Although the painting has repeatedly occupied iconographers of Fortuna (e.g. Schubring, *Cassoni*, p. 79; Van Marle, *Iconographie de l'art profane* II, 1932, p. 185; A. Doren, 'Fortuna im Mittelalter und in der Renaissance', *Vorträge der Bibliothek Warburg* II, i, 1924, p. 136 note; Wittkower, 'Chance, Time and Virtue', *Journal of the Warburg Institute* I, 1938, p. 318), the action performed by the figures has been either left unexplained or misunderstood. Paul Kristeller, *Mantegna* (1901), p. 457, ascribes the execution of the badly retouched fresco to Antonio da Pavia (?), but the invention may surely be regarded as Mantegna's.

round stone, so they placed Wisdom on a square one'.[16] But while the contrast between the firm socle and the mobile sphere is as unmistakable as between the characters of the women themselves, it is surely wrong, in the presence of these contrarious tutors of youth, to interpret 'the relation of these two forces as an irreconcilable feud'.[17] The youth, while placed under the protection of restraining Virtue, who significantly touches his breast, is quite intent in his pursuit of outward Chance, and the swift goddess is not unfriendly to him: for she keeps her forelock turned in his direction,[18] admonishing him as much towards speed as the attending Virtue does towards firmness. His action, at once eager and

16. Valeriano, *Hieroglyphica*, fol. 290ʳ, 'De quadrato'. For the juxtaposition of Chance and Wisdom, with sphere and cube as their respective seats, see frontispiece of Bovillus, *Liber de sapiente*, 1510–11, reproduced in E. Cassirer, *Individuum und Kosmos in der Philosophie der Renaissance* (1927), pl. II. Virtue in general, rather than Wisdom specifically, is characterized in Gyraldus, *Opera* I, 27, by a matronly aspect and a cubic pedestal: 'Sed enim Virtutem variis imaginibus conformatam ab antiquis fuisse advertimus: nunc enim *matronali habitu* honesto inaffectatoque, nunc *quadrato saxo* insistentem' (italics mine). A winged globe attached to a firm cube, with the inscription *virtute duce, comite fortuna* (from Cicero, *Ad familiares* X, iii) appears in the device of the printer Stephan Gryphius in Lyons, likewise of the Milanese printer Giovanni Antonio degli Antonii. Lomazzo's medal, inscribed UTRIUSQUE, shows Fortuna on a sphere and Hermes on a rock, both jointly invoked by the humble artist (reproduced in Hill, *The Gustave Dreyfus Collection: Renaissance Medals*, 1931, no. 443); cf. Alciati, *Emblemata* (1605, no. 98), where, following Galen, *Protrepticus* 3 (as quoted ibid., pp. 451 ff., Mignault's commentary), the globe of Fortuna is contrasted with Hermes's cube, symbol for the solidity of *ars*. In Plutarch, *De Fortuna Romanorum* 4, *Moralia* 318A (cf. Valeriano, *Hieroglyphica*, fol. 288ᵛ), Fortuna descends from her globe to indicate her steadiness – a motif adopted in an engraving by Hans Sebald Beham (Bartsch no. 140). Bocchi even placed a rectangular block under her foot (*Symbolicae quaestiones* no. xxiii: 'stabilis Fortuna'), the globe resting quietly next to her. For later examples, particularly in emblem literature, see W. S. Heckscher, 'Goethe im Banne der Sinnbilder', *Jahrbuch der Hamburgischen Kunstsammlungen* VII (1962), pp. 35 ff.: *mobile et fixum*, from Otto Vaenius, *Emblemata sive symbola* (1624), *virtute et fortuna*, from G. Rollenhagen, *Nucleus emblematum* (1611), finally the combination of sphere and cube in Goethe's altar to ἀγαθὴ τύχη.

17. Wittkower, loc. cit.

18. An unusually considerate action in a figure of Chance, for as Bacon observed, 'Occasion, as it is in the common verse, turneth a bald noddle, after she hath presented her locks in front, and no hold taken' (*Essays* xxi: 'Of Delays'). The common verse paraphrased by Bacon is *Catonis disticha* II, 26: 'Fronte capillata, post est occasio calva.'

steady, is a perfect embodiment of *festina lente*; he hastens slowly.[19]

The woodcuts of the *Hypnerotomachia* alone show more than eighty variations of *festina lente*, each one of them giving a new twist to the theme. Some of the designs are frankly comical, like the image of elephants turning into ants, and of ants into elephants, which demonstrates, on the authority of Sallust X, vi, a *discordia concors* between maximum and minimum.[20] Others are solemn, for example the obelisk of three facets, which bears triadic images and inscriptions relating the Holy Trinity to the three parts of Time.[21] Still others are puzzles for the eye: there is the half-seated, half-rising figure of a girl who has placed one foot firmly on the ground while lifting the other high into the air (fig. 54). On the side of the stationary foot she holds a pair of wings, on the side of the lifted foot a tortoise. The inscription informs us that she rises on the side of the tortoise to counteract its slowness, and at the same time remains seated on the side of the wings to offset their speed. And we are invited to do likewise: 'Velocitatem sedendo, tarditatem tempera surgendo.'[22] The union of contraries is here ciphered through an extravagant contrapost, whose very absurdity makes the image memorable. Through such ciphers, which entertain while they instruct, the hero of the *Hypnerotomachia* is cautiously and alluringly

19. I am glad to note that the interpretation given above has now been adopted by A. Chastel and his collaborator Robert Klein in *The Age of Humanism* (1963), p. 320, no. 50.

20. *Hypnerotomachia*, fol. p vi[v]. According to Valeriano, op. cit., fol. 19[r] (s.v. 'Concordiae discordiaeque effectus'), the combination of elephant and ant signifies not only growth and decline (Sallust, *Bellum Iugurthinum* X, vi) but the perfect intelligence that unites maximum and minimum in its grasp: '. . . perfectus etiam intellectus significari potest, quippe qui minimorum aeque ac maximorum cognitionem sit optime consecutus, omniumque unam quasi scientiam coniunxerit'. When Valeriano refers, as in this instance, to a *novum commentum* or, as on fol. 174[v], to a *iuniorum commentum*, he means the *Hypnerotomachia*, whose fifteenth-century hieroglyphs (e.g. 'goose attached to anchor' for *firma custodia*, fol c i[r]) he adopts with the same unconcern as Bocchi (see above, page 71 note 68).

21. *Hypnerotomachia*, fol. h v.

22. ibid., fol. h vii[v]. On the Fontana delle Tartarughe in Rome, as completed under Pope Alexander VII (cf. L. Càllari, *Le fontane di Roma*, 1945, p. 84), the ephebes, while pushing the tortoises upwards, step on the dolphins whom they hold back by their tails.

guided towards the more hidden arcana, learning on his way to combine prudence with daring. The plan of the novel, so often quoted and so little read, is to 'initiate' the soul into its own secret destiny – the final union of Love and Death, for which *Hypneros* (the sleeping *Éros funéraire*) served as a poetic image. The way leads through a series of bitter-sweet progressions where the very first steps already foreshadow the ultimate mystery of *Adonia*, which is the sacred marriage of Pleasure and Pain.[23]

One of the symbols for patience in the *Hypnerotomachia* – a bucranium or ox-skull (fig. 55)[24] – recurs in a painting of Amor attributed to Titian, in which Love sets the wheel of Chance into motion (fig. 51). Love, thus put between the symbols of Chance and Patience, is himself engaged in 'hastening slowly', and so lives up to his Platonic character – the son of painful Want and resourceful Affluence. 'He is always poor . . . and like his mother he is always in distress. Like his father too . . . he is always plotting . . . bold, enterprising, strong, a mighty hunter, always weaving some intrigue

---

23. The opinion still held by some of the best-informed scholars, that the *Hypnerotomachia* was conceived by an unphilosophical mind (M. T. Casella and G. Pozzi, *Francesco Colonna: biografia e opere* I, 1959, p. 29; II, p. 125), should perhaps be revised to read: an un-Thomistic mind. The notion, deliciously phrased in the *Hypnerotomachia* (g ivᵛ, l viiiʳ), that matter has an appetite for form and rejoices in it, is indeed *non rigorosamente tomistica* (Pozzi, op. cit. II, p. 28) but it occurs in Aristotle, *Physics* I, ix, 192A: matter desires form 'as the female desires the male' (ὥσπερ ἂν εἰ θῆλυ ἄρρενος), whence Giordano Bruno's sallies on *materia e femina* (cf. below, page 137, note 27). For other versions see Plutarch (*De Iside et Osiride* 53, 57 f., 78; *Moralia* 372E–F, 374D–375A, 383A) and also Plotinus (*Enneads* III, v, 9), both of whom toyed with the idea that prime matter, or 'the receptacle of all generation' as described in *Timaeus* 49A–53B, is identical with 'Penia' in *Symposium* 203B. In the words of Xylander's index to the *Moralia* (1572, s.v. 'materia'): 'materia semper appetit formam'. The discovery that much of the philological and antiquarian lore in the *Hypnerotomachia* derives from Niccolò Perotti (cf. Pozzi, op. cit. II, Index, s.v. Perotti), whose *Cornucopiae* Aldus published in the same year as the *Hypnerotomachia*, might be a hint for locating the source of some of the weirder philosophical speculations as well. Perotti was for many years Bessarion's secretary and *intimo confidente*, in which capacity he spent at least one year in Venice: see G. Mercati, *Per la cronologia della vita e degli scritti di Niccolò Perotti* (1925), pp. 50–4. An interesting list of members in the *divi Bessarionis Academia* appears in Perotti's dedicatory preface to his commentary on Statius's *Silvae*, Cod. Vat. lat. 6835, datable to 1472, fols. 54 f. (ibid., pp. 77 ff., 157 f.).

24. fol. d viiʳ.

or other, ... terrible as an enchanter, sorcerer, sophist. ... But that which is always flowing in is always flowing out, and so he is never in want and never in wealth.'[25] A perfect portrait of that desperate dialectician appears in an Italianate drawing of the sixteenth century ascribed to a German draughtsman (fig. 48). It shows the figure of an equilibristic Amor who has appropriated the sail and sphere of Fortuna.[26] Propelled by the force of his own breath which he blows into the sail, he throws the weight of his body in the opposite direction, stemming his feet against the sphere that carries him forward.[27] The demon driving the precarious engine is both its motor and its brake.

> *These contraries such unity do hold*
> *Only to flatter fools and make them bold.*

On the face of it, it would not seem unreasonable to cite Plato in support of a cunning folly, since his dialogues are filled with such contrarious characters. The philosopher who is both ignorant and knowing, the lover who is both wealthy and poor, the guardian who is both fierce and friendly (*Republic* 375), all would seem to exhibit a union of contraries. Yet Plato always criticized, in the *Republic* (436) as well as in the *Symposium* (187), the Heraclitean theory that opposites coincide; he regarded it as a verbal confusion. 'The way up' and 'the way down' may lead to the same point, but that does not make 'up' and 'down' identical. Laughter and tears, pleasure

25. *Symposium* 203.

26. E. Schilling, *Altdeutsche Meisterzeichnungen* (1937), no. 25: 'Zeichnungsweise eines deutschen Künstlers, der in Italien Wurzel geschlagen hat.' Attributed to Peter Vischer the Younger by E. Bock, *Die Zeichnungen in der Universitätsbibliothek Erlangen* (1929), no. 224. For the fusion of Amor and Fortuna see Valeriano, *Hieroglyphica*, fols. 288ᵛ, 410ʳ. The source is Pausanias VII, xxvi, 8. See also Dürer's *Kleines Glück* (Bartsch no. 78), a remarkably steady *Fortuna Amoris*: no flying forelock or 'bald noddle' but a veil so tied together at the back of her head that the hair falls over her shoulders. While precariously placed on her mobile globe, the goddess has a firm staff to lean on, a reassuring support for the flower of love (*eryngium*) in her hand. Clearly a variant of *stabilis Fortuna* (see above, page 102 note 16).

27. The posture resembles a classical gem (Gori, *Museum Florentinum* I, pl. 77, no. 1) where Amor navigates with a sail attached to an amphora on which he stands (cf. Reinach, *Pierres gravées*, 1895, pl. 37, no. 77¹). In Sigismondo Fanti's *Triompho di Fortuna* (1526), fol. A iiʳ, the same posture, with amphora and sail, is given to a Fortuna.

and pain, motion and rest, harmony and discord may become inter-fused in our experience, but this does not abolish the difference between them. In the 'royal craft of weaving', by which Plato illus-trated the art of statesmanship, the fierce nature of man should form the warp while his pliant nature serves as the woof: 'These, which are naturally opposed, she seeks to bind and weave together' (*States-man* 309), but that very attempt is based on the assumption that warp and woof are not the same. How to breed in man a dog-like capacity for being aggressive as well as friendly remained among the most formidable problems of an ideal republic; for it was not in the common nature of things to produce it, and when it did occur, it was something of a miracle, not unlike the philosopher-king, whose wisdom would not be clouded by his power.

A clear distinction between a conjunction and a coincidence of opposites was therefore one of Plato's basic postulates. While he favoured the development of opposite faculties in one person and in one state, and studied in the *Philebus* the ideal mixture of opposite principles in the *summum bonum*, he never conceded their coincidence anywhere, not even in the *Parmenides*, where the opposites are shown logically to entail each other. In that final and radical phase of Plato's dialectic, the One and the Many, Equality and Difference, still apply to the same things only in different respects, and so their own differ-ence does not vanish, because they continue to move each other back and forth in a relentless course of mutual irritation. In contra-distinction to some of the Neoplatonists, Plato did not allow the movement to come to rest in a theological *possest*[28] or a mathematical infinite – an infinite in which Cusanus was to demonstrate that the circle and the straight line become identical. For Plato the infinite remained the imperfect, a source of immeasurable confusion, which the dialectic was designed to cure. A theory which would let the dialectic be reabsorbed or halted by a coincidence of opposites, no matter whether defined as 'mature' or 'transcendent', would be, in Plato's terms, an admission of defeat.

28. A barbarism invented by Cusanus to indicate the coincidence of act and power in God. In any finite being, he explains in *De possest*, potentiality (= *posse*) and actuality (= *est*) are distinct; but in God the potential is always realized because infinite power *is* infinite act.

For Ficino, however, to whom the mysteries of Plato were revealed through Plotinus, Proclus, and Dionysius, the difference between a conjunction and a coincidence of opposites was merely one of degree. He was confident that 'our Plato in the *Parmenides* equally affirms and negates all possible opposites concerning the ultimate One',[29] and he attributed to Plato himself the opinion, of which there is no trace in Plato's text, that 'the Infinite and the End, which oppose each other when applied to particulars, are outside of particulars simply one and the same': *Infinitum igitur atque finis quae sunt in rebus opposita, extra res sunt ipsum simpliciter unum.*[30] On this theory of the 'infinite end', which is also to be regarded as the source of all being, the many conjunctions of opposites that Plato had favoured could be understood as emanations from their coincidence in the supreme One. Hence any practical believer in Augustan 'ripeness' could be hailed as a Platonic initiate; Ficino would greet him as *Complatonicus*. Even Erasmus thought that *festina lente*, that simple-sounding classical adage, had deep roots 'in the mysteries of ancient philosophy': *ex ipsis usque priscae philosophiae mysteriis profectum apparet* (*Adagia* II, i, 1). Although one would not expect to find Augustus in the company of Platonic mystagogues, his practical motto seemed to contain that balanced–unbalanced philosophy as in a cipher, visually illustrated on his coins by the combination of crab and butterfly:[31] the volatile animal joined to the crawling, the airiest to the most heavily armed. An excellent travesty of this inexhaustible subject is to be found in *Love's Labour's Lost* (III, I), where a dialogue between Armado and Moth, introduced by the phrase 'Bring him festinately hither', ends as follows:

29. *Opera*, pp. 1017 f.

30. ibid., p. 1175, *In Parmenidem*. On Ficino's reading of the *Parmenides*, see R. Klibansky, 'Plato's Parmenides in the Middle Ages and the Renaissance', op. cit., pp. 312–25.

31. Mattingly, op. cit. I, p. 11, no. 60. Reproduced as Augustus's emblem in Gabriel Symeone, *Le sententiose imprese* (1560), p. 11, inscribed *festina lente*. A recent article by Deonna, 'The Crab and the Butterfly', *Journal of the Warburg and Courtauld Institutes* XVII (1954), pp. 47–86, collects ancient prototypes and parallels to the coin of Augustus but is less rewarding for Renaissance iconography because, although citing significant examples, it does not penetrate to the Renaissance ideal of *maturitas*, nor to the source of the term in Gellius.

MOTH: As swift as lead, sir.

ARMADO: Thy meaning, pretty ingenious? Is not lead a metal heavy, dull, and slow?

MOTH: *Minime*, honest master; or rather, master, no.

ARMADO: I say, lead is slow.

MOTH: You are too swift, sir, to say so. Is that lead slow which is fir'd from a gun?

ARMADO: Sweet smoke of rhetoric! He reputes me a cannon. . . .

*

The cannon-ball that so aptly exploded at the climax of Shakespeare's quip was not a new conceit for *festina lente*; it was conventional, and that increased the satirical force of the image. In all earnestness, the duke of Ferrara, Alfonso d'Este, like Federigo da Montefeltro before him, had used a bomb-shell as a heroic emblem,[32] a symbol of concealed power propitiously released: A LIEU ET TEMPS. In Symeone's *Sententiose imprese*, a book not unlike Bruno's *Eroici furori*, the picture of the exploding 'ball of fire' (fig. 82) is accompanied by moral verses which are about as pleasing as the sentiment they express:

> *Come palla, in cui chiuso a tempo è foco*
> *per ingannar d'altrui l'incauta mente,*
> *tal l'huom si mostra all'hor saggio e prudente,*
> *ch'offende il suo nimico a tempo e loco.*[33]

The praise of this engine of destruction as a model of heroic prudence (*saggio e prudente*) contrasts with the sanity and courage of Ariosto who, although employed by these masters of artillery, did not fail to contradict their flatterers. In clear allusion to the cannon foundry of Alfonso d'Este, he foretold in *L'Orlando furioso* that the 'murderous engine' would destroy the virtues of chivalry. Orlando throws it to the bottom of the sea (IX, 88–91; also XI, 21–8). But however self-evident in retrospect, the idea that mechanical warfare must spell the end of the chivalrous tradition was blandly discounted by the Platonic emblem writers. Their books of heroic devices, so

32. Hill, no. 232; Giovio, *Dialogo dell' imprese*, p. 80. On Federigo da Montefeltro, see above, page 95.   33. Symeone, op. cit. p. 68.

rich in moral marvels and myths, are interspersed with pictures of mechanical inventions, admirable machines which harness the secret forces of nature in order to release them for a dramatic effect. Beside the classical columns and sirens, diamonds and laurels, salamanders, porcupines, and unicorns – symbols which continue to convey their heroic lesson in the language of fable – the new water-wheels, bellows, catapults, rockets, bombards, and barbacanes seem like brutally prosaic intruders, realistic contrivances in a setting of fantasy. Yet to the inventors themselves – Leonardo da Vinci among them – they exemplified the magical forces of nature, forces which man carries also in his own breast. Nature is man writ large; hence, if forces in nature produce miraculous effects when they are harnessed, collected, and propitiously released, they can set an example to the forces in man. In Bocchi's moral *Symbola*, the ancient observation quoted by Cusanus, that minimal spaces may conceal maximal forces, that the energy of a small spark is potentially that of a great fire,[34] was illustrated – in the midst of Socratic images of Silenus, Minerva, Hercules, and Venus – by a picture of the invention of gunpowder: 'Haec pulveris inventio bombardici':

> . . . *sic ignem saepe favilla,*
> *Ut minima, maximum facit.*[35]

In denouncing gunpowder as destructive of chivalry, Ariosto was old-fashioned. His view entailed a separation of mechanical from liberal arts; he distrusted their revolutionary fusion which the advanced spirits inclined to favour. He feared that if barbacanes, catapults, and bombards were freely admitted into the company of the muses, the mechanical arts would displace the liberal; the muses would be silenced by the engines. But the new Orlandos did not

34. See below, page 221.

35. *Symbolicae quaestiones*, no. cxiv. Emblematic frontispieces designed for treatises of military engineering (cf. John Hale, 'The Argument of Some Military Title Pages of the Renaissance', *The Newberry Library Bulletin* VI, 1964, pp. 91–102) amplify the moral of the cannon-ball: quick-witted *Ingenio* joined to patient *Labor* (ibid., pl. vi), a volatile Mercury to a ponderous Hercules (pl. v), a feather on a casket to a tortoise on a shield (pp. 99 f.). The ambivalent Mars appears over his two astrological houses, the ram and the scorpion, and between the lightning of Jupiter and the hourglass of Saturn (pl. vi): *festina lente* varied *ad nauseam*.

think of throwing their firearms into the sea. They embroidered them on their waistcoats. Alfonso wore a flaming bomb on his cuirass; his medals portray him in that chivalrous outfit (fig. 81). And in Titian's painting he places his hand, a fine and courtly hand, with possessive elegance on a cannon, not only the proud symbol of an artillery expert and manufacturer, but his emblem of statecraft, of prudent *virtù* (fig. 83). In the opinion of the emperor Charles V, the duke of Ferrara was outstanding among Italian princes for his skill in civic administration and diplomacy, to which he knew how to apply a tactic of propitious explosion, patiently accumulating the forces which he would unexpectedly release. 'Sweet smoke of rhetoric! He reputes me a cannon.' It is essential to the stylishness of Titian's portrait that the duke, while touching the cannon as his emblem, is dressed in civilian attire, with a courtier's sword on his hip (a *finesse* abandoned in some of the copies). Conceived as a personal attribute, the cannon signifies a princely virtue not confined to military strategy, a combination of force and prudence.

These mechanistic models for a moral virtue, which distantly resemble Cusanus's beryl, his *ludus globi*, his 'all-seeing' icon, or his 'experiments with the scales',[36] belong to a phase of Renaissance imagination which was classed as *magia naturalis*. Distinct from necromancy by its enlightened methods of inquiry, natural magic was a part of natural philosophy, even its consummation according to Pico, because it was natural philosophy in action.[37] Pico defined this discipline as 'a science concerned with the virtues and actions of natural forces and their effect on each other and on their natural dependents, and by which is known what natural forces can achieve by their own virtue, and what not'.[38] But despite his cautious definition, which he offered in the *Apologia*, Pico ascribed an enormous range to natural magic. 'There is no latent force in heaven or earth which the magician cannot release by proper inducements.'[39] In reflecting on the foundations of this titanic science, Pico explained that man is the vital link between the skill of magic and the works of nature: 'What the human magician produces through art, nature

36. See below, pages 222 f., 227. 37. *Conclusiones magicae*, nos. 3 and 4.
38. *Apologia* (*Opera*, p. 168) 39. *Conclusiones magicae*, no. 5.

produces naturally by producing man.'[40] And that explains why magic is a moral force: it makes man recognize in himself the forces of nature, and in nature the model of his own force. By properly inserting his magical art into nature, he can release forces that are greater than his own.

Pico regarded that power as purely beneficial. Natural magic, 'in calling forth into the light as if from their hiding-places the powers scattered and sown in the world by the loving-kindness of God, does not so much work wonders as diligently serve a wonder-working nature'.[41] By 'applying to each single thing the suitable and peculiar inducements (which are called the ἴυγγες of the magicians)', natural magic 'brings forth into the open the miracles concealed in the recesses of the world, in the depths of nature . . . ; and as the farmer weds elms to vines, even so does the *magus* wed earth to heaven. . . .'[42]

His disdain of necromancy notwithstanding, this is the mood in which Leonardo da Vinci explored the secret recesses of nature, releasing and harnessing its concealed forces by 'suitable and peculiar inducements'. The episodic method of his experimentation, so baffling to modern scientists because of its unconsecutive, conjectural style,[43] is a pursuit of elective affinities that are of magical power – inconspicuous causes that produce amazing effects. Disinterested science, discovery for its own sake, lay outside Leonardo's ambition. His spirit of inquiry was spectacular like a magician's; and hence his diction tended towards oratory, even his arguments aimed at effect. One wonders whether that famous and mysterious sentence, 'la natura è piena d'infinite ragioni che non furono mai in esperienza',[44] means anything more than this: Nature is full of latent causes which have never been released.

40. 'Quod magus homo facit per artem, facit natura naturaliter faciendo hominem,' ibid., no. 10.

41. '. . . non tam facit miranda quam facienti naturae sedula famulatur,' *De hominis dignitate*, ed. Garin, p. 152; tr. E. L. Forbes.

42. ibid.: '. . . et sicut agricola ulmos vitibus, ita magus terram coelo . . . maritat.'

43. cf. Leonardo Olschki, *Geschichte der neusprachlichen wissenschaftlichen Literatur* I (1919), pp. 346–413.

44. Institut de France MS J, fol. 18ʳ; Richter, *The Literary Works of Leonardo da Vinci*, no. 1151.

As for Pico, it is remarkable that in describing the magician's art as a 'marriage of heaven and earth' he drew his simile from Virgil's *Georgics* I, 2: the farmer's skill in wedding elms to vines, *ulmisque adiungere vites*.[45] The quotation vividly points to the fact, too easily overlooked, that 'natural magic' extends its method to the study of organic marvels. The sympathetic skill of 'applying to each single thing the suitable and peculiar inducements' achieves its 'maturest' triumph in the art of planting and husbandry. For it is here, in the exploration of growth, rather than of mechanical cataclysms, that 'ripeness' returns to its poetic homeland and supplies truly 'natural' models for *festina lente*. Lodovico il Moro's device of the mulberry-tree might be taken for a purely verbal allusion to his person; for the Latin name of the tree was *morus*, the Italian *moro celso*. But in Pliny the mulberry was described as 'the wisest of trees' – *morus ... sapientissima arborum* – because it develops its bloom very slowly, but then matures so fast that it bursts forth with dramatic vigour: 'Sed cum coepit, intantum universa germinatio erumpit, ut una nocte peragat etiam cum strepitu.'[46] An ideal of statecraft attached to a name (*Morus*)[47] was thus illustrated by the natural wisdom of a plant – 'symbol, in its long delay and sudden yielding of flowers and fruit together, of a wisdom which economizes all forces for an opportunity of sudden and sure effect'. The description is Walter Pater's.[48] Inadvertently it recalls the moral of the cannon-ball, but translated into the language of the tenuous alliance between dialectic and pastoral poetry.

45. Also *Georgics* II, 221. The image recurs, beautifully expanded, at the conclusion of Politian's *Manto* ('. . . amicitur vitibus ulmus. . . . / O vatum preciosa quies, ó gaudia solis / Nota piis, dulcis furor, incorrupta voluptas'). Further sources listed in Ripa, *Iconologia*, s.v. 'Benevolenza'.

46. Pliny, *Natural History* XVI, xxv. Applied by Ripa to *Diligenza*: 'Così sapientissimo sarà riputato colui che unirà la prestezza con la tardanza, trà le quali consiste la diligenza', a slightly lop-sided rendering of Gellius X, xi: 'ut ad rem agendam simul adhiberetur et industriae celeritas et diligentiae tarditas'.

47. Paolo Giovio, *Elogia virorum bellica virtute illustrium* IV (Basle 1596), p. 128: 'Ludovicus Sfortia.' Cf. a marble relief portraying Lodovico il Moro, his coat embroidered with the mulberry emblem, in the small cloister of Santa Maria delle Grazie, Milan (Malaguzzi Valeri, *La corte di Lodovico il Moro* II, p. 202, fig. 236).

48. *The Renaissance*: 'Leonardo da Vinci'.

CHAPTER VII

BOTTICELLI'S PRIMAVERA

e segue l'occhio ove l'orecchio tira
per veder tal dolcezza d'onde è nata.
– Lorenzo de' Medici, *L'altercazione*

FOR some time there has been among historians of art a remarkable unanimity about the literary sources relevant to Botticelli's *Primavera* and *The Birth of Venus*. As both pictures are known to have come from the villa of Castello, a property of the younger branch of the Medici, it is practically certain that they were painted for Lorenzo di Pierfrancesco (fig. 22), who was brought up under the guardianship of his cousin Lorenzo the Magnificent.[1] There is documentary evidence that he was a pupil of Politian and Ficino,[2] and that he became a patron of Botticelli.[3] The constellation Ficino–Politian–Botticelli should therefore be amply sufficient to explain these pictures. But, strange to say, only the component deriving from Politian has been established with complete success.[4] Botticelli's poetical trappings are unmistakably indebted to Politian's muse and to those ancient poems (particularly the Homeric Hymns, Horace's

1. On Lorenzo di Pierfrancesco as the patron of these paintings, see H. P. Horne, *Botticelli* (1908), pp. 49 ff., 184 ff.; J. Mesnil, *Botticelli* (1938), p. 198 note 46, with reservations; C. Gamba, *Botticelli*, tr. Chuzeville (n.d.), pp. 135, 160; N. A. Robb, *Neoplatonism of the Italian Renaissance* (1935), p. 217 (where 'uncle' should read 'second cousin'); Gombrich, 'Botticelli's Mythologies: a Study in the Neoplatonic Symbolism of his circle', *Journal of the Warburg and Courtauld Institutes* VIII (1945), pp. 7–60, with particular emphasis on Ficino's *Epistolarium*. For an explanation of Lorenzo di Pierfrancesco's medal (Hill, no. 1054, our figs. 21 f.), which represents him at a more advanced age, see below, page 266.

2. cf. Politian's *Silvae* (dedication of *Manto*), *Opera* II, fol. 84ʳ; Ficino's *Epistolarium*, *Opera*, pp. 834 f., 843 f.

3. It was for him that Botticelli made the famous illustrations to Dante; see Mesnil, op. cit., p. 122. On other employments of Botticelli by the same Lorenzo, ibid., pp. 151, 210 notes 152 f.

4. Warburg, *Sandro Botticellis 'Geburt der Venus' und 'Frühling'* (1893), reprinted in *Erneuerung der heidnischen Antike*, pp. 1–57, with additions pp. 307–28.

Odes, and Ovid's *Fasti*) with which Politian and Ficino had made him conversant;[5] but in none of these cases do the parallels extend beyond single traits or episodes. They establish a connexion of mood and taste, and a community of literary interests, but they do not explain the programme of the paintings. The *Primavera* in particular has remained a riddle.[6] If I dare to propose a solution, it is because the presence of the three Graces (fig. 26) may offer a clue to the programme of the picture as a whole (fig. 25). When Pico wrote that 'the unity of Venus is unfolded in the trinity of the Graces', he added that the same form of dialectic pervades the entire universe of pagan myth.[7] It is legitimate, therefore, to inquire how the triad of figures on the right of the painting, which derive from a passage in Ovid, is related to the formal triad of the Graces on the left, and whether these two contrasting groups, being placed on either side of Venus, perhaps represent two consecutive phases of one coherent theory of love.

*

5. Politian, carrying imitation to the point of virtuosity, composed in Ovid's manner a versified commentary on the *Fasti*, presumably intended as one of the *Silvae* but not preserved. It is mentioned in a letter from Michael Verinus to Piero de' Medici (F. O. Mencken, *Historia vitae Angeli Politiani*, 1736, p. 609; Warburg, op. cit., p. 34 note 3), a document showing the high estimation of the *Fasti* in fifteenth-century Florence: 'qui est illius divini vatis liber pulcherrimus'.

6. That the picture belongs to the context of Florentine Neoplatonism, as had been suspected by Warburg and many others, was recently reaffirmed, with particular reference to Ficino, by Gombrich in the article cited page 113 note 1. Unfortunately, the arguments he has found in Ficino (not to mention Apuleius) lead all around the programme of the picture but not to its centre, perhaps because they have lost their original focus. In dealing with philosophical propositions, enumeration is not a substitute for analysis. The triads loosely listed by Gombrich and regarded by him as unconnected (p. 36: 'our difficulty is obviously not that we do not know any meaning but that we know too many') derive, without exception, from a basic Neoplatonic principle (*emanatio–raptio–remeatio*) which is absent from his article. The resulting aggregate of Neoplatonic quotations, unrelated to their formative principle, amounts to an error of description like mistaking a vertebrate for a jelly-fish. In part this confusion may have been caused by a superficial flabbiness in Ficino's style. As Festugière remarked, '. . . il y a bien du fatras dans les Commentaires de Marsile' (*Studia Mirandulana*, p. 162): for although Ficino can be quite succinct in formulating a principle, he reveals, in the expansion of detail, the diversionary habits of a vast compiler and talker. The problems posed by this peculiarity have been admirably stated by Kristeller, *The Philosophy of Marsilio Ficino*, pp. 6 f. ('Methodological Questions').

7. See above, page 36.

1. Apollo and Marsyas. Drawing after a Roman sarcophagus.
Eton College

2. Raphael: Apollo and Marsyas. Stanza della Segnatura, Vatican

3. Michelangelo: Leda (copy). Gemäldegalerie, Dresden

4. Leda. Renaissance drawing after a Roman relief (reversed). Coburg Castle

5. Michelangelo: Night. Medici Chapel, Florence

6. Leonardo da Vinci: Leda (copy). Spiridon Collection, Rome

7. Leda and the Eggs, from *Discours du songe de Poliphile*, 1546

VNI GRATVM
MARE
ALTERVM GRATVM
MARI

8. Apollo's Oracle on the Eggs of Leda, from *Discours du songe de Poliphile*

9. The Three Graces (Pompeian fresco). Museo Nazionale, Naples

10–11. Medal of Pico della Mirandola:
PULCHRITUDO–AMOR–VOLUPTAS

12–13. Medal of Giovanna Tornabuoni:
CASTITAS–PULCHRITUDO–AMOR

14. Medal of Giovanna Tornabuoni:
VIRGINIS OS HABITUMQUE GERENS...

15. Titian: The Blinding of Amor. Galleria Borghese, Rome

16. Correggio: The Three Graces. Camera di San Paolo, Parma

17. The Three Graces
from Pierio Valeriano's *Hieroglyphica*

18. The Three Graces,
detail from the *Tarocchi*

19. The Three Graces. Stucco from Raphael's Logge, Vatican

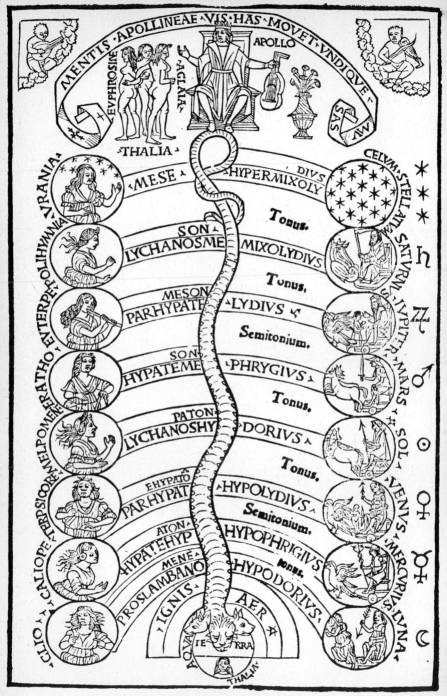

20. The Music of the Spheres, from Gafurius's *Practica musice*, 1496

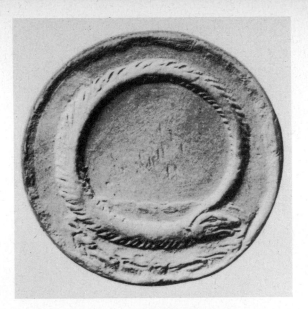

21–22 Medal of Lorenzo
di Pierfrancesco de' Medici

24. Hermes as *divinus amator*, from Bocchi's *Symbolicae quaestiones*

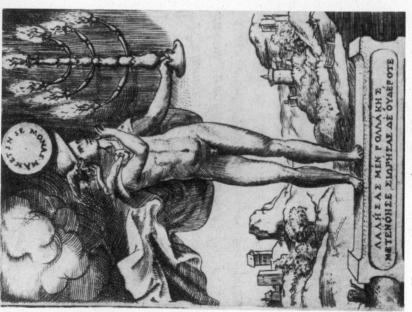

23. Hermes as Mystagogue, from Bocchi's *Symbolicae quaestiones*

25. Botticelli: Primavera. Uffizi, Florence

26. Botticelli: The Three Graces, from the Primavera

27. Botticelli: Blind Amor, from the Primavera

28. Botticelli: The Grace VOLUPTAS, from the Primavera

29. Botticelli: The Grace CASTITAS, from the Primavera

30. Botticelli: The Grace PULCHRITUDO, from the Primavera

31. Botticelli: Flora, from the Primavera

32. Botticelli: Mercury, from the Primavera

33. Botticelli: Flora, Chloris, and Zephyr, from the Primavera

34. Venus de' Medici. Uffizi, Florence

35. Venus rising from a shell.
Graeco-Roman gem.
Antiquarium, Berlin

36. Venus rising from a shell. Detail from a
Roman sarcophagus. Louvre, Paris

37. Titian: Sacred and Profane Love.
Galleria Borghese, Rome

38. Marcantonio Raimondi: Clio and Urania.
Engraving after Raphael

39. Botticelli: The Birth of Venus. Uffizi, Florence

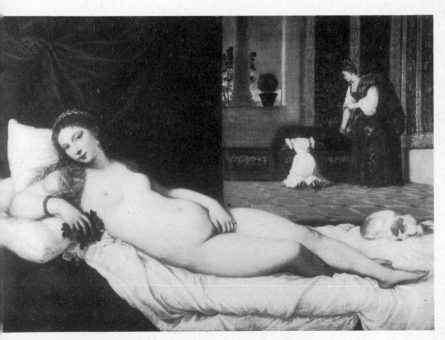

40. Titian: Venus of Urbino. Uffizi, Florence

Symb. CXVII.

41. The Taming of the Passions. From Bocchi's *Symbolicae quaestiones*

42. Titian: Scenes of chastisement, from Sacred and Profane Love

43. Veronese. The Chastening of Love. National Gallery, London

44–45. Epiphany of Venus, from a pair of Florentine marriage chest

46. Veronese: Epiphany of Venus. National Gallery, London

Collection Earl of Crawford and Balcarres

47. Veronese: The Tripartite Life. National Gallery, London

48. Peter Vischer the Younger (?): *Fortuna amoris*. Universitätsbibliothek, Erlangen

The scene on the right is not easy to decipher (fig. 33). Here Zephyr, the wind of spring, swiftly pursues, as in Ovid's *Fasti*, the innocent earth-nymph Chloris.[8] With blowing cheeks he rushes from behind a tree which bends under his impact. Chloris tries to escape his embrace, but as Zephyr touches her, flowers issue from her breath, and she is transformed into Flora, the resplendent herald of spring. *Chloris eram quae Flora vocor*: 'I once was Chloris who am now called Flora.'

In the *Fasti*, the transformation was introduced as a playful piece of etymology. The poet supposed that the Greek name Chloris, which belonged to a simple-minded nymph of the fields (*nympha campi felicis*), had changed into the Roman name of the goddess Flora. But when we see how Chloris, at the touch of the spring breeze, produces flowers from her breath (*vernas efflat ab ore rosas*), how her hands reach behind the flowers that decorate the garment of the new Flora,[9] and how the two figures converge in their rapid motion so that they would seem to collide, we can hardly doubt that the metamorphosis was represented by Botticelli as a change of nature. The awkwardness of the shy and primitive creature, caught against her will by the 'gale of passion', is transformed into the swift poise of victorious Beauty. 'Till then,' according to the *Fasti*, 'the earth had been but of one colour.'

In Ovid, Chloris herself confesses that when Zephyr first saw her she was so unadorned that she hardly dared, after her transformation, to reflect on what she had been:

Quae fuerit mihi forma, grave est narrare modestae.

But with becoming humour she concedes that it was the bareness of her form that secured for her a proper husband (literally, 'a son-in-law for my mother'), who gave her the realm of flowers as a bridal gift.[10]

8. *Fasti* V, 193-214. Cf. Warburg, op. cit., p. 32.

9. In Chloris's left hand some of these flowers appear between thumb and forefinger; and also her open right hand has the tip of the third finger overlapped by the end of a twig or leaf, which might be mistaken for a slip of the brush, did not the other hand show the same motif.

10. *Fasti* V, 200, 212.

. . . questa novella Flora
fa germinar la terra e mandar fora
mille vari color di fior novelli.[11]

The interpretation here offered combines two traditional views which have been regarded as incompatible: first, that the figure strewing flowers is Flora, which it seems difficult to deny; secondly, that the nymph pursued by Zephyr is Ovid's Chloris, whom Ovid himself identified with Flora, as did also Politian.[12] The contradiction vanishes if the scene is recognized as a metamorphosis in Ovid's style, suggested by Ovid's own phrase: 'Chloris eram quae Flora vocor.' That the flowers issuing from the mouth of Chloris fall on to Flora's garment and into her lap has always been noticed; but the spatial relation between the two figures, which is so ambiguous as to verge on confusion, has been accepted as an oddity of style rather than a calculated effect. And yet the scene has reminded more than one observer of the pursuit and transformation of Daphne.[13]

As for Vasari's recollection that the picture 'signifies spring' (*dinotando la primavera*), this does not imply, as has been occasionally supposed, a separate personification of Primavera herself. In the poems of Lorenzo de' Medici, spring is the season 'when Flora adorns the world with flowers' – *la primavera quando Flora di fiori adorna il mondo*.[14] This passage alone would speak against the suggestion that the figure strewing flowers needs to be renamed Primavera. She is Flora, whose advent is a sign of spring. Flowers

11. Lorenzo de' Medici, *Comento sopra alcuni de' suoi sonetti*, in *Opere* I (ed. A. Simioni, 1939), p. 117. On Lorenzo's device *Le temps revient* see Luigi Pulci's verses in *La giostra di Lorenzo de' Medici* (1468), lxiv, 7 f., where the words 'tornare il tempo e 'l secol rinnovarsi' allude of course (like stanza xxvii: 'tornar Saturno e 'l mondo d' auro') to Virgil's Fourth Eclogue: *redeunt Saturnia regna . . . surget gens aurea mundo*. A fresh shoot growing from a dry tree (*Giostra* lxv, 7 f.: 'et era questo alloro parte verde / et parte secho') was a common formula for 'renascence', used also in Laurana's medal for René d'Anjou (Hill, no. 59, dated 1463), with allusion to the name, Renatus. On a Renaissance cameo in the Bibliothèque Nationale (Cabinet des Médailles, no. 402; reproduced in E. Babelon, *La gravure en pierres fines*, 1894, p. 246, fig. 177) the same motif illustrates religious rebirth. Further examples in G. B. Ladner, 'Vegetation Symbolism and the Concept of Renaissance', in *Essays in Honor of Erwin Panofsky* (1961), pp. 303–22. On the related concept of palingenesis, see below, page 257.

12. *Giostra* I, lxviii.   13. Warburg, op. cit., p. 33.   14. *Comento*, ed. cit., p. 122.

burst forth when the cold earth is transformed by the touch of Zephyr.

In the guise of an Ovidian fable, the progression Zephyr–Chloris–Flora spells out the familiar dialectic of love: Pulchritudo arises from a *discordia concors* between Castitas and Amor; the fleeing nymph and the amorous Zephyr unite in the beauty of Flora. But this episode, *dinotando la primavera*, is only the initial phase in the Metamorphoses of Love that unfold in the garden of Venus.

*

Despite her modesty and restraint, Venus was recognized by Vasari in the central figure of the painting. Above her is a passionate, blindfolded Cupid, whose impetuous action supports by contrast the deliberate gesture of her hand. Although ostensibly blind, the energetic little god appears to be a most accurate marksman (fig. 27). He aims his burning arrow with absolute precision at the central dancer among the Graces,[15] who is characterized as Castitas.

To distinguish her from her sisters, the central Grace is unadorned, her garments fall in simple folds, and her hair is carefully bound together (fig. 29). The sadness of her face, a shy and wistful melancholy, contrasts with the wilful expression of her left neighbour who steps forth against her with a kind of determined passion (fig. 26). The unruly nature of this opponent is apparent through her attire as a Grace. A flamboyant coiffure (fig. 28), which surrounds the head in snake-like tresses and allows flaming curls to play in the wind, a gorgeous brooch on a heaving chest, and swelling curves in body and garment convey a sense of overflow and abundance and of a voluptuous energy.

The third Grace (fig. 30) is the most comely of the group and

15. He is clearly *not* shooting at Mercury, although it has occasionally been claimed. The old-fashioned description of the picture in F. von Reber and A. Bayersdorfer, *Klassischer Bilderschatz* I (1889), p. x, no. 140, is correct, as we shall see, in every detail: 'In the centre Venus; above her, Amor shooting burning arrows toward the Graces who dance on the left. Next to these, Mercury dispelling with his caduceus the mists in the treetops. On the right, Flora walks forward, strewing roses, while flowers issue from the mouth of the fleeing earth-nymph as she is touched by Zephyr.' Quoted by Warburg, op. cit., pp. 26 f.

exhibits her beauty with a judicious pride. She wears a jewel of moderate size, with a thin chain resting on a braid of hair. Her locks, which are set off by a veil surmounted by an ornament of pearls, produce an effect both more varied and more composed, and hence of a considerably greater splendour, than either the loose tresses or the tight coiffure that characterize her companions. The Latinized names of the three Graces – *Viriditas, Splendor, Laetitia Uberrima*, which signify Juvenescence, Splendour, and Abundant Pleasure – may have suggested some of the traits and ornaments which amplified the abstract triad of Castitas–Pulchritudo–Voluptas.[16]

That the Graces are not represented naked, but wearing loose, transparent garments, shows how much the painter was inspired by literature: for they are thus described in Horace and Seneca: 'solutis itaque tunicis utuntur; perlucidis autem ...',[17] 'solutaque ac perlucida veste',[18] 'et solutis Gratiae zonis'.[19] Also the exquisite maze in which they interlace their gestures recalls Horace's famous 'knot of the Graces':

segnesque nodum solvere Gratiae.[20]

Even the incidental solecism that the two lateral Graces are facing inward, in contradistinction to the classical group, is supported by a literary variant: '... unam aversam, reliquas duas se invicem contueri'.[21] Above all, the choreography of the dance seems to follow Seneca's rule: 'Ille consertis manibus in se redeuntium chorus.'

But however diversified the literary sources that may have supplied this or that descriptive detail, the sense of the action is only strengthened by these elegant poetical attributes. While 'juvenescent' Castitas and 'abundant' Voluptas step forth against each other, Pulchritudo in her 'splendour' stands firm and poised, siding with Castitas whose hand she clasps, and at the same time joining Voluptas in a florid gesture. In so far as dialectic can be danced, it has been

16. For the names of the three Graces, see Orphic Hymns LX, 3 (= Hesiod, *Theogony* 907; Pausanias IX, xxxv, 5; Plutarch, *Moralia* 778E); for their Latin translation Ficino, *De amore* V, ii (cf. above, page 39 note 14).

17. Seneca, *De beneficiis* I, iii, 5.

18. ibid. I, iii, 2. 19. Horace, *Carmina* I, xxx.

20. ibid. III, xxi. 21. Gyraldus, *Opera* II, 731.

accomplished in this group. 'Opposition', 'concord', and 'concord in opposition', all three are expressed in the postures and steps and in the articulate style of joining the hands. Placed palm against palm to suggest an encounter but quietly interlocked in the absence of conflict, they rise up high to form a significant knot when they illustrate the Beauty of Passion.

That this gesture is made to hover like a crown above the head of Castitas defines the theme of the dance as her initiation. Castitas is the neophyte, initiated into Love by the ministrations of Voluptas and Pulchritudo. Protected by Venus and assailed by Cupid, she adopts some of the traits which she resists. Her garment has fallen from her left shoulder, this being the side on which she is joined by Voluptas; and in deference to Pulchritudo, on her right, a rich flowing tress escapes from the knot of her hair. Yet as she acts the part of the 'enraptured' Grace who unites the opposites in her person, the whole dance becomes imbued with her own spirit of chastity which she imparts to her two companions. In this she appears to have the sanction of Venus; for however recklessly Cupid may shoot his fire, Venus tempers the dance and keeps its movements within a melodious restraint.

The idea of Venus as a goddess of moderation may seem mythologically odd. Yet when Pico della Mirandola defined her as the source of *debiti temperamenti* and called her the goddess of concord and harmony, he followed Plutarch almost to the letter.[22] The concept of a beneficent, peaceable, guarded Venus was one of the more refreshing paradoxes of Neoplatonism. In Plotinus's *De amore*,[23] which was translated and explained by Marsilio Ficino, the contrast between her placid nature and the restiveness of her son was brought out in a definition which seems to explain their divergent roles in Botticelli's picture: 'If the soul is the mother of Love [εἴπερ ψυχὴ μήτηρ Ἔρωτος], then Venus is identical with the soul, and Amor is the soul's energy [ἐνέργεια ψυχῆς].'[24] In this view, Venus holds the

---

22. See above, pages 86 ff.   23. *Enneads* III, v, 4.

24. In Ficino's translation, 'siquidem anima est mater Amoris, Venus autem est anima, Amor vero est actus animae ...' Also *Enneads* VI, ix, 9: καὶ ἔστι πᾶσα ψυχὴ Ἀφροδίτη (Ficino: *est autem omnis anima Venus*).

powers of love in abeyance, while they are released by the wantonness of Amor. And it follows that the precious choreography of the Graces is both sustained and moved by these contending forces, the two gods conveying to the triadic dance their proportionate characters of passion and restraint:

> . . . and where you go,
> So interweave the curious knot,
> As ev'n the observer scarce may know
> Which lines are Pleasure's, and which not. . . .
>
> Then as all actions of mankind
> Are but a labyrinth or maze:
> So let your dances be entwined,
> Yet not perplex men unto gaze:
>
> But measured, and so numerous too,
> ·As men may read each act they do;
> And when they see the graces meet
> Admire the wisdom of your feet.[25]

In contrast to the pursuit and transformation of Chloris, the dance of the Graces is in a decorous style: *iunctaeque nymphis Gratiae decentes*.[26] There is no trace of that forthright vitality which animated Chloris and Zephyr, and which gave to the face of the transfigured Flora the sturdy air of a country bride (fig. 31). The 'harmony in discord' is now a studied knot, a balanced symmetry between three sisters. In the argument of the painting, this elevation of mood is combined with an elevation of meaning. When Passion (in the character of Zephyr) transforms fleeing Chastity (Chloris) into Beauty (Flora), the progression represents what Ficino called a 'productive triad' (*trinitas productoria*).[27] Hence the group appears in a forward, descending movement, issuing into the figure of Flora who firmly and jubilantly treads the earth. But when the Graces resume and develop the theme, they reverse the sequence as in a

25. Ben Jonson, *Pleasure Reconciled to Virtue*.
26. Horace, *Carmina* I, iv.   27. *Opera*, pp. 1559 ff.

musical palindrome: Castitas, taking Pulchritudo as her term of departure, moves towards an encounter with Voluptas, and the resulting group is a 'converting triad' (*trinitas conversoria sive ad supera reductoria*) in which Castitas, as the central figure, turns her back to the world and faces the Beyond. Her glance is in the direction of Mercury who has turned away from the scene and plays with clouds. For it has been repeatedly and justly observed that the objects which Mercury touches with his staff are not golden apples in the trees, but a band of clouds that have collected there.[28]

*

The crux of any interpretation of the *Primavera* is to explain the part played by Mercury (fig. 32). By tradition he is 'the leader of the Graces';[29] but while that would seem to explain his place next to them, it is hard to reconcile with his disengaged – not to say, indifferent – attitude. Mercury is also the 'guide of souls' (*Psychopompos*) whom he conducts to the Beyond; but although he is here represented as nostalgic and bears on his cloak a symbol suggestive of 'death (inverted flames),[30] there is nothing funereal about this

28. Writers on the *Primavera* who have read of these clouds in other writers have occasionally questioned their existence; but they are clearly visible in the original, at least in its present condition and light, as is also the top of Mercury's staff entwined with serpents. The outfit of the god, however unclassical in appearance, is mythographically irreproachable. The high boots with wings rising from the heel like spurs are typical of a Quattrocento Mercury (cf. Hind, *Early Italian Engraving* IV, pl. 361, *Tarocchi*; Hill, nos. 1068, 1089). The shoes are often open to give the impression of a sandal showing the toes (Mantegna's *Parnassus*). On the sword as a legitimate attribute of Mercury, see above, page 76 note 77; for Mercury's helmet, cf. Petrarch, *Africa* III, 174 ff., also Boccaccio, *Genealogia deorum* II, vii, who refers to Statius (*Thebais* I, 305). However enigmatic in other respects, there is no ground for doubting that this figure is Mercury.

29. Gyraldus, *Opera* I, 419; II, 734. Cartari, *Imagini*, p. 563 (s.v. 'Gratie'): 'come ci insegnarono gli antichi parimente nella imagine delle Gratie, facendo che fosse loro scorta e duce Mercurio'. Also Ripa, s.v. 'Venustà'. The ancient monuments of that type are listed in Daremberg-Saglio, s.v. 'Gratiae'.

30. Tongues of flame on the chlamys of Hermes were an 'authentic' attribute, as shown in a drawing of an archaic Greek Hermes in Cyriacus of Ancona, Bodl. MS Can. Misc. 280, fol. 68ᵛ (*Italian Illuminated Manuscripts from 1400 to 1550, Catalogue of an Exhibition*, Oxford, 1948, no. 44). The drawing is reproduced in Panofsky–Saxl, 'Classical Mythology in Mediaeval Art', *Metropolitan Museum Studies* IV (1933), p. 265,

youth who seems too relaxed, in his quiet contrapost, to suggest a ghost-like journey. His detachment and poise also seem to contradict an important passage in Virgil which might otherwise explain his action. 'With his staff,' we read in the *Aeneid*, 'he drives the wind and skims the turbid clouds':

> *Illa [scil. virga] fretus agit ventos et turbida tranat*
> *Nubila.*[31]

But this is an agitated passage. Virgil describes how the swift messenger of the gods, by lifting his magic staff, gains control over the clouds and winds, and sails through them like a bird. That the most volatile of gods stands quietly on the ground, combining the part of a 'skimmer of clouds' with that of a pensive deity, points surely to a very particular, 'philosophical' idea of Mercury.

Not only was Mercury the shrewdest and swiftest of the gods, the god of eloquence, the skimmer of clouds, the psychopompos, the leader of the Graces, the mediator between mortals and gods bridging the distance between earth and heaven; to humanists Mercury was above all the 'ingenious' god of the probing intellect, sacred to grammarians and metaphysicians, the patron of lettered inquiry and interpretation to which he had lent his very name (ἑρμηνεία),[32] the revealer of secret or 'Hermetic' knowledge, of which his magical staff became a symbol. In a word, Hermes was the divine *mystagogue*. Because 'he calls the mind back to heavenly things through the

---

fig. 44, where the adornment of the chlamys is visible and appears similar to Botticelli's. Through a copy in the possession of Schedel (Cod. Monac. lat. 714) Cyriacus's sketch became known to Dürer (cf. O. Jahn, 'Cyriacus von Ancona und Albrecht Dürer', *Aus der Altertumswissenschaft*, 1868, pp. 349 ff.) who derived from it a design of Hermes (Vienna, Kunsthist. Mus., L. 420), again with flames on the chlamys. Engraved as a woodcut-frontispiece to Apianus, *Inscriptiones sacrosanctae vetustatis*, 1534; cf. H. W. Davies, *Devices of the Early Printers*, frontispiece and p. 55.

31. IV, 245 f. Cf. Warburg, op. cit., p. 320.

32. Plato, *Cratylus* 407B ff.; Diodorus Siculus I, xvi; Orphic Hymns XXVIII, 6; Macrobius, *Saturnalia* I, xvii. On these etymologies see Festugière, *La révélation d' Hermès Trismégiste* I (1944), pp. 71 f.; Dieterich, *Abraxas*, p. 72 note 2. The tradition survives in Isidorus, *Etymologiae* VIII, xi, 49: 'Hermes autem Graece dicitur ἀπὸ τῆς ἑρμηνείας, Latine interpres.'

power of reason', Ficino assigned to him the first place in the 'converting triad which leads back to the upper world': *trinitas conversoria sive ad supera reductoria in qua primum Mercurius tenet gradum animos per rationem ad sublimia revocans.*[33] The removal of clouds would indeed be a proper occupation for a god who presides over the reasoning soul, particularly as Ficino himself used the simile to characterize in Plotinus's *Enneads* the enlightening force of intellectual contemplation: 'Animus affectibus ad materiam *quasi nubibus procul expulsis* ad intellectualis pulchritudinis lumen extemplo convertitur.'[34] And power to dispel mental clouds was explicitly ascribed also by Boccaccio to the staff of Mercury: 'Hac praeterea virga dicunt Mercurium . . . et tranare nubila, id est turbationes auferre.'[35]

Even so, one may doubt whether Mercury's concern with clouds is to be understood in the *Primavera* entirely in a negative sense, as if he were purging the mind or the air of an obstruction. For that his gaze is too contemplative (fig. 32), his bearing too poetical. He plays with the clouds rather as a Platonic hierophant, touching them but lightly because they are the beneficent veils through which the splendour of transcendent truth may reach the beholder without destroying him. To 'reveal the mysteries' is to move the veils while preserving their dimness, so that the truth may penetrate but not glare. The transcendent secret is kept hidden, yet made to transpire through the disguise. 'Nec mysteria quae non occulta,' wrote Pico in the *Heptaplus*;[36] or, in his Commentary on Benivieni's *Amore*: 'Divine things must be concealed under enigmatic veils and poetic dissimulation.'[37] As an *interpres secretorum* (Boccaccio's phrase for Mercury),[38] Mercury looks upward and touches the

33. *Opera*, p. 1559.

34. Ficino's heading to *Enneads* I, vi, 7; see Plotinus, *Opera* (1492), fol. 48ᵛ (italics mine).

35. *Genealogia deorum* XII, lxii. See also III, xx: 'Ventos insuper hac virga medicus [i.e. Mercurius] amovet, dum stultas egrotantium opiniones suasionibus et rationibus veris removet, auferendo timorem.'

36. Prooemium, ed. Garin, p. 172.

37. III, xi, 9 (ed. Garin, p. 581). See also the discussion on *nubes* in Ripa, s.v. 'Sapienza divina'; also s.v. 'Bellezza'.

38. *Genealogia deorum* XII, lxii.

clouds. 'Summus animae ad Deum ascendentis gradus caligo dicitur atque lumen.'[39] The highest wisdom is to know that the divine light resides in clouds.

If it is the hidden light of intellectual beauty (*intellectualis pulchritudinis lumen*) to which Mercury raises his eyes and lifts his magic wand, then his posture also agrees with his role as 'leader of the Graces'; for in turning away from the world to contemplate the Beyond, he continues the action begun in their dance. The Grace of Chastity, who is seen from the back, looks in his direction because it is the transcendent love – *amore divino* – towards which she is driven by the flame of the blindfolded Cupid. While she remains linked to her sisters by the 'knot which the Graces are loth to loosen', she unites and transcends the peculiarities of Beauty and Passion by following Mercury, the guide of spirits. And perhaps divine love, as a variant of death, is also intended by the falling flames on Mercury's cloak, since flames like these appear also on the mantle of the Madonna Poldi-Pezzoli, and fill the heavenly spheres in Botticelli's illustrations of the *Paradiso*. 'Amor che nella mente mi ragiona. . . .'[40] In Bocchi's *Symbolicae quaestiones* a youthful Mercury, silently contemplating the mysteries above while walking through flames, is defined as an image of the *divinus amator* (fig. 24).[41]

*

If Platonic Love were understood only in the narrow, popular sense in which it means a complete disengagement from earthly passions, the solitary figure of Mercury would be the only Platonic lover in the picture (fig. 25). But Ficino knew his Plato too well not to realize that, after gazing into the Beyond, the lover was supposed to return to this world and move it by the strength of his clarified passion. The composition of the painting is therefore not fully under-

39. Ficino, *Opera*, p. 1014 (*In Dionysium Areopagitam*).

40. Dante, *Convivio* III, 1 f.; *Purgatorio* II, 112.

41. Symbolon no. cxliii (ed. 1574): 'Fert tacitus, vivit, vincit divinus amator.' For the association of Hermes with Eros, see Gyraldus I, 302 ('Hermerotes'). Also *Symposium* 202E: ἑρμηνεύειν as a power of Eros. An illustration of Hermeros in Hill, no. 975 (medal of Francesco Filarete). On the usefulness of Bocchi in Quattrocento studies, cf. above, page 71 note 68.

stood, nor the role of Mercury quite comprehended, until he and Zephyr are seen as symmetrical figures. To turn away from the world with the detachment of Mercury, to re-enter the world with the impetuosity of Zephyr, these are the two complementary forces of love, of which Venus is the guardian and Cupid the agent: 'Reason the card, but passion is the gale.'

For the interplay between Mercury and Zephyr it must also be remembered that their mythological roles are related. As a mover of clouds Mercury is a kind of wind-god. 'Ventos agere Mercurii est,' writes Boccaccio in the *Genealogia deorum*;[42] and when Jupiter invites Mercury in the *Aeneid* to take to the sky and drive the winds, he explicitly names the winds as zephyrs:

Vade age, nate, voca zephyros et labere pinnis.[43]

Since breath and spirit are but one afflatus (the Latin word *spiritus* signifying both), Zephyr and Mercury represent two phases of one periodically recurring process. What descends to the earth as the breath of passion returns to heaven in the spirit of contemplation.

Between these extremes unfold the triadic movements characteristic of the *Theologia Platonica*. Not only do the groups 'driven' by Zephyr and 'guided' by Mercury exhibit mutations of a triadic pattern, but the entire picture seems to spell out the three phases of the Neoplatonic dialectic: *emanatio–conversio–remeatio*; that is, 'procession' in the descent from Zephyr to Flora, 'conversion' in the dance of the Graces, and 'reascent' in the figure of Mercury. (Or to put it in terms of Proclus's 'three causes', by which Pico preferred to describe the cycle: *causa efficiens, causa exemplaris*, and *causa finalis*.)[44] Since an orientation towards the Beyond, from which all things flow and to which they all return, is the primary tenet of this philosophy, the composition and mood of the painting are pervaded

42. II, vii.

43. IV, 223. See also W. H. Roscher, *Hermes der Windgott* (1878).

44. As it is the *causa exemplaris* which determines the Platonic 'participation' between divine models and earthly images, this would also explain why Venus and Amor, who dominate the action of all the figures, attend more specifically to the action of the Graces.

by a sense of that invisible world towards which Mercury turns and from which Zephyr enters.[45]

The three verbs *ingredi*, *congredi*, and *aggredi* were effectively used by Ficino to distinguish between the different disguises under which transcendent Beauty holds converse with the soul: 'aggreditur animum admiranda, ut amanda congreditur, ingreditur ut iucunda'.[46] And tracing each phase through a new modulation he defined *Veritas* as the aim of the first, *Concordia* of the second, and *Pulchritudo* of the third. Although Botticelli's painting is composed in a different key, being held throughout in the mood of Venus, it would be legitimate to infer that, within the limitations of that mood, the detachment of Mercury aims at *Veritas*, the dance of the Graces at *Concordia*, and the gift of Flora at *Pulchritudo*. But it is questionable to what extent such excursions into minor refinements of Ficino's system may contribute to an understanding of the painting. Being composed in a didactic style, the picture is governed by the kind of schematism which it delighted Ficino to spin out. The marvel is that, in Botticelli's treatment, philosophical pedantry has become so infused with lyrical sentiment that, for many generations of beholders, the sentiment of the picture has extinguished the thought, with the result that the mood itself has been too loosely interpreted. To restore the balance it is necessary to stress the intellectual character of Botticelli, which induced Vasari to call him *persona sofistica*. This process should sharpen our sense of the *lyrisme exact*, but stop as soon as it begins to blunt it.[47]

45. cf. Lorenzo the Magnificent's device *Le temps revient* (above, page 116 note 11). Reduced to the simplest formula, the cycle of perfection descending from the Beyond and producing an earthly image of Eternity is illustrated on the medal of Lorenzo di Pierfrancesco de' Medici (who commissioned the *Primavera*) by a fully rounded serpent *not* biting its tail (fig. 21): 'non tota descendit anima quum descendit' (see below, page 266).

46. *Opera*, p. 1559.

47. If, for example, Venus represents the soul as defined by Plotinus and Ficino, the groups in the foreground, in unfolding the phases of the soul, might possibly conform to one of the traditional divisions: as for instance *anima vegetativa* (Flora), *anima sensitiva* (Graces), *anima intellectiva* (Mercury). But although that classification occurs in Aristotle, Plotinus, Dante (*Convivio* III, ii), and Ficino (e.g. *In Timaeum* xxvii, *Opera*, p. 1452), it cannot be regarded as vital to the picture because no pictorial

Concerning Ficino it is important to remember that, as a philosopher, he systematically placed the visual medium below the verbal. Divine names, he explained, deserve greater veneration than divine statuary 'because the image of God is more expressively rendered by an artifice of the mind than by manual works'.[48] Surprising though it may seem in a philosopher whose arguments were so often clothed in allegories and apologues that lent themselves easily to visual translation, Ficino's own visual sensibility was slight, and he speaks of painting as though he were a stranger to it.[49] His case might be compared to that of a poet who, endowed with a sensitive ear for words but no ear for music, writes poetry that inspires musicians.

---

feature is lost if we forget it, or gained if we remember it. The theory first proposed, I believe, by J. A. Symonds and still tenaciously held by L. P. Wilkinson, Boyancé, and others, that the painting refers to Lucretius V, 736-9, should be qualified. The passage describes a procession of Spring (*Ver*) which is led by Amor who 'walks ahead' of Venus joined to Ver, while Zephyr and Flora play around them. Although some of the *dramatis personae* are the same, which is almost inevitable in an allegory of Spring, their grouping bears no relation to the picture; and above all, some of the chief characters are different. Mercury and the Graces do not appear in Lucretius, while Ver, whom he explicitly joins to Venus (*it Ver et Venus*), is not personified by Botticelli. Politian, on the other hand, did certainly have the Lucretius passage in mind when he wrote *Giostra* I, lxviii, but more specifically he remembered Horace and Ovid; and it is from this compound, reorganized by a philosophic argument, that the *Primavera* descends.

48. *In Philebum* I, xi, *Opera*, p. 1217. The statement flatly contradicts Gombrich's suggestion that in Ficino's system 'the visual symbol ... is superior to the name' ('Icones symbolicae', op. cit., p. 170), and that Ficino's sense for 'the special virtues inherent in the visual symbol would have contributed to the enhanced status of the figurative arts' (ibid., p. 184). A case in point is Ficino's medal, Hill, no. 974. In marked contrast to Renaissance custom, its reverse shows no visual symbol at all but only the name PLATONE.

49. See Kristeller, *The Philosophy of Marsilio Ficino*, pp. 305 ff. Although a slight overstatement, Panofsky's remark that Ficino had 'no interest whatever in art' (*Dürer* I, p. 169) comes closer to the truth than the reverse opinion. It is important to draw a clear distinction, which one misses in Chastel's *Marsile Ficin et l'art*, between Ficino's impact on the arts and his estimation of them.

CHAPTER VIII

THE BIRTH OF VENUS

A SINGULARLY arid part of Ficino's doctrine is his theory of per-
mutations. Had he explained it more fully in one of his letters, we
might have heard the conversational tone by which he made it
pleasing to his listeners. But apparently the theory was so elementary
that the letters took the knowledge of it for granted. As a result we
are reduced to learning it for ourselves from the long-winded commentary on Plotinus. Since the theory is basic to the invention and
composition of Botticelli's pictures, at least one example of it may
be given here.

In explaining the third book of the first *Ennead*, which in the
original is called 'On Dialectic' but for which Ficino introduced
the more elaborate title 'On the Threefold Return of the Soul to the
Divine' (*De triplici reditu animae ad divinum*),[1] Ficino started with a
triad of gods – Mercury, Venus, and Apollo – and expanded it into
an ennead, that is a ninefold series, because each of the three gods
asserts his power for himself and also in combination with one of
the others. The nine possible variations are listed by Ficino in this
sequence: (1) Mercury, (2) Mercury–Venus, (3) Mercury–Apollo,
(4) Venus, (5) Venus–Mercury, (6) Venus–Apollo, (7) Apollo, (8)
Apollo–Mercury, (9) Apollo–Venus. In this list the constellation of
Venus–Mercury, which Botticelli represented in the *Primavera*,
occupies the centre (5), and that is perhaps more than an accident
since it is a combination greatly praised in Plotinus's *De amore* when
he speaks of the soul (ψυχή) conjoined to the mind (νοῦς) as the most
perfect form of Aphrodite.[2] The constellation was also well chosen

1. *Opera*, p. 1559. In his translation of Plotinus he called it *De triplici ad mundum
intelligibilem ascensu*, but seems to have avoided the original (that is Porphyry's) title
Περὶ διαλεκτικῆς.

2. *Enneads* III, v, 9, in Ficino's translation: 'Anima [ψυχή] cum mente [νοῦς] simul
existens et ab ipsa mente subsistens, rursus rationibus hinc imbuta, ipsaque pulchra

for a youth, the owner of the picture, whose growing sensibility and intellect or, in Ficino's words, *pulchritudo et ingenium*, should be placed under the joint tutelage of Venus and Mercury. That would secure for him the double character of *philosophus et amator*, a most Platonic quality.[3]

But however auspicious, Platonic, and profound the combination of Aphrodite and Hermes may have appeared,[4] the fact remains that it is only one of nine, or, if one takes the full system of Ficino's triads into account, only one of (at least) twenty-seven combinations. This implies not only that the picture must have been keyed to a particular mode, but that for a fuller awareness of that mode it would be helpful, if not necessary, to have some sense for the complementary keys, that is, for the possible modulations of which the theme was susceptible. Of the many historical disfigurations to which Renaissance art has been subjected, one of the saddest is that pictures which were conceived in a cyclical spirit have come down to us as solitary paintings. In the case of the *Primavera*, the spectator was probably meant to sense that the grouping here so clearly dominated by Venus and guided by Mercury was capable of an Apollonian translation, of the kind proposed by Ficino; and of this there is an example in a contemporary musical source.

At the top of the frontispiece to the *Practica musice* of Gafurius, which pictures the musical universe (fig. 20), Apollo is so placed that the Three Graces appear on his right and a pot of flowers on his left. The latter attribute looks like a gratuitous ornament, but when we remember from the *Primavera* how Venus was placed between

---

pulchris admodum exornata, affluentiaque luxurians, adeo ut in ea iam splendores varios liceat contueri pulchrorumque omnium simulacra: id, inquam, totum Venus ipsa censetur ['Ἀφροδίτη μέν ἐστι τὸ πᾶν].'

3. For similar configurations see Ficino, *Opera*, p. 1619: '. . . a Mercurio inquisitio quaelibet et expressio, a Venere charitas et humanitas. . . . Sic eorum opinio confirmatur qui Veneri Mercurium anteponunt'; *Supplementum Ficinianum* I, p. 56: 'Picus heros ingeniosus et pulcher Mercurio et Venere natus. . . .' See also Cartari, *Imagini*, p. 541, 'Venere con Mercurio.' On a medal, Hill, no. 219, Mercury points upward to the star of Venus: EGO INTUS, VENUS EXTRA, a compliment to the intelligence and beauty of a woman (certainly not satirical, as Hill surmises).

4. On the 'blest Hermaphrodite', see below, pages 200 ff., 211 ff.

the Graces and Flora to indicate her spiritual and her sensuous manifestations, we may suspect that Apollo was to be endowed with a
similar inclusiveness of powers.[5] The correspondence becomes more
explicit in the system of musical intervals illustrated below this
headpiece and explained in the book.[6] Here the note associated with
Apollo or Sol is again placed 'in the centre' (*in medio residens
complectitur omnia Phoebus*) but in such a way that there are three
notes below it and four notes above, and the last of these transcends
altogether the planetary music and belongs to the sphere of the
fixed stars:

$$8 \quad 7 \quad 6 \quad 5 \quad 4 \quad 3 \quad 2 \quad 1$$
$$\cdot \quad \cdot \quad \cdot \quad \odot \quad \cdot \quad \cdot \quad \cdot$$

The resulting division of the octave, with the fourth note treated as
central and the eighth as transcendent, and the remaining six forming symmetrical triads, corresponds very closely to the composition
of the *Primavera*. It is possible therefore that the painting was meant
to carry a musical suggestion, the eight figures representing, as it
were, an octave in the key of Venus. Transposed into the key of
Apollo, the highest note of the octave would belong to the muse
Urania, who was frequently represented turning away to gaze at
the stars,[7] while the first and lowest note (Clio) was compared by
Gafurius to 'the sigh of Proserpina', breaking (as he said) the silence
of the earth. If we recall that on her return in the spring Proserpina
was pictured as strewing flowers, it becomes likely that an echo of
that myth, or of its musical equivalent, was meant to be sensed in

5. In a more abundant form the same combination, the Graces placed against a
rich foliage of laurel, which makes them look like dryads, recurs in Agostino di
Duccio's relief of Apollo in the Tempio Malatestiano in Rimini. Since the Greek and
Latin words for 'matter' signify sylvan vegetation (ὕλη, *silva*), it was not illogical to
suggest the musical animation of matter (νοῦς ὑλικός) by placing the Graces in a
sylvan setting.

6. See below, Appendix 6, pages 265–9. Originally published as a frontispiece to
Gafurius, *Practica musice* (1496), the woodcut was reprinted with commentary in
Gafurius, *De harmonia musicorum instrumentorum* IV, xii (1518), fol. 94ᵛ. Cf. Warburg,
op. cit., pp. 271, 412 ff., 429 f.

7. For example on the title page of Hyginus, *Poeticon astronomicon* (1502), where
Urania turns her back. See also the averted Urania in Raphael's *Parnassus*.

the progression from Zephyr to Flora. Whether these themes were to be resumed, transposed, and more fully developed in a picture of Apollo presiding over the Muses, much as Venus presides over the Graces and Nymphs, we do not know. It is certain, on the other hand, that the *Birth of Venus* came from the same villa as the *Primavera*; and this picture in its turn is an example of a change of key, or modulation.

After the labyrinth of the *Primavera* it is something of a relief to discover how simply the same philosophy of love has been re-stated in the *Birth of Venus* (fig. 39). Four figures in the place of eight, and so grouped that a plain triad emerges from their con-figuration. Driven by the blowing winds, who are represented as a pair of lovers – Politian's *zefiri amorosi*[8] – Venus glides on a huge shell (*sopra un nicchio*) towards the shore where the Hour of Spring spreads out a flowered mantle to receive her, while the roses that fall from the breath of the Zephyrs perfume the foaming sea. Had not Pico della Mirandola declared that the biblical words 'spiritus ferebatur super aquas' refer to the moving spirit of Eros ('spiritus amoris'),[9] one would hesitate to apply the phrase to the Zephyrs, for they clearly represent the breath of passion by which the new-born Venus is moved and inspired – *da' Zefiri lascivi spinta a proda*;[10] but on the shore the mantle prepared for her protection is held out by the chaste Hour. The goddess's own posture, that of the classical *Venus pudica*, expresses the dual nature of love, both sensuous and chaste, of which her attendants represent the separate aspects. But as the transcendent 'union of contraries' is rendered by a moment-ary gesture, the universal symbol demanded by the dialectical pro-gramme becomes a transitory scene:

> Giurar potresti che dell'onde uscisse
> La Dea premendo con la destra il crino,
> Con l'altra il dolce pomo ricoprisse.[11]

8. *Giostra* I, cxiii, 4, as in xcix, 7 f.
9. *Heptaplus* III, ii.
10. *Giostra* I, xcix, 7. On Venus's shell see below, Appendix 5, pages 263 f.
11. ibid. I, ci, 1–3.

The transient effect of Botticelli's Venus, the more surprising in view of the static quality of its ancient prototypes (fig. 34),[12] was prepared for Botticelli by Politian's mastery in ostensibly describing a plastic monument while actually dissolving it into a sequence of episodes. Both poet and painter aimed at recapturing the spirit of the lost *Venus Anadyomene* of Apelles, which was known from ancient descriptions.[13] In addition to its poetical and didactic character, Botticelli's painting must therefore also be classed among those attempts at antiquarian revival by which the vision of a lost painting of antiquity was to be conjured up before the beholder. While the *Calumny of Apelles* by Botticelli is a strained example of these learned ambitions,[14] in the *Birth of Venus* the archaeological burden is absorbed by a lucid elegance. Considering all the literary refinements that were to be satisfied by the picture – philosophical, poetical, antiquarian – its freshness and successfully feigned naïveté remain a singular achievement. It is as if the high spirits of Politian had for once outdistanced the prolixities of Ficino and Pico.

Even so, a new poetic dimension will be felt in the picture, and also in the myth as related by Politian, when they are compared with the peculiarly laboured interpretation which Pico offered for 'this mystery' of the Birth of Venus.[15] Since Venus signifies beauty (*bellezza la quale si chiama Venere*), she represents for Pico a composite principle: for 'whenever several diverse things concur in constituting a third, which is born from their just mixture and temperation, the bloom which results from their proportionate composition is called beauty'. Composition, however, presupposes

12. On the acquaintance of the Quattrocento with the type of statue now best known from the Medici Venus, see Warburg, op. cit., p. 308, note to p. 10. J. J. Bern-ouilli, *Aphrodite* (1873), pp. 237 f., lists eighteen bronze statuettes of that type.

13. The classical texts are listed in Pauly–Wissowa I, 2020, s.v. 'Anadyomene'. In imitation of *Anthologia graeca* XVI, 178–82, Politian wrote a Greek epigram on the Venus Anadyomene of Apelles (*Opera* II, fol. 102ᵛ), which he imagined as a *Venus pudica;* cf. Frey–Sallmann, op. cit., pp. 119 f., with reference to Botticelli.

14. R. Förster, 'Die Verleumdung des Apelles in der Renaissance', *Jahrbuch der preussischen Kunstsammlungen* VIII (1887), pp. 29–56; 89–113; XV (1894), pp. 27–40; also 'Wiederherstellung antiker Gemälde durch Künstler der Renaissance', ibid. XLIII (1922), pp. 126–36. Further literature in Wind, *Bellini's Feast of the Gods*, p. 18, note 38.

15. *Commento* II, xvi f. (ed. Garin II, xviii ff., pp. 509–12).

multiplicity, which cannot be found in the realm of pure being, but only in the chaotic realm of change. Venus must therefore arise from 'that formless nature of which we have said that every creature is composed':[16] and this is signified by the waters of the sea 'because water is in a continuous flux and easily receptive of any form'. But in order to produce the beauty of Venus, the Heraclitean element of mutability requires transfiguration by a divine principle of form; and that need is signified by the barbarous legend, which Pico quoted from Hesiod's Theogony, that the foam of the sea (ἀφρός) from which the heavenly Aphrodite arose was produced by the castration of Uranus. Being the god of heaven, Uranus conveys to formless matter the seed of ideal forms: 'and because ideas would not have in themselves variety and diversity if they were not mixed with formless nature, and because without variety there cannot be beauty, so it justly follows that Venus could not be born if the testicles of Uranus did not fall into the waters of the sea'.[17]

The unpleasant machinery of the myth, which is far remote from Botticelli, will seem less pedantic and far-fetched when it is understood that 'dismemberment' is a regular figure of speech in the Neoplatonic dialectic. The castration of Uranus is of one type with the dismemberment of Osiris, Attis, Dionysus, all of which signify the same mystery to the neo-Orphic theologians: for whenever the supreme One descends to the Many, this act of creation is imagined as a sacrificial agony, as if the One were cut to pieces and scattered. Creation is conceived in this way as a cosmogonic death, by which the concentrated power of one deity is offered up and dispersed: but the descent and diffusion of the divine power are followed by its resurrection, when the Many are 'recollected' into the One.[18]

16. cf. above, page 88.

17. While Boccaccio, Genealogia deorum III, xxiii, followed Cicero in assuming that the Venus born from the sea was the 'second' Venus (De natura deorum III, xxiii, 59), Pico adopted the more common view and identified her with Venus Urania, the foam being the seed of Uranus (Heaven).

18. See Macrobius, In Somnium Scipionis I, xii; also Gyraldus, Opera I, 273, on 'Macrobius ex Orphica theologia.' Boyancé, Le culte des Muses, pp. 83–8, believes Olympiodorus was justified in reading the Neoplatonic allegory of the dismemberment and resurrection of Dionysus–Zagreus into Phaedo 67c ff. (the soul as 'divided' throughout the body, from where it has to be 'recollected into itself'). But while it

Why the dialectical rhythm of the One and the Many should be invested with such fearful ritualistic emotions was explained quite clearly and sensibly by Proclus. These fables, he said, serve the purpose 'that we may not only exercise the intellectual part of the soul through contending reasons, but that the divine [intuitive] part of the soul may more perfectly receive the knowledge of beings through its sympathy with more mystic concerns. For, from other [rational] discourses we appear similar to those who are [soberly] compelled to the reception of truth; but from fables we suffer in an effable manner ... venerating the mystic information which they contain.'[19] Pico also made it a practice thus to twist abruptly a seemingly rational figure of speech into a violent myth, as when he compared 'the art of discourse or reasoning' first to the steps of a ladder, and then added that on those steps 'we shall sometimes descend, with titanic force rending the unity like Osiris into many parts, and we shall sometimes ascend, with the force of Phoebus collecting the parts like the limbs of Osiris into a unity'.[20] The static image of a ladder, incongruously combined with the agony and resurrection of Osiris, produces that ambiguous state of understanding in which reason becomes charged with ritual.

---

might be argued that the Neoplatonic elaboration of the myth was sanctioned by that passage among others, it is difficult to prove that the passage actually implies the myth, or is meant to recall the corresponding ritual. On the other hand, Plato's use of the myth in other places is so veiled, and yet so undeniable (cf. Dodds, *The Greeks and the Irrational*, pp. 155 f., 176 ff. notes 131-5), that an outright rejection of Boyancé's view seems as difficult as a simple acceptance. All that may (and possibly must) be said is that Plato's thoughts on the relation of body and soul, as seen by his frequent references to catharsis, are shot through with Dionysiac allusions. But in contrast to Neoplatonic ritualism, the image of 'breaking' for 'making a singular into a plural' occurs in Plato only as a jest, *Meno* 77A.

19. *Theologia Platonica* I, vi; tr. Taylor, p. 18. On the belief in the efficacy of myths through sympathy, see Boyancé, *Le culte des Muses*, p. 163, with reference to Proclus, *In Rempublicam* II, 108, and Julian, *Orationes* VII, 216C. See also Julian, ibid. 222A–B: 'But when I say ... "torn to shreds" no one must consider the bare meaning of the words and suppose that I mean ... a thread of linen, but he must understand these words in another sense, that used by Plato, Plotinus, Porphyry, and the inspired Iamblichus.'

20. *De hominis dignitate* (ed. Garin, p. 116), tr. Forbes.

Perhaps the clearest description of this poetico-theological device is in Plutarch's *On the εἶ at Delphi*. Because of his sane, unperturbed way of facing these awkward arguments, Plutarch is of invaluable help in their study. 'We hear from the theologians,' he writes, 'both prose writers and poets, that the god is by nature indestructible and eternal, but yet, under the impulsion of some predestined plan and purpose, he undergoes transformations in his being. . . . When the god is changed and distributed into winds, water, earth, stars, plants, and animals, they describe this experience and transformation allegorically by the terms "rending" and "dismemberment". They apply to him the names Dionysus, Zagreus, Nyctelius, Isodaites, and they construct allegorical myths in which the transformations that have been described are represented as death and destruction followed by restoration to life and rebirth.'[21]

These mystical Ultimates, being extremes, cannot be pictured except as catastrophes;[22] and Plato suggested, with little success, that it is best not to picture them at all. In the *Republic* (378A), the Castration of Uranus takes the first place among the prohibited fables: '. . . If possible, they had better be buried in silence. But if there is an absolute necessity for their mention, a chosen few might hear them in a mystery (δι' ἀπορρήτων), and they should sacrifice not a common pig, but some huge and unprocurable victim; and then the number of hearers will be very few indeed.' It might be thought that Botticelli and Politian had followed Plato's rule and, unlike the

---

21. *On the* εἶ *at Delphi* 9 (*Moralia* 388F–389A), tr. Linforth, op. cit., pp. 317 f.

22. Since dispersal through death is conceived here as an act of creation, it follows logically that resurrection from death must appear as a destructive force. The end of the world, when all things return to the One, is pictured as a supreme conflagration, Plutarch, op. cit., 388B, 389C, διακόσμησις being reversed in ἐκπύρωσις, the god 'sets fire to nature and reduces all things to one likeness' (tr. Linforth, loc. cit.). By the same logic the myth of Saturn eating his children was greeted as a promise of redemption: the Many returning to the One, a reversal of primeval 'dismemberment', cf. *Enneads* V, i, 7; also Sallustius, *Concerning the Gods and the Universe* §iv (ed. A. D. Nock, 1926, p. 4), where κατάποσις is a symbol of ἐπιστροφή. The Neoplatonic artifice of lifting the primitive impulses of cannibalism and castration to the level of philosophical mysteries is a remarkable instance of *évolution régressive*. An illustration of Saturn in *Les échecs amoureux* (Bibl. Nat., MS fr. 143, fol. 28ʳ) stresses the symmetry between 'divine swallowing' and 'divine dismemberment' by showing them as pendants. On the substitution of Saturn (Cronus) for Uranus, cf. *Enneads* III, v, 2.

meticulous illustrators of mythographical text-books,[23] or an occasional minor painter who left nothing unsaid,[24] had omitted any allusion to the Castration of Uranus from their depiction of the Birth of Venus; but it is not so.[25] Politian describes the white foam as the divine seed fallen from the sky in the opening stanza of the episode:

> *Nel tempestoso Egeo in grembo a Teti*
> *si vede il fusto genitale accolto,*
> *sotto diverso volger di pianeti*
> *errar per l'onde in bianca schiuma avvolto;*

but before the stanza is ended, the *fusto genitale* has already been superseded by the pleasing image, from the Homeric Hymns, of Venus driven to the shore by zephyrs:

> *E dentro nata in atti vaghi e lieti*
> *una donzella non con uman volto,*
> *da' Zefiri lascivi spinta a proda,*
> *gir sopra un nicchio; e par che 'l ciel ne goda.*[26]

23. In two Vatican manuscripts of the fifteenth century – *Libellus de deorum imaginibus* (Cod. Reg. lat. 1290, fol. 1ʳ) and *Fulgentius metaforalis* (Cod. Pal. lat. 1066, fol. 226ʳ) – the Birth of Venus is combined in one picture with the castration scene. Also as jest in Cardinal Bibbiena's bathroom (engraved after Raphael by Marco da Ravenna).

24. An otherwise attractive little picture in the Castello Sforzesco in Milan (no. 55), formerly ascribed to Andrea Schiavone, now classified as Venetian School, shows the foam-born Venus carried to the shore by a dolphin (cf. Nonnus, *Dionysiaca* XIII, 439) while the castration of Uranus takes place in the sky (illustrated in A. Venturi, *Storia dell' arte italiana* IX, iv, 1929, p. 704, fig. 498, where Venus is misnamed Galatea, despite the celestial events). I am indebted to Ernest O. Hauser for drawing my attention to this painting.

25. Ficino followed the rule more faithfully than either Politian or Pico. In *De amore* II, vii, and VI, vii (*Opera*, pp. 1326, 1345), where the nature of Venus Urania is so fully discussed, the circumstances attending her birth are passed over in silence. Obedience to a prohibition of Plato seems the most likely explanation for this remarkable omission, which occurs again in Ficino's commentaries on *Euthyphro* 6A, 8B, and *Republic* 377E–378A. The rare instances in which he brings himself to mention the Castration of Uranus show a brevity of style uncommon in Ficino; e.g. *In Plotinum* V, viii, 13 (*Opera*, p. 1769), *In Platonis Philebum* I, xi (ibid., p. 1217), *De amore* V, xii (ibid., p. 1340, explaining Agathon's dismissal of 'the ancient doings among the gods', *Symposium* 195C).

26. *Giostra* I, xcix.

The concluding phrase – 'the sky rejoiced' – entirely blots out the initial horror, for it suggests, as do also the succeeding stanzas, that Uranus is no longer a solitary god but takes pleasure in finding himself incarnated in his new-born daughter ('In thee I am well pleased').

In Botticelli's painting, the accents are distributed with the same care and in the same order of importance. As in Politian's poem, the white foam on the waves is emphatically stressed, but it is incidental to the main scene. While the general atmosphere is that of a cosmogonic myth, and shows how the divine spirit, in the words of Plutarch, is 'changed and distributed into winds and water', the moment chosen for representation is that following the cosmic birth: the new-born Venus, already risen from the sea, is blown to the shore by the winds of spring. And as if to suggest, through a poetic after-image, that the sea has been fertilized by the sky, a mystical rain of roses issues from the breath of the wind-god – 'the spirit moving over the waters'.[27]

*

27. The rain of flowers, as a symbol of divine impregnation, recurs in Signorelli's *Immaculata* (Il Gesù, Cortona). Robert Boyle's philological comment on 'the operation of the Spirit of God who is said [Genesis i, 2] to have been moving Himself, as hatching females do (as the original, *Merhephet*, is said to import ...) upon the face of the waters' (*The Sceptical Chymist*, Part II) is of patristic origin: see St Basil, *Hexameron* ii, 6; St Augustine, *De Genesi ad litteram* I, xviii, 36. On comparable thoughts in a Paracelsian vein cf. A. A. Barb, 'Diva Matrix', *Journal of the Warburg and Courtauld Institutes* XVI (1953), pp. 205, 219 note 75. The common source (sought by Barb, ibid., p. 202) of Paracelsus, *Opus paramirum* IV ('De matrice'), and Hippolytus, *Refutatio omnium haeresium* V, xix, 11 ff., may be found in *Timaeus* 49A–53B, on 'the receptacle of all generation' (πάσης γενέσεως ὑποδοχή). Paracelsus's term *matrix quattuor elementorum* corresponds exactly to the argument in the *Timaeus*. A variant of the doctrine in Aristotle (*Physics* I, ix, 192A, on which see above, page 104 note 23) gave Giordano Bruno, who knew the original in Plato, the chance for a long comical digression on the equation of *materia e femina* by one of the Aristotelian pedants in *De la causa, principio et uno* IV, introduced by the biblical quotation: *Et os vulvae numquam dicit: sufficit* (from Proverbs xxx, 16), which he interprets as meaning: 'materia recipiendis formis numquam expletur'. Rubens and Peiresc, when they discussed the *vulva deificata* on Graeco-Egyptian gems (Barb, op. cit., p. 194; C. Bonner, *Studies in Magical Amulets*, 1950, pp. 80 f.), were certainly acquainted with Plutarch *De Iside et Osiride* 53–6 (*Moralia* 372E–373F), where Plutarch expanded the passage from the *Timaeus* into a vast Graeco-Egyptian allegory of creation. The pleasure that Rubens took in this type of speculation may have prompted him to copy (see Brussels Museum, no. 388) a Flemish portrait of Paracelsus (Louvre, no. 2567A).

The self-division by which the Orphic gods unfold their powers and multiply diminishes in violence as the emanations descend from the highest to an intermediate level. In the supreme One, which is simple and ineffable, division appears as 'dismemberment' because it is only by a kind of self-immolation, a logical μετάβασις εἰς ἄλλο γένος, that the One can be made over into the Many. But particular deities who, like Venus, are inherently composite and contrarious contain multiplicity within their own natures and are hence not agonized when their power is spread out, or paired with that of other deities in a new combination. This is important for the understanding of the harmonious relation in which the *Venus Urania*, born from the sea, stands to the sheltered Venus, who, in a grove illumined by golden fruits, gently presides over the rites of *Primavera*. The transition from the elemental to the pastoral setting is defined by the flowered mantle of Spring which is spread over Venus as she approaches the earth. In the Platonic scale of things this is a descent, a vulgarization; for the wealth of colours and variety of shapes that delight the eye when it perceives beauty on earth are but a veil behind which the splendour of the pure celestial beauty is concealed. But in recognizing that the clothed Venus is the *Venere vulgare* or *Aphrodite Pandemos*, whom Plato and the Platonists opposed to the *Aphrodite Urania* (*Venere celeste*),[28] we must beware of oversimplifying the contrast by assuming that the vulgar Venus is purely sensuous and does not share in the celestial glory. Pico himself, who developed the theme that the 'two Venuses' in Plato were meant to illustrate the distinction between a celestial and an earthly vision of beauty, warned his readers that the desire of love aroused by earthly beauty is in its turn of two opposite kinds, 'de' quali l'uno è bestiale, e l'altro è umano'.[29] While a purely sensuous instinct will incline to misplace the source of visual beauty in the body and seek the fruition of beauty in animal pleasures alone, the human lover will recognize

---

28. *Symposium* 180D–E; Ficino, *De amore* II, vii; Pico, *Commento* II, viii (ed. Garin II, x, p. 498). As early as 1433, Carlo Marsuppini referred to the *duas Veneres, Uraniam et Pandemon*, in a letter to Lorenzo Valla written in praise of Valla's *De voluptate* which had just been reissued under the new title *De vero bono*; cf. L. Barozzi and R. Sabbadini, *Studi sul Panormita e sul Valla* (1891), p. 66.

29. *Commento* II, xxiv (ed. Garin III, ii, p. 524).

that the Venus who appears clothed in an earthly garment is an 'image' of the celestial. 'And observe that Plotinus in his book *De amore* does not speak of the first celestial Love but only of this, and similarly he does not speak of the first Venus, but of the second', and far from characterizing her as the Venus Urania, he makes her descend into the 'prima anima', declaring 'che questa anima è chiamata Venere in quanto è in lei un certo amore splendido e specioso'.[30] If the distinction is overlooked, Pico warns, 'it might appear as if Plato and Plotinus were in disagreement on this matter, whereas he who studies them carefully will notice that the complete and perfect cognition of celestial love was held by both of them together, because Plato dealt with that which is the first and pure celestial love, and Plotinus with the second which is its image'. Quite consistently Pico was led by these observations to go beyond the simple dichotomy of 'celestial' and 'vulgar', by expanding it into a triple division: *amore celeste, umano, e bestiale*.[31] And as the last of these was declared too low to deserve of philosophical consideration, from those at least who refused to 'profane the chaste amorous mysteries of Plato' (*profanare e' casti misteri amorosi di Platone*), it follows that the Platonic doctrine of 'two Venuses' no longer designated two opposite kinds of love, one chaste and noble, the other sensuous and vain, but two noble loves called *Amore celeste e umano*, of which the second, confined to the variegated medium of sensibility, was but the humbler image of the first. 'Amore umano è proprio quello che disopra fu detto essere immagine dello amore celeste.'[32]

It was an inspired device in Botticelli to represent the *amore*

---

30. *Commento* II, xxii (ed. Garin III, i, pp. 521 f.). The argument refers to *Enneads* III, v, 5–9. Pico slightly overstates his case since Plotinus begins by discussing both Venuses (III, v, 1–4), but it is true that the bulk of his argument, and particularly that part which interprets the myth of Poros and Penia, is confined to the second Venus.

31. loc. cit. (ed. Garin, pp. 524–31). Ficino, *De amore* VI, viii (*Opera*, pp. 1345 f.), had also discussed *amor divinus, humanus, ferinus* with regard to the 'two Venuses' in Plato, but without distinguishing Plato's celestial Venus from the noble but worldly Venus in Plotinus. Pico's insistence on this point was one of his many digs at the 'distinguished Platonist' whom he found, as may easily be the case with an assiduous compiler, both informative and muddle-headed.

32. loc. cit. (ed. Garin, p. 525).

splendido e specioso of the second Venus by endowing her with matron-like features (fig. 25). She who is the source of earthly splendour, and whose role as a goddess of fertility is modestly suggested by her bulb-like figure, appears, in contrast to the wealth which she administers, as a restraining and moderating force, aware of her part as the vicar of a higher Venus of whom she is only an image or shadow (*ombra*),[33] although she exercises in her own realm an undisputed sovereignty. 'Motrice de' corpi ed alligata a questo ministerio',[34] she is the power that moves the visible world, infusing the transcendent order into the corporal: 'subietta a quella e padrona di questa'.[35]

---

33. *Commento*, ed. Garin, p. 537.   34. ibid., pp. 463, 469.

35. 'Two Venuses, one draped, the other nude', were mentioned in a letter by Calandra in which he described Mantegna's painting of Comus, finished by Costa after Mantegna's death and now in the Louvre. In this picture (cf. Wind, *Bellini's Feast of the Gods*, p. 47, with further literature), the characterization of the two Venuses leaves no doubt that the clothed Venus, while inferior to the naked, is also the more humble of the two. Horne, *Botticelli* (1908), p. 56, guessed at the right solution by a happy instinct while reading of the two Venuses in Junius, *De pictura veterum* (1637), a book so far distant in style from Botticelli that Horne referred to it with appropriate hesitation: 'Perhaps, in the two paintings of Venus, which Botticelli executed for Lorenzo di Pierfrancesco de' Medici, is to be traced that double conception of Aphrodite; of Aphrodite Urania, the Heavenly Venus, the daughter of Uranus, born of the sea without mother; and of Aphrodite Pandemos, the daughter of Zeus and Dione, the Venus of universal nature, spiritualized by Botticelli in his painting of the "Spring", which certain later writers have sought to emphasize; and notably Franciscus Junius in his work "De Pictura Veterum" ...'

CHAPTER IX

SACRED AND PROFANE LOVE

IF we remember that Pico della Mirandola, in describing 'la vio-
lenzia dello amor celeste',[1] borrowed his images from a flaming
passion, it seems not surprising, nor is it un-Platonic, that Divine
Love should in the end have fostered a spiritual cult of the senses.
This tendency was latent in it from the start. In so early a dialogue
as Lorenzo Valla's *De voluptate* (1431), the Christian in his spiritual
fervour and the Epicurean of sensuous fantasy and caprice find it
possible to come to terms with each other, whereas neither is able
to tolerate the frigidity which the Stoic mistakes for virtue. Some of
the characteristic glow of Renaissance Platonism is due to this anti-
stoical bias:

> *Witnesse the father of Philosophie,*
> *Which to his Critias, shaded oft from sunne,*
> *Of love full manie lessons did apply,*
> *The which these Stoick censours cannot well deny.*[2]

While the Epicurean strain in Venetian life might otherwise
dissuade it from Florentine dialectics, the praise of Pleasure in
Ficino's Platonism could have been invented for Venetians.[3] In
Titian's *Venus of Urbino* (fig. 40) the goddess is stretched out in
sumptuous repose, facing the beholder with the placid air of a
Venetian odalisque. It would seem, despite the reminiscence of a
Venus pudica, that an undisguised hedonism had at last dispelled the
Platonic metaphors. But in the background, by way of a gloss, two
servants are occupied with a *cassone* out of which they have taken
the mantle of Venus. In this marginal episode, which might be a

---

1. *Commento* III, ii (ed. Garin, p. 537).   2. *Faerie Queene* IV, Proem, 3.
3. In this connexion it is interesting to note again that Ficino's *De voluptate* was
separately published in two Aldine editions, Venice 1497 and 1516, together with
selections from Iamblichus and Proclus.

Dutch interior, the cosmic mantle designed to cover the celestial Venus (cf. fig. 39) has been reduced to comfortable domestic apparel befitting a *toilette de Vénus*, and if there is a touch of *drôlerie* in the vernacular rendering of such a well-known mythological attribute, the change of style is the right accompaniment to the luxurious figure in the foreground. Epicurean Pleasure in its pure form, which Ficino reserved for the joys of heaven, is readmitted to earth in Titian's paintings; but its effect is heightened by an echo of Platonism which enters as an accompanying theme into these hymns of physical well-being. In a book entitled *L'œil écoute*, the orthodoxy of Paul Claudel discerned a trace of spirituality in Titian's 'paradis de la chair': 'On dirait que le monde spirituel est, sinon découvert, au moins reconnu et ouvert à notre désir sous les espèces de l'affection, en même temps que la grâce s'étend au corps humain, qu'elle pénètre, sous les espèces de la beauté.'

One wonders whether it is because a Stoic frost has so often invaded the garden of Plato that one of the most gracious Platonic-Epicurean pictures, a figured dialogue *de voluptate*, has acquired the title of *Sacred and Profane Love* (fig. 37). Inevitably the inappropriate name, of which no trace has been found earlier than 1700, has engendered futile and self-contradictory attempts to affix a sacred or profane character to one or the other of the two figures. To a conventional view of Christian virtues, there could be no doubt that Sacred Love should be decently clothed, and that the naked figure represented the profane.[4] But against that reading it has been justly observed that the composition of the picture gives the superior role to the figure that is nude. Her greater height, her more vigorous posture, her lifted arm, her condescending address, all seem to raise her above the listening figure whom she appears to persuade or admonish; and as if to stress her sacred nature, Titian painted a church in the background behind her, whereas a castle appears opposite, as an accompaniment to the figure elegantly clothed. Since furthermore, according to a well-established tradition, the absence of adornment is a sign of virtue and candour ('naked Truth', 'intrinsic Beauty'), there would seem to be an excellent case for

4. A. Venturi, *Il museo e la galleria Borghese* (1893), p. 104.

ascribing a nobler character to the naked figure, and a more worldly nature to the figure that is clothed.[5] However, when that inference was first drawn, the visual evidence was again intercepted by a sanctimonious prejudice. It was assumed that the naked figure could not be the 'higher' and more sacred unless she represented the chaster love, and *vice versa*.[6] But regardless of the question to what extent an abstemious morality was favoured by Renaissance Platonists, the characters in the painting express the opposite. The red of the cloak that spreads behind the figure on the right intensifies the sense of her passionate nature, while the colours of the clothed figure appear subdued by comparison, the red tones being here confined to the undergarment which shows only in the right sleeve and near the left foot, while the dress is otherwise a simple white.

It should therefore be admitted at the outset that the clothed figure combines two traits which 'these Stoic censors' are always inclined to separate: she is the more worldly of the two, and also the more restrained.[7] The beauty of her garment does not depend for its effect on embroideries, pearls, gold braid, or brocades, which so often

---

5. On all these points Panofsky's argument in *Studies in Iconology*, pp. 150–60, and, more fully, *Hercules am Scheidewege*, pp. 173–80, seems to me conclusive. E. Petersen, 'Zu Meisterwerken der Renaissance: Bemerkungen eines Archäologen', *Zeitschrift für bildende Kunst* XVII (1906), pp. 182–7 ('Tizians *Amor sacro e profano*') was the first to associate the painting with the two Venuses in Ficino's *De amore* (p. 186).

6. Essentially this is still Panofsky's view.

7. The same 'philosophy of clothes' can be studied in Giorgione's *Fête champêtre* in the Louvre. The nymphs, distinguished from the musicians by the absence of clothes, are meant to be recognized as 'divine presences', superior spirits from whose fountain the mortal musicians are nourished. In the Holkham *Venus* (Metropolitan Museum of Art, New York), and the corresponding paintings by Titian in Madrid and Berlin, the disparity between mortal and goddess is heightened by a paradox of posture. While the courtier plays music under the inspiration of love (cf. Erasmus, *Adagia* s.v. *musicam docet amor*), he does not face the goddess directly, but turns his head over his shoulder to 'look back' at her; he thus enacts the Platonic ἐπιστροφή, the reversal of vision by which alone a mortal can hope to face transcendent Beauty. O. Brendel, 'The Interpretation of the Holkham *Venus*', *Art Bulletin* XXVIII (1946), pp. 65–75, suspected a Neoplatonic argument in these paintings, but adhered to the mistaken restriction of supreme Platonic love to *amor intellectualis* – clearly not Titian's theme. Although the composition seems specifically Venetian, the idea of juxtaposing a clothed mortal to a 'transcendent' nude representing Venus can be traced back to Florentine marriage *cassoni* (our figs. 44 f.); cf. below, page 273, also Schubring, *Cassoni*, pl. xxx, nos. 156 f.; pl. xxxviii, nos. 184 f.

predominate in Renaissance dress:[8] for the splendour is achieved entirely by the generous draping of the garment, and it should be noticed that its chief ornament is a locked girdle.[9] The absence of any other jewels,[10] the fact that she prefers flowers for her adornment, wearing a small wreath of myrtle (*myrtus coniugalis*) in her hair and holding a few flowers on her lap, would suggest a gentle rather than an ambitious sensibility; and that is confirmed by her meditative expression. To convict her of an undue addiction to the vanities of the world, there remains only the suspicious fact that her gloved hand is resting on a closed vessel which has been supposed, on the analogy of Ripa's 'Short-lived Happiness', to contain gems and other riches.[11] But this surmise reminds us of Plutarch's reflection 'that the Stoics rave worse than the poets'; for if Titian had intended us to understand that the vessel is filled with earthly treasures, presumably he would not have hesitated to paint them.[12] Instead he painted a vessel which is closed, and that is in itself

8. It is the more surprising that Scipione Francucci, a poet of the seventeenth century (on whom see L. Venturi, 'Note sulla Galleria Borghese', *L'arte* XII, 1909, pp. 37 ff.), should have found her barbarously overdressed, *di barbarica pompa*; quoted by Panofsky, *Studies in Iconology*, pp. 159 f.

9. cf. *Faerie Queene* IV, v, 3: 'That girdle gave the virtue of chaste love . . .' See also Boccaccio, *Genealogia deorum* III, xxii; and Ripa, *Iconologia*, s.v. 'Venustà', 'Piacere honesto'; Valeriano, *Hieroglyphica* XL, fol. 299ʳ. Holbein played on this theme in his curious little painting of *Magdalena Offenburg as Venus* (Basle Museum no. 322), which shows the goddess wearing the girdle, whereas the companion piece, *Magdalena Offenburg as Laïs* (Basle Museum no. 323), portrays the same sitter as courtesan. This spirited pair of pictures (comparable to Dürer's double portrait of Katharina Fürlegerin) literally represents, with an appropriate variation of gesture, Love sacred and Love profane, Venus Urania and Pandemus. The historical Laïs, as Holbein knew, had favoured Apelles, the painter of Venus (cf. Athenaeus XIII, 582 ff.; also Winckelmann, *Geschichte der Kunst des Altertums* I, iv).

10. In photographs she appears to wear a bracelet, but this is actually the fringe of the glove.

11. Panofsky, *Hercules am Scheidewege*, p. 174.

12. How little Titian's figure corresponds to *Felicità breve* in Ripa may be seen from Ripa's description: 'A woman dressed in white and yellow, who wears a golden crown on her head and is adorned with various jewels. Raising her right arm high, she holds a sceptre entwined with the leaves of a gourd that rises from the ground near her feet, while with her left hand she holds a vessel full of coins and gems.' To save the 'close resemblance' that has been discovered between this figure and Titian's, at least five of the attributes listed by Ripa would have to be disregarded. The same applies to *Felicità eterna* in relation to Titian's nude.

meaningful, particularly as it contrasts with the open vessel near the other figure; and between the two there is a plucked rose.[13]

To understand the symbolism it may be helpful to inquire at what kind of fountain the two women are met.[14] That it is a fountain of love is shown by the presence of Amor, who bends over the water and plays with it; but the reliefs with which the fountain is decorated have a severe, forbidding aspect. A man is being scourged, a woman dragged by the hair, and an unbridled horse is led away by the mane (fig. 42). As the horse is a Platonic symbol of sensuous passion or *libido* (cf. fig. 41),[15] or of what Pico called *amore bestiale*, the fierce

13. On the symbolism of the rose, as a token of love, see C. Joret, *La rose dans l'antiquité et au moyen âge. Histoire, légendes et symbolisme* (1892). Also L. F. Benedetto, *Il 'Roman de la rose' e la letteratura italiana* (1910), pp. 9, 186, etc. A closer connexion with the *Roman de la rose*, which has occasionally been suspected in Titian's painting, I have been unable to detect. The nearest approach, in the Italian version by Durante, is the sonnet no. xvii (*Il fiore*, ed. F. Castets, Paris, 1881, p. 9) in which Venus admonishes *Bellaccoglienza*, but this reference is as inconclusive as W. Friedländer's identification of the two figures ('La tintura delle rose', *Art Bulletin* XX, 1938, pp. 322 ff.) with Venus and Polia, the heroine of the *Hypnerotomachia*. Although the symbolism of the novel draws from the same sources as Titian's painting, he did not illustrate its incidents (see below, page 147 note 24). Nor is the surmise that the closed vessel contains white roses (Friedländer, p. 324 note 16) any superior to the suggestion that it contains gems.

14. Although the shape of the fountain resembles a sarcophagus and might thus recall the Italian custom of using ancient sarcophagi as fountains, Titian did not introduce in this instance any of those traces of fragmentation by which he generally characterizes a piece of sculpture as antique (cf. the fractured statue in the background of the fresco St Anthony healing a Child, Scuola del Santo, Padua; or the torso in the right corner of the *Presentation of the Virgin*, Accademia, Venice). Since all the figures and mouldings are intact, and the relief includes a Renaissance coat-of-arms, there is no justification for regarding the sculpture as 'ancient', and consequently any iconographic inferences drawn from that assumption ('a fountain of life made out of a tomb', 'originally destined to hold a corpse but now converted', etc.) are open to question. The subjects of the relief in fact exclude a funerary significance.

15. Bocchi, *Symbolicae quaestiones*, no. cxvii: 'Semper libidini imperat prudentia' (horsetamer); Valeriano, *Hieroglyphica*, fol. 34ᵛ: 'Immoderatus impetus'. Derived from the horse of ἐπιθυμία in *Phaedrus* 253D, to which Petersen refers op. cit., p. 187. On *Cupido* as a name for Roman racehorses (kindly brought to my attention by Eduard Fraenkel) see A. Alföldi, *Die Kontorniaten* (1942–3), p. 178, no. 446 (pls. xlix, 5; liv, 13). A witty allegory of horse-taming by Piero di Cosimo (National Gallery of Art, Washington, no. 271) represents the chaste goddess Hippo training a young stallion on an island in a siren-infested lake: cf. Ermolao Barbaro, *Castigationes Plinianae* V, iv (1492, fols. k 5ᵛ–6ʳ); Gyraldus, *Opera* I, 46C–D (s.v. 'Hippo'), 343D (s.v. 'Hippia').

scenes of chastisement on the fountain of love show how animal passion must be chastened and bridled. Such violent scenes, conceived as a phase in the mysteries of love, were not uncommon in pagan rites of initiation; and the Renaissance may have known their representation in Roman mystery chambers, of which perhaps many more, and certainly others, were accessible then than are preserved at present.[16] But while the exact degree of a visual acquaintance with these secret traditions would be difficult to ascertain, the chief source was probably again of a literary nature. Both Ficino and Pico professed to know that in the pagan initiatory rites of love the first stage was a purge of the sensuous passion, a painful ritual of purification by which the lover was prepared for his communion with the god.[17] It was surely as an allusion to these propitiatory ordeals, rather fully described in Apuleius, that symbols of chastisement were so frequently introduced by Renaissance artists into an amorous context, as shown for example by the mysterious whip in Mantegna's Camera degli Sposi,[18] or by the emblematic figure of the 'tortured Cupid'.[19] For Ausonius the *Cupido cruciatus* was still a

16. The frescoes in the Villa Item, which seem relevant, are of course a very late discovery, but a like cycle, of which a sixteenth-century record survives in a sketch-book by Francisco d'Ollanda (Cod. Escor. 28–1–20, fols. 13 f., reproduced in *Os desenhos das antiqualhas que vio Francisco d'Ollanda*, ed. E. Tormo, 1940, fols. 13ᵛ–14ʳ), existed in the Golden House of Nero; cf. F. Weege, 'Das Goldene Haus des Nero', *Jahrb. d. deutsch. archäol. Inst.* XXVIII, 1913, pp. 179 f., pl. 9. On the range of ancient fresco painting still preserved in the Renaissance and now lost, see Weege, 'Der malerische Schmuck von Raffaels Loggien in seinem Verhältnis zur Antike', in T. Hofmann, *Raffael als Architekt* IV (1911), pp. 140–203; Salis, op. cit., pp. 203–7.

17. Ficino, *Opera*, p. 1018: 'Quomodo purgetur animus'; also his commentary on *Enneads* VI, vii, 36: 'primus [gradus] est purgatio animi', ibid., p. 1793. Pico, *De hominis dignitate*, ed. Garin, pp. 112 ff.: 'Impuro, ut habent mysteria, purum attingere nefas.' On the relevant passages in Plato, Plotinus, Proclus, and Dionysius, see H. Koch, *Pseudo-Dionysius Areopagita in seinen Beziehungen zum Neuplatonismus und Mysterienwesen*, s.v. 'Reinigung', pp. 136, 144, 155, 174. Pico adopts Dionysius's sequence *purgari–illuminari–perfici* (cf. above, page 24 note 25).

18. See also the scourges in Mantegna's *Parnassus*.

19. In Hellenistic gems and epigrams (*Anthol. graec.* V, 195–9) Eros seems to undergo as many agonies as Psyche, both of them victims of the 'pains of love' – pains which the unsuccessful lover tries to 'pin' on the cool object of his passion by the use of poetic invocations or amulets. A famous late-antique love spell (Preisendanz, *Griechische Zauberpapyri* I, 1928, pp. 126–31: Bibl. Nat. suppl. gr. 574, fols. 20 f.; cf. Reitzenstein, *Das Märchen von Amor und Psyche*, p. 80) prescribes that a gem be engraved

victim of revengeful passion, but on Renaissance medals, as in Petrarch's *Trionfi* (II, 120 ff.),[20] he appears as a symbol of chastity, inscribed *Virginitas amoris frenum*, or *Virtuti ac formae pudicitia praeciosissimum*, or combined with an anagram addressed to the *Castitatis dea*.[21] 'La castità', writes Ripa following Thomas Aquinas, 'è nome di virtù detta dalla castigatione', and represents Chastity swinging a scourge.[22] To illustrate the 'Tortures of Love' as a refining ordeal, Veronese boldly juxtaposed *Castigatione* and *Castità* (fig. 43).[23] Unquestionably, the reliefs of chastisement on Titian's fountain of love are to show how love is chastened.[24]

If the reliefs on the fountain thus demonstrate that animal passion has been exorcized, it would follow that the water in the fountain of love is pure, although it is gently stirred by Amor; and it follows further that the two women conversing at the fountain in the presence of the god are both representatives of a love above the

---

on one side with the tortures of Psyche imposed by Eros and Aphrodite, on the other with the group of Eros and Psyche embracing. The same contrast on Roman sarcophagi, where the agony of Love is identified with that of Death, cf. below, page 160.

20. Panofsky, *Studies in Iconology*, p. 126 note 79; with further literature on the Hellenistic epigrams. Also 'Der gefesselte Eros', *Oud Holland* L (1933), pp. 193–217.

21. Hill, nos. 992, 1011, 233–5.

22. Ripa, s.v. 'Castità'.

23. See below, Appendix 8, pages 272 ff.

24. Hill, no. 1019, shows the chastisement of Love joined to the chastisement of Fortune; and it is not impossible that both these unbridled forces were to be tamed in the scenes on the fountain. The woman pulled by the flying forelock (near the left edge of the design) is more likely a Fortuna, who is supposed to be caught in just this way, than a nightmare-vision of Polia pulled by the hair (Friedländer, cited above, note 13). The horse also has no immediate connexion with Polia's dream, whereas a *Fortuna a cavallo* is listed by Cartari, *Imagini*, s.v. 'Fortuna', as a Renaissance symbol of fugacious fortune. Verbally derived from the Roman *Fortuna equestris*, but only rarely used as an emblem of knighthood or noble fortune (see S. Béguin, 'A Lost Fresco of Niccolò dell'Abbate at Bologna in Honour of Julius III', *Journal of the Warburg and Courtauld Institutes* XVIII, 1955, pl. 32a), the *Fortuna a cavallo* chiefly suggested the *immoderatus impetus* of the Platonic horse (cf. Bocchi, symbolon no. cxvii), and thus changed into the *equus infoelicitatis* of the *Hypnerotomachia* (fols. b iiiiᵛ–b vʳ), a demonic horse throwing off *amoretti* who try to ride it. All these are fickle and uncontrolled powers, and Virtue chastises them as companions of an unchaste Amor. In the *Hypnerotomachia*, the chastisement of Adonis (with which Friedländer seeks to identify the scene on Titian's fountain) is itself understood as a purification rite, *Adonia* being the atonement for *impura suavitas*, fols. z viᵛ ff.

'profane', their dialogue rising to those *casti misteri amorosi di Platone* which allow for two forms of chastened love, *Amore celeste e umano*.[25] Human Love, while beautifully adorned, is the more restrained of the two because she knows her adornments to be vicarious, whereas Celestial Love, who is unadorned, is the more passionate and ardent, holding in her hand a vase from which a flame rises.[26] Between the two, Amor is seen setting the water of the fountain in motion, an idyllic version of the 'spirit moving over the waters', which changes chastity into love.[27] As the movement of the group is from left to right, the three figures again illustrate the progression from *Pulchritudo* through *Amor* to *Voluptas*, with Amor playing his traditional part as a mediating or converting power. The theme of the picture is therefore exactly what the untutored eye has often suspected – an initiation of Beauty into Love.[28]

Since there is little chance that the popular title *Amore sacro e profano* will be abandoned very soon for the more just *Amore celeste e umano*, or the less attractive *Pulchritudo–Amor–Voluptas*, we should be grateful that it does at least retain the tone of a mystical initiation and allows that the two main figures represent an allegory rather than a myth. To call either or both of them by the name of Venus seems to me too positive; for although the theory of love which they embody was unquestionably associated with the two Venuses in Plato, 'one draped, the other nude',[29] it is important to observe that, in contradistinction to Botticelli and Mantegna, Titian endowed the figures with attributes and characters which transcend the mythological idiom. Neither the red cloak behind the nude figure, nor the flaming vase in her hand, or the closed vessel held

25. See above, page 139.

26. cf. *Hypnerotomachia*, fol. h v^v, where 'il vaso igneo' (illustrated fol. h v^r) signifies 'una participatione d'amore'.

27. The importance of the action of Amor for the interpretation of the painting was first stressed in a lecture by O. Brendel. On 'the spirit moving over the waters' as *spiritus amoris*, see above, page 131.

28. Aldo de Rinaldis, *La Galleria Borghese*, p. 46: 'Si tratterebbe, ad ogni modo, di una scena di "persuasione all'amore"; e non v'è dubbio che questo titolo sarebbe il più appropriato al famosissimo quadro di Tiziano.'

29. See above, page 140 note 35. Also pages 138 ff., 143 note 5.

by the other figure, occur, to my knowledge, as attributes of Venus.[30]

The picture belongs rather to the same class as an allegory by Garofalo (fig. 63) in which the growth of love is pictured as a configuration of Amor, Pulchritudo, and Voluptas. In this painting Amor is represented by the presiding Cupid, Pulchritudo by the two lovers contemplating each other's beauty, and Voluptas by the pair who embrace.[31] It is evident, however, that the poetry inherent in the subject is heightened by Titian's more figurative mode of expression. If the poetical virtues of allegory required a defence, comparison of these two pictures might show how the more allegorical of the two is also the more poetical.

Perhaps because Titian's allegory is so economically contrived, despite the richness of the setting, it resembles a design of Roman style and didactic rigour, engraved by Marcantonio Raimondi after Raphael (fig. 38). Mistakenly called *The Two Sibyls*, the engraving represents the muses of history and astronomy, *Clio and Urania*. Touched by the celestial music of the spheres, Urania has closed her book and appears to be seized with an ecstatic rapture, whereas Clio, bound to the earth, records the deeds to be remembered. The zodiacal signs of the Scales and the Scorpion, which appear to inspire the astral muse, are quoted as harbingers of death in Horace: *Seu Libra seu me Scorpios adspicit*,[32] and the same idea, in an earthly form, is probably also intended by the slab of stone on which Clio

---

30. R. Freyhan, in *Journal of the Warburg and Courtauld Institutes* XI (1948), p. 86, has pointed out that the flaming vase, as it appears in Titian, was in Christian iconography an attribute of Caritas signifying *amor dei*, although derived from the flaming torch held by Venus in medieval illustrations; but while this observation supports the association of Titian's figure with *amore celeste*, it seems to me to contradict her identification with Venus, since the attribute is clearly not a torch.

31. The animals in the upper right, a timid lizard and an aggressive goat, are *imprese amorose*, to be combined in the perfect lover. On the lizard (*ramarro*) as symbol of shyness or coolness in love, but also of constancy, see Jacopo Gelli, *Divisi, motti e imprese di famiglie e personaggi italiani* (1928), nos. 124, 972, 1499, 1575, 1629. The goat's amorous passion is of course proverbial.

32. *Carmina* II, 17. As astrological 'houses' *Libra* and *Scorpio* belong to Venus and Mars, whose combination again signifies *concordia discors*, that is, Harmony. See Plutarch and Pico as quoted above, pages 86 ff.

rests her foot.[33] The picture thus represents a dual philosophy of death, by combining a quiet and careful remembrance on earth with an enthusiastic abandon at the thought of heaven. To invoke a conformity of human deeds with the destiny written in the sky is a Stoic rather than a Platonic maxim; and the willing acceptance of the fateful sentence, as expressed in the concordance between the two muses, has more of the spirit of Stoical heroism than of Plato's elusiveness. Yet the ecstatic joy expressed by Urania, whose posture is modelled after a Bacchante, is quite the opposite of Stoic apathy. Her enraptured attitude induced Achille Bocchi to reproduce her figure among his pedagogical symbols under the name and in the role of *felicitas*,[34] which was Ficino's synonym for divine Joy or *voluptas urania*.[35]

In the background of Titian's painting, the landscape is animated by little idyllic scenes which echo, or parody in the musical sense of the word, the theme of the *misteri amorosi*. A pair of rabbits, animals sacred to Venus (but not necessarily profane since they also attend the Madonna), relieve the heroic image of the castle on the left which is approached by a knight on horseback. In front of the lake, two riders with dogs are hunting a hare; a shepherd guards a flock of sheep; and near the edge of the painting a pair of rustic lovers engage in a passionate embrace. These three episodes, so loosely juxtaposed as if they were freely improvised and unconnected, yet

33. Her posture is taken from an ancient Nike inscribing a shield, a figure that recurs also among the *stucchi* of Raphael's Logge. In Poussin's frontispiece to the Bible (Wildenstein, op. cit., no. 169) the two Muses are boldly transmogrified into allegories of 'Word' and 'Spirit'.

34. Bocchi, symbolon no. cxxvii. He added a man on the side of Clio, whom he redefined as *virtus*, so that the group resembles a feeble Hercules at the Crossroads. The title, however, reads *virtutis et felicitatis formula*, in which *felicitas* is the reward, not the opponent, of *virtus*.

35. That Titian's picture was designed as a bridal gift is, on the face of it, not an unreasonable hypothesis, since Plotinus, and Ficino with him, regarded the 'passions of lovers' as an image or copy of the celestial ecstasy (as in the Catholic 'sacrament of marriage'). But since allusion to a marriage would require two coats-of-arms, not one, Petersen (op. cit., p. 183) was justified in questioning the theory. The coat-of-arms on the fountain, reproduced and described in A. Venturi, *Il museo e la galleria Borghese*, pp. 103 f., appears to be that of Niccolò Aurelio (cf. A. L. Mayer, in *Art Bulletin* XXI, 1939, p. 89), or possibly of another member of his family.

carry a suggestion of three phases of life which, if they were expressed in terms of Greek mythology, would be governed by three gods – Diana the chaste huntress, Hermes the shepherd, and Venus the goddess of love. That the peaceful shepherd is placed in the centre, separating the hunters from the lovers, gives a sense of the benign protective power which mediates between passion and chastity. But although the theme of the foreground is thus restated in the language of pastoral elegy, the argument is not stressed but rather made to evaporate. A poetic mood completely absorbs the philosophical construction, and a piece of landscape painting emerges, so remote in tone from the models of antiquity that it would seem to be the reverse of an ancient revival, although it was inspired by a Platonic mystery and served to heighten a dialogue. To borrow a phrase applied by Reynolds to the Arcadian landscapes of Poussin, Titian reveals in this painting 'a mind naturalized in antiquity'.

CHAPTER X

AMOR AS A GOD OF DEATH

BY one of those accidental conjunctions that Hegel might have ascribed to the cunning of history, the ancient monuments with which Renaissance Platonists were faced exactly suited their predisposition. Most of the objects were of a late date and lent themselves to a mystical reading, for with rare exceptions Greek art was inaccessible, and works of the classical period were virtually unknown. It is impossible to say, and hence futile to ask, what would have been the effect on minds steeped in the mysteries of Plotinus had they encountered the pagan myths on Greek vases of the fifth century B.C., rather than on Roman sarcophagi. As the myths appeared to them in a sepulchral setting, it was only natural, and perhaps legitimate, to inquire into their secret meaning, and to read them not as simple tales but as allusions to the mysteries of death and after-life, conceived in Neoplatonic terms.

In 1529, when Michelangelo had temporarily abandoned work on the Medici Tombs, he designed for Alfonso d'Este a figure of *Leda*, which is preserved in several copies (fig. 3).[1] It is interesting to compare this painting with the statue of *Night* (fig. 5). That the two designs are variations of one theme is suggested not only by their formal resemblance but by the fact that they were derived from a common model, an ancient image of *Leda and the Swan* (fig. 4), which frequently recurs on Roman sarcophagi.[2] It is certain, there-

1. The copy attributed to Rubens (fig. 3), on which see R. Oldenbourg, 'Rubens in Italien', *Jahrbuch der preussischen Kunstsammlungen* XXXVII (1916), pp. 272 ff., is presumably closer to the tone of the original than the more elegant replicas in the Fontainebleau style, of which one ascribed to Rosso (now in the National Gallery, London) was formerly in the collection of Sir Joshua Reynolds.

2. A. Michaelis, 'Michaelangelos Leda und ihr antikes Vorbild', *Strassburger Festgruss an Anton Springer* (1885), pp. 31 ff.; C. Robert, *Die antiken Sarkophag-Reliefs* II (1890), pp. 6–9. Our fig. 4, from a sixteenth-century codex of drawings in Coburg

fore, that the theme of Leda was not introduced by Michelangelo as an afterthought; he had found it on the ancient sepulchre from which he took his idea for the *Night*. Nor was the association accidental. 'The name Leda,' according to a curious etymology encouraged by Plutarch, 'is generally associated with Leto and explained as the Night, the mother of luminary gods.'[3]

Although this verbal connexion is too superficial to explain the mysterious affinity between the two figures by Michelangelo, it shows that he interpreted the ancient sarcophagus in the literary spirit implanted in him by his early training; for he himself mentioned to Condivi that when he first studied the antiques in the Medici garden he did so under humanist guidance. Politian, in particular, 'spurred him on in his studies, always explaining things to him and giving him subjects'.[4]

It could hardly have been otherwise. To secure correctness in copying these ancient images, or in reconstructing the missing parts, the Renaissance artist needed the advice of an antiquarian whose mind was formed by the study of ancient authors. A literary atmosphere thus enveloped the draughtsman who 'copied from the antique'. Literary knowledge, which he required to guide his eye, ended by dominating his mind, particularly as the literary records were so much better preserved than the visual. While in the recovery of plastic monuments a sense of ruins and fragments prevailed, the solid body of classical literature, however partially preserved or regained, offered a spectacle of incomparable splendour. Had the visual imagination been less vigorous and bold, the overwhelming presence of ancient letters might easily have enslaved it. But what

---

Castle (described by F. Matz, 'Über eine dem Herzog von Coburg-Gotha gehörige Sammlung alter Handzeichnungen nach Antiken', *Monatsberichte der Berliner Akademie*, 1871, p. 486, no. 150), is a detail from a Renaissance reconstruction of a Roman sarcophagus which combines twisted flutings with figured reliefs. Robert infers that the figured reliefs, while unquestionably ancient, did not originally belong to this piece, but were inserted by a Renaissance restorer acquainted with other Leda and Ganymede sarcophagi.

3. Roscher, *Lexikon der griechischen und römischen Mythologie* II, ii, col. 1924: 'Der Name Leda wird gewöhnlich mit Leto zusammengestellt und erklärt als die Nacht, die Mutter von Lichtgöttern.' See also A. B. Cook, *Zeus*, III, ii (1940), p. 1042 note 5.

4. Ascanio Condivi, *Life of Michelangelo*, tr. Holroyd (1911), p. 12.

in any weaker period would have produced obfuscation and fears released in the Renaissance artist an inquisitive impulse which made him the most undismayed of explorers.

If trained in this spirit of exploration, an artist seeing the figure of *Leda and the Swan* on a Roman sarcophagus would not be satisfied just to copy the design. He would also inquire why it was that an amorous adventure of Jupiter should have been chosen to decorate a tomb. He could not fail to notice that the loves of the gods appeared on sarcophagi with remarkable frequency. The love of Bacchus for Ariadne, of Mars for Rhea, of Zeus for Ganymede, of Diana for Endymion – all these were variations of the same theme; the love of a god for a mortal. To die was to be loved by a god, and partake through him of eternal bliss. 'As there are many kinds of death,' a Renaissance humanist explained engagingly, 'this one is the most highly approved and commended both by the sages of antiquity and by the authority of the Bible: when those ... yearning for God and desiring to be conjoined with him (which cannot be achieved in this prison of the flesh) are carried away to heaven and freed from the body by a death which is the profoundest sleep; in which manner Paul desired to die when he said: I long to be dissolved and be with Christ. This kind of death was named the kiss by the symbolic theologians [the *mors osculi* of the Cabbalists, for which Pico claimed to have found a parallel also among the Chaldeans],[5] of which Solomon also appears to have spoken when he said in the Song of Songs: *Osculetur me osculo oris sui*. And this was foreshadowed in the figure of Endymion, whom Diana kissed when he had fallen into the profoundest sleep. ...'[6]

---

5. *Conclusiones ... de intelligentia dictorum Zoroastris et expositorum eius Chaldaeorum,* no. 7. For the text of the so-called Chaldean Oracles see Franciscus Patricius, *Zoroaster et eius 320 oracula chaldaica* (1591); W. Kroll, *De oraculis chaldaicis* (1894), with additions in Hans Lewy, *Chaldaean Oracles and Theurgy,* pp. 8–65. On the legendary ascription to Zoroaster see Bidez and Cumont, *Les mages hellénisés* I, pp. 158–63; II, pp. 251–62; also below, pages 243 and 250.

6. Valeriano, *Hieroglyphica,* fol 430ʳ (appendix by Celio Agostino Curione); cf. Cicero, *De finibus bonorum et malorum* V, xx, 55: 'Endymionis somnum ... mortis instar putemus'; *Tusculanae disputationes* I, xxxviii, 92: 'Endymion. ... Habes somnum imaginem mortis'. On the ancient twin brothers Death and Sleep, see below, page 165.

While proposing to deal with the subject 'more fully in our Poetic Theology', Pico introduced already in the *Commento* a long excursus on the *morte di bacio*, in which he associated the death of Alcestis, and even 'the kisses of Agathon', with the translation of Enoch, Abraham, and other patriarchs, and compared their tragic ecstasies to the Song of Songs.[7] With remarkably few omissions, the same arguments were repeated in Leone Ebreo's *Dialoghi d'amore*,[8] in Celio Calcagnini's *Orationes*,[9] in Francesco Giorgio's *De harmonia mundi*,[10] in Egidio da Viterbo's *Libellus*,[11] in Castiglione's *Cortegiano*,[12] in Bruno's *Eroici furori*,[13] etc. And invariably the 'most joyous

7. *Commento* III, viii (ed. Garin IV, iv, pp. 557 ff.): 'Through the first death, which is only a detachment of the soul from the body, . . . the lover may see the beloved celestial Venus . . . and by reflecting on her divine image, nourish his purified eyes with joy; but if he would possess her more closely . . . he must die the second death by which he is completely severed from the body. . . . And observe that the most perfect and intimate union the lover can have with the celestial beloved is called the union of the kiss . . . and because the learned Cabbalists declare that many of the ancient fathers died in such a spiritual rapture, you will find that, according to them, they died . . . the death of the kiss: which they say of Abraham, Isaac, Jacob, Moses, Aaron, [Elijah], and several others. . . . This is what our divine Solomon desired . . . in the Song of Songs. . . . This Plato signified by the kisses of his Agathon' (which refers not to the *Symposium* but to an epigram ascribed to Plato in Diogenes Laertius III, 32 and *Anthologia graeca* V, 78). The notion of 'two deaths', as developed in *Phaedo* 61E–68A, underwent shifting elaborations by later Platonists. The account given, for example, by Plutarch, *De facie in orbe lunae* 28 (*Moralia* 943A–B), differs from that in Macrobius, *In Somnium Scipionis* I, xiii, which Cumont believes to derive from a lost text by Porphyry: 'Comment Plotin détourna Porphyre du suicide', *Revue des études grecques* XXXII (1919), pp. 113–20. Pico seems to follow Macrobius.

8. op. cit., ed. Caramella, pp. 46 f.; tr. Friedeberg-Seeley and Barnes, pp. 49–51. In these passages the 'union and copulation with God Most High' is defined as a spiritual delight perfected in death: 'Hence some, that have achieved such conjunction in this life, could not continue in perpetual enjoyment thereof, because of the bonds of the flesh; . . . only, as they reached the limit of life, the soul in the embrace of God would abandon the body altogether, remaining in supreme bliss, conjoined with the Godhead.'

9. 'Nam et in arcanis Hebraeorum legitur, Abraham, Aaron, Enoch, et Heliam atque alios qui ad caelestium rerum contemplationem ita rapti sunt, ut in se mortui, extra se viverent, non alia morte quam brasicae, id est osculi deperisse. Ob id clamat Salomon in principio Canticorum, Osculetur me osculo oris sui.' *Opera aliquot*, p. 552.

10. *De harmonia mundi* III, vi, 18 (ed. cit., vol. II, fol. 68r).

11. Cod. Vat. lat. 5808, fol. 46 (ed. Secret, p. 53).

12. Castiglione, *Il cortegiano* IV, lxx (Cian).

13. '. . . quella morte d'amanti, che procede da somma gioia, chiamata da' cabalisti *mors osculi*'. *Eroici furori* II, i, 7: *mors et vita*.

and vital death' (*felicissima e vital morte*) was illustrated – as in the *Cortegiano*'s hymn to Platonic love, where one would least expect it – by the 'enraptured patriarchs' of the Old Testament: 'come già morirono quegli antichi padri, l'anime dei quali tu [Amor] ... rapisti dal corpo e congiungesti con Dio'.

Although based on the fantastic assumption that Hebrew sources could be used to elucidate the pagan mysteries of love,[14] the inference drawn in these arguments from the *mors osculi* of the Cabbala comes remarkably close to a modern opinion that the pagan mysteries culminated in a *hieros gamos*, an ecstatic union with the god which was experienced by the neophyte as an initiation into death.[15] 'And from this we may understand,' wrote Pico in describing the

14. Not without parallel in modern philology. R. Reitzenstein, *Die hellenistischen Mysterienreligionen* (1927), pp. 34–8 ('Gottesbrautschaft'), also pp. 99–102, and pp. 245–52 ('Die Liebesvereinigung mit Gott'), observes on this subject a concordance between Plutarch (*Quaestiones conviviales* VIII, i, 3; *Vita Numae* 4) and Philo (*De cherubim* 42 ff.), also confirmed by Norden, *Die Geburt des Kindes*, p. 98: 'Es kann ja nicht auf Zufall beruhen, dass sich uns Zeugnisse Philons und Plutarchs zu einer Einheit ergänzten.'

15. In a famous fragment (Stobaeus, *Florilegium* 120, 28, quoted by Cornford in *Classical Review* XVII, 1903, p. 439) Themistius refers to those initiatory rites (τελεταί) which 'in fact, as well as in name, resemble death (τελευτᾶν)'. On the ἱερὸς γάμος cf. Kern and Hopfner, 'Mysterien' in Pauly–Wissowa, loc. cit. Of earlier literature see Lobeck, *Aglaophamus* (1829), pp. 609 f., 648–52 (still unsurpassed as a collection of sources); E. Petersen, 'Sepolcro scoperto sulla via Latina', *Annali dell'instituto di corrispondenza archeologica* XXXII (1860), pp. 392 f.; Dieterich, *Eine Mithrasliturgie* (1903), pp. 121–34 ('Die Liebesvereinigung des Menschen mit dem Gott'); Harrison, *Prolegomena to the Study of Greek Religion* (1903), pp. 535 ff.; O. Gruppe, *Griechische Mythologie und Religionsgeschichte* (1906), I, p. 55; II, p. 1900 s.v. 'Ehe mit der Gottheit'. To what extent the subject has occupied recent scholarship may be seen from the following list, which is far from complete: E. Strong, *Apotheosis and After Life* (1915), pp. 202 f., 209, 276 note 31; R. Pettazzoni, *I misteri* (1924), p. 51; F. Noack, *Eleusis* (1927), pp. 241 ff.; M. Rostovtzeff, *Mystic Italy* (1927), p. 46, bibliography pp. 159 f.; J. Carcopino, *La basilique pythagoricienne de la Porte Majeure* (1943), p. 121; W. K. C. Guthrie, *The Greeks and their Gods* (1950), pp. 53–64, 177; Gilbert Murray, *Five Stages of Greek Religion* (3rd ed. 1951), pp. 17 f., 150. The complete absence of the theme from Cumont's chapter 'Les mystères' in *Lux perpetua*, pp. 235–74, and the less than passing reference to it in his *Recherches sur le symbolisme funéraire des Romains*, pp. 247 f., lead one to infer that, however much he otherwise agreed with Carcopino and Rostovtzeff, he preferred, on this particular point, to practise the *ars nesciendi*. A sceptical view also in M. P. Nilsson, *Geschichte der griechischen Religion* I (1941), pp. 110 ff., 627, and in Festugière, *L'idéal religieux des Grecs*, pp. 136 f., who inclines to reduce the ritual of hierogamy to a religious convention devoid of intense mystical emotions.

mirabili e secreti misterii amorosi, 'with what mystery the story of Alcestis and Orpheus is endowed by Plato in the *Symposium*, ... where we shall find a spiritual sense conforming to our explanation, by which both the meaning of Plato and the profundity of this matter will become perfectly apparent. ... Alcestis achieved the perfection of love because she longed to go to the beloved through death; and dying through love, she was by the grace of the gods revived. ... And Plato could not have suggested this more lightly or subtly than by the example he gave of Orpheus, of whom he says that, desiring to go and see his beloved Eurydice, he did not want to go there through death but, softened and refined by his music, sought a way of going there alive, and for this reason, says Plato, he could not reach the true Eurydice, but beheld only a shadow or spectre. ...'[16]

How widely the doctrine was accepted in the Medici circle is shown by Lorenzo de' Medici's commentary on his own sonnet sequence, in which he explained why, in singing of love, he had started with a sonnet on death. 'He that examines these matters more closely,' he wrote, 'will find that the beginning of the *vita amorosa* proceeds from death, because whoever lives for love, first dies to everything else. And if love has in it a certain perfection, ... it is impossible to arrive at that perfection without first dying with regard to the more imperfect things. This very rule was followed by Homer, Virgil and Dante: for Homer sent Ulysses into the Underworld, Virgil sent Aeneas, and Dante made himself wander through the Inferno, to show that the way to perfection is by this road (*che alla perfezione si va per queste vie*).' And because Orpheus did not really die (*non essere veramente morto*), he was 'debarred from the perfection of felicity', and unable to regain Eurydice.[17]

With the Platonic theory of love as the key to a philosophy of death, some of the funerary images on Roman sarcophagi seemed to reveal their secrets. The observation which in the eighteenth century so bitterly irritated Lessing – that the learned Klotz could mistake

16. *Commento*, loc. cit. (ed. Garin, pp. 554 f.). On Plato's version of the myth, *Symposium* 179D, see C. M. Bowra, 'Orpheus and Eurydice', *Classical Quarterly* II. (1952), pp. 120 ff.

17. *Opere*, ed. cit. I, pp. 24 f.

the winged genius of death for the god of love although he held his torch downward[18] – would not have troubled these Renaissance humanists. They argued, perhaps not unjustly, that Thanatos and the funerary Eros were one, and that the image of Love was the Platonic and very poetical answer to the question 'wie die Alten den Tod gebildet'. And perhaps that answer might even offer a correction of some recent studies of Roman sepulchral art. No scholar has been more eloquent than Cumont in transcribing the symbolic mood of the winged funerary figures that flank the central panels of many Roman sarcophagi: 'ces figures d'Éros funéraires, qui, immobiles, les jambes croisées, et tristement appuyés sur leur flambeau renversé ... deviennent ... une représentation allégorique de la mort'.[19] Yet when the love of Diana for the mortal Endymion is shown on the central panels of the same sarcophagi, Cumont interprets that image in a different sense. Intent on reducing funerary symbols to an astral topography of the Beyond,[20] he sees

18. As Lessing knew (*Wie die Alten den Tod gebildet*, in *Schriften*, ed. Lachmann-Muncker, XI, 1895, p. 10), Bellori had anticipated Klotz in explaining a winged genius with inverted torch on a funerary relief as Eros (*Admiranda romanarum antiquitatum*, 1693, pl. 79). In Ovid, *Remedia amoris* 551 f., an Amor extinguishing the torch is worshipped as Lethaeus Amor; cf. Servius, *In Aeneidem* IV, 520; λυσέρως.

19. *Textes et monuments figurés relatifs aux mystères de Mithra* I (1899), p. 206; restated in *Symbolisme funéraire des Romains*, pp. 409 f., 444. Similar views in Petersen, 'Eros und Psyche oder Nike', *Römische Mitteilungen* XVI (1901), p. 59; Furtwängler, *La Collection Sabouroff* (1883–7) I, pp. 39, 49, 55; II, pp. 19 ff. etc.; also in Roscher I, 1370 ('Eros ... bezeichnet den Tod als einen seligen'); Collignon, 'Éros funèbre', in Daremberg–Saglio I, pp. 1609 f.; Deonna, 'Éros jouant avec un masque de Silène', *Revue archéologique* 1916 (i), pp. 74–97. It is worth noting that in Philostratus, *Imagines* I, 2, the figure of Κῶμος ('Revelry') standing at the gate of a nuptial feast is described in the posture of a funerary Eros, slumbering though he stands, καθεύδων ὀρθός, holding his torch downward and crossing his legs. In picturing his dead son among the blessed, Himerius wrote: 'Above, playing with the gods, you perceive all things, jesting with Eros, revelling (κωμάζων) with Hymen. ...' (*Orationes* XXIII, 23; cf. Cumont, *Symbolisme funéraire*, p. 345). The association of Hymen with death also in Servius I, 651 (the model for *Hypnerotomachia*, fol. r iiiʳ). Nock, 'Sarcophagi and Symbolism', p. 160 note 81, quotes several passages from Artemidoros 'for the parallelism of marriage and death'. The prevalence of wedding ceremonies on funerary monuments was noted by W. Furtwängler, *Die Idee des Todes in den Mythen und Kunstdenkmälern der Griechen* (1860), pp. 293–5: 'Der Todesakt unter der Form der Hochzeit'; also pp. 295–9: 'Der Totengott unter der Gestalt des Eros'.

20. The general assumptions of Cumont's method are concisely stated in his two essays, 'Le mysticisme astral dans l'antiquité', *Bulletin de l'académie royale de Belgique*,

in the conjunction of Endymion with the goddess of the moon primarily a sign of the soul's location after death, 'la lune séjour des morts'.[21] The Endymion-sarcophagi thus become a separate lunar class, unrelated to the cognate funerary types of Leda or Ganymede loved by Zeus, of Rhea loved by Mars, Psyche by Eros, and so forth. But since in all of these, however varied in their mythological connotations, Death appears as communion with a god through Love, it seems odd that this particular form of apotheosis, so completely in accord with third-century Neoplatonism, should be disregarded in Cumont's discussion of sarcophagi of that very period.[22]

For the immediate and 'faithful' pupils of Plotinus, susceptible though they were to *mysticisme astral*, cosmology remained one of the 'lesser spectacles',[23] not to be confused with the real destination of the soul. The meditations in *Enneads* I, vi, 8, on the voyage to the Beyond, leave no doubt that their author did not expect to travel through the spheres; he hoped to unite with the Godhead as 'one to one' (φυγὴ μόνου πρὸς μόνον). And because of the feigned simplicity of his writing, and his calculated use of traditional myths to circumscribe the experience of reunion with the Divine, his symbolism was inherently more poetic and flexible than any fixed dogma of 'lunar or luni-solar immortality'.[24] If some of the sarcophagi of his time seem to exhibit, as such products of a manufacturing

---

classe des lettres (1909), pp. 256–86; and 'La théologie solaire du paganisme romain', *Mémoires de l'académie des inscriptions et belles-lettres* XII (1913), pp. 447–79.

21. *Symbolisme funéraire*, p. 249. Although it did not escape Cumont (ibid., p. 247 note 2) that on some Endymion-sarcophagi 'Sélène se présente *nubentis habitu*', or that 'Endymion endormi, à qui l'on a prêté le visage du mort, est entouré de deux Amours portant les torches de l'hyménée', he does not accept the nuptial union between mortal and god as a funerary symbol in its own right: Endymion is wedded to Selene only to indicate that dead men migrate to the moon.

22. K. Lehmann-Hartleben and E. C. Olson, in *Dionysiac Sarcophagi in Baltimore* (1942), p. 38 note 107, observe that 'the iconography of the sleeping Ariadne [approached by Dionysus] is certainly very closely related to that of Endymion [approached by Selene]: in at least one case, sarcophagi with these themes were used in a tomb as companion-pieces.' A strictly lunar theology could hardly account for that symmetry.

23. δεύτερα θεάματα, cf. *Enneads*, VI, ix, 11.

24. Cumont, op. cit., p. 252.

industry inevitably would, a taste for the poetic commonplace,[25] this very fact would bring them closer to the *Enneads* than, say, to the Chaldean Oracles.[26]

Conversant with the idea of Eros as a power that loosens or breaks the chains that bind the soul to the body, the Renaissance antiquarians may also have had a more correct understanding of the *Éros funèbre* than some of the great archaeologists of the recent past who, like Collignon, Wiegand,[27] or Furtwängler, thought of Eros in a funerary context as representing only 'life after death', the 'joys of the blessed'.[28] The Renaissance identified him with Death itself, in its painful no less than its joyous aspect, as is shown so clearly on the Roman sarcophagi which represent the agonies inflicted on Psyche by Eros as a prelude to their ultimate embrace.[29] A god of pain and

25. It is on this point that Nock's critique is most relevant and salutary.

26. On meditation as a subject of funerary art, see G. Rodenwaldt, 'Zur Kunstgeschichte der Jahre 220 bis 270', *Jahrb. d. deutsch. arch. Inst.* LI (1936), pp. 101–5; Marrou, Μουσικὸς ἀνήρ (Grenoble 1937); also Boyancé, *Le culte des Muses*, p. 2, where he argues, against Cumont, that the sarcophagi of the Muses need not be related to a spatial voyage through the astral spheres in order to yield a funerary meaning. The Muses suggest *per se* a sense of unison with the Divine. An extreme case of cosmographic reduction is Cumont's interpretation of the Marsyas sarcophagi, in which he sees not only, as the Renaissance did, an image of musico-religious catharsis, but a reference to the element of air, as the 'location' of the purgatory of impure souls, because Marsyas hangs from a tree while being flayed – *l'atmosphère séjour des âmes* (pp. 19, 147).

27. cf. 'Eros und Psyche auf einem Bronzerelief aus Amisos', *Jahrbuch für Kunstwissenschaft* I (1923), pp. 23–9.

28. See the literature quoted above, page 158 note 19. A notable exception is Eduard Gerhard, *Über den Gott Eros*, read at the Berlin Academy 20 July 1848 (published 1850), p. 15, where the funerary concept of Love is suggested in a few sentences.

29. Sarcophagus from Tarsus, Metropolitan Museum of Art, New York. On a gem illustrated in Lessing, *Wie die Alten den Tod gebildet* (ed. cit., p. 5), the funerary Eros, carrying a cinerary urn on his right shoulder and an inverted torch in his left hand, is attended by a butterfly (*psyche*), symbol of the liberated soul. The image was included by Pier Leone Ghezzi among his sketches of 'Amore e Psiche', Cod. Vat. Ottob. 3101, fol. 33, inscribed 'Il Genio della Morte, . . . espresso con savio giudizio dagli Antichi.' Despite his contempt for Apuleius, Herder listed the many funerary motifs in the story of Eros and Psyche with remarkable astuteness (*Sämtliche Werke*, ed. B. Suphan, XV, 1888, pp. 429–85: 'Wie die Alten den Tod gebildet. Ein Nachtrag zu Lessings Abhandlung desselben Titels und Inhalts', particularly pp. 462 ff.). He also noticed (p. 432) that Philostratus's figure of Comus (*Imagines* I, 2; cf. above, page 158 note 19) is a variant of the funerary Eros.

sadness he remained,[30] but no persistent terror could be attached to Death if he appeared in the image of Amor:

> *Natura insegna a noi temer la morte,*
> *ma Amor poi mirabilmente face*
> *suave a' suoi quel ch'è ad ogni altro amaro.*[31]

The mood of this verse by Lorenzo de' Medici is that of the *dulce amarum*[32] or γλυκύπικρον ('bitter-sweet') which Ficino, apparently unaware that the phrase is derived from Sappho,[33] introduced as a Platonic-Orphic term to define the equation of Love with Death: 'Love is called by Plato bitter (*res amara*), and not unjustly because death is inseparable from love (*quia moritur quisquis amat*). And Orpheus also called Love γλυκύπικρον, that is, *dulce amarum*, because love is a voluntary death. As death it is bitter, but being voluntary it is sweet. *Moritur autem quisquis amat. . . .*'[34] Or in Lorenzo's words: '. . . intendendo questa morte nella forma che abbiamo detto morire li amanti, quando tutti nella cosa amata si trasformono'.[35] A peculiarly morbid painting by Lorenzo Lotto (fig. 50) shows Amor

---

30. Perhaps no group of sarcophagi is more explicit in uniting the agonies of love and death than those representing the death of Penthesilea. F. Missonnier, 'Sur la signification funéraire du mythe d'Achille et Penthésilée', *Mélanges d'archéologie et d'histoire* XLIX (1932), pp. 111–31, recognized clearly a *catégorie des monuments funéraires où l'amour est associé à la mort*.

31. Lorenzo de' Medici, ed. cit. I, p. 87.

32. ibid., p. 90, 'la mistione sopradetta della amaritudine colla dolcezza'.

33. Sappho, fr. 137 (Diehl), γλυκύπικρον, from Hephaestion (= Bergk fr. 40; Lobel-Page fr. 130). Although Hephaestion is quoted by Gyraldus as a source for Sappho (*De historia poetarum* ix, *Opera* II, 459), this particular fragment seems to have escaped his attention: for in discussing the union of pain and pleasure as an attribute of Eros, he quoted Alexander of Aphrodisias, Phornutus, and Proclus as sources, but not Sappho (*Historia deorum gentilium*, syntagma xiii: 'Cupido', *Opera* I, 407). Nor is Sappho mentioned in Erasmus, *Adagia*, s.v. *dulce et amarum*, where the phrase is traced back only as far as Plautus. Since Erasmus, in collecting the *Adagia*, was assisted by the best humanists on both sides of the Alps, it would seem that Sappho's use of γλυκύπικρος was virtually unknown in the Renaissance, despite Politian (see below, page 162 note 39).

34. *De amore* II, viii, *Opera*, p. 1327. Festugière, *La philosophie de l'amour de Marsile Ficin et son influence sur la littérature française au XVIᵉ siècle* (1941), pp. 94–140, quotes a representative series of French verses on *amère doulceur* and *mort vive*, notably by Maurice Scève, Antoine Héroët, and Marguerite de Navarre.

35. op. cit., p. 139. But see also the bitter verses of Politian, *Rispetti spicciolati* xcv ff.

crowning a death's head that rests on a cushion (emblem of *dolcezza* or *voluptas*).[36]

The assurance with which Ficino declared that 'Orpheus called Love γλυκύπικρον' is the more remarkable since Ficino is the only source for the attribution. Kern therefore, in his *Orphicorum fragmenta*, classed the passage among the *Spuria vel dubia*;[37] but in a more recent book on Orpheus it has been proposed that Ficino must have known an Orphic text now lost, and that Sappho's phrase therefore should be accepted on his authority as of Orphic descent.[38] However, this places too much confidence in Ficino. Since he regarded all Neoplatonic mysteries as derived from Orpheus, the presence of γλυκύπικρος in a Neoplatonic text would be sufficient for him to consider it Orphic. Now the intrusion of the term into Neoplatonic writings can be traced through at least two stages. Maximus of Tyre, in his discourse 'On the amatory art of Socrates', drew an explicit and lengthy parallel between the loves of Socrates and of Sappho, in which he remarked that, if Socrates says that love flourishes in abundance and dies in want, 'Sappho conveys the same meaning when she calls love bitter-sweet (γλυκύπικρος) and a painful gift'.[39] The second stage is represented by Hermias's *Commentary on the Phaedrus*, 251D, which was one of Ficino's 'Orphic' sources. Here the transference of the Sapphic term to Socratic love was made

36. For a stiff German version inscribed MORTEM NON TIMEO, see H. W. Janson, 'The Putto with the Death's Head', *Art Bulletin* XIX (1937), pp. 423–49, fig. 20. A bitter-sweet union of love and death appears also in the famous *Dead Putto on a Dolphin* (Hermitage, Leningrad) ascribed in the eighteenth century to Raphael, and still remembered as such by Yeats: 'Do you know Raphael's statue of the Dolphin carrying one of the Holy Innocents to Heaven?' (*W. B. Yeats and T. Sturge Moore: their Correspondence*, 1953, p. 165). Yeats used the image in *Byzantium* (stanza 5), and again in *News for the Delphic Oracle* (stanza 2). On the ancient and Renaissance sources for this conceit, see Wind, 'Raphael: The Dead Child on a Dolphin', *The Times Literary Supplement*, 25 October 1963, p. 874.

37. op. cit., p. 344, fr. 361.

38. Böhme, *Orpheus: Das Alter des Kitharoden* (1953), pp. 93 f.

39. *Philosophumena* XVIII, 9 (ed. Hobein, 1910, p. 232). The passage was known to Politian, who wrote it into the margin of *Heroides* XV ('Sappho to Phaon') in his copy of the Parma edition (1477) of Ovid's *Opera* (Bodleian Library, Oxford, Auct. P. 2.2, fol. gg ii^v; observation by A. Perosa). It is the more remarkable that Sappho's use of γλυκύπικρος remained unknown to Ficino, on whose strained relations with Politian see above, page 48 note 49; also page 75 note 74.

without any mention of Sappho: ὅθεν γλυκύπικρόν τινες εἰρήκασι τὸν ἔρωτα.[40] It is almost certain that in this passage Ficino would take the anonymous τινες as a concealed reference to the Orphic initiates. Unfortunately Ficino's translation of the Orphic Hymns, although famous in its day, remained unpublished[41] except for a few extracts in his *Epistolarium*[42] and in the *Theologia Platonica*;[43] but there can be no doubt that the cult of ambivalent love as defined by Sappho, and now proclaimed by Ficino as an Orphic tradition, had an influence on the 'bitter–sweet' style of Renaissance Petrarchists who regarded themselves as Platonic poets. Politian's *Orfeo* too would deserve to be re-examined in the light of the 'Orphic' revival; and the prevalence of that fashion might also be traced in Botticelli's bitter–sweet physiognomies: they seem to reflect the spectral amalgamation of Sappho, Plato, and Orpheus. In the *Hypnerotomachia*, where the precious diction is an extreme instance of the bitter–sweet style in literature, the Great Jupiter himself blesses Amor in these very words: σύ μοι γλυκύς τε καὶ πικρός,[44] 'you are sweet for me and bitter'. By the power of love the immortal gods acquire a semblance of mortality, and beloved mortals survive death because they live 'entombed' in the hearts of their lovers:

Felix Polia quae sepulta vivis.

In later emblem literature, these sweet agonies of love appeared reduced to moral anecdotes, idylls, and epigrams. Alciati, for example, applied the title *Dulcia quandoque amara fieri* to Theocritus's story of Cupid stung by bees while tasting honey;[45] and under the title *De morte et amore* he introduced the fable of Love and Death exchanging their arrows, so that young people die and the old fall

---

40. Hermias Alexandrinus, *In Platonis Phaedrum*, ed. P. Couvreur (1901), p. 185, line 11 (referring to *Phaedrus* 251D). In Ficino's translation: 'Quapropter quidem vocant amorem dulce amarum' (Cod. Vat. lat. 5953, fol. 258ʳ); cf. above, page 58 note 18.

41. On an anonymous MS in the Laurenziana, Plut. 36, 35, which is attributed to Ficino in Bandini's catalogue (II, 240), see *Supplementum Ficinianum* II, pp. cxlii note 8, also pp. 87 f.

42. *Opera*, pp. 933 ff.
43. XIII, ii (*Opera*, p. 294).
44. fol. liʳ.
45. *Emblemata*, no. 89.

in love.[46] It would be difficult to decide whether these trivialities displaced, or merely disguised, the mysteries still preserved in their titles. 'Le lecteur ... s'émerveille ... d'une prétention qui place ces futilités sous le patronage du Sphinx',[47] but the mystification may also explain the popularity of Alciati, and was in any case regarded as essential to emblems.[48] Although as impatient with obscurity as he was with platitude, Erasmus relished in a good emblem (like his own *Terminus*) the art of suggesting a thought by withholding it;[49] and the busy Politian, who had solved the ancient *aenigmata* of Varro and Ausonius,[50] included in the list of his 'little employments' (*occupatiunculae*) the invention of cryptic symbols for lovers, which would be understood by the lovers only, and 'exercise in vain the conjectures of others' (*caeterorum frustra coniecturas exerceat*).[51]

Since Michelangelo grew up in the Medicean circle among the Orphic poets of the *dulce amarum*, and was guided in his early studies by Politian himself, it is remarkable how completely his *terribilità* was able to divest the 'bitter-sweet' mysteries of their gentleness. In

46. *Emblemata*, no. 65. For other poems on that fable see C. Dionisotti, 'Amor; morte', *Italia medioevale e umanistica* I (1958), pp. 419–26.

47. Seznec, *La survivance des dieux antiques*, p. 94.

48. Emblems belong to the irritating sort of learned game described by A. Delatte, *Études sur la littérature pythagoricienne* (1915), p. 112: 'ces jeux savants où la part de la niaiserie et du mensonge est égale à celle des bonnes intentions et qui transforment des légendes délicieusement humaines en récits stupides, honnêtes et édifiants'. On the avowed ambition of emblem writers to dispense the ancient mysteries, see M. Praz, *Studies in Seventeenth-Century Imagery* I (1939), pp. 25, 50 f., 53 f., 159, etc.; also G. Boas in *The Hieroglyphics of Horapollo* (1950), p. 36. One of Jacob Cats's emblem books bears the title *Silenus Alcibiadis, sive Proteus* (1618), which he explains in the preface, fol. i ivᵛ ff.

49. cf. Wind, 'Aenigma Termini', *Journal of the Warburg Institute* I (1937), pp. 66 ff. In his defence of the emblem Erasmus wrote: '... in huiusmodi symbolis captari etiam obscuritatis aliquid quod coniecturas intuentium exerceat'. And again: '... quod geminam haberet gratiam; alteram ex allusione ad priscam ac celebrem historiam, alteram ex obscuritate quae symbolis est peculiaris'. Letter to Alfonso Valdes, 1 August 1528, *Epistolae*, ed. cit., no. 2018.

50. *Miscellanea* xxxvi, xxxix; *Epistolae* VII, i (*Opera* I, fol. 59ᵛ).

51. *Epistolae* II, xi (ibid., fol. 19ʳ). Averse to obscurantism though he was, Politian in the preface to his translation of Plato's *Charmides* (of which only a fragment has survived) praised the transmission of philosophical knowledge in the cryptic form of fables and riddles 'ne religiosa quodammodo Eleusinarum dearum mysteria profanarentur' (*Opera* I, fol. 123ʳ). A surprising statement for one more attuned to the formula *ex elegantia voluptas* than to Iamblichus, *De vita pythagorica* xvii, 75.

part that may be due to a change of scale. The heroic proportions to which he enlarged the image of Leda (fig. 3) would invariably dispel the lyricism of a myth which was so beautifully rendered by Spenser[52] and admired by Goethe as the most amiable of scenes, *die lieblichste von allen Szenen*.[53] The gloom of death which the idyllic image on the sarcophagus was designed to lighten (fig. 4) seems now condensed into a euphoric stupor.

Without removing the image from its sepulchral context, Michelangelo could not have produced such a ruthless picture. Conversely, when he retained the figure for a tomb, he transformed the Leda into an allegory of Night. Thus the funerary symbolism and the pagan myth, which he had found combined on the Roman sarcophagus, were split by him into separate images, of which each retained some of the traits of the other, although the attributes and the meaning were changed. In the place of the swan, the *Night* has an owl, curiously lodged below the angle of her knee, and she rests on a mask and a bundle of poppies, symbols of Death and Sleep,[54] the ancient twin-brothers who were children of Night.[55]

52. *Faerie Queene* III, xi, 32; cf. D. Bush, *Classical Influences in Renaissance Literature* (1952), p. 45.

53. *Faust* II, Act ii, Scene 2 (repeated in Scene 4). Goethe's description of the setting as a woodland idyll, with bathers frightened away by swans, recalls Correggio's *Leda*, acquired in 1755 by Frederick the Great.

54. The Latin word for mask is *larva*, which also suggests death in its fearful aspect (skeleton, ghost, shadow); cf. Plato's 'bogey' in *Phaedo* 77B: τὸν θάνατον ὥσπερ τὰ μορμολύκεια, translated as *larvae* by Ficino (*Platonis Opera*, 1548, p. 340), interpreted as 'masks' (προσωπεῖα) also in *Scholia Platonica* (ed. Greene, p. 145, on *Gorgias* 473D) and Plutarch, *De exilio* 5 (*Moralia* 600E): whence 'Children frightened by a Mask' as a sepulchral image (cf. Deonna, 'Éros jouant avec un masque de Silène', op. cit.; F. Altheim, 'Maske und Totenkult', *Terra mater*, 1931, pp. 48–65). In Horapollo, *Hieroglyphica* (1551), p. 223, the word *Manes* is rendered by a mask (our fig. 85). See also Jacob Cats, *Proteus* (1658), p. 557: *mors larvae similis*. Ripa (s.v. 'Morte') shows Death wearing a mask, but only to suggest Death's disguises, *le maschere della Morte*.

55. On Sleep and Death as children of Night, see Pausanias V, xviii, 1. Poetic allusions to the myth in Homer (*Iliad* XIV, 231; XVI, 454, 672, etc.), Hesiod (*Theogony* 211 f., 758 f.), and the Orphic Hymns (lxxxv, 8) are discussed and illustrated in Carl Robert, *Thanatos* (1879), pp. 6 ff.; E. Pottier, 'Thanatos', *Mélanges Piot* XXII (1916), pp. 35–55; C. Ramnoux, *La Nuit et les enfants de la Nuit dans la tradition grecque* (1959). For the Renaissance view, cf. Gyraldus, *Opera* I, 60, 310 f. A survey of the iconographic tradition in H. von Einem, *Asmus Jacob Carstens, Die Nacht mit ihren Kindern* (1958), pp. 11–20.

Designed as one of four gigantic *pleureurs*, she no longer celebrates death as the love of a god, but mourns it as the work of destructive Time, in which she laments her own part, as Michelangelo said in a poetic note on Night and Day in the Medici Chapel.[56]

In view of this transformation it might be argued that, however significant for Michelangelo's method of working, the association of Night and Leda is irrelevant to the works themselves. Rather than juxtapose the *Leda* with the *Night*, we should study the *Night* in the context of the Medici Chapel and consider the *Leda* as a separate work, designed for a Ferrarese patron of neo-pagan tastes. Unquestionably, this should be the primary approach, and there is no obligation to go beyond it. Aesthetically the two works are separate, and it is a form of antiquarian curiosity to look at them together. Yet the question remains whether Michelangelo himself did not intend to arouse this curiosity. As both works became widely known, and were not produced without that intention, Michelangelo must have counted on their resemblance being observed. No one seeing the *Leda* could help thinking of the *Night*, and wondering what Michelangelo had intended. The use of such closely related forms for incompatible purposes might appeal to his admirers as a *tour de force*, or it might offend his critics as a sign of parsimony (one of the accusations levelled against Michelangelo by the Venetians, who found his inventions forceful, strained, and repetitious). But as long as the astonishment did not penetrate below the surface, the designs were not understood for what they were: variations of one symbolic theme. In poetic theology, Leda and Night were one, and their figures represented two aspects of a theory of death in which sorrow and joy coincide.[57]

56. C. Frey, *Die Dichtungen des Michelagniolo Buonarroti* (1897), p. 14, no. xvii; *Rime*, ed. Girardi, pp. 8, 166 f., no. 14.

57. Did Baudelaire know both designs? In 'L'idéal' (*Les fleurs du mal* I, xviii) he pictured Michelangelo's *Night* in the attitude of Leda: '. . . toi, grande Nuit, fille de Michel-Ange, / Qui tors paisiblement dans une pose étrange / Tes appas façonnés aux bouches des Titans!' It is well, however, to dissociate the Renaissance equation of love with death from the similar mysteries in Wagner or Rilke or Conrad Ferdinand Meyer, since these have passed through the denser mists of German romanticism. In *Resignation*, Schiller's vision of death was still the same as Lessing's: 'Der stille Gott – o weinet, meine Brüder – / Der stille Gott taucht meine Fackel nieder, / Und die Erscheinung

Although Leonardo's famous design of Leda,[58] conceived in the style of a joyful idyll, does not prepare us for the gloom on which Michelangelo insisted, the presence in it of the four children of Leda – Castor, Pollux, Helen, and Clytemnestra, issuing pair-wise from the eggs (fig. 6) – would seem to confirm an ambivalent interpretation of the theme: *concordia* represented by Castor and Pollux, *discordia* by Helen and Clytemnestra.[59] As they break through the shells, the two amiable and the two obstreperous infants appear as antithetical twins.[60] The *Hypnerotomachia* illustrates the same

---

flieht.' But when he wrote *Die Götter Griechenlands*, he attached the image to a didactic *Liebestod*, as if to prepare for Karoline von Günderode: 'Liebe heisset dies Band, das an den Tag mir geknüpft / Hat die erebische Nacht, Tod mit dem Leben vereint' (cf. W. Rehm, *Götterstille und Göttertrauer*, 1951, pp. 142 ff.). The precipitation of these developments by Creuzer and Schelling, both steeped in Neoplatonism, is perhaps less surprising than Schopenhauer's 'patient' reading of Plotinus, Porphyry, Proclus, and Iamblichus, on which he reports in *Parerga und Paralipomena* I, ii, § 7; also II, xviii, § 203. As for Nietzsche, despite his professed anti-Platonism, he was literally on the trail of Pico's *Conclusiones . . . de intelligentia dictorum Zoroastris*, no. 6, 'de duplici ebriatione', when he wrote *Das trunkene Lied*; that is, he did not revive the Persian Zarathustra, but only the *mage hellénisé*. The song begins with a praise of darkness 'Was spricht die tiefe Mitternacht? . . . Die Welt ist tief, und tiefer als der Tag gedacht') and ends with what Pico, in *Heptaplus* V, i, called *voluptas, qua nulla maior, qua nulla verior, nulla est permanentior*: 'alle Lust will Ewigkeit.'

58. The copies at Wilton House and in the Spiridon Collection, Rome (fig. 6), correspond to Cassiano del Pozzo's description of the lost original, which he saw in 1625; cf. Kenneth Clark, *Leonardo da Vinci* (1939), pp. 123 ff.

59. 'And I recall,' wrote Yeats in *A Vision* (1937), pp. 67 f. (see also pp. 51, 267 f.), 'that Love and War came from the eggs of Leda.' Remarkable for its mythographic accuracy, Yeats's idea of Leda was supported by Neoplatonic readings casually listed by him, pp. 19 f. In the poem *Leda*, Helen and Clytemnestra are engendered first ('. . . the burning roof and tower / And Agamemnon dead'), while the conception of the demigods is left in doubt ('Did she put on his knowledge with his power / Before the indifferent beak could let her drop?'). Clearly, 'his knowledge' and 'his power' refer to the superhuman vision and force bestowed by the god (G. Melchiori, *The Whole Mystery of Art*, 1960, p. 145), but if we were to argue that *for that reason* the phrase does not allude to the Dioscuri (ibid., p. 161 note 1), we might as well deny that Helen and Clytemnestra are meant by 'the burning roof and tower and Agamemnon dead'. For the variant adopted in *A Vision*, p. 51, where Castor is combined with Clytemnestra, and Pollux with Helen, see Gyraldus, 'Castores vel Dioscuri', *Historia deorum gentilium*, syntagma v, *Opera* I, 184 ff., where several variants are listed.

60. If the union of Discord and Concord, as the Orphic–Neoplatonic 'principle of generation', is implied in the mystery of Leda, then the theme is, like the figure of the

'mystery of Leda' by showing a flame issuing from one egg, two stars from the other (fig. 8).[61] Calcagnini, transcribing a passage from Pliny's *Natural History*, refers to Castor and Pollux as the twin stars who dispel the dire threats embodied in their sister Helen.[62]

The legend that only three of Leda's children came from Jupiter, Clytemnestra being a daughter of Tyndareus,[63] does not apply to Leonardo's design, which (except for the copy in the Borghese Gallery) shows all four as cygnet-homuncles. But Michelangelo seems to have preferred the other version. There is little doubt that the children of Leda figured in his original design. Condivi described it as 'Leda and the Swan, and near by the egg from which Castor

---

swan, essentially musical, which might explain the iconographic affinity between Leonardo's *Leda* and Filippino Lippi's *Allegory of Music*. It would also account, in Correggio's *Leda*, for the presence of Amor and *putti* as musicians, playing the lyre and flute and thus offsetting the turmoil of the bathers frightened by swans. In a delightful engraving by the so-called 'Master I.B. with the Bird' the *discordia concors* has become a bustling family game: the two affectionate children fondle their mother while the two naughty ones have attacked the Swan, who engages them in a rough mock-battle. Less dramatic, the painting of *Leda* ascribed to Pontormo (Uffizi, no. 1556) shows the amiable twins embracing each other, and opposite to them a divided pair.

61. fols. k vi^r–vii^v. Our illustrations (figs. 7 and 8) are taken from the French edition, 1546.

62. 'Equitatio', *Opera*, p. 571, after Pliny II, xxxvii; see also Perotti, *Cornucopiae*, s.v. 'gratum nautis', and Gyraldus, *De re nautica*, in *Opera* I, 618. Navigation is again the subject of the cryptic oracle about the eggs of Leda in the *Hypnerotomachia* (our fig. 8): 'To the one the sea is pleasing, the other is pleasing to the sea' – unless (as Eduard Fraenkel suggests) *mari* is here to be read, for the sake of Helen, as the dative of *mas*; that is, 'pleasing to men'. In the plan of the novel, the story of Leda belongs to a sequence of four theogamies which represent the Four Elements subject to the *physizoa Venere* (fol. m vii^r); namely, Europa and the Bull (Earth), Leda and the Swan (Water), Danaë and the golden rain falling from the Sky (Air), and Semele consumed by Fire. On the rare adjective *physizoos*, which occurs in Greek poetry only five times, and of which the two most famous instances refer to the Dioscuri (*Iliad* III, 243; *Odyssey* XI, 301), while a third, in the Homeric Hymn to Aphrodite (125), introduces her ἱερὸς γάμος with Anchises, see Gilbert Murray, 'What English Poetry may still learn from Greek', in *Essays and Studies* by members of The English Association III (1912), pp. 8 ff.; T. F. Higham and C. M. Bowra, *The Oxford Book of Greek Verse in Translation* (1953), p. xlii. The authors of the *Hypnerotomachia* used the word exactly in the sense here defined.

63. cf. Gyraldus, 'Castores vel Dioscuri', *Opera* I, 186.

and Pollux were born, as is fabled by ancient writers',[64] but his recollection may have been incomplete; for if we trust the contemporary engraving made in Italy by Cornelis Bos, which has strong marks of authenticity,[65] two eggs appeared in Michelangelo's painting: one broken, with a pair of twins issuing from it, the other still intact but transparent, showing the outline of a dormant infant, Helen.[66]

In representing an Orphic mystery, it was permitted to add a touch of the bizarre. Plato had set the example for it by admitting Aristophanes among the allegorists of Love. 'These and many other things,' Ficino explained in his commentary on Aristophanes' speech in the *Symposium*, 'Aristophanes tells in a form resembling monsters and portents, behind which, as behind a veil, divine mysteries are meant to be hidden. For it was the custom of ancient theologians to protect their sacred and pure arcana by hedges of metaphor (*figurarum umbraculis*) in order to prevent them from being defiled by the profane and impure.'[67] The eggs of Leda belong to that genre of sacred *drôlerie*, for which Aristophanes had created the classical model in the 'Orphic' cosmogony of the *Birds*:

> *Of Darkness an egg, from the whirlwind conceived,*
> *was laid by the sable-plumed Night,*
> *And out of that egg, as the Seasons revolved,*
> *sprang Love, the entrancing, the bright.*[68]

64. op. cit., tr. Holroyd, p. 53.

65. Bos worked in Rome during Michelangelo's lifetime.

66. The inscription on the engraving explicitly mentions Castor and Pollux as issuing from one egg, Helen from the other: *Ex illo gemini Pollux cum Castore fratres, / Ex isto erumpens Helene pulcherrima prodit.* Cf. also Ronsard, *Odes* III, xxi (ed. 1584): 'L'un, deux jumeaux esclorra. . . . Dedans l'autre germera la beauté'. Ronsard's *Leda* resembles Michelangelo's also in posture ('ses membres tombent' . . . 'dedans la mort voisine' . . .). The painting was at that time in Fontainebleau.

67. *De amore* IV, ii, *Opera*, p. 1331.

68. 695 f., tr. B. B. Rogers. It is interesting that the memorable attack by Wilamowitz on Orphism in the Classical Age stopped short of the theogony parodied by Aristophanes; cf. *Glaube der Hellenen* II, p. 193, with reference in note 2. See also Guthrie, *Orpheus and Greek Religion* (1935), pp. 92 ff. On the cosmic egg as discussed by Plutarch, *Quaestiones conviviales* II, iii (*Moralia* 636D ff.), and Macrobius, *Saturnalia* VII, xvi, see M. P. Nilsson, *The Dionysiac Mysteries of the Hellenistic and Roman Age* (1957), pp. 140 ff., with further literature.

Phanes-Eros, first-born of Night, is hailed as 'egg-born' (ᾠογενής) in the Orphic Hymns,[69] and of a 'double nature' (διφυής).

69. *Hymn to Protogonos.* On Phanes-Eros see now K. Preisendanz in Pauly–Wissowa XIX (1938), 1761–74; for the Renaissance view, Gyraldus I, 409, with references to Orpheus, Hermias, Lactantius, Macrobius. Drawings ascribed to Perino del Vaga and to Peruzzi (Panofsky, *Hercules am Scheidewege*, p. 9 note 2, fig. 9) suggest that the ancient relief of Phanes in Modena (ibid., fig. 8) was known and understood in the sixteenth century. The two halves of the cosmic egg, which, in the Modena relief, is split apart by the apparition of Phanes, represent the celestial and the subterranean 'hemispheres' which were identified with the caps or *pilei* worn by Castor and Pollux; see Cumont, *Symbolisme funéraire*, pp. 68–73, with texts. A curiously corrupted version, perhaps a deliberate travesty (?), in Valeriano, *Hieroglyphica*, fol. 294ᵛ, s.v. *forma pilei*, where, on the authority of a jest in Lucian's *Dipsas* about 'sufficient covering for a man's head', the ovoid shape of the *pileus* is derived from the halving of an ostrich egg – an object unrelated to the Dioscuri but occupying a curious place in Christian iconography (M. Meiss, '*Ovum Struthionis*, Symbol and Allusion in Piero della Francesca's Montefeltro Altarpiece', *Studies in Art and Literature for Belle da Costa Greene*, pp. 92–101). Inevitably, the idea of egg-born deities became a target for Renaissance jests. Gyraldus cites the 'speciosa interpretatio' of one of his friends that amphitheatres were built in an oval shape because Pollux, the god of pugilists, was egg-born (*Opera* I, 184 f.).

CHAPTER XI

THE FLAYING OF MARSYAS

WHILE Michelangelo made a cult of melancholy, Raphael, himself of a melancholy complexion,[1] was opposed to the school of night. His friend Calcagnini, in an *Encomium umbrae*,[2] introduced the parable of a man who felt threatened by his shadow because this dark attendant persistently followed his steps, mimicked his gestures, withdrew when he approached, but never left him. In fear that the sly pursuer would kill him, he consulted an oracle and received the advice: *Cole perspicua*, study clarity. The parable fits the genius of Raphael. In approaching the gloomy mystery of Marsyas, he attacked the subject with a passionate lucidity and freed it from its inherent obliqueness. The fresco of *Apollo and Marsyas* in the Stanza della Segnatura (fig. 2) transforms a gruesome tale into a Socratic metaphor.

His model was again a Roman sarcophagus, perhaps the very fragment which was also copied by a less intelligent artist (fig. 1).[3] Whether or not the model, now lost,[4] was quite so mediocre as it looks in this perfunctory drawing, it surely had nothing of the verve and economy which Raphael gave to the design. The crowning of Apollo and the flaying of Marsyas appear on the sarcophagus as two separate episodes. On the left, the crown is proffered by a

---

1. On Raphael's melancholy, see V. Golzio, *Raffaello nei documenti* (1936), p. 97, no. 10.

2. 'Ne quis se a sua umbra vinci sinat', *Opera*, p. 325.

3. An early-eighteenth-century drawing from the collection bequeathed by Richard Topham to Eton College in 1736 (Bm I 55); by an unimaginative draughtsman. The instrument in Apollo's hand is not restored as a lyre, and the knife of one of the executioners is rendered like a twig.

4. The fragment belonged at one time to the Villa Borghese, where it was seen by Jacopo Manilli (*Villa Borghese*, 1650, pp. 42 f.) and Domenico Montelatici (*Villa Borghese*, 1700, p. 161). Cf. Robert, *Die antiken Sarkophag-Reliefs* III, ii (1904), p. 249, no. 199.

winged Victory, with a contemplative river god at her feet;[5] on the right, two henchmen turn their backs to her while they attend to the torture of Marsyas. In Raphael's painting the double action of torturing and crowning is carried out by one pair of ephebes, remarkably alike in type. Their heads, both wreathed with ivy, a plant sacred to Dionysus, are so closely juxtaposed that, as agents of glory and agony, they appear inspired by one common command, which issues from Apollo. Marsyas is made to face the god. The insipid corpse which on the sarcophagus was frontally attached to the tree has been changed into a living figure, drawn in profile from another antique.[6] His limbs firmly stretched as on a rack, the knife of the flayer touching his chest, Marsyas awaits his 'living death' which, in Ovid's *Metamorphoses*, makes him cry out to Apollo: Why do you tear me from myself? *Quid me mihi detrahis?*[7]

Readers of Plato who studied the *Symposium* as a secret compendium of mysteries would remember that, in the drunken speech of Alcibiades, Socrates himself was called a Marsyas, and that this dubious appellation followed immediately after the description of him as a 'Silenus figure', in which he was compared to a deceptive contraption in statuary shops which shows outwardly the face of an ugly man, but, when opened, proves to be full of gods.[8] Like Silenus, Marsyas was a follower of Bacchus, and his flute was the Bacchic instrument for arousing the dark and uncontrollable passions that

5. In the drawing the river god has been mistaken for a shepherd, see Robert, loc. cit.

6. Raphael's figure corresponds almost literally to a profile view of the famous statue of Marsyas (Capitoline Museum, and others); but a similar figure appears also as the corner-piece of some Marsyas sarcophagi, Robert, op. cit., pp. 247 ff., no. 198 (Louvre); Cumont, *Symbolisme funéraire*, pl. I.

7. *Metamorphoses* VI, 385.

8. cf. Erasmus, *Adagia*, s.v. *Sileni Alcibiadis*: 'Haec nimirum est natura rerum vere honestarum: quod habent eximium, id in intimis recondunt abduntque; quod contemptissimum, id prima specie prae se gerunt, ac thesaurum ceu vili cortice dissimulant, nec prophanis ostendunt oculis.' Erasmus infers that not only Socrates, Diogenes, and Epictetus, but also Christ and the Apostles, the Holy Scripture, and the very Sacraments of the Christian Church, reveal, if properly understood, a Silenus-nature, whereas the official administrators of these mysteries are too often 'inverted Sileni', *praeposteri Sileni*, outwardly rich and inwardly poor.

conflict with the purity of Apollo's lyre.[9] The musical contest between Apollo and Marsyas was therefore concerned with the relative powers of Dionysian darkness and Apollonian clarity; and if the contest ended with the flaying of Marsyas, it was because flaying was itself a Dionysian rite, a tragic ordeal of purification by which the ugliness of the outward man was thrown off and the beauty of his inward self revealed. That Socrates, who was a disciple of Apollo and had adopted from an inscription on Apollo's temple at Delphi his own maxim 'Know thyself', should be figuratively described as a Silenus and a Marsyas meant that his ruthless pursuit of bewildering questions was but the disguise of an inward clarity – a disguise which was indispensable because it reckoned with the twofold nature of man. To bring out the hidden clarity in others, whose souls were covered and confused by their bodies, required a cathartic method, a Dionysian ordeal by which the 'terrestrial Marsyas' was tortured so that the 'heavenly Apollo' might be crowned. 'If you consort with singers and harpists, you may trust your ears,' wrote Pico ironically, 'but when you go to philosophers', whose proper style is *Silenorum nostri Alcibiadis*, 'you must withdraw from the senses, you must return into yourself (*redeas ad te ipsum*), you must penetrate into the depths of your soul and the recesses of your mind, you must acquire the ears of the Tyanean (*Tyanei aures*)[10] with which, because he was no longer in his body, he heard not the terrestrial Marsyas but the heavenly Apollo, who on his divine lyre, with ineffable modes, tuned the melodies of the spheres.'[11]

The cry: 'Why do you tear me from myself?' expresses then an agonized ecstasy and could be turned, as it was by Dante, into a prayer addressed to Apollo: 'Enter my breast, and so infuse me with your spirit as you did Marsyas when you tore him from the cover of his limbs.'

9. cf. *Republic* 399D–E, with reference to Apollo and Marsyas. On the flute as lugubrious or confusing, in contrast to the lyre, see also Plutarch, *On the εἰ at Delphi* 21 (*Moralia* 394B–C). In a lighter vein, concerning Apollo and Marsyas, *Quaestiones conviviales* VII, viii, 4 (*Moralia* 713D).

10. The 'Tyanean' is Apollonius of Tyana, whose philosophical warning against pleasing sounds is recounted in Philostratus, *Vita Apollonii Tyanei* V, xl. See the commentary on Pico's passage by Franciscus Sylvius, in *Opera Politiani* I (1519), fol. 77ᵛ.

11. *Opera*, p. 354. Letter to Ermolao Barbaro, cf. above, page 10 note 29.

> O buono Apollo, all'ultimo lavoro
> Fammi del tuo valor sì fatto vaso,
> Come domandi a dar l'amato alloro.
> Infino a qui l'un giogo di Parnaso
> Assai mi fu, ma or con ambedue
> M'è uopo entrar nell'aringo rimaso.
> Entra nel petto mio, e spira tue
> Sì come quando Marsia traesti
> Della vagina delle membra sue.[12]

To obtain the 'beloved laurel' of Apollo, the poet must pass through the agony of Marsyas. The words of Lorenzo de' Medici apply also here: 'The way to perfection is by this road.'

As Raphael's painting of the Flaying of Marsyas is placed in the corner between the *Parnassus* and the *Disputa*, it is flanked on either side by the figure of Dante, who appears in the *Disputa* among the followers of St Thomas and St Bonaventura, and in the *Parnassus* in the company of Homer and Virgil. In the entire cycle of the Stanza della Segnatura, Dante is the only author represented twice: and since his two portraits appear at the corner in which Theology and Poetry are joined, it is only consistent that the picture in that corner is an example of Poetic Theology, representing a mystery of the pagans with which Dante opened the first Canto of the *Paradiso*.

In explaining some of the Bacchic mysteries in *De hominis dignitate*, Pico suggested that inspiration by Apollo always requires in us the dismemberment of Osiris, whom he identified with Bacchus ('Nunc unum quasi Osirim in multitudinem vi titanica discerpentes descendemus, nunc multitudinem quasi Osiridis membra in unum vi Phoebea colligentes ascendemus').[13] 'These two powers residing

---

12. *Paradiso* I, 13–21.

13. *De hominis dignitate* (ed. Garin, p. 116). On the identification of Osiris with Bacchus, cf. Herodotus II, 48; Plutarch, *De Iside et Osiride* 28 (*Moralia* 362B); Servius, *In Georgica* I, 166; Valeriano, *Hieroglyphica*, fol. 234ʳ. For Orphic initiates there could be no doubt that death by dismemberment, as suffered by Orpheus, was but the ritual re-enactment of the dismemberment of the god (cf. Proclus, *In Platonis Rempublicam* I, 174, 30, tr. Linforth, *The Arts of Orpheus*, p. 229). Pinturicchio's painting *The Dismemberment of Osiris*, in the Sala de' Santi of the Borgia Apartments, is discussed, with

in our souls, by one of which we are raised to heaven while the other throws us into hell', are like Empedocles' 'strife and friendship, or war and peace', which persistently divide and harmonize the universe. The cruelty inflicted on Marsyas by Apollo, while he himself is crowned the victor in their contest, therefore expresses the supreme sense of disproportion by which the god attacks the human frame, which is agonized as it succumbs to the divine ecstasy. 'Let us be driven,' Pico concluded in his reflections on the Bacchic mysteries,[14] 'let us be driven by the Socratic frenzies, which so may place us outside of our minds, that they will place our minds and ourselves in God.' 'Quis talibus sacris initiari non appetat? ... Quis Socraticis illis furoribus ... afflari non velit ... ?' The words recall the Virgilian *numine afflatur* which is inscribed over Raphael's *Parnassus*. In Virgil these words – *adflata est numine*[15] – express the frenzy of the Sibyl as she becomes possessed by the approaching god, whom she tries vainly to shake off from her anguished breast:

> *At Phoebi nondum patiens, immanis in antro*
> *Bacchatur vates, magnum si pectore possit*
> *Excussisse deum; tanto magis ille fatigat*
> *Os rabidum, fera corda domans, fingitque premendo.*[16]

The torture of the mortal by the god who inspires him was a central theme in the revival of ancient mysteries, its illustration in *Apollo and Marsyas* being only one of many variations. Its most elaborate development was in the story of Amor and Psyche, in which the ordeals suffered by Psyche to regain Amor were understood as stages of a mystical initiation. Her descent to Orcus and the Styx, so that she might rise to heaven, again confirmed and illustrated Lorenzo's moral: 'The way to perfection is by this road.' Had the scenes in the lunettes of the Farnesina cycle survived, we

---

reference to Pico, by D. R. de Campos, *Itinerario pittorico dei Musei Vaticani* (1949), p. 49. Alexander VI, who, it may be noted, revoked the indictment of Pico in 1493, had in Annius of Viterbo a mentor in Egyptian mysteries, on whom see Giehlow, 'Die Hieroglyphenkunde des Humanismus', op. cit., pp. 44 ff.

14. *De hominis dignitate* (ed. Garin., p. 122).
15. *Aeneid* VI, 50.   16. ibid., 77–80.

would know how Raphael pictured the sombre ritual, which is the necessary counterpart to the Olympian mood of the ceiling.[17] Yet even within the celestial zone, the division between a trial and a triumph of Love is illustrated in the centre by the two large pictures, the tribunal of the gods preceding the marriage feast. The surrounding spandrels are also divided into two sets: six scenes of divine anger and complaint, which entail mortal trials for Psyche, are followed by four scenes of divine acceptance and rejoicing which signify Psyche's ascension.[18] So richly and variedly is the dual theme developed, and so well disguised in a humorous Apuleian style, that one hardly becomes aware that this exuberant cycle unfolds the same duality of triumph and agony which Raphael epitomized in *Apollo and Marsyas*.

When Shaftesbury wrote 'that Wit and Humour are corroborative of Religion', he may not have thought of the gods of the Farnesina. Their humour is perhaps more frivolous than he would have thought proper, and their underlying seriousness too grim for his irony. But the Renaissance mystagogues cultivated a combination of gloom and banter. The comic mask of the fluting Silenus, which must be opened to reveal the perfection of the gods, represented the same mystery as Marsyas flayed. The final note of the *Symposium* was that tragic and comic catharsis are one. Dionysus, the dispenser of copious joy, is himself the god of tragic frenzy.

17. An attempted reconstruction of the lower sequence in Salis, *Antike und Renaissance*, p. 200. See also G. Hoogewerff, 'Raffaello nella Villa Farnesina', *Capitolium* XX (1945), pp. 9–15, with reference to an important set of engravings based on Raphael's lost designs (Bartsch XV, 'Maître au Dé', nos. 39–70). It is a mistake, however, to assume that the lower scenes would have extended below the nine lunettes now disguised with painted windows. Like the cycles of Amor and Psyche in the Castel Sant' Angelo in Rome and in the Palazzo Doria in Genoa, which are so clearly derived from the Farnesina, Raphael's cycle must have ended above the wall itself. This is also confirmed by the documents (Golzio, op. cit., p. 65), which speak only of a decoration of the ceiling ('volta'), a term extending, as we know from the Sistine Ceiling, down to the lunettes, but not further.

18. The architectural disposition of the loggia was utilized to bring out the contrast; for while the six episodes of divine displeasure, accompanied by Psyche's trials below, occupy the pendentives between the lunettes, the scenes of triumph and apotheosis appear between the open arcades.

CHAPTER XII

A BACCHIC MYSTERY BY MICHELANGELO

AMONG the more confusing achievements of Michelangelo's youth was his consummate forgery of a Sleeping Cupid, which was exhibited in Rome as a genuine antique. The work, successively owned by Cesare Borgia, Guidobaldo of Urbino, and Isabella d'Este and now lost, is supposed to have aroused the interest of Cardinal Riario: for he invited the young virtuoso to visit Rome.

That Michelangelo was attached to Riario's household in Rome is made certain by his correspondence; but it has caused surprise that during this period he should have made a *Bacchus* for Jacopo Galli and a *Pietà* for the Cardinal de Villiers, whereas he received no major commission from Riario himself. Perhaps Riario considered him still an apprentice. From a complimentary poem by Antonio Flaminio it appears that Riario maintained in his Roman palace, which was filled with antiques, a school for artists similar to that of the Medici in Florence.[1] Here Michelangelo continued to study from the antique, and that may well have been the real purpose of Riario's invitation. As is shown by the style of the LIBERALITAS on his medal, Riario had a taste for the pseudo-antique which he shared with Pontano, Sannazaro, and other academicians whom he befriended.[2]

A pseudo-antique statue was also the first work Michelangelo produced under these auspices in Rome. The *Bacchus* that he made for the garden of Jacopo Galli, a friend of Riario and his immediate

---

1. M. Vattasso, 'Antonio Flaminio e le principali poesie dell'autografo Vaticano 2870', *Studi e testi* I (1900), p. 51, no. xxxii: *Pictor ad card. S. Georgii, in cuius aedibus picturam didicit.* On Riario's collection, see Lanciani, *storia degli scavi*, I, p. 94.

2. Like the Ciceronian letters exchanged between academicians, these medals show a neo-classical style not confined to one locality. The attempt to attribute them all to one artist, Adriano Fiorentino, whose travels would account for their wide and thin distribution, has not been entirely successful. Hill, *A Corpus of Italian Medals* I, p. 83.

neighbour,[3] has not met with much favour from poetical critics (fig. 97). Shelley found that the figure is 'abundantly inharmonious', 'has an expression of dissoluteness the most revolting', and is altogether a 'mistake of the spirit and meaning of Bacchus'. Holroyd, lenient among adverse critics, felt that this 'ugly, but marvellously finished statue' inspired a mixture of admiration and discomfort: 'The finish and the truth to nature of the unpleasant youth are exquisite.'

That the posture was meant to suggest a precarious balance, which is apt to attend a state of inebriation, surely does not contradict the divine nature of Bacchus. The *ratio causae*, Pico explained, presupposes in a deity the *ratio perfecti*[4] so that a god is always filled with the powers he dispenses. Apollo could not convey the gift of music if he were not himself inspired by music, nor would Venus inspire love, were she not moved by love.[5] It follows that for Bacchus to convey drunkenness, he must be drunk. And yet, though Michelangelo's logic was impeccable, the criticism of the statue is more justified than its defenders have admitted: for it can be shown, I believe, that the awkward and heavy cup which gives to the gesture a patent vulgarity, is a clumsy restoration.

It would be difficult to imagine Michelangelo patiently cutting into the surface of the cup the series of insipid rosettes which serve

3. The Casa Galli adjoined the palace of Riario (*Cancelleria*): 'ad angulum posteriorem huius palatii', Boissard, *Topographia romanae urbis* II (1627), p. 18. On the extent of the grounds belonging to the Galli, and the presumable location of their palace and garden, see C. Hülsen and H. Egger, *Die römischen Skizzenbücher von Marten van Heemskerck* I (1913), pp. 39 f.; cf. also P. Romano, *Roma nelle sue strade e nelle sue piazze*, n.d., p. 222; B. Blasi, *Stradario romano* (1933), p. 132. According to R. Rufini, *Dizionario etimologico storico delle strade, piazze, borghi e vicoli della città di Roma* (1847), pp. 86 f., the Galli assisted Riario in financing the construction of his new palace. Its location in the immediate vicinity of the Casa Galli is confirmed also by Ulisse Aldrovandi, 'Delle statue antiche che per tutta Roma in diversi luoghi e case si veggono', appended to Lucio Mauro, *Le antichità della città di Roma* (1558), p. 167.

4. *Conclusiones . . . in doctrinam Platonis*, no. 4.

5. In Plato's *Symposium* 196E, Agathon says of Eros that he is 'the source of poetry in others, which he could not be if he were not himself a poet'. Cf. Plotinus about Venus (*Enneads* III, v. 2): καὶ ἐρασθεῖσα ῎Ερωτα ἐγέννησε, et Amorem amando genuit (Ficino's translation). Another example of the same principle is Raphael's Apollo, the inspirer of music, who appears in the *Parnassus* as inspired by music. Archaeological notes for 'diese Bildung des seiner selbst vollen Gottes' in Petersen, 'Eros und Psyche oder Nike', op. cit., p. 59.

as its decoration, or modelling the two realistic handles that stick out at unfortunate angles while the cup is precariously held with a lifted thumb and two fingers. It is also curious that although the statue is composed in the round, as befits a garden figure, the approach from the left offers a ridiculous aspect because the face vanishes behind the cup. The restorer's work is marked by two breaks, one of which runs straight through the wrist, the other through the thumb and forefinger. The original state, if it may be so called, is preserved in several drawings of the sixteenth century, which show the statue without the right hand (figs. 98, 99).

Of these drawings, the most important is by Heemskerck, the Flemish admirer of Michelangelo, who visited Rome in 1532–5, that is, during Michelangelo's lifetime.[6] He made a sketch of the statue in its original place, the garden of the Casa Galli, where it then stood as a semi-classical ruin, surrounded by genuine antiques in a ruinous state (fig. 98). Another drawing made some twenty years later for an Englishman in Rome (1551–2)[7] shows that the statue had by that time been restored unsuccessfully, for there is a peg in the stump of the right arm (fig. 99). No reproduction or description of the statue with the hand and cup has been found that can be dated before 1551–2, when this unsuccessful restoration had already been made. While it is not impossible that Michelangelo himself was asked on his return to Rome in 1535 to restore the hand, it is very unlikely that, broken off again by 1551–2, the remaining fragment or group of fragments would have survived the transport from the Casa Galli to the Villa Madama and from there to Florence in 1572. A drawing inscribed 'in the house of Madama without Rome' shows the statue in the same ruinous condition, with the peg sticking out of the right arm.[8]

6. Hülsen and Egger, loc. cit.

7. Trinity College, Cambridge, MS R 17, 3, fol. 14 (M. R. James, *The Western Manuscripts in the Library of Trinity College, Cambridge* II, 1901, no. 989). For the date, see P. G. Hübner, *Le statue di Roma* (1912), pp. 59 f., as against Michaelis, 'Römische Skizzenbücher nordischer Künstler des XVI. Jahrhunderts', *Jahrb. d. deutsch. archäol. Inst.* VII (1892), p. 95, no. 14.

8. Michaelis, op. cit., p. 98, no. 54: 'in the hous of madama we thowt rom [i.e. without Rome]'. The drawing shows the statue in profile and is therefore independent of the drawing in our fig. 99. It is stuck into the same sketch-book on fol. 54. I am

It cannot be seriously questioned, therefore, that the *Bacchus* is in a disfigured condition.[9] That he originally did hold a cup appears to me certain, but the workmanship was surely more fluent, and the hand was probably bent at the wrist, as was Michelangelo's custom; this would also explain why it broke so easily at the wrist.[10] But more conclusive and revealing than any of these inferences is the direct evidence contained in Heemskerck's drawing that the statue was regarded as pseudo-antique. The drawing shows that, in Michelangelo's own lifetime, the owners of the statue were content to let it stand in their garden as a classical ruin, and that it was so recorded by one of Michelangelo's admirers. By the middle of the century, still during Michelangelo's life, this curious condition had already occasioned a legend which was inscribed on the sketch of fig. 99: 'Scoltur de michelangeli the which was buried in the grownd and fo[u]nd for antick.' Boissard, a few years later, embellished the legend by a further detail. Supposedly to confound Raphael, 'Buonarroti made . . . this Bacchus out of ancient marble, and from the finished

---

indebted to Dr A. Scharf, who called my attention to this sketch-book many years ago when I first suggested that the hand was restored.

9. C. de Tolnay, *Michelangelo* I (1943), p. 142, observes that the hand and cup 'are of the same marble as the figure and *seem to be* by Michelangelo himself' (italics mine). From so critical an author one might have expected a commitment whether the workmanship is Michelangelo's or not. The words 'the same marble' are also ambiguous since they can either mean 'the same kind of marble', which would not prove anything, or 'the same piece of marble', which would be decisive. Tolnay's description of the condition of the statue, although very long, is incomplete: the second break in the hand is not mentioned, nor are any of the other injuries listed, for example in the nose and the tail of the satyr, in the ivy leaves of Bacchus, etc. The two sixteenth-century drawings after the Bacchus in the Cambridge Sketch-book are confused by Tolnay with each other and treated as one, the inscription 'in the hous of madama . . .', which belongs to fol. 54, being falsely referred to the drawing on fol. 14. The important fact that the Bacchus is represented in both these drawings without a hand and with a peg in the stump of the arm is altogether omitted. The carelessness in Tolnay's report on the Cambridge Sketch-book is matched in vol. III by repeated confusions between Cod. Pighianus and Cod. Coburgensis with reference to the *Leda*. Hence it is not made clear that Tolnay's fig. 250 (= Jahn, op. cit., no. 156) is a copy of his fig. 281 (= Matz op. cit., no. 150). The latter, from Cod. Coburgensis, is misnamed throughout Cod. Pighianus.

10. In some of the small bronze copies of the *Bacchus* made in the sixteenth century, the hand holding the cup is bent (for example, Tolnay's fig. 172), while in others (his fig. 171) the cup is raised as high as the head. Tolnay does not consider their difference.

statue he broke off an arm, which he kept . . . and he had the work
buried in the grounds of a certain citizen, who was soon to build a
house on it. And when in the following year the statue was found
by those who were laying the foundation of the house . . . it was
greatly praised', particularly by Raphael (who, incidentally, was not
yet in Rome). Michelangelo then produced the missing piece and
proved his authorship.[11] From the point of view of a Roman or
Florentine *cicerone*, the story could not have been better invented.
It not only explained why the right arm was fractured and repaired,
but it also proved the authenticity of the restoration. Inadvertently
it also recalled an undeniable fact; namely, that the statue had
existed for some time without a hand.

While it would not be wise to accept any of these tales uncritically,
they deserve attention for the spirit in which they were told, particularly as they represent a type of story which was repeatedly
fastened on Michelangelo. That he was able to 'prepare' a statue 'as
one from whom no craft was hidden, so that it looked as if it had
been made many years ago', was confidently asserted by his pupil
Condivi, who intended it as a compliment;[12] and the praise was
extended by Vasari to the forgery of old drawings, in which he
extolled Michelangelo's proficiency.[13] The pleasure the Renaissance

11. Boissard, loc. cit. In the first part of his Treatise on Painting, completed in 1548,
Francisco d'Ollanda, who knew Michelangelo personally, told a similar story. He
claimed that the *Bacchus* (which he actually remembered so badly that he described
the satyr as carrying a basket on his back) was shown to him in Rome as an ancient
sculpture, but that he recognized it as not antique, 'although the colouring of the
marble and all the details of execution seemed to suggest it. . . . The master learned that
he had not deceived me.' *Francisco de Hollanda, Vier Gespräche über die Malerei, geführt
zu Rom 1538*, ed. J. de Vasconcellos (1899), pp. 193 f.

12. Condivi, *Life of Michelangelo*, tr. Holroyd, p. 18.

13. Vasari, *Life of Michelangelo*: 'He also forged [*contraffece*] sheets by the hands of
various old masters [*maestri vecchi*] with such similitude that no one recognized it; for
he tinged and aged them with smoke and various other means, and so dirtied them
that they looked old [*che elle parevano vecchie*] and, when compared with the originals,
they could not be distinguished from them: and he did this so that, by giving his
copies, he might retain the originals for himself, which he admired for the excellency
of their art and tried to surpass by his own: by which he acquired a great name.'
The enthusiastic spirit of Renaissance forgers was stressed by Louis Courajod, *L'imitation et la contrefaçon des objets d'art antiques aux XV et XVI siècles* (1889). Also F. von
Bezold, *Aus Mittelalter und Renaissance* (1918), p. 119, with reference to the literary
forgeries of Celtes, Trithemius, and Annius of Viterbo.

took in this kind of make-believe was too intense to be restrained by any scruples. Moral doubts were thrown only on the character of the merchant who had paid Michelangelo too little for the Sleeping Cupid which was to be passed off for antique. The artist's own part was not plain fraud but emulation. He desired to compete with the silent masters, and if he could imitate them to the point of deception, it proved that he fully understood their craft. In this respect, Michelangelo's pseudo-antique sculpture is the exact parallel to certain literary performances which, while removed from the temptations of the market-place, aimed at a similar deception. No greater compliment could be paid to Bembo than to mistake one of his Latin epigrams for ancient. Alberti's comedy *Philodoxus* passed for a genuine Latin work, and a number of false Lucians also seem to have issued from his pen.

To understand the passionate tone of the Renaissance debates *De imitatione*,[14] one must abandon the common prejudice that imitation is always a cold and uninspired performance, and hence incompatible with a creative spirit. Burckhardt, himself a neo-classical poet, observed that intense admiration, an overpowering sense of another's superiority, invariably engenders imitation. Under an irresistible and quite irrational impulse the enthusiastic admirer turns into a mime. The phenomenon is known in daily life by the ludicrous behaviour of devoted disciples who acquire the mannerisms of their master, repeating his intonation, his gestures, even his gait. These are but the travesties of an imaginative power of self-transformation which can be refined to a religious discipline, as was shown for example by the Franciscans. In vowing to imitate their founder, because St Francis himself had imitated Christ, they demonstrated how a spiritual communion can be established on a persistent practice of devout imitation. Machiavelli, who was not prejudiced

14. The camps were sharply divided between the purists and those favouring, or tolerating, a composite style, as shown by the controversies between Politian and Paolo Cortese, Giovanni Pico and Ermolao Barbaro, Gianfrancesco Pico and Bembo (cf. G. Santangelo, *Le epistole 'de imitatione' di Giovanfrancesco Pico della Mirandola e di Pietro Bembo*, 1954), Erasmus and Longueil or Navagero, etc. Castiglione sympathized with the Erasmian view in the *Cortegiano*, but sided with Navagero when he was in Spain. Michelangelo, from his first visit to Rome, clearly belonged to the intransigent party, Raphael to the eclectic.

in favour of monks, explained that 'for a sect or a commonwealth to last long, it must often be drawn back to its beginning', and he observed that 'the need for that kind of renovation is shown by the example of our religion, which would have been utterly extinguished, had it not been drawn back to its beginning by St Francis and St Dominic. ... By returning to the example of the life of Christ, they re-established religion in the minds of men. ... And it is this renovation which has maintained religion, and still maintains it.' The passage occurs in the *Discourses on Livy*,[15] and serves as a parallel to political attempts at reviving the ancestral Roman virtues.

A like discipline was required to revive the Bacchic mysteries of Plato. These rites were distinguished by their convivial nature, in which the 'furor' of the god was disguised by irony. For combining a Bacchic with a Socratic spirit, the *Symposium* of Plato and the Bacchic passages in the *Phaedrus* were the venerated ancient models. An accomplished imitation of this genre, a dialogue by Sadoleto entitled *Phaedrus*, is located in the suburban Roman villa of Jacopo Galli, and gives a picture of the kind of conviviality in which the owner of Michelangelo's *Bacchus* took part as host and chief interlocutor.[16] The role of Phaedrus was here played by Tommaso Inghirami, whose nickname Fedro, originally derived from a performance of Phaedra, was turned into a compliment to his oratorical gifts. With an abundance of pointed illustration, the new Phaedrus was pictured as dismissing philosophy as useless and extolling the glories of rhetoric in its place, while his amused but unconvinced opponents compared him to the sophist Gorgias. In a second dialogue, Sadoleto himself took up the case for philosophy and argued it out against the animadversions of Phaedrus. Needless to say, philosophy was saved,[17] but Sadoleto was too elegant and gracious a writer not to allow the jests of Phaedrus to conclude the feast. Against

15. III, i.
16. Sadoleto, *Opera omnia* III (1738), pp. 128–79. The villa was located 'in campo feniculario secundum Adriani molem' (ibid., p. 131), that is, near the Castel Sant' Angelo. The dialogue opens showing Inghirami in conversation with Jacopo Galli: 'cum ipso Gallo sermocinantem'.
17. 'De laudibus philosophiae', ibid., pp. 179–244.

the background of some very solemn reflections, a ruthless gaiety was allowed to prevail and provided the pleasures of what Gyraldus called *rhetoricae ludicrae exercitatio*, a form of oratory for which the classical example was again the drunken speech of Alcibiades.

Some of the demonic Alcibiadic spirit may be detected in the expression of Michelangelo's *Bacchus* (fig. 101), admirably described by the innocent Condivi, who even revealed, in a singularly childish passage, that he had been made aware of some tragic mystery which he was unable to fathom. 'This work in form and bearing in every part corresponds to the description of the ancient writers – his aspect, merry; the eyes, squinting and lascivious, like those of people excessively given to the love of wine. He holds a cup in his right hand, like one about to drink, and look at it lovingly, taking pleasure in the liquor of which he was the inventor; for this reason he is crowned with a garland of vine leaves. On his left arm he has a tiger's skin, the animal dedicated to him, as one that delights in grapes; and the skin was represented rather than the animal, as Michelangelo desired to signify that he who allows his senses to be overcome by the appetite for that fruit, and the liquor pressed from it, ultimately loses his life. . . .'[18]

Errors of description in Condivi are so frequent that, although he is supposed to have written under Michelangelo's direct supervision, it is impossible to trust him on any detail. But compared to the blunders he committed in other instances,[19] the errors about the *Bacchus* are slight. The leaves in the hair, although intertwined with grapes, are ivy, and the flayed animal does not look like a tiger but rather like a *leopardus*, a fabulous beast described by Pliny as a hybrid between lion and panther.[20] That Condivi saw the *Bacchus* holding a cup is possible because the first restoration antedates the publication of his book (1553); but implicit faith should not be placed in his

18. Condivi, op. cit., pp. 20 f.

19. The *Madonna of Bruges* he described as a bronze, the *Sacrifice of Noah* in the Sistine Ceiling as a *Sacrifice of Cain and Abel*, the diadem of *Leah* he mistook for a mirror (which, if represented at all, would have belonged to *Rachel*), and the *Moses* at San Pietro in Vincoli he remembered as 'supporting his chin with his left hand, like one tired and full of cares'.

20. Pliny, *Natural History* VIII, xvi.

statement since Aldrovandi, who saw the statue about the same time, did not mention the cup in his detailed description.[21]

And yet, whatever Condivi's minor errors, one feels how close he was to the master to whom he endeared himself by his simplicity. Unlike Vasari, who posed as a man of letters, Condivi was never baffled by Michelangelo's cryptic manner. Ambiguous remarks were accepted by him without any of that sense of frustration which Vasari revealed in an unguarded moment: 'E stato nel suo dire molto coperto ed ambiguo, avendo le cose sue quasi due sensi.'[22] When Condivi asked, for example, why Michelangelo had represented the Virgin in the *Pietà* of St Peter's as younger than Christ, Michelangelo, instead of giving the theological reason, which can be gathered from the sermons of Bernardino da Siena,[23] replied with a grim joke at the expense of old spinsters which Condivi understood to be a new contribution to morals and theology. On the *Bacchus* Condivi seems to have been favoured with an equally suitable remark. One can hear this determined young Boswell asking what the skin of the flayed animal signified, and receiving the kind of answer which he bravely recorded: Do you not know that people who drink too much die?

In any case, the flayed animal signified death, and as we saw in the Flaying of Marsyas, that kind of death is associated with Bacchus. The god offering the cup of rejoicing introduces a ritual of cruel destruction, and his twofold gift is illustrated in the figure of the little satyr. While he 'furtively enjoys', as Condivi says, the grapes which are enveloped in the flayed skin, he is so placed that the skin and head of the tortured animal emerge between his own goat feet (fig. 100). Half-human, half-animal, he himself willingly holds and supports the horrid symbol of agony because in it is laid the fruit of rejoicing which he smilingly touches with his lips. As the mysteries of Bacchus are both destructive and consoling, because he

21. 'Delle statue antiche', op. cit., p. 168, written in 1550; cf. Hülsen, 'Römische Antikengärten des XVI. Jahrhunderts', in *Abhandlungen der Heidelberger Akademie*, philos.-histor. Klasse, XIII, iv (1917), p. viii.

22. First edition of the *Vite* (1550), p. 989; cf. E. Steinmann, *Michelangelo im Spiegel seiner Zeit* (1930), p. 11 note 2.

23. cf. Mâle, *L'art religieux de la fin du moyen âge en France* (1922), p. 128.

conveys the power to draw life out of death, he fittingly presides over a garden of ruins, the desolate site of enthusiasm.

*

It has been asked how it was possible that the young Michelangelo, professedly a believer in Savonarola, could produce, at the very height of Savonarola's influence, an undisguisedly pagan statue of Bacchus. A full answer to this question would require a more detailed analysis than can be attempted here of Savonarola's critique of the pagan revival.[24] It may suffice, however, to observe that while he attacked a literal-minded, popular, wordly paganism, Savonarola himself was so profoundly affected by the mystical Platonism of Ficino and Pico that there are demonstrable traces of it in his writing. The dialogue *De veritate prophetica* not only starts out in a pseudo-Socratic tone of doubt, and introduces, in the names of the interlocutors, some of the Hebrew acrostics that were so dear to Pico, but the pleasing setting of the conversation is copied from Plato himself: the inspiring plane tree on the bank of the Ilissus, under which Socrates invites Phaedrus to sit, reappears as a plane tree on the outskirts of Florence.

Exactly how far, within a mystical context, Savonarola would favour the imitation of pagan models was perhaps too nice a question for the young Michelangelo to ponder, particularly while he was working for Roman patrons who were politically not on Savonarola's side. Riario was cardinal-protector of the Augustinian order, and on close terms with its general, Fra Mariano da Genazzano, who was Savonarola's powerful and very vocal opponent. In their circle, which was also Jacopo Galli's, an Augustinian revival of Christian mysticism was combined with a formal cult of Cicero and Virgil. It is important, for an understanding of Michelangelo's Roman style, to picture him in that neo-classic atmosphere, whose peculiarly Roman mood (reflected in the epigrams of the *Coryciana*) was so markedly different from the Florentine. Egidio da Viterbo

24. The legend of Savonarola's hostility to art has been disproved by G. Gruyer, *Les illustrations des écrits de Jérôme Savonarole*, 1879. On the misinterpretation of the 'burning of the vanities', merely a variant of the 'burning of Carnival', see P. Villari, *Life and Times of Savonarola* III, vi.

referred with pride to his Roman friends of Sant'Agostino when he claimed that, while in other ages piety was combined with an unpolished manner, and elegance tended to be impious, it was the distinction of his own age that it knew how to be at once pious and elegant: 'ut denique summae pietati summam elegantiam copulaverit'.[25] The fact that Michelangelo produced the *Pietà* of St Peter's almost simultaneously with the *Bacchus*, and again under the sponsorship of Jacopo Galli,[26] proves that neither he nor his patrons felt any difficulty in shifting from pagan to Christian poetry, or from devout to elegant modes of speech.

Nor did Michelangelo abandon in his later years, despite the growth of a more narrow and contracted piety, his relish for the Bacchic mysteries he had learned in his youth. The Dionysian ritual of flaying recurs in a love poem, addressed presumably to Cavalieri. The *morta spoglia*, or the *irsuta pelle*, are to be shed by the lover and offered to the beloved as a trophy of passion, sacrifice, and transformation, a token of renewal through death:

> *Così volesse al mie signior mie fato*
> *Vestir suo viva di mie morta spoglia,*
> *Che, come serpe al sasso si discoglia,*
> *Pur per morte potria cangiar mie stato.*
> *O fussi sol la mie l'irsuta pelle*
> *Che, del suo pel contesta, fa tal gonna*
> *Che con ventura stringe sì bel seno....*[27]

An ostensibly Christian form was given to this symbol in the St Bartholomew of the *Last Judgement*. The 'flayed apostle' (*lo Apostolo scorticato*) threateningly lifts the knife with which he was martyred, while in his left hand he holds the gruesome skin on which

25. *Historia viginti saeculorum*, Biblioteca Angelica, Rome, MS. 502, fols. 197^v–198^r.

26. The contract for the *Pietà* (cf. *Le lettere di Michelangelo Buonarroti, coi ricordi ed i contratti artistici*, ed. G. Milanesi, 1875, p. 614) includes the following pledge to the Cardinal de Villiers: 'And I, Jacopo Galli, promise to His most Reverend Lordship, that the said Michelangelo shall execute the said work in a year, and that it shall be the most beautiful work of marble in Rome, and that no master living could do it so well' (tr. C. Heath Wilson, *Michelangelo*, 1876, p. 570).

27. *Rime*, ed. Girardi, p. 278, no. 94; 'Sembra dedicato al Cavalieri'; Frey, op. cit., p. 55, no. LXVI.

Michelangelo painted an agonized self-portrait (fig. 102).[28] As in Dante, of whom Michelangelo was known to be a profound expositor, the Marsyas-like portrait is a prayer for redemption, that through the agony of death the ugliness of the outward man might be thrown off and the inward man resurrected pure, having shed the *morta spoglia*.[29]

This was one of those 'secrets' in the *Last Judgement* which filled Pietro Aretino with dismay. 'If Michelangelo desires that his pictures be understood only by the few and learned, I must leave them alone since I do not belong to these.'[30] Actually, he understood them to perfection. In a letter of 1538, addressed to Vittoria Colonna, he declined to accept her noble advice that he should confine his writing to his religious tracts, which she had found immensely edifying. 'I admit,' he answered mockingly, 'that I render myself less useful to the world, and less acceptable to Christ, by producing trifles rather than true works; but of every evil the cause is in the pleasure of others, and in my indigence: for if the piety of the princes were as great as my penury, I would write nothing but *Misereres*.'[31] To illustrate his point he chose St Lawrence and St Bartholomew, the two most prominent saints symmetrically placed in Michelangelo's *Last Judgement*, and compared them to what he conceived to be their pagan counterparts. The princes, he claimed, would rather see Hercules burning on his funeral pyre than St Lawrence roasting on his grill; and to the sight of 'the flayed apostle' they would prefer 'Marsyas without skin': *Marsia senza pelle*.[32]

Whatever the personal aspects of Aretino's enmity, no critic has been more penetrating than he in defining the nature and limitations of Michelangelo's art. Animated by a hatred of obscurantism in any form, he detected in Michelangelo's cult of the enigmatic a detestable spirit of evasion. While Michelangelo professed to have turned

28. First observed by Francesco La Cava, *Il volto di Michelangelo scoperto nel Giudizio Finale*, 1925.   29. See above, pages 173 ff.

30. Lodovico Dolce, *L'Aretino ovvero Dialogo della pittura*, ed. C. Teoli (1863), p. 51.

31. *Il secondo libro de le lettere di M. Pietro Aretino*, Paris (1609), fol. 9ʳ.

32. It would be tempting to regard the date of this letter as a *terminus ante quem* for the completion of Michelangelo's cartoons. But while that inference is not contradicted by any of the available evidence, it should be taken into account that the presence of St Lawrence and St Bartholomew in a prominent place was prescribed by the dedication of the Chapel (see Wind, *Gazette des beaux-arts* XXVI, p. 223 note 32).

away from the pagans, and to have become as *chietino* as Vittoria Colonna herself, his work was still of pagan inspiration, and his imagery pagan in disguise. It was the disguise that Pietro Aretino was determined to expose. He himself had advocated a new freedom of letters, of which he had made an uninhibited use; but with a purism not incompatible with a licentious spirit, he did not believe in the mixing of genres. Like the princes he preferred his Marsyas plain.

This master of the bizarre could be relied upon to detect a bizarrerie in others. His correspondence with Michelangelo, in which he displayed his peculiar art of resolving flattery into caricature, shows Michelangelo's own skill in Aretino's idiom. We hear much about Michelangelo's sombreness and depth, but too little is said about his grim sense of humour and his genius for the grotesque. The sonnet about shedding his skin, for example, is only half understood if it is read solely as a tragic expression of passion and longing, which it unquestionably is. But these emotions are rendered by a preposterous image which is meant to strike the reader as grotesque. And surely, there is also an ingredient of bizarrerie in his picturing San Baccio (= Bartolommeo) as a Bacchic saint, his portentous skin inscribed with the tragic mask of the artist.

FABRINI: I hear it said that in the design of his stupendous Last Judgement there are some allegorical senses of great profundity which are understood only by a few.

ARETINO: In this he would deserve praise because it would appear that he had imitated those great philosophers who concealed under the veil of poetry the deepest philosophical mysteries both human and divine so that they might not be understood by the vulgar: not wishing, as it were, to throw pearls before swine. And this I would also believe was Michelangelo's intention. . . . [Yet] to me it does not seem so very praiseworthy that the eyes of children, matrons, and maids should openly see in these figures the improprieties which they exhibit, and only the learned understand the profundity of the allegories which they conceal.[33]

It would be difficult to deny that this criticism strikes at a basic paradox of cryptic art, which frequently addresses itself to the very

33. *L'Aretino*, pp. 50 f.

audience from which it professes to be hidden.[34] And yet, the aim to combine a didactic with a secretive manner, which has been described as a self-contradiction in Renaissance emblems,[35] should perhaps rather be defined as a rule of Platonic pedagogy. 'No one denies,' wrote St Augustine, 'that things sought with a certain difficulty are found with much greater pleasure. . . . *Facile investigata plerumque vilescunt.*'[36] Aretino evaded the problem by skilfully dividing the spectators of the *Last Judgement* into the devoutly uninformed on the one hand, and an élite of omniscient experts on the other. He cut out the intermediate phase of suspense, presupposed in any initiation – the wide middle region between knowledge and ignorance, which is the chosen state of the Platonic enthusiast who yearns for wisdom because he does not have it. It was by squarely placing himself on this middle ground that Pico could adopt the rule of withholding the pagan mysteries from the public, and at the same time offer to debate them publicly in Rome. How a debate might be both public and secret, his own propositions were able to illustrate by their teasingly enigmatic form.[37] Designed to arouse surprise, curiosity, and contradiction, they were conceived as part of an *exercitatio*, a solemn game of intellectual wrestling *in hac quasi literaria palaestra.*[38]

But the contest was not confined to letters. 'Try to reduce your inquiry to figures,' wrote Cusanus in *De coniecturis*, 'so that under the guidance of sensibility (*sensibili manuductione*) you may turn your conjecture toward the arcana.'[39] While he intended the advice for philosophers, it may be of benefit to the historian also. At least, it has been my assumption in these pages that in studying the Renaissance mysteries through the medium of art one may approach them *sensibili manuductione.*

34. cf. Boas, *The Hieroglyphics of Horapollo*, p. 23.

35. Praz, *Studies in Seventeenth Century Imagery*, p. 155.

36. Marrou, *Saint Augustin et la fin de la culture antique*, pp. 488 f.

37. For example, *Conclusiones . . . de modo intelligendi hymnos Orphei*, no. 1: 'Sicut secretam Magiam a nobis primum ex Orphei hymnis elicitam fas non est in publicum explicare, ita nutu quodam, ut in infrascriptis fiet conclusionibus, eam per aphorismorum capita demonstrasse utile erit ad excitandas contemplativorum mentes.'

38. *De hominis dignitate*, ed. Garin, p. 134.   39. *De coniecturis* I, xi.

CHAPTER XIII

PAN AND PROTEUS

In Pico's oration *On the Dignity of Man*, man's glory is derived from his mutability. The fact that his orbit of action is not fixed, like that of angels or of animals, gives him the power to transform himself into whatever he chooses and become a mirror of the universe. He can vegetate like a plant, rage like a brute, dance like a star, reason like an angel, and surpass them all by withdrawing into the hidden centre of his own spirit where he may encounter the solitary darkness of God. 'Who would not admire this chameleon?'[1]

In his adventurous pursuit of self-transformation, man explores the universe as if he were exploring himself. And the farther he carries these metamorphoses, the more he discovers that all the varied phases of his experience are translatable into each other: for they all reflect the ultimate One, of which they unfold particular aspects. If man did not sense the transcendent unity of the world, its inherent diversity would also escape him. Pico expressed this cryptically but unmistakably in one of the Orphic *Conclusiones*: 'He who cannot attract Pan approaches Proteus in vain.'[2]

The advice to seek for the hidden Pan in the ever-changing Proteus refers to the principle of 'the whole in the part', of the One inherent in the Many. And it is worth while to watch the principle in operation because it explains the nature of Orphic polytheism, the Renaissance scheme of a pluralistic universe. While the preceding chapters have drawn attention to certain mysteries in their particular

1. 'Quis hunc nostrum chamaeleonta non admiretur?' *De hominis dignitate*, ed. Garin, p. 106. The argument occurs also in Ficino, *Theologia Platonica* XIV, iii, as the sixth among sixteen *signa immortalitatis* (*Opera*, pp. 309 ff., cf. Kristeller, op. cit., p. 118).

2. *Conclusiones ... de modo intelligendi hymnos Orphei*, no. 28. Also *De hominis dignitate*, loc. cit.: 'Quem [hominem] ... versipellis huius et se ipsam transformantis naturae argumento per Proteum in mysteriis significari. ...' Repeated in Rhodiginus, *Antiquae lectiones* I, xxxix: 'tamquam Proteus aut Chamaeleon'.

setting, an attempt will be made here to survey the Orphic pantheon as a system, and to see by what logical rules, if any, its mysteries are governed.

When Pico wrote that 'the unity of Venus is unfolded in the trinity of the Graces', he added that he who understands that operation clearly and fully holds the key to the whole of Orphic theology.[3] Indeed, the unfolding of a divine unit into a triad is but an inverse expression of the Neoplatonic law that 'the contraries coincide in the One' (*contradictoria coincidunt in natura uniali*).[4] While this resolution is final only in the supreme One, whose names are legion because it is nameless, each subordinate being, in so far as it has unity, repeats the process of the One and generates triads; that is, it unfolds its nature by exhibiting its extremes and holding them together through a common centre.

The argument has a disconcertingly modern ring,[5] and because it sounds Hegelian it would be tempting to dismiss it as anachronistic; but the similarity is not adventitious. If the notorious triads of Hegel resemble those employed in the Orphic theology of the Renaissance, it is because he drew in part from the same ancient sources. In Hegel's opinion, Plato's *Parmenides* was 'perhaps the greatest masterpiece of ancient dialectic';[6] and he also recalled that it was from that dialogue that some of the late-antique and Renaissance Neoplatonists professed to derive their fusion of dialectic with ecstasy:

Inzwischen kann ich bedenken, dass ... es auch Zeiten gegeben, welche sogar Zeiten der Schwärmerei genannt werden, worin ... der Parmenides des Plato, wohl das grösste Kunstwerk der alten Dialektik, für die wahre Enthüllung und den positiven Ausdruck des göttlichen Lebens gehalten wurde, und sogar bei vieler Trübheit dessen, was die Ekstase erzeugte, diese missverstandene Ekstase in der Tat nichts anderes als der reine Begriff sein sollte.

---

3. *Conclusiones ... de modo intelligendi hymnos Orphei*, no. 8.
4. *Conclusiones paradoxae*, no. 15.
5. 'Il faut que notre pensée se développe,' wrote Valéry, 'et il faut qu'elle se conserve. Elle n'avance que par les extrêmes, mais elle ne subsiste que par les moyens.'
6. *Phänomenologie des Geistes*, Vorrede (Glockner edition II, pp. 64 f.).

In this passage, from the *Phänomenologie des Geistes*,[7] Hegel claims that his own dialectic was darkly foreshadowed in Neoplatonic dithyrambs, which would only need to be freed from the confusions of ecstasy to reveal Hegel's 'Selbstbewegung des Begriffs'. Later he developed the comparison more fully in the *Vorlesungen über die Geschichte der Philosophie* by analysing the *Parmenides* in the light of Proclus,[8] whose system of triads he recorded in detail, praising it as 'die Spitze der neuplatonischen Philosophie' while stressing its demonstrable affinity to his own system.[9]

Nor was Hegel alone in these observations. In 1820 two separate editions of Proclus began to appear in Frankfurt and Paris, one by Creuzer, the other by Cousin, and both with dedications to Hegel and Schelling.[10] Creuzer reports in his autobiography that he was guided by Hegel in the work on the edition;[11] and although, in penning his formidable dedications, he extolled Hegel and Schelling indiscriminately among 'the foremost interpreters of Platonic texts',[12] he noted in his autobiography this difference between them, that 'Hegel cared less for Plotinus than for Proclus', and that Hegel ascribed, in contrast to Schelling, the greatest importance to the *Institutio theologica*, in which Proclus had reduced the Neoplatonic triads to a rigid system of deduction.[13] Cousin, in his turn, observed

7. loc. cit. Hegel's reference to 'Zeiten der Schwärmerei' should be compared with W. G. Tennemann, *Geschichte der Philosophie* (1789–1819), the sixth volume of which, published in 1807, deals with 'Schwärmerische Philosophie der Alexandriner und Neuplatoniker' (pp. 284–352: Proclus).

8. Glockner edition XVIII, pp. 243 f.

9. ibid., XIX, pp. 78–93.

10. Cousin's edition (*Procli philosophi platonici opera*) was the first to appear, and despite his attempt to appease the *amicissimum Creuzerum* (I, pp. xlix f.), Creuzer attacked it spitefully in his own preface (*Initia philosophiae ac theologiae ex platonicis fontibus ducta* I, pp. viii f.). Cousin replied in vol. III, pp. viii f.

11. *Aus dem Leben eines alten Professors*, pp. 123 ff. In the edition of Proclus (*Initia* II, p. 82 note 6) he introduced an emendation by Hegel with the words: 'Hoc vult philosophus.' Fuller quotations from Hegel, ibid. II, pp. 325 f.

12. Vol. I was dedicated to Boissonade and Schelling as 'Platonicorum monumentorum philosophiaeque interpretibus primariis'; vol. II to Hegel and van Heusde as 'Philosophiae veteris cum universae tum eius imprimis quae platonicis monumentis continetur interpretibus primariis'.

13. op. cit., p. 124, a capital document on Hegel and Schelling, as well as on Creuzer. 'Hegel hielt weniger auf Plotin als auf Proclus, und legte besonders diesem

the same distinction between the two 'leaders of present philosophy': for while he hailed Schelling and Hegel together as 'the restorers of the Parmenidean and Platonic One',[14] he noticed particularly in his 'friend Hegel' (*amicus Hegelius*) a striking resemblance to Proclus himself: *qui et ipse cum Proclo nostro tantam similitudinem refert*.[15] Less sympathetic, Schleiermacher looked upon the Platonic affinities of Hegel with undisguised malice. In the preface to his translation of Plato's *Parmenides* he observed that 'this is certainly the oldest attempt in philosophy to construe cognition through a union of contraries (*der ... gewiss in der Philosophie älteste Versuch, durch Verknüpfung von Gegensätzen Erkenntnis zu konstruieren)*',[16] and he added caustically that 'few may have guessed the age of that method' which is 'so similar to certain things that have turned up among us'. If we add that in a dialogue by Schelling, entitled *Bruno, oder über das göttliche und natürliche Princip der Dinge*, the great rival of Hegel adopted for himself Giordano Bruno's use of the coincidence of opposites, declaring it to be 'das Symbolon der wahren Philosophie',[17] we may conclude that the

---

Buche des letzteren [*Procli Institutio theologica*] einen grossen Wert bei. Daher er, wissend, dass ich handschriftliche Hülfsmittel dazu habe, dringend mir anlag, es neu zu bearbeiten. Ich willfahrte ihm unter der Bedingung, dass ich ihm die Druckbögen zusende, und er mir seine Bemerkungen dazu mitteile. Dies ist denn auch ... brieflich von ihm geschehen, und ich habe sie in einem Epimetrum zu der im folgenden Jahre erschienenen Ausgabe abdrucken lassen. ... Dagegen schrieb mir Schelling in einem Briefe (Erlangen den 13 Sept. 1822) unter anderm: "Ich werde nun versuchen, mich mit Ihrer Hilfe auch in diese *Institutionem theologicam* des Proclus hineinzuarbeiten, wiewohl ich nicht leugne, dass ich mich vor der Eintönigkeit der Darstellung und dem Dogmatischen des Vortrags einigermassen fürchte." Und dies war und ist [Creuzer adds on his own] auch meine Empfindung; weshalb ich aus eigner Bewegung auch schwerlich jemals diese Schrift bearbeitet haben würde.'

14. IV (1821), p. v. The volume is devoted to Proclus's *Commentarii in Parmenidem Platonis* and bears a dedication to Boissonade: 'nec non amicis et magistris F. W. J. Schelling et G. W. F. Hegel, philosophiae praesentis ducibus, unius Parmenidei et Platonici restitutoribus'. Cf. recently Klibansky, Preface to *Plato latinus* III ('Parmenides ... nec non Procli commentarium'), p. x, with further quotations from Hegel.

15. I, pp. xlix f.

16. It is interesting that Schleiermacher, aware of Plato's opposition to Heraclitus, spoke of 'Verknüpfung von Gegensätzen', not of 'Koinzidenz von Gegensätzen'.

17. The reference is to Bruno, *De la causa, principio et uno* V, quoted by Schelling in Jacobi's translation: 'Um in die tiefsten Geheimnisse der Natur einzudringen, muss

revival of Platonism in the Renaissance was echoed in the early nineteenth century by a Romantic revival of certain Renaissance arguments.[18]

The great difference in climate, however, should warn us against treating the two revivals as identical: for nothing could be farther apart in temperament than Schelling's 'philosophy of mysteries' and that of Bruno, or Pico's and Hegel's 'union of contraries'. The *Weltseele* of Schelling, although more effeminate, was no less voracious than Hegel's *Weltgeist*: both lived on a diet of tortuous positivism which would have killed Poetic Theology. But in so far as all these divergent philosophies of transmutation suffer, to put it negatively, from the same logical idiosyncrasies, they may exhibit certain typical deviations from classical logic, which it would be

---

man nicht müde werden, den entgegengesetzten und widerstreitenden äussersten Enden der Dinge, dem Maximum und Minimum nachzuforschen; den Punkt der Vereinigung zu finden, ist nicht das Grösste, sondern aus demselben auch sein Entgegengesetztes zu entwickeln, dieses ist das eigentlichste und tiefste Geheimnis der Kunst' (Schelling, *Sämtliche Werke* I, iv, 1859, p. 328, after F. H. Jacobi, *Über die Lehre des Spinoza, in Briefen an den Herrn Moses Mendelssohn*, 1789, Beilage I, p. 305). The same passage from Bruno was singled out by Hegel, *Geschichte der Philosophie*, ed. cit. XIX, p. 233: 'Dies ist ein grosses Wort.' But he expounded it in the manner of Proclus: 'in Proklus' Manier' (p. 237), '. . . auch bei Proklus das Dritte im Ersten' (p. 238). And he reproached Schelling (ibid., p. 667) for having accepted the Neoplatonic Absolute without penetrating to it through the 'movement' of Plato's dialectic. On the other hand, the ritualistic aspects of Neoplatonism appealed to Schelling more than to Hegel. The following passage from Schelling's *Bruno* (op. cit., p. 329) should be compared with Pico's 'Osiris ladder' (above, pages 134 f.): 'Diesem folgend werden wir . . . auf dieser geistigen Leiter frei und ohne Widerstand auf und ab uns bewegen, jetzt herabsteigend die Einheit des göttlichen und natürlichen Prinzips getrennt, jetzt hinaufsteigend und alles wieder auflösend in das Eine, die Natur in Gott, Gott aber in der Natur sehen. . . . Auch die Schicksale des Universums werden uns nicht verborgen bleiben . . ., noch werden uns die Vorstellungen von den Schicksalen und dem Tode eines Gottes dunkel sein, die in allen Mysterien gegeben werden, die Leiden des Osiris und der Tod des Adonis.'

18. Ficino occupies the first place in Creuzer's essays 'Zur Geschichte der Classischen Philologie seit Wiederherstellung der Literatur' (*Deutsche Schriften* V, ii, 1854, pp. 10–21), in the preface of which he says, 'Ich hatte einmal den Gedanken, ihr [dieser Schrift] den metaphorischen Titel: *philologische Ahnenbilder* vorzusetzen.' See also *Prolegomena literaria de Plotino* in Creuzer's Oxford edition of Plotinus I (1835), pp. xxxvi ff. note 4: 'De restituta per Italiam philosophia platonica eiusque restitutionis causis auctoribusque'.

useful to record. Hegel was certainly not the first to flout in his logic the classical principles of identity, contradiction, and the excluded middle. The same use, or abuse, of ambiguity by which he made identity unfold itself as contrarious was also at the root of Pico's parable that Pan is hidden in Proteus. Mutability, in Pico's view, is the secret gate through which the universal invades the particular. Proteus persistently transforms himself because Pan is inherent in him.

All the particular gods, in the Orphic theology as outlined by Pico, seem animated by a law of self-contrariety, which is also a law of self-transcendence. The chaste Diana, despite her coldness, is a mad huntress and changeable as the moon; the mad Dionysus not only rages, but through his rage he purifies and consoles; Apollo inspires by his music poetic frenzy as well as poetic measure; Hermes, the god of eloquence, advises silence,[19] and Minerva, the goddess of peace, favours a martial garb; Mars, the god of war, is enamoured of Venus who, as the goddess of Concord, loves Strife. In short, all the gods, without exception, appear in Orphic theology both as inciters and as moderators, they are *dei ambigui* (to use a phrase from the *Hypnerotomachia*);[20] and because each god thus shares in the temperament of other gods, they are able to assist and also to offset each other. The wild Dionysus, on Mount Parnassus, finds himself checked by a stern Apollo, who in his turn, when he appears opposite to Minerva, softens her severity.[21] Apollo thus resembles a tenor who would sing the second voice in a duet with a soprano, and the first voice in a duet with a bass: except that, in this particular music, each voice mysteriously includes all others, although, when externally juxtaposed, they tend to bring out each other's peculiarities.

In the *Eroici furori*, Giordano Bruno illustrated the principle by

19. Our fig. 23; cf. above, page 12 note 40.
20. *Hypnerotomachia*, fol. b v^r.
21. For Dionysus–Apollo see the portrait of Alberto Pio (Mond Collection, National Gallery, London), which should be ascribed, I believe, to Giacomo Francia. It shows the Muses divided between Apollo and Dionysus, whose temples, inscribed with their names, occupy the two peaks of Parnassus. For Apollo–Minerva see Raphael's *School of Athens*.

Ficino's old example, the Judgement of Paris. The three goddesses, Bruno explained, did not represent three mutually exclusive perfections: for it would be a denial of their divinity to say that the beauty of Venus was without majesty or wisdom, the wisdom of Minerva without beauty or majesty, or the majesty of Juno without wisdom or beauty. Since all three were perfect, they could not be wholly deprived of any of these attributes; but their perfection was finite because, in each goddess, one of the three attributes which they all held in common prevailed over the other two. And for that reason alone, because of their finite perfection, discord arose between them. And therefore Paris ought not to have given the apple to any finite power in which beauty prevailed over wisdom, or wisdom over majesty, or majesty over beauty, but only to that infinite power in which they coincide: 'For in the simplicity of the divine essence ... all these perfections are equal because they are infinite.'[22] The fable teaches, according to Bruno, that when divine perfections become finite, they disclose through their discord an overruling harmony, of which each is only a partial expression. Their finite collisions carry the overtone of their coincidence in the infinite; and thus one dominant consonance emerges from a variety of discords.[23]

Bruno hardly needed to go back to Cusanus to learn that particular argument,[24] since Ficino had already drawn from it the cogent

22. I, v, 11 (Sonnet xxxv, *pulchriori detur*). Bruno must have been aware that exactly the same argument was used by Augustine, *De Trinitate* VI, x, 12, to distinguish the supreme and infinite Trinity, in which the parts are equal to the whole, from any subordinate and finite trinity, in which they are necessarily unequal.

23. The pedantry of Conrad Celtes (cf. below, page 252) may be of use in elucidating the argument. The Judgement of Paris, which he placed at the bottom of his pyramid of learning (A. Burkhard, *Hans Burgkmair d. Ä.*, 1932, pl. 9, no. 10), includes an allegorical figure, inscribed *Discordia*, who brings the apple of strife to Paris, while Mercury, placed on the other side of Paris, lifts the caduceus as the emblem of concord. The interaction between these contrary forces, as they enter into the Judgement of Paris, is explained by the inscription: *errando discitur philosophia*. Paris's error is but the first step in the process of drawing concord out of discord. In the *Sigillum collegii poetarum Viennae*, again invented by Celtes and engraved by Burgkmair (op. cit., no. 7), Apollo killing the python is juxtaposed to Mercury playing the flute, another illustration of *discordia concors*.

24. Bruno's references to Cusanus listed in F. I. Clemens, *Giordano Bruno und Nicolaus von Cusa* (1847), pp. 134 f.

lesson that it is a mistake to worship one god alone. In order to invoke the help of Minerva, it is wise to pay homage also to Juno and Venus; and it would be impossible to secure the protection of Venus without facing some aspect of Diana or of Mars. By calling one god, we call his affiliates; and by calling a few, we call them all. Polytheism leads to the Pantheon.

> Nimmer, das glaubt mir, erscheinen die Götter,
> Nimmer allein.[25]

The mutual entailment of the gods was a genuine Platonic lesson. Plato called it κοινωνία τῶν γενῶν, and he explained that the members of the divine community are alternately divided and conjoined by a dialectical 'movement' (κίνησις) which brings out their 'sameness' and 'otherness' through a series of changing configurations.[26] With every shift of argument a new harmony or discord may thus be discovered between the gods, and it was expected of a Renaissance humanist, when he contrived the programme of a new mythological image, that his genius would surprise, enlighten, and satisfy the spectator by the persuasive twist of his 'invention'. The range and freshness of some of these turns, no less than their occasional deviousness, are the despair of iconographical mechanics. As in a good musical composition, the developments are both logical and unforeseen. In the presence of a bluntly aggressive Venus we may see Diana join the fight on the side of Minerva, as in Perugino's *Battle of Love and Chastity*;[27] but when Minerva, in Tritonius's *Melopoiae*, represents the rational

25. Schiller, *Dithyrambe*. A clear statement of the philosophical implications in Schiller, *Über die ästhetische Erziehung des Menschen*, vi: '... so fein und scharf sie [die Vernunft der Griechen] auch trennte, so verstümmelte sie doch nie. Sie zerlegte zwar die menschliche Natur und warf sie in ihrem herrlichen Götterkreis vergrössert auseinander, aber nicht dadurch dass sie sie in Stücken riss, sondern dadurch dass sie sie verschiedentlich mischte, denn die ganze Menschheit fehlte in keinem einzigen Gott.'

26. *Sophist* 252 ff. On *theomachies* as symbols of the κοινωνία τῶν γενῶν, from which issue both union and division between the gods, see Proclus, *In Rempublicam* 373, translated in Taylor, *The Mystical Initiations; or Hymns of Orpheus*, pp. 158 ff., note. Also Proclus, *In Parmenidem* V, 1028 (Cousin²).

27. Painted for the *grotta* of Isabella d'Este, now in the Louvre; cf. Wind, *Bellini's Feast of the Gods*, p. 19 note 41.

aspect of Apollo, we find that Diana has taken the side of Dionysus and enacts the part of a sylvan fury.[28] It makes for the logic and liveliness of the Orphic gods that they partake of what the Marquess of Halifax called *the character of a trimmer*. ('This innocent word *trimmer*,' Halifax explained, 'signifies no more than this, that if men are together in a boat, and one part of the company would weigh it down on one side, another would make it lean as much to the contrary.'[29]) In the ever-changing *balance des dieux* the gods reveal their Protean nature: but the very fact that each god contains his opposite in himself, and can change into it when occasion demands, makes him shadow forth the nature of Pan in whom all opposites are one.

*

In the Orphic Hymns the duplicity of the gods was emphatically praised as a divine power:

> *War's parent, mighty, of majestic frame,*
> *Deceitful saviour, liberating dame.*[30]

Such compliments were addressed in the Hymns not only to Rhea (whom they fit because she saved Jupiter by deceiving Saturn), but also to Minerva, to Diana, to Apollo, whose powers were celebrated as ambivalent. Philosophers committed to the coincidence of opposites of course seized on that fact as confirming their view;[31] which helps to explain why 'composite gods' became the rule rather than the exception in Orphic theology. Whatever may be said against the divine hybrids, the curious crossbreeds that people the Orphic

---

28. The illustration of Parnassus in the *Melopoiae*, however unattractive in itself, is important as an iconographic link between Raphael's *Parnassus* and the portrait of Alberto Pio (above, page 196 note 21). The association Diana–Dionysus also in Gyraldus I, 267, dedication of Syntagma viii, 'De Baccho'.

29. *The Character of a Trimmer* (1699).

30. Taylor's translation of the *Hymns of Orpheus* (1787), p. 139, 'To Rhea'.

31. cf. Ficino, *Opera*, p. 1374: '. . . Iamblichus . . . eiusmodi daemones [i.e. mundi rectores] inquit partim quidem alligare nos fato, partim vero solvere. Hinc Orpheus saepe numina claves tenere canit, quibus videlicet claudant pariter et aperiant.' On the affinity of the Orphic gods to Janus, see below, pages 201, 230.

pantheon, they express the Orphic spirit at its fullest, and it is remarkable with what persistence and shrewdness the Renaissance antiquarians justified a predilection for them. An incidental passage in Virgil or Statius, a passing reference in Pausanias, Lucian, Cicero, or Ausonius, a capricious epigram in one or two of the elegiac poets, were sufficient to 'prove' the authenticity of a Venus–Diana, a Hermathena, a Hermeros, a Hypneros, a Hermercules, a Hercules Musagetes, a Fortuna–Nemesis, a Nemesis Amoris, a Venus Armata or Venus Victrix bearing the weapons of Mars or of Minerva.[32] Even the wanton statues of the Hermaphrodite, which inspired the jocular sallies of Beccadelli,[33] did not escape a mystical reading: 'ad superiorem intellectum referri debent', wrote the impervious Pierio Valeriano.[34] A secretive, esoteric tone attended all these mythological compounds, and often also a tone of mockery. The title of the *Hypnerotomachia* recalled the titles of Homeric burlesques, of the classical *Batrachomyomachia* or Prodromus's *Galeomyomachia*:

> For through the Janus of a joke
> The candid psychopompos spoke.[35]

If the spirit of sacred *drôlerie* was responsible, in mystical Renaissance language, for some remarkably ugly neologisms (like Cusanus's *possest* or the hieroglyphic *paedogeron*),[36] it also gave rise to a Neoplatonic reinterpretation of that most symmetrical of monsters, the double-headed Janus. Mindful of the opening passages of Ovid's

32. Valuable observations on 'theocrasy', that is, on the fusion of the gods as a recurrent feature of Greek mythology, in Gruppe, *Griechische Mythologie und Religionsgeschichte* (1906), pp. 1093–6.

33. Beccadelli's *Hermaphroditus*, dedicated to Cosimo de' Medici, was meant to amuse (like Beccadelli's reckless talk in Valla's *De voluptate*) a circle of humanists steeped in syncretism. In reading these poems it is well to remember that it was presumably for the same circle that Donatello made the polymorphous Cupid (now in the Bargello) who, although he has the face and wings of a classical Eros, wears the tail of a Pan, the trousers of Attis, the belt of Hypnos, and the sandals of Mercury. On *Eros Pantheos* see Pauly–Wissowa XVIII, iii, 746, s.v. *Pantheion*; also Gyraldus I, 409 on *Eros pandamator.*

34. *Hieroglyphica* XVIII, fol. 135ʳ.   35. W. H. Auden, *New Year Letter.*

36. The *paedogeron*, or *puer senex*, is explained above, page 99 note 8, as a fusion of Youth (παῖς) and Old Age (γέρων). On Cusanus's *possest*, which unites *est* and *posse*, see above, page 106 note 28.

Fasti, where Janus presides over the gates of heaven,[37] Pico reserved the symbol of Janus for the 'celestial souls', that is, for the souls that animate the firmament. 'In ancient poetry,' he claimed, 'these souls were signified by the double-headed Janus, because, being supplied like him with eyes in front and behind, they can at the same time see the spiritual things and provide for the material.'[38] But our inferior souls cannot do both at the same time. 'Before they fall into this earthly body, our souls also have two faces . . . but when they descend into the body, it is for them as if they were cut in half [*se fussino per mezzo divise*], and of the two faces there remains only one, whence every time that they turn the one face that is left to them toward sensible beauty, they remain deprived of the vision of the other.'[39] And thus a Platonic dilemma was read into the comic fable told by Aristophanes in the *Symposium* that man was originally double, but lost his perfection when he was cut in half.

On a medal of the Paduan philosopher Marcantonio Passeri, the comic monster of Aristophanes – like a pair of Siamese twins, with heads joined in Janus-fashion – appears with the inscription: PHILOSOPHIA DUCE REGREDIMUR (fig. 68).[40] This unattractive

37. *Fasti* I, 125.   38. *Commento* II, xxv (ed. Garin III, iv, pp. 527 ff.).

39. *Commento,* loc. cit., ed. Garin, p. 529. The chapter ends (p. 531) with an explicit reference to 'la fabula di Aristofane, posta nel *Convivio* di Platone'. As so often in Pico, the passage reads like a tightening-up of Ficino's system. The twofold animation of the spheres was quoted by Ficino from the 'theology of Orpheus', but in that context he did not speak of Janus (*Theologia Platonica* IV, i, *Opera,* pp. 130 f.). On the other hand, when he did compare the soul to Janus, because it connects the eternal with the temporal, he did not restrict the image to celestial souls but spoke of the soul in general (*Theologia Platonica* XVI, v, *Opera,* p. 375; also *Epistolae* I, ibid., pp. .657 f.; cf. Kristeller, *The Philosophy of Marsilio Ficino,* pp. 393 ff.), and without reference to Aristophanes' fable, or his own interpretation of it (*De amore* IV, *Opera,* pp. 1330–4).

40. The woodcut, after a medal by Cavino, appears in I. P. Tomasinus, *Illustrorum virorum elogia* (Padua 1630), p. 104, where the ground-line is mistaken for a staff and the figure placed upright. For the correct position see *Museum Mazzuchellianum* I (1761), pl. lxix, 4. The same medal appears also with the inverse motto PHILOSOPHIA COMITE REGREDIMUR (fig. 67, cf. G. Habich, *Die Medaillen der italienischen Renaissance,* 1924, pl. lxxvi, 12), suggesting that in a bifrontal man it makes little difference whether philosophy 'leads' or 'follows' (cf. Hill, no. 1159: EADEM DUX EADEMQUE COMES, medal of Agostino Chigi showing a double-headed Prudence). Because of his Genoese descent, Passeri adopted the byname *De Ianua,* to which his Janus-like emblem undoubtedly refers (cf. Isidorus, *Etymologiae* VIII, xi, 37: 'Ianum dicunt quasi mundi vel caeli vel mensuum ianuam'). It would be tempting to recognize Passeri's features

picture represents the perfect man; and the irony was intentional, an Orphic portent. In Ficino's Commentary on the *Symposium*, the explanation of this particular myth was assigned to Cristoforo Landino, 'whom we recognize as the foremost Orphic and Platonic poet of our time'.[41] An Orphic poet could not doubt that the monstrousness of Aristophanes' fable was a sign that it concealed a sacred mystery; and in that he followed, perhaps more than he knew, the distant precedent of Alexandrian Platonism. The biblical passage: 'and he divided them in the midst' (Genesis xv, 10) had been cited by Philo as crucial evidence for the λόγος τομεύς, the 'Logos as cutter', who produces 'creation by dichotomy' but is the 'joiner of the universe' as well.[42] In Aristophanes' fable the divided man longs to regain his original integrity; and as Landino is made to explain in Ficino, that benefit is conferred on him by the power of Love: 'quod nos olim divisos in integrum restituendo reducit in coelum'.[43] Instead of having to turn around to see the light, like the prisoners in Plato's allegory of the cave, the Aristophanic man can attend to the upper and lower worlds simultaneously. He no longer requires the ἐπιστροφή. For Ficino the ridiculous monster thus concealed a promise of celestial bliss. Aristophanes' rather explicit moral appeared to him obscure and foreshortened (*obscura et implicita Aristophanis sententia*), requiring some elucidation and unravelling (*enodationem adhuc aliquam lucemque*).

---

and character in an emblematic portrait ascribed to Girolamo Mazzola (fig. 65) of a philosopher holding an hour-glass almost run out. The word EXI ('seek a way out') is inscribed on a labyrinth in the background while the homophone ECCE ('behold') refers to a Janus-head embossed on an amphora. The body of the urn, below the Janus, shows a procession of figures looking back over their shoulders (ἐπιστροφή). Pierio Valeriano dedicated the thirty-ninth book of the *Hieroglyphica* to Passeri. Andreas Vesalius mentions him in the preface to *Tabulae sex* (1538). Rabelais appreciated his preposterous emblem: the young Gargantua wears it on his cap as a huge medallion (I, viii).

41. *De amore* IV, i, *Opera*, p. 1330.

42. E. R. Goodenough, 'A Neo-Pythagorean Source in Philo Judaeus', *Yale Classical Studies* III (1932), pp. 115–64, with further literature. Also the same author's *By Light, Light* (1935), p. 66, and, on the singular and plural in Philo, *Jewish Symbols in the Greco-Roman Period* I (1953), pp. 49 f.

43. *De amore* IV, vi, *Opera*, pp. 1333 f. ('Amor animas reducit in coelum').

Since the ordinary rules of evidence were reversed by the Orphic rule of concealment, it is not surprising that the Orphic theologians managed to extract their hybrid gods from texts unsuspected of mysticism. The more inauspicious a classical reference was, the more acceptable it became as a sacred witness: for if Venus–Diana represented a mystery, it was very proper of Virgil not to dwell on the figure, and mention her only once in the whole of the *Aeneid*.[44] Plato did even better by never mentioning at all that Athena and Eros were worshipped jointly in the grounds of the Academy (the fact was casually revealed by Athenaeus).[45] Nor did Cicero, when he acquired a Hermathena for his Tusculan villa, display any of his usual volubility;[46] but that was all the more reason for Bocchi, when he adopted the emblem for his academy, to interpret it as a secret admonition in the style of *festina lente*: Combine the swiftness of the god of eloquence (Hermes) with the steadfastness of the goddess of wisdom (Athena)![47]

The belief that because a thing is not stressed it must be important is not entirely without merit, but it can lead to exegetic madness. Gibbon ridiculed a faith which taught its adherents that a 'contradictory doctrine *must* be divine since no man alive could have thought of inventing it'. By the same token it is a prejudice to assume that a thing must be central because it looks marginal. Yet, the supposition that some things which look marginal *may* be central is one of those judicious reflections that rarely fail to open up new fields of knowledge because they introduce a change of focus. Not only is it true that great discoveries have generally 'centred' on the 'fringes' of knowledge but the very progress of knowledge may be regarded as a persistent shift of centre. In Cusanus and Pico, a sharp

44. *Aeneid* I, 315.

45. *Deipnosophists* XIII, 561D–E. The union of Athena and Eros recurs in Pico, *Conclusiones . . . in doctrinam Platonis*, no. 14; also in Rhodiginus, *Antiquae lectiones* IX, xxiv, p. 449.

46. *Ad Atticum* I, i, 5; I, iv, 3.

47. In Bocchi's *Hermathena* (symbolon no. cii) the two gods are joined by Eros (like Hermes and Heracles in the *Deipnosophists*, loc. cit.). A combination of Hermes and Athena, with the suggestion that it typifies the Academy, figured also in Ficino's dedication of Plato's *Statesman* to Federigo da Montefeltro (*Opera*, pp. 855, 1294). See also Cartari, *Imagini*, p. 356, s.v. 'Minerva'.

instinctive awareness of the rule, that any given knowledge may be transcended, was condensed into a mystical superstition: a belief that all important truths are cryptic. But from this bleak, retardative axiom of faith, perhaps the most perilous vestige of Neoplatonism, they drew a prophetic rule of learning: that it is more profitable to explore the hidden bypaths of knowledge than to tread the common highways. Enlightenment and obscurantism were tightly linked in the method of *docta ignorantia*.

Perhaps it is possible now to understand more clearly why the 'hybrid gods', who were at best a bypath of classical mythology (if not a remnant of a pre-classical phase),[48] seemed so important to the humanists of the Orphic persuasion. These gods seemed closer to the secret centre of myth than the plain gods, of well-defined character, who occupied the common highways. If they resembled monsters and abnormal portents, it was not because of a wilful preference for the grotesque. The unusual subject demanded an unusual tone: for it would be nonsense to make *mirabilia* look familiar. Like all valid symbols, the fabulous Orphic images reveal what they appear to conceal. Their meaning requires, to be properly expressed, a transcendent and hence implausible vocabulary which may produce laughter as well as awe, and even a Christian kind of reverence. For it should be noticed that in composite gods the tension between chastity and passion, or penitence and pleasure, which is generally associated with the conflict between Christianity and paganism, was revealed as a phase of paganism itself.

*

But however irregular and unfamiliar to the outward view, the hybrid gods of Orphic theology consistently follow a logic of their own, which is the logic of concealment. And by that logic their meaning can be 'unfolded' or made more explicit, provided the rule of 'infolding' has been mastered first, which Cusanus distinguished from *explicatio* by the quaint but fitting name of

48. cf. Jessen's article 'Hermaphroditos' in Pauly–Wissowa VIII (1913), pp. 714–21; also Usener, 'Zwillingsbildung', *Strena Helbigiana* (1900), pp. 315–33; Hermann Baumann, *Das doppelte Geschlecht* (1955). On the revival of hybrid gods in Hellenistic mysteries, see below, page 213 note 66.

complicatio. When the Venus–Virgo becomes 'unfolded' in the three Graces, as we have seen, each Grace represents a less 'complicated' state of mind than the 'infolded' Venus from whom they descend. Theoretically, the process of explication could be continued indefinitely; and the farther it proceeds, the plainer are the elements obtained. But so long as the elements remain interdependent, they all partake of each other's nature, and pure externality is never reached. Absolute plainness is therefore an illusion produced by a severance of that universal link through which even the most 'explicit' members of this expanding series retain an inherent 'complication'. *Castitas*, as represented by one of the Graces, would become 'pure and simple' only if she gave up her part as a Grace. Only then would she merge with the stock figure of purity, a plain Diana or Minerva alien to Venus. And the same applies, *mutatis mutandis*, to the plain Venus herself, the stock figure of Pleasure. Thus a marked and critical breach remains, which separates even the lowest or plainest of unfolded terms from a literal-minded statement.

It is useful to look at the breach from the opposite side by studying the logic of an exoteric fable. In *The Choice of Hercules*, for example, which is the perfect instance of a popular moral, the terms of the argument are literal and fixed. Voluptas is appointed to tempt the hero with her specious allurements, while Virtus acquaints him in all her austerity with the arduous prospect of heroic labours: and it may be expected of a reliable Hercules that he will not remain suspended between them. The choice is clear because the two opposites, having been introduced in a complete disjunction, obey the logical principle of the excluded middle: *tertium non datur*. It is the absence of any transcendent alternative which renders the moral so respectable; but although the humanists used it profusely in their exoteric instruction,[49] they left no doubt that, for a Platonic initiate, it was but the crust, and not the marrow.[50] 'So far, indeed, we are

49. As is shown by the comprehensive collection in Panofsky, *Hercules am Scheide-wege*. It is the more remarkable that in the mystical interpretation of Hercules (cf. Marcel Simon, *Hercule et le Christianisme*, 1955) the labours of Hercules and his self-immolation are the chief subjects, while the fable of his Choice receives little attention, the Pythagorean cipher for the crossroads notwithstanding.

50. Always to the point, even in his errors, Carlyle's Teufelsdröckh mistook

in the light,' wrote Pico, 'but God has placed his dwelling in darkness.' In Ben Jonson's *Pleasure Reconciled to Virtue*, a sequence of 'knots' is introduced by the dancing master Daedalus, who interweaves the two opposites in a perfect maze; and his labyrinthian designs are accompanied by a warning that, while the 'first figure' should suggest the contrast of Virtue and Pleasure as in the Choice of Hercules,[51] it is the purpose of the dance to 'entwine' Pleasure and Virtue beyond recognition:

> *Come on, come on! and where you go,*
> *So interweave the curious knot,*
> *As ev'n the observer scarce may know*
> *Which lines are Pleasure's, and which not.*

In the course of tying the knot, the 'unfolded' figures, which appeared familiar because they were closer to exoteric terms, are united – 'infolded' – in a mysterious cipher which comprises the contraries as one; and when 'complication' reaches its height, and the opposites become indistinguishable, all multiplicity vanishes in the One beyond Being – the absolutely unfamiliar, for which there is no fitting image or name.

It follows that all mystical images, because they retain a certain articulation by which they are distinguished as 'hedges' or *umbraculae*, belong to an intermediate state, which invites further 'complication' above, and further 'explication' below. They are never final in the sense of a literal statement, which would fix the mind to a given point; nor are they final in the sense of the mystical Absolute in which all images would vanish. Rather they keep the mind in continued suspense by presenting the paradox of an 'inherent transcendence'; they persistently hint at more than they say. It is a mistake, therefore, to overlook a certain ambiguity in the praise of hieroglyphs which Ficino, and after him Giordano Bruno, adopted from

---

conversion (in Greek ἐπιστροφή) for a word and experience unknown to the ancients: 'they had only some *Choice of Hercules*' (*Sartor Resartus* II, x). Against such a view see Nock, *Conversion*, pp. 23–32; Festugière, *Personal Religion among the Greeks* (1954), pp. 42 ff.

51. 'First figure out the doubtful way, / At which a while all youth should stay, / Where she [Pleasure] and Virtue did contend, / Which should have Hercules to friend.'

an incidental remark by Plotinus.[52] In a famous passage of the fifth *Ennead*, Plotinus had suggested that Egyptian ciphers are more suitable for sacred script than alphabetic writing because they represent the diverse parts of a discourse as implicit, and thus concealed, in one single form.[53] Since Pico ascribed the same virtue to the writing of Hebrew without vowels,[54] it is legitimate to suspect that the Renaissance speculations on 'implicit signs' were not concerned with a positive theory of optical intuition,[55] but with that far less attractive subject called steganography, the cryptic recording of sacred knowledge. Because God, in the opinion of Ficino, 'has knowledge of things not by a multiplicity of thoughts about an object, but by a simple and firm grasp of its essence', it seemed only right that the Egyptian priests had imitated the divine comprehension in their script, signifying 'the divine mysteries not by the use of minutely written letters, but of whole figures of plants, trees, and beasts'.[56] But as Erasmus observed in the *Adagia*, the content of these figures was not meant to be open to direct inspection, or 'accessible to anyone's guess' (*ut non cuivis statim promptum esset conjicere*); they

52. Ficino, *In Plotinum* V, viii (*Opera*, p. 1768); Giordano Bruno, *De magia* (*Opera latina*, ed. F. Tocco and H. Vitelli, III, 1891, pp. 411 f.).

53. *Enneads* V, viii, 6. Cf. Boas, in *The Hieroglyphics of Horapollo*, pp. 21 f. It should be remembered that the passage develops the praise of 'undrawn images', ἀγάλματα οὐ γεγραμμένα (*Enneads* V, viii, 5), a term not too partial to the visual arts. Plotinus clearly distinguishes between ἄγαλμα and εἴδωλον, and he applies the term ἀθρόον ('implicit') only to the former. Since his use of language is always paraphrastic and hinting, it should not be pressed for a downright 'theory of hieroglyphs'.

54. *Conclusiones cabalisticae numero LXXI*, no. 70: 'Per modum legendi sine punctis in lege, et modus scribendi res divinas et unialis continentia per indeterminatum ambitum rerum divinarum nobis ostenditur.' Reuchlin, *De verbo mirifico* (1514), fols. g iv^v–h iv^v, shows in some detail how the writing of Hebrew without vowels, which allows for multiple verbal expansion, has the same cryptic virtue as the designing of hieroglyphs.

55. The exaggerated inferences recently drawn concerning 'the visual image in Neoplatonic thought', now summarized in Chastel, *Marsile Ficin et l'art*, pp. 72, 77 notes 5 f., rest on a confusion between the 'intuitive' as the implicit, and the 'intuitive' as the visual, which is scarcely improved by the suggestion that the two 'could easily merge' (Gombrich, 'Icones symbolicae', op. cit., p. 171). For the assumption that Ficino's philosophy taught or implied 'the superiority of *visual* intuition over discursive reason' (ibid., p. 184, italics mine), there is no evidence in his writings. Ficino placed the visual medium below the verbal, a sacred name being higher and holier for him than a sacred image; see above, page 127 note 48.   56. Ficino, loc. cit.

presupposed in the reader a full acquaintance with the properties of each animal, plant, or thing represented: 'is demum collatis eorum symbolorum coniecturis aenigma sententiae deprehendebat.'[57] Thus, contrary to the divine intelligence which the reading of hieroglyphs is supposed to foreshadow, the intuitive grasp of them depends on discursive knowledge. Unless one knows what a hieroglyph means, one cannot *see* what it says. But once one has acquired the relevant knowledge, 'unfolded' by more or less exoteric instruction, one can take pleasure in finding it 'infolded' in an esoteric image or sign.[58]

Thus the rules of 'explication' and 'complication', by which we

57. *Adagia*, s.v. *festina lente* (digression on hieroglyphs). See also Crinitus, *De honesta disciplina* VII, ii; Caelius Rhodiginus, *Antiquae lectiones* XVI, xxv; Gyraldus, *De poetarum historia* I (*Opera* II, 18). In a sketch by G. A. Dosio of an Egyptian obelisk, the hieroglyphs are being deciphered by four classical commentators whose names are inscribed below the scene: Diodorus Siculus, Strabo, Tacitus, Pliny (cf. C. Hülsen, *Das Skizzenbuch des Giovannantonio Dosio*, 1933, p. 42, pl. cxvi, fol. 88ʳ). The relevant passages are Diodorus III, iv; Strabo XVII, i, 27, 46; Tacitus, *Annals* II, lx; Pliny, *Natural History* XXXVI, lxiv–lxxiv.

58. It follows that Ficino's praise of the *Hieroglyphica* of Horapollo, however interesting as a scholium to Plotinus (loc. cit., *Opera*, p. 1768), gives only an incomplete account of their Renaissance use. It is noticeable, for example, that while Plotinus had stressed the implicit understanding of hieroglyphs, and Ficino had praised them for their power of contracting many thoughts into one single form, those who designed 'authentic hieroglyphs' after classical monuments were particularly attracted by the reverse possibility, that of expanding the symbols into an additive picture-script, whose parts were to be read like words and sentences of a discursive language; cf. Hülsen, 'Le illustrazioni della *Hypnerotomachia Polifili* e le antichità di Roma', *Bibliofilia* XII (1910), pp. 172 f., figs. 22 f.; L. Volkmann, *Bilderschriften der Renaissance* (1923), p. 16, fig. 5. The *Hypnerotomachia* carried that method to extremes by translating Latin sentences, word by word, into hieroglyphic designs which, contrary to Ficino's argument, consisted always of several symbols, never of one alone. Even the famous compound of anchor and dolphin for *festina tarde* was not left to itself, but juxtaposed to a circle, for *semper*, so as to produce a discursive sequence: 'semper festina tarde' (our fig. 55). In an instructive woodcut from the *Weisskunig*, in which Burgkmair represents himself as painting hieroglyphs under the dictation of Maximilian (Burkhard no. 125, pl. 45), the canvas is filled with eleven symbols. To suggest that their meaning, hitherto undisclosed, is meant to be grasped 'in a flash', is a *reductio ad absurdum* of that theory. Dürer's *Mysterium der aegyptischen Buchstaben*, designed as a eulogy of Maximilian, is a compound of thirteen separate hieroglyphs corresponding to 'every single phrase in Pirckheimer's Latin and Stabius's German text' (Panofsky, *Dürer* I, p. 177). The disturbing effect of the crowded design recalls the *ars memorativa*, and may have been intended, in this particular instance, to serve the same purpose, cf. above, page 27 note 3.

found the Orphic images to be governed, apply to Renaissance hieroglyphs as well. They are, all of them, 'hedges' or *umbraculae*, infested with the paradox of self-transcendence. For it is a general rule of Neoplatonic symbolism, because Pan is always inherent in Proteus, that any figure tends to engender others; they abhor isolation. This explains why the mystical language so easily grows luxuriant, and produces the kind of cumulative verbiage which disfigures many Neoplatonic tracts, and is often carried over into visual imagery.[59] The Neoplatonic discipline tried to restrain and direct the unruly impulse without depriving it of its poetry. The contraction and expansion of metaphors were subjected to a few simple dialectical rules which were to secure a rich but reasonable 'genealogy of the gods', a succession of steps which, broadening downward and narrowing towards the top, promised ecstasy while advising prudence.

'Now the Supreme, because within it are no differences,' says Plotinus in the sixth *Ennead*, 'is eternally present; but we achieve such presence only when our differences are lost. . . . We have at all times our centre There, though we do not at all times look Thither. We are like a company of singing dancers, who may turn their gaze outward and away, notwithstanding they have the choirmaster for centre; but when they are turned towards him, then they sing true and are truly centred upon him. Even so we encircle the Supreme always, and when we break the circle, it shall be our utter dissolution and cessation of being; but our eyes are not at all times fixed upon the Centre. Yet in the vision thereof is our attainment and our repose and the end of all discord, God in his dancers and God the true Centre of the dance.'[60]

There is no question, though, that in the absence of discretion a

59. A characteristic example is a double triad engraved by Robetta (Hind, *Early Italian Engraving*, no. D.II.33, pl. 296), which goes under the wrong title *The Choice of Hercules*, although the sky in the picture is filled with *amoretti* and *erotes* swinging arrows and strewing flowers, which does not fit Xenophon's moral in the least. In both triads Voluptas and Amor clearly outweigh the solitary Virtus, whose chastity is parodied by the 'chaste book' which covers one of the frivolous Graces. Panofsky, *Hercules am Scheidewege*, pp. 104 f. (pl. 48), after an inconclusive attempt to vindicate the traditional title, dismisses the engraving (p. 144) as 'eine ziemlich wilde Kompilation'.

60. *Enneads* VI, ix, 8, tr. Dodds.

perfunctory handling of the Orphic rules could change a poet into a pedant. In the *Faerie Queene* the 'unfolding' of Agape into her three sons (IV, ii, 41–3) is no more than a didactic exercise. The three Graces could hardly have been more circumspect in their dance than these three knights are in the display of their martial equipment; but despite the fatuity of the verses, it may be instructive, as a schoolroom lesson in mystical 'explication', to quote them here in full:

> Amongst those knights there were three brethren bold,
>   Three bolder brethren never were yborn,
>   Born of one mother in one happy mold,
>   Born at one burden in one happy morn;
>   Thrice happy mother, and thrice happy morn,
>   That bore three such, three such not to be found;
>   Her name was Agape whose children werne
>   All three as one, the first hight Priamond,
> The second Diamond, the youngest Triamond.
>
> Stout Priamond, but not so strong to strike,
>   Strong Diamond, but not so stout a knight,
>   But Triamond was stout and strong alike:
>   On horseback used Triamond to fight,
>   And Priamond on foot had more delight,
>   But horse and foot knew Diamond to wield:
>   With curtax used Diamond to smite,
>   And Triamond to handle spear and shield,
> But spear and curtax both us'd Priamond in field.
>
> These three did love each other dearly well,
>   And with so firm affection were allied,
>   As if but one soul in them all did dwell,
>   Which did her power into three parts divide;
>   Like three fair branches budding far and wide.
>   That from one root deriv'd their vital sap:
>   And like that root, that does her life divide,
>   Their mother was, and had full blessed hap,
> These three so noble babes to bring forth at one clap.

But if Spenser seems unduly obvious in tracing the logic of 'unfolding', he is also quite fearless in tracing the reverse, the 'infolding' of opposites into one. The goddess of Concord, whom he encounters at the entrance to the temple of Venus (IV, x, 31–6), he finds attended by Love and Hate,

> Begotten by two fathers of one mother,
> Though of contrary natures each to other.

And the veiled statue of Venus herself, in whom these contraries are united (IV, x, 41), is mysteriously described by the poet as Hermaphrodite:

> The cause why she was covered with a veil,
>   Was hard to know, for that her priests the same
>   From people's knowledge labour'd to conceal.
>   But sooth it was not sure for womanish shame,
>   Nor any blemish, which the work might blame;
>   But for, they say, she hath both kinds in one,
>   Both male and female, both under one name:
>   She sire and mother is herself alone,
> Begets and eke conceives, nor needeth other none.[61]

It might be thought that at this point the Renaissance mystic had really surrendered to 'the abominations of the heathen': the barbarous belief, that the monstrous is higher and more divine than the normal, would seem impossible to reconcile, even by the most

---

61. Mythographical sources for the *Venus biformis* in Gyraldus I, 394 f.; also Cartari, s.v. 'Venere barbata'. At the entrance to Spenser's temple of Venus, the goddess of Concord adroitly coaxes the hero to pass slightly off-centre between Love and Hate, whom she holds in precarious balance: 'By her I entring halfe dismayed was', etc. (IV, x, 36). Although 'Peace and Friendship' are named as twin-offspring of Concord (IV, x, 34, line 2) and serve as twin-reconcilers in other parts of Book IV by supplying 'double mean terms' between Hate and Love (cf. Alastair Fowler, *Spenser and the Numbers of Time*, 1964, pp. 26 ff.), it should be noted that Spenser did *not* introduce them as allegorical actors into the dramatic pageant of Love, Hate, and Concord: here Concord performs her difficult office unassisted. It would indeed have been absurd to complete the tetrad on the *threshold* of Venus, hardly the place for a 'stable balance' (cf. K. Henniger, Jr, 'Some Renaissance Versions of the Pythagorean Tetrad', in *Studies in the Renaissance* VIII, 1958, pp. 7–35).

dexterous of poetic theologians, with the Judeo-Christian code of propriety. And yet, any reader of Ezekiel or the book of Revelation will know that their accounts are filled with miracles and visions which would sustain the anti-classical faith that, when God appears to His prophets, His supernatural powers are displayed through monstrous apparitions. The hope that the transition from the One to the Many might take place 'simply' and 'normally' would have to dispense with the supreme disproportion between Pan and Proteus, with that 'friendly enmity' in the universe, of which Pico said that without it there would be no creation but only God.[62] In the Bible itself, the transition from the singular to the plural is mysteriously abrupt in Genesis i, 27: 'So God created man in his own image, in the image of God created he him; male and female created he them.' Philo and Origen inferred from this passage – and their authority ranked high with Renaissance Platonists[63] – that the first and original man was androgynous; that the division into male and female belonged to a later and lower state of creation; and that, when all created things return to their maker, the unfolded and divided state of man will be re-infolded in the divine essence.[64]

Pico, who had expounded in the *Commento* that man was originally of a Janus-nature, eagerly seized on Origen's interpretation. 'It

62. *Commento*, quoted above, page 88.

63. Wind, 'The Revival of Origen', loc. cit., pp. 412–24; D. P. Walker, 'Origène en France au début du XVIᵉ siècle', *Courants religieux et humanisme* (1959), pp. 101–19. For the revival of Philo see the comprehensive bibliography by H. L. Goodhart and E. R. Goodenough, appended to Goodenough, *The Politics of Philo Judaeus* (1938), pp. 125–321, particularly pp. 180 f., 'Codices containing the Latin translation of Lilius Typhernas', and pp. 308 f., 'Mention of Philo in Printed Books of the Fifteenth Century', nos. 1508–79.

64. Origen, *In Genesim* I, 15 (*Patr. graec.* XII, 158): 'Videamus autem etiam per allegoriam quomodo ad imaginem Dei homo factus masculus et femina est', etc. *In Canticum Canticorum* II, xi (ibid. XIII, 134) on Adam as prophet of the *magnum mysterium*: 'et erunt ambo in carne una' (Christus-Ecclesia). A related statement in Augustine, *De Trinitate* XII, vii. For the Jewish–Platonic exegesis, from which Origen's view derives in part, see Philo, *De opificio mundi* 76; *Quis rerum divinarum heres* 164, both with reference to Genesis i, 27 as proof of the androgynous Adam. In his theory of 'creation by dichotomy' or the 'Logos as cutter' (λόγος τομεύς) Philo relied (cf. above, page 202) on Genesis xv, 10: 'and he divided them in the midst'. These niceties did not escape Sir Thomas Browne, *Pseudodoxia epidemica* III, xvii; *Religio medici* I, xxi. For a weird selection from pietistic texts in praise of the androgynous Adam, see E. Benz, *Adam, der Mythus vom Urmenschen* (1955).

is not without mystery' (*non item vacat mysterio*), he wrote in the *Heptaplus* on Genesis i, 27, 'that He created man [the celestial Adam] male and female. For it is the prerogative of celestial souls that they fulfil simultaneously the two functions of mental contemplation and of physical care, without either of them obstructing or impeding the other. And the ancients in particular, as we may observe also in the Orphic Hymns, adopted the custom of designating these two forces inherent in the same substance ... by the names of male and female.'[65] In *De occulta philosophia*, Agrippa of Nettesheim listed the Orphic and Hermetic passages at which Pico had merely hinted;[66] and Leone Ebreo added, in the *Dialoghi d'amore*, that Aristophanes' fable of the 'androgynous man' was 'translated' from the Bible: 'male and female created he them'.[67] Among French humanists of the sixteenth century *l'androgyne de Platon* became so acceptable an image for the universal man[68] that a painter could apply it without

65. *Heptaplus* II, vi (Garin, p. 242).

66. *De occulta philosophia* III, viii, p. 222: '[Mercurius Trismegistus] vocat etiam deum utriusque sexus foecunditate plenissimum ... et Orpheus naturam mundi Iovemque mundanum marem simul appellat et foeminam: adseritque utrunque diis sexum inesse. Hinc in Hymnis Minervam sic alloquitur: Vir quidem et foemina pro- ducta es. Et Apuleius in libro quem scripsit de Mundo, ex Orphica theologia hunc versiculum traduxit de Iove: Iuppiter et mas est et foemina, nescia mortis.' On the phoenix as hermaphrodite cf. Festugière, 'Le symbole du phénix et le mysticisme hermétique', *Monuments Piot* XXXVIII (1941), pp. 148 f. In the *Corpus Hermeticum*, ed. Nock–Festugière, see particularly *Poimandres* I, 9; 12; 15; *Asclepius* 20 f. Further examples in Guthrie, *Orpheus and Greek Religion*, pp. 101 f. (on the androgynous Phanes); Dieterich, *Abraxas*, p. 79, with reference to Servius, *In Aeneidem* IV, 638; Nock, *Conversion*, p. 115 f., after a document preserved in Hippolytus, *Refutatio omnium haeresium* V: 'It expounds the content of various legends on the first man, throws light on the triple nature of the soul from "Assyrian mysteries" ... and refers to Phrygian, Egyptian, and Greek mysteries, the Phrygian and the Greek both giving the concept of a bisexual Heavenly Man.' A useful survey in M. Delcourt, *Hermaphro- dite: mythes et rites de la bisexualité dans l'antiquité classique* (1958), pp. 104–29: 'Le symbole androgyne dans les mythes philosophiques.' On the Romantic revival of these speculations, see Fritz Giese, *Der romantische Charakter* I (1919): 'Die Entwicklung des Androgynenproblems in der Frühromantik.'

67. '... la favola è tradutta da ... la sacra istoria di Moïse de la creazione. ... Maschio e femina creò essi.' *Dialoghi d'amore*, ed. Caramella, pp. 291 f. See also Francesco Giorgio, *De harmonia mundi totius* II, v, 4.

68. cf. Festugière, *La philosophie de l'amour de Marsile Ficin et son influence sur la littérature française*, p. 42 note 3, with references to Tyard, Du Bellay, Marguerite de Navarre, and above all (pp. 122 ff.) to Héroët's *L'androgyne de Platon* (1536). Ronsard's

impropriety to an allegorical portrait of Francis I (fig. 80). The shock of seeing the bearded warrior display the anatomy of a *virago* is lessened by the emblematic style of the painting which reduces the portrait to a hieroglyphic design, a mystical cipher of divine perfection:

> *O France heureuse, honore donc la face*
> *De ton grand roi qui surpasse Nature:*
> *Car l'honorant tu sers en même place*
> *Minerve, Mars, Diane, Amour, Mercure.*[69]

In their extravagance these courtly compliments revert to a primitive way of picturing the numinous: they conceive of the supernatural as composite.[70]

Perhaps it should also be mentioned here that in alchemy the Hermaphrodite, called *Rebis*, represents the apex of transmutation; which accounts for his regular appearance in alchemical books – in Paracelsus, 'Trismosin', or 'Basil Valentine'. As Bidez observed in the preface to his Catalogue of Alchemical Manuscripts,[71] alchemical symbols are a deposit (perhaps the *caput mortuum*?) of Neoplatonism; Cumont's *disciples infidèles de Plotin* being the lineal ancestors of Paracelsus. The spiritualization of matter attempted by Plotinus (in

---

attitude was less tolerant. Although much given to Platonic conceits, he could treat them (like Donne) with refreshing impatience: 'Bien que l'esprit humain s'enfle par la doctrine de Platon ...' (*Sonnets pour Hélène* I, L; *Œuvres complètes*, ed. Gustave Cohen, I, 1950, p. 236). On Leone Ebreo he wrote a brilliantly coarse and mocking sonnet (ed. cit. II, p. 674); and in presenting a copy of that author to Charles IX, he advised the king to attend to earthly love and leave the celestial to the gods (*Odes* V, viii: 'Au roi Charles, lui donnant un Léon Hébrieu', ed. cit. I, p. 611). These acid reflections come close to Montaigne, *Essais* III, v: 'Mon page fait l'amour, et l'entend: lisez lui Léon hébreu et Ficin; on parle de lui, de ses pensées et de ses actions, et si n'y entend rien. ... Si j'étais du métier, je naturaliserais l'art autant comme ils artialisent la nature. Laissons là Bembo et Equicola.'

69. Bibliothèque Nationale, Cabinet des Estampes; cf. Exhibition catalogue *L'Europe humaniste* (Brussels 1955), pl. 49.

70. E. H. Kantorowicz, *The King's Two Bodies* (1957), pp. 10, 390, 502; Wind, 'In Defence of Composite Portraits', *Journal of the Warburg Institute* I (1937), pp. 138–42.

71. *Catalogue des manuscrits alchimiques grecs* I (1924), p. iv.

the fourth *Ennead*)[72] was understood by the alchemists as a material-
ization of spirits, to be achieved by a series of concoctions and ceremonious conflagrations that mimicked a mystical purification rite.
The spiritual ingredient in the alchemist's furnace was appreciated
by Sir Thomas Browne: 'The smattering I have of the Philosophers
Stone (which is something more than the perfect exaltation of Gold)
hath taught me a great deal of Divinity, and instructed my belief,
how that immortal spirit and incorruptible substance of my soul
may lie obscure, and sleep awhile within this house of flesh.'[73] In
an illustration of Henricus Khunrath's alchemical kitchen the
words *festina lente* and *maturandum*, employed by Gellius and
Erasmus to designate a moral ideal of adventurous prudence, are
inscribed on the vessels of transmutation,[74] to suggest that slow
heat, a controlled sort of boiling, is conducive to the 'exaltation of
gold'.[75]

72. A universe of elective affinities emerges from *Enneads* IV, iii, 11 f. and IV, iv,
32–41, summarized by Ficino in *De amore* VI, x, and elaborated in his Plotinian commentary *De vita coelitus comparanda* (*Opera*, pp. 493–572), on which see Garin, 'Le
"elezioni" e il problema dell'astrologia', in *Umanesimo e esoterismo*, ed. E. Castelli
(1960), pp. 19 ff. Cf. also Ficino's translation of a relevant extract from Proclus, *De
sacrificio et magia* (*Opera*, pp. 1928 f.).

73. *Religio medici* I, xxxix. On pastoral edification through alchemy see J. Ruska,
Tabula Smaragdina (1926), pp. 23 ff.: 'Verquickung von Alchemie und Seelsorge';
raised to a system by C. G. Jung, *Psychologie und Alchemie* (1944).

74. Reproduced in G. F. Hartlaub, *Der Stein der Weisen* (1959), fig. 40; also John
Read, *Prelude to Chemistry* (1936), pl. 52, from Henricus Khunrath, *Amphitheatrum
sapientiae terrenae* (1609). On *festina lente* or *maturandum* as a moral rule, see above,
pages 98 ff.

75. Is it accidental that this debased form of the Neoplatonic tradition should have
lent itself in recent years to psychological probings that rely on Janet's *abaissement du
niveau mental*? On the use of that principle, see Jung and Kerényi, *Essays on a Science
of Mythology* (1949), p. 103; also M. Éliade, *Méphistophélès et l'androgyne* (1962), on
'expériences religieuses diffuses' (p. 10) belonging to 'la phase présystématique de la
pensée' (p. 99). A few critical comments in Wind, *Art and Anarchy* (1963), pp. 177 ff.
What attracted Jung to a book like the *Hypnerotomachia* was a debased French version
of 1600, whose editor, Béroalde de Verville, had brought the argument down to an
alchemical level (*Psychologie und Alchemie*, p. 66). On the same principle Jung reduced
Cartari's *Occasione*, with flying forelock, sphere, and razor (ibid., p. 447), to an alchemical 'Mercurius auf der Erdkugel'; Sebastian Brant's mnemonic figure for the
gospel according to John (p. 561) to an alchemical *coniunctio*, a 'Bruder–Schwester-
Paar' (p. 559); Jean Thenaud's *dame Nécessité* governing the Fates (= Plato, Republic
616C–617C) to a 'mütterliche Figur' (p. 76). In short, an erosion of categories.

But it would be false to conclude this account without referring, however elliptically, to Donne, who managed to distil and assimilate the mystical tradition so completely to his own spirit that he created it afresh, both as a poet and as a religious critic, thus rescuing it from degradation. Paracelsus, Cusanus, Pico della Mirandola, not to forget 'our singular Origen', are repeatedly cited in the writings of Donne.[76] And from Donne's whimsical remark about 'Gregory's and Bede's spectacles, by which one saw Origen, who deserved so well of the Christian Church, burning in Hell',[77] it would seem certain that he approved of Pico's defence of Origen in the *Disputatio de Origenis salute*. In the humorous portrait which Donne drew of Pico in the *Catalogus librorum*, the 'Judeo-Christian Pythagoras' is engaged in demonstrating the coincidence of opposites by an irresistibly felicitous image: he proves 'the numbers 66 and 99 to be identical if you hold the leaf upside down'.[78] But the doctrine here ridiculed by Donne is one to which he himself was so passionately committed that he engraved it on his tomb. In the Latin epitaph he composed for himself, HIC LICET IN OCCIDUO CINERE ASPICIT EUM CUIUS NOMEN EST ORIENS,[79] the words *oriens* and *occiduus*

76. A few examples chosen at random from *Essays in Divinity* (ed. E. M. Simpson, 1951): Origen, pp. 8, 25, 45; Cusanus, p. 9; Pico, pp. 10, 13 f.; Paracelsus, p. 11. Other or similar examples could be drawn from *Biothanatos, Pseudo-Martyr, LXXX Sermons, Catalogus librorum, Ignatius his Conclave*, or the *Letters*. On Paracelsian images in Donne's poetry, see W. A. Murray, 'Donne and Paracelsus', *Review of English Studies* XXV (1949), pp. 115–23.

77. *Ignatius his Conclave*, in John Donne, *Complete Poetry and Selected Prose*, ed. J. Hayward (1936), p. 363.

78. *Catalogus librorum*, ed. E. M. Simpson (1930), p. 32. Donne's admiration of Pico, it should be remembered, was never uncritical. The principle of the whole in the part, for example, by which Pico, in the *Heptaplus*, 'found all Moses's learning in every verse of Moses', Donne rejected as bad exegesis. 'Since our merciful God hath afforded us the whole and entire book, why should we tear it into rags, or rend the seamless garment?' (*Essays in Divinity*, p. 14). But *contradictoria coincidunt in natura uniali* was to him, as to Pico, the ultimate wisdom, and from that opinion he never varied. How the perfect parody, quoted above, on the very part of Pico's doctrine of which Donne approved, could have suggested to a reader of Donne an 'apparent reversal of opinion on Pico della Mirandola' (C. M. Coffin, *John Donne and the New Philosophy*, 1937, p. 248) is difficult to understand. Surely, men less brilliant and paradoxical than Donne have enjoyed parodies of doctrines they held in esteem.

79. Izaak Walton, *The Life of Dr John Donne* (Oxford 1950), p. 79.

answer each other, meeting like 'the farthest East and the farthest West'[80] – 'so death doth touch the Resurrection'.[81]

> *There I should see a sun, by rising set,*
> *And by that setting endless day beget.*[82]

On the word *oriens*, East, he wrote a curious commentary in which he explained it as a name with two opposite prophetic meanings: '*Oriens nomen eius*, the East is one of Christ's names in one prophet; and *Filius Orientis est Lucifer*, the East is one of the devil's names in another, and these two differ diametrically.'[83] (In the epitaph, the use of the indicative *aspicit* might seem strangely positive in a dying man, writing about himself: for how could Donne feel assured of the beatific vision? But if *cuius nomen est Oriens* refers alternatively to the Lord of Heaven whom Donne hoped to face, and to the doom of hell, then the indicative mode is right.) To evoke by one word these contradictory prospects is perhaps the acme of dialectical suspense; but in writing *To Mr Tilman after he had taken orders*, Donne did not shrink from claiming for his own profession the 'prerogative' of Pico's celestial Adam:

> *How brave are those who with their engines can*
> *Bring man to heaven and heaven again to man . . .*
> *Both these in thee are in thy calling knit*
> *And make thee now a blest Hermaphrodite.*

80. Letter to Sir Robert Ker (Gosse, *Life and Letters* II, 1898, p. 191); also in *LXXX Sermons*, no. 55, cf. *The Divine Poems*, ed. H. Gardner (1952), p. 108.

81. *Hymn to God my God, in my sickness.*

82. *Goodfriday, 1613. Riding Westward.*

83. Letter to Sir Robert Ker, loc. cit.

CHAPTER XIV

THE CONCEALED GOD

THE doctrine that Pan is hidden in Proteus, that mutability is the secret gate through which the universal invades the particular, deserves credit for a peculiar philosophic achievement: it supplied a cogent mystical justification for an eminently sensible state of mind. 'It is written,' Cusanus said, 'that God is hidden from the eyes of all sages.'[1] But because the ultimate One is thus invisible, His visible manifestations must be manifold. Poetic pluralism is the necessary corollary to the radical mysticism of the One. To Renaissance Platonists, as to Plato himself, a generous and varied use of metaphor was essential to the proper worship of the ineffable god. 'All these names,' wrote Cusanus about the many names given to the deity by the pagans, 'are but the unfolding of the one ineffable name, and in so far as the name truly belonging to God is infinite, it embraces innumerable such names derived from particular perfections. Hence the unfolding of the divine name is multiple, and always capable of increase, and each single name is related to the true and ineffable name as the finite is related to the infinite.'[2]

Although stated in the terminology of the *Docta ignorantia*, the argument echoes a view current among ancient Neoplatonists: 'I have been initiated into many sacred mysteries in Greece,' said Apuleius, 'I learned worship on worship, rites beyond number, and various ceremonies in my zeal for truth and in my dutifulness to the gods.'[3] The same praise was bestowed on Proclus by Marinus,[4] on Julian by Libanius;[5] and before them Philo had extended the same principle to a multiple Hebrew revelation: 'If ye meet with any of

1. *De ludo globi* II (*Opera*, 1514, fol. 166ʳ).
2. *De docta ignorantia* I, xxv.
3. *Apologia* 55; cf. Nock, *Conversion*, pp. 114 f.
4. *Vita Procli* xix.
5. *Orationes* XXIV, 36. See also Julian, *Orationes* VII, 237A.

the initiated, press him closely and cling to him lest he conceal from you some newer Mystery. Cling to him until ye have mastered it clearly. For I myself have been initiated by the God-beloved Moses into the Greater Mysteries. Yet when I saw the prophet Jeremiah and recognized that he was not only an initiate but a capable hierophant, I did not shrink from his company.'[6]

The charge has been made that these philosophers were illogical in their desire 'to be initiated into as many mysteries as possible', because 'logically, on the theory that the various divine names belonged to one unity, one mystery might suffice'.[7] But exactly the opposite premise was assumed, logically, by the Neoplatonists; namely, that multiple revelation is the necessary counterpart to 'the One beyond Being'. With some justice they argued that belief in a unique revelation of the One would be contrary to Plato's teaching. The *Symposium* had warned against worshipping transcendent Beauty in one embodiment only; and in the *Parmenides* (also in the seventh Letter) Plato fought the danger, of confusing the One with one of its exemplars, by introducing the method of διαγωγή, the running through of all the possible alternatives of asserting and denying the One in the Many. The pathos of the Platonic position was expressed with remarkable force by Maximus of Tyre when he concluded his defence of idols by an invocation of the hidden God:

God Himself, the father and fashioner of all that is, older than the Sun or the Sky, greater than time and eternity and all the flow of being, is unnameable by any lawgiver, unutterable by any voice, not to be seen by any eye. But we, being unable to apprehend His essence, use the help of sounds and names and pictures, of beaten gold and ivory and silver, of plants and rivers, mountain-peaks and torrents, yearning for the knowledge of Him, and in our weakness naming all that is beautiful in this world after His nature – just as happens to earthly lovers. To them the most beautiful sight will be the actual lineaments of the beloved, but for remembrance' sake they will be happy in the sight of a lyre, a little spear, a chair, perhaps, or a running-ground, or anything in the world that wakens the memory of the beloved. Why should I further examine and pass judgement about Images?

6. *De cherubim* 48 f., tr. Goodenough, *By Light, Light*, p. 231.
7. Nock, loc. cit.

Let men know what is divine (τὸ θεῖον γένος), let them know; that is all. If a Greek is stirred to the remembrance of God by the art of Pheidias, an Egyptian by paying worship to animals, another man by a river, another by fire – I have no anger for their divergences; only let them know, let them love, let them remember.[8]

Very much the same reasoning pervades Cusanus's *De pace seu concordantia fidei*. Although indispensable to a finite mind, no finite image or ritual, he argued, can be adequate to represent the infinite. But the recognition that 'between the finite and the infinite there is no middle' should not only humble the believer but also supply him with a key to religious peace; for while all religions agree in acknowledging the infinite, it is only in the finite that their differences arise. *Una religio in rituum varietate.*[9] The finite perfections of each rite, which are the cause of its collision with other rites, conceal and imply an infinite perfection, of which they are limited symbols. 'The signs vary, but not the signified.'[10]

In meditating on the 'face of God' (*De visione Dei*) Cusanus marvelled, without distress, at the many different faces ascribed to God by his votaries. 'If the lion were to ascribe thee a face, he would imagine the face of a lion, the ox would imagine that of an ox, the eagle, of an eagle.[11] Oh Lord, how marvellous is thy face, which youths cannot conceive but as youthful, men but as manly, and the aged as aged! ... Oh marvellous face, whose beauty all those who see it are insufficient to admire! The face of faces is veiled in all faces and seen in a riddle. Unveiled it is not found until one has entered, beyond all visions, into a state of secret and hidden silence,

8. *Philosophumena*, ed. Hobein, II, 10; tr. Gilbert Murray, *Five Stages of Greek Religion* (1951), p. 77 note 1. For a Renaissance translation, by Cosimo de' Pazzi, archbishop of Florence, dedicated to Julius II, see Cod. Vat. lat. 2196; also above, page 162 note 39, on Politian's reading of Maximus of Tyre.

9. *De pace seu concordantia fidei*, § 1.   10. ibid., § 17.

11. The animals mentioned (lion, ox, and eagle) are symbols of the evangelists Mark, Luke, and John. The symbol of the fourth, Matthew, is 'a man'; and the passage actually opens with the phrase 'Homo non potest iudicare nisi humaniter.' But while recalling the biblical tetramorph (cf. Ezekiel i, 10), the argument was modelled on a famous fragment of Xenophanes: 'If oxen and lions had hands and could make images, they would fashion their gods as oxen and lions' (fr. 15).

in which nothing is left of knowing or imagining a face. For so long as this obscurity is not reached, this cloud, this darkness – that is, the ignorance into which he who seeks thy face enters when he transcends all knowledge and understanding – so long can thy face be encountered only veiled. This darkness itself, however, reveals that it is here, in the transcending of all veils, that the face is present. . . . And the more densely the darkness is felt, the truer and closer is the approach, by virtue of this darkness, to the invisible light.'[12]

The union of contraries in the 'absconded God', whose blinding light is impenetrable darkness,[13] is repeated by the multifarious 'visions of God' in minor and more imperfect degrees. Hence Cusanus did not object to polytheism, or to the polymorphic views of the deity.[14] Like Proclus he regarded them as preparatory stages of initiation. 'Those who are introduced into the mysteries,' wrote Proclus, 'at first meet with manifold and multiform gods, but being entered and thoroughly initiated . . . they participate the very Deity.'[15] In *De ludo globi* Cusanus compared this law of regression, from many outward images to the inward One, with a law of nature observed by Aristotle. 'Elemental forces, according to Aristotle, have the smallest extension and the greatest power. . . . The force inherent in a spark is that of the whole fire. . . . A small seed has the strength of many grains. . . . The core of the apparent is in the occult, the outward depends on the inward. The skin and crust

---

12. *De visione Dei* vi: 'De visione faciali.'

13. 'Thy throne is darkness in the abyss of light, / A blaze of glory that forbids the sight.' Dryden, *The Hind and the Panther* I, 66 ff.

14. *De docta ignorantia* I, xxv; *De pace*, § 6. Cf. Cassirer, *Individuum und Kosmos*, p. 32.

15. *Theologia Platonica* I, iii (ed. Portus, p. 7), here quoted from the translation in Berkeley's *Siris*, § 333. Public worship in More's *Utopia* (Book II) is addressed only to the hidden deity: 'they call upon no peculiar name of god, but only Mithra [the 'Mediator' between light and darkness in Plutarch, *De Iside et Osiride* 46; *Moralia* 369E, where that supposedly Zoroastran invocation is dated 'five thousand years before the Trojan War'], in the which word they all agree together in one nature of the divine majesty whatsoever it be.' Their churches are 'all somewhat dark; howbeit that was not done through ignorance of building but, as they say, by the counsel of the priests', who held views akin to those of Donne: 'Churches are best for prayer, that have least light: / To see God only, I go out of sight.' *A Hymn to Christ, at the author's last going into Germany.*

are there because of the muscles and marrow, and these because of the invisible force that is concealed in them.'[16]

Erasmus repeated the argument in the *Adagia*, under the heading *Sileni Alcibiadis*: 'Thus the most important is always the least conspicuous. A tree flatters the eye with flowers and foliage, and exhibits the massiveness of its trunk: but the seed, from which these have their strength, what a small thing it is, and how hidden. ... Gold and gems have been concealed by Nature in the recesses of the earth. ... What is most divine and immortal in man is inaccessible to perception. ... And also in the temperament of the physical body, while phlegm and blood are familiar to the senses and tangible, that which contributes most to life is least patent, namely the spirit. And in the Universe the greatest things are invisible, like the so-called separate substances. And the supreme among these is furthest removed. ... God, unintelligible and unthinkable because He is the unique source of all.'

*

In order to guide the mind towards the hidden God, Cusanus invented experiments in metaphor, semi-magical exercises which would solemnly entertain and astonish the beholder. These serious games (*serio ludere*) consisted in finding within common experience an unusual object endowed with the kind of contradictory attributes which are difficult to imagine united in the deity. The motionless eye of God, for instance, is said to follow us everywhere. But can an eye stay at rest while it moves? In *De visione Dei* Cusanus observed that if in the painting of a head the eyes are fixed on the spectator – and having seen heads painted in that fashion, he supplied the reader with an icon of this kind[17] – the eyes will follow the spectator through

16. *De ludo globi* II, loc. cit. Also Ficino, *Theologia Platonica* VI, ii (*Opera*, pp. 161 f.). In Pierio Valeriano's *Hieroglyphica* VI, fol. 48ᵛ, the words *divina in occulto* are inscribed on a picture of Silenus.

17. Although Cusanus included the picture of an archer among his examples, and also an ill-described panel which has caused a lively debate as to whether or not it showed a self-portrait of Roger van der Weyden (cf. recently Panofsky, 'Facies illa Rogeri maximi pictoris', *Late Classical and Mediaeval Studies in Honour of A. M. Friend, Jr*, 1955, pp. 392–400, with further literature), there is no doubt that the icon which accompanied the treatise sent to the monks of Tegernsee was an image of Christ. See

a room without moving. If there are several spectators in the room, each will feel the eyes looking at him. And yet, although the eyes in the painting appear to see all and everything (*figura cuncta videntis*), it is obvious that they do not move. Of a comparable nature, we may conjecture, is the mystical 'eye of God', in which motion and rest coincide. In *De beryllo* Cusanus chose a lens, and in *De ludo globi* a newly invented toy, to show how immanence and transcendence may be combined, how an object within the world can embrace the world from without, and how the overwhelming paradoxes of God's 'absent presence' can be reflected in a harmless game, in the throwing of a bowl which runs with a bias and must be propelled slantingly to come out straight, or in the spinning of a top which, when it comes to a stand, combines a state of rest with the greatest speed of rotation.[18] Several of these paradoxes recur in a masque by Ben Jonson, in which the Sphinx proposes the following riddle to Cupid:

> *First, Cupid, you must cast about*
> *To find a world the world without,*
> *Wherein what's done, the eye doth do;*

---

preface: 'Ne tamen deficiatis in praxi, quae sensibilem talem exigit figuram, quam habere potui charitati vestrae mitto tabellam, figuram cuncta videntis tenentem, quam eiconam dei appello.' In some manuscripts of the treatise, and in letters relating to it, such images of Christ were inserted, either in the type of an *Ecce Homo* or of *Veronica's Napkin*. They are listed in E. Bohnenstaedt's translation *Von Gottes Sehen* (1944), p. 163 note 4.

18. Cusanus described the 'beryl' as a white transparent stone cut in the shape of a lens, concave and convex, to enlarge our vision by that union of opposites. In *De ludo globi* the game consists in throwing a spheroid or bowl, oblate on one side and prolate on the other. The association of this game with the *Tarocchi* (proposed by H. Brockhaus, 'Ein edles Geduldspiel', *Miscellanea in onore de I. B. Supino*, 1933, pp. 397 ff., and quoted by Hind, *Early Italian Engraving* I, pp. 221 ff.) is mistaken, since it is obviously not a game of cards. Its didacticism is strictly mechanical, how to make a slanted propulsion come out straight. 'Haec est vis mystica ludi,' says Cusanus, 'studioso exercitio posse etiam curvum globum regulari, ut post instabiles flexiones motus in regno vitae quiescat' (*Opera*, 1514, fol. clviii^v). The moral of spinning a top is discussed by Cusanus in *De possest*. Combined with more hackneyed moral precepts, both games recur in Francis Quarles's *Emblems* (1635), I, 5 and 10. From a recent study of Renaissance games of perspective it appears that some of them are based on the same principle as Cusanus's games, 'l'égalité est obtenue par l'inégal, et la stabilité par l'ébranlement' (J. Baltrušaitis, *Anamorphoses ou perspectives curieuses*, 1955, p. 7).

And is the light and treasure too.
This eye still moves, and still is fixed,
And in the pow'rs thereof are mix'd
Two contraries; which time, till now,
Nor fate knew where to join, or how.
Yet, if you hit the right upon,
You must resolve these, all, by one.[19]

Had the riddle been proposed to an immediate disciple of Cusanus, he would have answered 'God', or perhaps an 'icon' of God, a beryl, or a game of bowls. But for a Cupid addressing the court of James I God's icon was present in the person of the king, and the Sphinx aimed no higher than patriotism:

'Tis done! 'tis done! I've found it out –
Britain's the world the world without.
The king's the eye, as we do call
The sun the eye of this great all.
And is the light and treasure too:
For 'tis his wisdom all doth do.
Which still is fixed in his breast,
Yet still doth move to guide the rest.
The contraries which time till now
Nor fate knew where to join, or how,
Are Majesty and Love; which there,
And no where else, have their true sphere.[20]
Now, Sphinx, I've hit the right upon,
And do resolve these all by one:
That is, that you meant Albion.

The transference of divine traits to King and Country need not detain or disturb us here. It is a familiar subject. The interest of this particular example is that it still retains the mystical arguments of Cusanus to the letter, but already anticipates the outlook of

19. *Love Freed from Ignorance and Folly.*
20. cf. Ovid, *Metamorphoses* II, 846 f.: 'non bene conveniunt nec in una sede morantur / maiestas et amor.'

that emancipated trimmer who drew consolation from the British climate.

A direct line of descent from Cusanus to Halifax would require some audacious interpolations; but it is safe to infer that there actually were some historical links between them. Not only was the knowledge of Cusanus spread in England by the visit of Giordano Bruno, but there were other vehicles besides. The correspondence between Harvey and Spenser, for example, shows that they were studying the works of Gianfrancesco Pico, which abound in quotations from Cusanus.[21] And since Lefèvre d'Étaples had edited and published Cusanus in France,[22] the knowledge of his doctrines and method in England did not have to rely exclusively on Italian sources. Donne found Cusanus's *Cribratio Alchorani* in a collection of tracts prefaced by Luther.[23] But subsidiary influences notwithstanding,[24]

21. See above page 47 note 45; also Appendix 1, page 240.

22. Paris (Badius) 1514, ed. Faber Stapulensis. The preface, fol. aa ii^v, draws an illuminating parallel between Cusanus and Pacioli. By a curious coincidence, a physician from Pavia, named Niccolò Cusano, is also mentioned in Pacioli's *Divina proportione*, but since Pacioli says that he took part in a learned assembly at Milan on 9 February 1498, he was alive thirty-four years after the great Cusanus's death. The identity of names has caused occasional confusions, set right in Cassirer, *Individuum und Kosmos*, p. 54 note 2, but newly confounded in *Journal of the Warburg and Courtauld Institutes* XVI (1953), p. 302. On Cusanus in France, with particular reference to Faber Stapulensis, see A. Renaudet, *Préréforme et humanisme à Paris* (1953), pp. 661–5 and Index, s.v. 'Cues'.

23. Quoted in *Essays in Divinity*, p. 9. Cusanus is mentioned also in Foxe's *Acts and Monuments* (1563); cf. F. A. Yates, 'Queen Elizabeth as Astraea', *Journal of the Warburg and Courtauld Institutes* X (1947), p. 43.

24. Since those who were interested in Neoplatonic texts knew either Latin or Italian or both, the English translations are not a safe criterion of popularity. Pico was of course, as Donne put it, 'happier in no one thing in this life than in the author which writ it to us'; namely Thomas More (*The Life of Johan Picus, Earl of Mirandula, c.* 1510). Still, the *Commento* did not appear in English, under the title *A Platonic Discourse on Love*, until 1651, translated by Thomas Stanley, who also included it in his *History of Philosophy* II (1656), pp. 94–118. A translation of Cusanus's *De visione Dei* by Giles Randall was published in 1646 under the suggestive title *The Single Eye*; and the *Idiota*, 'by the famous and learned Cusanus', appeared in English in 1650. Pico's *Heptaplus*, however, had been accessible in French since 1579 in the translation of Nicolas Lefèvre de la Boderie, published in one volume with Francesco Giorgio's *Harmonia Mundi* in the translation of Guy Lefèvre de la Boderie, a combination which may possibly account for the close association of these two books in Donne's mind (e.g. *Essays in Divinity*, p. 10), although, as Garin recently observed in his introduction

Bruno's *Eroici furori*, with its dedication to Sidney, played a crucial role in 'naturalizing' the coincidence of opposites among Elizabethan writers. The book includes, under the heading *manens moveor*,[25] an emblem for the coincidence of motion and rest with which Ben Jonson's sphinx entertained her audience; and even 'the world outside the world' is already interpreted by Bruno as a compliment to England. The biblical 'separation of the waters' is associated by him with Elizabeth's island kingdom, governed by the influx of 'the prime intelligence which is like Diana among the nymphs'. These sacred waters, Bruno says, 'are not to be found on the continent of the world but *penitus toto divisim ab orbe*'.[26] They derive their supreme virtue from the secluded position of the British Isles, which seemed 'out of the world' to Virgil's shepherd:

Et penitus toto divisos orbe Britannos.

(*Eclogues* I, 66)

By the time of Halifax this famous phrase was trimmed. The seal of Charles II, which shows him as ruler of the sea, bears the altered legend:

Et penitus toto regnantes orbe Britannos.[27]

But could that proud emendation have been designed to supplant the memory of Virgil's verse? Did its effect not rather depend on evoking it? That *divisos* was the clue to *regnantes* was not too esoteric a lesson for Charles's minister. Halifax, imbued with a contrapositive

---

to the *Heptaplus* (ed. cit., p. 32 note 3; also 'Noterelle di filosofia del Rinascimento', *Rinascita* IV, 1941, pp. 419 f.), the historical connexion between Pico and Francesco Giorgio is in fact very intimate. Chiefly known to historians of art because of his musico-architectural expertise on how to build the church of San Francesco della Vigna in Venice (Schlosser, *Die Kunstliteratur*, 1924, pp. 224, 226 with further literature; now also Wittkower, *Architectural Principles in the Age of Humanism*, 1949, pp. 90-4), Francesco Giorgio, a Venetian Franciscan, transmitted his veneration for Pico to his pupil Arcangelo da Borgonuovo, another Franciscan, who wrote a defence and explanation of Pico's cabbalistic theses. Cf. Blau, *The Christian Interpretation of the Cabala*, pp. 25 ff., 119 f., 153 (s.v. 'Puteus'); Secret, *Les kabbalistes chrétiens*, pp. 268 f.

25. *Eroici furori* II, i, 5.   26. ibid., dedication.
27. See Warburg, *Die Erneuerung der heidnischen Antike*, pp. 258, 393.

49. Veronese: Concord of Love. National Gallery, London

50. Lorenzo Lotto: Love crowning Death (*dulce amarum*). Alnwick Castle

51. Titian (?): Amor between the symbols of Chance and Patience.
National Gallery of Art, Washington

52. Aldine Emblem: *Festina lente*

53. Mantegna (school): *Festina lente*. Palazzo Ducale, Mantua

54. Antithetical figure, from the *Hypnerotomachia*

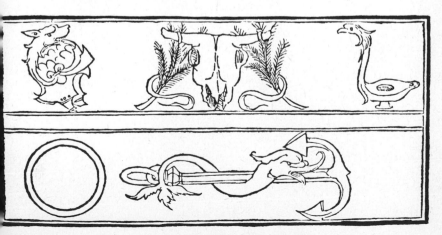

55. Hieroglyphs, from the *Hypnerotomachia*

CVM VIRTVTE ALMA CONSENTIT
VERA VOLVPTAS.

Symb. X.

56. Minerva and Venus reconciled, from Bocchi's *Symbolicae quaestiones*

57. Medal of Altobello Averoldo, Governor of Bologna:
MATURA CELERITAS

58. 'Advice to a Governor', from Bocchi's
Symbolicae quaestiones

59. Scipio. Fifteenth-century Florentine relief. Louvre, Paris

60. Raphael: The Dream of Scipio. National Gallery, London

61. Raphael: The Three Graces, Musée Condé, Chantilly

62. The Graces playing Ball. Ex-libris of Johannes Cuspinianus (detail)

63. Garofalo: Amor-Pulchritudo-Voluptas. National Gallery, London

64. Lovers with Apples. Fifteenth-century Florentine engraving

65. Girolamo Mazzola: Portrait of a Philosopher (Marcantonio Passeri?).
Galleria Nazionale, Parma

66–67. Medal of Marcantonio Passeri:
PHILOSOPHIA COMITE REGREDIMUR

68. Medal of Marcantonio Passeri:
PHILOSOPHIA DUCE REGREDIMUR
Woodcut from Tomasini's *Elogio*

69-70. Medals of Maria Poliziana: CONSTANTIA and CONCORDIA

71. Medal of Federigo da Montefeltro by Clemente da Urbino:
MARS FERUS ET SUMMUM TANGENS CYTHEREA TONANTEM . . .

72. Medal of Paolo Dotti: CONSTANTIA

73. Marco Zoppo: *Venus armata*. British Museum, London

74. Botticelli: Mars and Venus. National Gallery, London

75. Piero de Cosimo: Mars and Venus. Staatliche Museen, Berlin-Dahlem

76. Veronese: Mars and Venus (*Fortezza* submissive to *Carità*).
Metropolitan Museum of Art, New York

77. Francesco Cossa: Mars enchained by Venus (detail)
Palazzo Schifanoia, Ferrara

78–79. Medal of Rodrigo de Bivar: Mars and Venus,
QUORUM OPUS ADEST

80. Androgynous portrait of Francis I. Bibliothèque Nationale, Paris

81. Medal of Alfonso d'Este, with bombshell on cuirass

82. Impresa of Alfonso d'Este: A LIEU ET TEMPS, from Symeone's *Sententiose imprese*

83. Titian (copy?): Portrait of Alfonso d'Este. Metropolitan Museum of Art, New York

Quo modo Deum.

Quo modo Manes.

84–85. Divine eyes and mask of death, from Horapollo's *Hieroglyphica*

86. Medal of Leone Battista Alberti by Matteo de' Pasti: QUID TUM

87. Medal of Savonarola: GLADIUS DOMINI SUPER TERRAM . . .

88. Medal of Pietro Pomponazzi:
DUPLEX GLORIA

89. Medal of Galeotto Ferreo Orsini:
DUMQUE SENEX PUER

90. Quellinus the Elder:
Good Counsel. Town Hall, Amsterdam

91. The Three Faces of Prudence. Fifteenth-century Florentine relief.
Victoria and Albert Museum, London

92.–93. Syncretic medals by Giovanni dal Cavino

Sopra il porreɗo đgli anguli della ob
scura petra, rimando uidi uno monſtro
ægyptio aureo, Iacente quadrupedo. Lu-
no degli quali hauea la facia tutta huma-
na. Laltro femihumana & femibellua. La
tertia tutta belluale. Cú una uitta el fronte ambiente, cum dui lemniſci contegen
do lorechie dependuli, Et al collo & pe-
ɗo ſimilmente perlambenti. Et uno per
el dorſo deſcendente, Cum il corpo di Le
ena, cum il uolto al protenſo.

Dunque ſopra el tergo di ciaſcuno,
præmeua una maſſicia Pyra aurea trian-
gulare, fina al ſuo ſupremo propilato, li-
nee cinque del faciale imo, o uero del ſuo
diametro. In qualunque fronte era inſcal
pto uno circulo tanto, & di ſopra il circu
lo una litera græca. O. Nella laltra facia
uno circulo, & ſopra una littera. Ω. Nella
tertia planitie uno circulo, & ſopra ſe una
litera. N.

Incomício e quiui la Theophraſta Lo
giſtica præconizare & adire. Per queſte figure la cœleſte harmonia cóſiſte. Et a duer
tiſci Poliphile, che queſte figure cú perpe
tua affinitate & coniúɗione, ſono præcla
riſſimi monumenti antiquarii, & ægyptii
hieraglyphi, gli quali inſinuare uolendo
ti dicono. DIVINAE INFINITAE-
QVE TRINITATI VNIVS ES-
SENTIAE. La iſima figura alla diuini-
tate e cóſecrata, perche dalla unitate e pro-

94. Egyptian monument to the Trinity, from the *Hypnerotomachia*

95. Pagan Trinity, from Tritonius-Celtes's *Melopiae*, 1507

96. Christian Trinity. Detail from Raphael's Disputation of the Sacrament.
Stanza della Segnatura, Vatican

97. Michelangelo: Bacchus. Bargello, Florence

98. Heemskerck: Garden of the Casa Galli in Rome, with Michelangelo's Bacchus.
Kupferstichkabinett, Berlin

99. Drawing of Michelangelo's Bacchus, from a Renaissance sketch-book.
Trinity College, Cambridge

100. Michelangelo: Satyr. Detail from the Bacchus

101. Michelangelo: Head of Bacchus

spirit of
lation. 'I
dox to s
from wl
It has
part in t
Experin
by its d
dox ha:
Cusanu
era

102. Michelangelo: St Bartholomew. Detail from the Last Judgement.
Sistine Chapel, Vatican

spirit of statecraft, ascribed the world-power of Britain to its isolation. 'Happy confinement that has made us free. . . . It is no paradox to say that England has its root in the sea, and a deep one too,
from whence it sendeth its branches into both the Indies.'[28]

It has since become habitual to say that England owes her central
part in the balance of power to her marginal position. As in Cusanus's
Experiments with the Scales, 'one pound can lift a thousand pounds
by its distance from the centre of the scales'.[29] But while that paradox has tended to harden into a dangerous political commonplace,
Cusanus, primarily interested in theology, derived it from a more
general and queer-sounding postulate: that periphery and centre are
interchangeable in God. Like many other Renaissance thinkers
Cusanus had a liking for the pseudo-Hermetic notion of comparing
God to an infinite sphere whose circumference is nowhere and
whose centre is everywhere;[30] and in so far as 'everywhere' and
'nowhere' amount to the same, the contraries of periphery and
centre become interchangeable.[31] God is in all the world, that is, in
the smallest part of it; and yet all of the world is also in God, since

28. 'The Trimmer's Opinion in relation to Things Abroad', op. cit., pp. 68 f., is
as unmistakable on that point as Halifax's *Rough Draught of a New Model at Sea* (1694).

29. *De staticis experimentis* (*Opera*, 1514, fol. 98ᵛ).

30. Cusanus, *De docta ignorantia* I, xii (cf. ed. Hoffmann–Klibansky, p. 25 note 11);
Ficino, *Theologia Platonica* XVIII, iii, *Opera*, p. 403; Francesco Giorgio, *De harmonia
mundi* I, iii, 2; Giordano Bruno, *De monade* (*Opera latina*, ed. F. Fiorentino, I, i, 1884,
p. 342). Among Neoplatonists the figure had become a commonplace, long before
Pascal made it even more famous; cf. D. Mahnke, *Unendliche Sphäre und Allmittelpunkt*
(1937). Thomas Browne was not entirely wrong in calling it 'Trismegistus his circle'
in *Christian Morals* III, ii, and referring to it as 'that allegorical description of Hermes'
in *Religio medici* I, x, with marginal note, 'sphaera cuius centrum ubique, circumferen-
tia nullibi'; for it occurs for the first time in the *Liber xxiv philosophorum* (ed. C.
Baeumker, *Studien und Charakteristiken zur Geschichte der Philosophie*, 1927, pp. 194–
214) as *propositio ii* (ibid., p. 208). Presumably written about 1200, the text bears in
Cod. Vat. lat. 3060 and other MSS the inscription *liber ... qui dicitur Termegisti
Philosophi* (ibid., p. 207), and is quoted as Trismegistus not only by St Bonaventura and
St Thomas (ibid., p. 201), but also by Francesco Giorgio, loc. cit., and other Renaissance
authors. Donne, who meditated on the image in the *Devotions* (ed. J. Sparrow, 1923,
p. 4), parodied it in the *Catalogus librorum* no. 5 (ed. Simpson, p. 31). For the idea that
the supreme One is everywhere and nowhere, cf. Plotinus, *Enneads* V, ii, 2: ὁ μηδαμοῦ
καὶ πανταχοῦ οὕτως ἐστίν.

31. According to Cusanus, op. cit., I, xxi, the centre and the periphery of an infinite
circle are exchangeable also with its diameter.

he embraces and transcends it. Maximum and minimum are one.[32] By pushing the contraries to their extremes Cusanus thought that he made them vanish; but whatever may be said against his claim on the grounds of logic, it has been pragmatically confirmed on at least one point: the conclusions of the extreme mysticism of Cusanus agree with the observations of practical politics. To be placed outside a political situation is to occupy a privileged position within it. As transcendence and inherence coincide in God, so the central position of a worldly power is often secured by its eccentricity.[33]

Halifax would not have been pleased to hear his policy defended by such reasonings. He had no taste for 'the frenzy of Platonic visions'. Bruno's triumphant demonstration in the *Eroici furori* 'that there is no difference between the most evident and the most concealed, between the beginning and the end, between the most lucid height and the profoundest abyss, between infinite power and infinite act'[34] would only have brought to his mind a verse from *Hudibras*:

> *The extremes of glory and of shame*
> *Like east and west become the same.*[35]

32. Cusanus, op. cit., I, ii, iv, xvi; II, iii.

33. It would be of interest to examine Cusanus's politics in relation to his metaphysics. Like Halifax, he could easily be called inconstant because he seemed to trim his sails to the wind; but Macaulay's defence of Halifax supplies an adequate answer: 'As well might the pole star be called inconstant because it is sometimes to the east and sometimes to the west of the pointers.' Cusanus's shift from the Council of Basle to the Eugenian party, or from a tolerant to an intransigent policy towards the 'Bohemian heretics', is perhaps less revealing than his explicit statement, in the Epilogue to the *De docta ignorantia*, that the dialectical principle underlying the book had occurred to him during a diplomatic mission. On the ship which carried him back from Byzantium, where he had helped to persuade the emperor John Palaeologus to embark on a journey to the West for the purpose of reuniting the Greek and Roman Churches, he was vouchsafed an overwhelming intuition into the union of contraries as a universal principle. To what length he was willing to carry this rule, he had the opportunity to show under Pius II: for it was in support of a bold and desperate papal stratagem, that of offering the supreme secular power of Christendom to the conquering sultan, against whom the Christian princes were unwilling to unite, that Cusanus wrote his 'Scrutiny of the Koran' (*Cribratio Alchorani*), a book designed to demonstrate the compatibility of the two conflicting faiths.

34. *Argomento*, referring to II, v.

35. *Hudibras* II, i, 271 f. Did Butler intend to travesty Donne's 'physicians grown cosmographers'? 'What shall my West hurt me? As West and East / In all flat maps

Halifax's own metaphysics of trimming were less extravagant. He was satisfied to observe 'that our climate is a trimmer between that part of the world where men are roasted, and the other where they are frozen; that our Church is a trimmer between the frenzy of Platonic visions and the lethargic ignorance of popish dreams; that our laws are trimmers between the excess of unbounded power and the extravagance of liberty not enough restrained; that true virtue has ever been thought a trimmer and to have its dwelling in the middle between the two extremes; that even God Almighty himself is divided between his two great attributes, his mercy and his justice'.[36]

In the last sentence the word 'divided', which Halifax extends to 'even God Almighty', would have profoundly offended the Renaissance Neoplatonists. In Cusanus's and Ficino's and Pico's idea of God (and on this point they were supported by a solid theological tradition) the opposites of justice and mercy coincide. 'Thy anger is love, Thy justice mercy.'[37] It is man's limitation to conceive of them as 'divided'; and as long as he fails to recognize his limitation, man (in the Neoplatonic view) is unable to rise to the idea of God, and falls short of his own perfection. His natural weakness, as a creature below the moon, may force him to alternate and compromise between the opposites, this being a temporal way of mediating between them. Yet the aim of mediation is union; and while turning his face from one side to the other, the sage should comprise both sides at once. 'Sapiens haud simplex, sed geminus homo est,' wrote Bovillus, and pictured the sage as a Janus (*sapiens bifrons*).[38]

The 'character of a trimmer' thus leads us back to the Renaissance

---

(and I am one) are one, / So death doth touch the Resurrection.' Donne's geographical illustration of the coincidence of opposites may, incidentally, preserve an original feature of the new discoveries. The wide-flung speculations on the coincidence of opposites, which are an outstanding feature of Quattrocento thought, may well have prepared the intellectual climate for conceiving of a westward voyage to the East.

36. op. cit., p. 97.
37. Cusanus, *De pace seu concordantia fidei*, § 1.
38. *De sapiente* xxxi; cf. Cassirer, op. cit., p. 369.

'mystery of Janus' which Pico had cited as a symbol of reintegration, and which Passeri associated with the Aristophanic Man: 'philosophia duce regredimur'.[39] Admittedly, acquisition of completeness in such an extraordinary form is no easy matter. Mystics who yearn for union with God often fail in circumspection; and prudent men, while they may be skilled in the art of trimming, are rarely propelled by mystical ardours. Yet only those who can combine these two qualities in one person would be said, at least in some measure, to achieve the Janus-face of perfection, which is to know the invisible God as One, and recognize him in the visible Many. The confident belief of Halifax, 'that true virtue has ever been thought a trimmer and to have its dwelling in the middle between the two extremes', applies to every step of the Neoplatonic scale, but not to the scale itself. As Spenser put it, *in medio virtus – in summo felicitas*.[40]

*

Perhaps it was largely for etymological reasons, because the word 'initiation' suggests a door or gate, a threshold over which the neophyte passes in being admitted to a secret mystery, that Janus, Ovid's celestial 'janitor' who has the power to open and to close,[41] was defined by George Wither, in his book of emblems, as the god of mysteries in general.[42] But with perfectly good religious logic, and with the cunning that distinguishes some of the emblem writers, Wither extended the character of the god to his votaries, and so the double face, originally meant for the janitor who protects the door, was transferred to those whom he lets in:

> He that concealèd things will find
> Must look before him and behind.

39. See above pages 201 f.
40. cf. above, pages 47 f.
41. *Fasti* I, 63–288; cf. Bocchi, *Symbolicae quaestiones*, no. cli: 'Ianitor immensus superis et manibus imis.' How widely this mystery could be expanded is shown by the Janus frieze over the entrance to the Medici villa at Poggio a Caiano, a Neoplatonic monument of the first importance, on which see A. Chastel, *Art et humanisme à Florence au temps de Laurent le Magnifique* (1959), pp. 217–25.
42. George Wither, *Emblems* (1635), p. 138.

102. Michelangelo: St Bartholomew. Detail from the Last Judgement.
Sistine Chapel, Vatican

101. Michelangelo: Head of Bacchus

With this rhyme Wither expanded the motto *pando recondita*, and declared himself pleased that prudence in man and omniscience in God should thus both be represented by the same secret figure.[43]

Not unlike the triadic faces of Prudence, which imitate the divine Trinity,[44] Wither's double-faced Prudence is a vestige of God in man. Yet, like Halifax, Wither told only half the story. The Renaissance mystics were not so timid as to recognize a divine vestige only in a cautious approach to the Ultimate;[45] nor were they so bold as to trust their prudence to the last, and to envisage with equanimity the prospect of meeting the deity face to face. The 'all-seeing eye' which Cusanus introduced as an experimental parable in *De visione Dei*, had also its terrifying aspects; and perhaps no Renaissance hieroglyph conveys a sense of *terribilità* more clearly than the famous 'winged eye', the emblem of Leone Battista Alberti, which appears on his medal with the motto QUID TUM (fig. 86).[46] What does the puzzling figure mean? And what is meant by its Ciceronian motto?

An earlier version of Alberti's emblem showed the figure of an eagle, again with the inscription QUID TUM.[47] As the imperial bird of Zeus, the eagle was credited with virtues that Plutarch, in *De Iside et Osiride*, had ascribed originally to the falcon, the symbol of Horus and Osiris: 'This bird,' he said, 'is distinguished by the

43. 'In true divinity,' Wither explains, "tis God alone / To whom all hidden things are truly known. / He only is that ever present being / Who, by the virtue of his pow'r all-seeing, / Beholds at one aspect all things that are, / That ever shall be, and that ever were. / But in a moral sense we may apply / This double-face that man to signify / Who, whatsoere he undertakes to do, / Looks both before him and behind him too.'

44. See below, pages 260 f.

45. A century before Wither, a humanist printer in Lyons, named Hughes de la Porte or Hugo a Porta, had used the same emblem as a printer's mark – a gate with Janus-head inscribed *recondita pando* (cf. L.-C. Silvestre, *Marques typographiques* II, 1867, nos. 731, 983); but far from being approached with circumspection, the doors are carried off, like the gates of Gaza, by a bold Samson with a defiant motto, LIBERTATEM MEAM MECUM PORTO. Both the image of the gate (*porta*) and the act of carrying it (*porto*) were allusions to the printer's name.

46. Hill, no. 161.

47. Giehlow, 'Die Hieroglyphenkunde des Humanismus', op. cit., p. 36.

sharpness of its vision and the speed of its wings';[48] and it therefore signifies the union of supreme insight and supreme power. Ripa said the same of the eagle: 'havendo egli (scil. l'aquila) la vista acutissima e il volo di gran lunga superiore a gl'altri animali volatili',[49] an argument borrowed from Pierio Valeriano who, although committed by the Egyptian character of his Hieroglyphica to retain these attributes for the falcon,[50] was sufficiently generous and inconsistent to ascribe them to the eagle as well.[51] The description fits so exactly the later version of Alberti's medal, where the piercing eye and the rapid wings are combined in one cipher, that most probably the meaning is the same as that of the whole figure of the eagle, particularly as the inscription has remained unaltered. But not only does the compactness of the hieroglyph single out the two essential traits (which in a figure of the whole bird would be suggested only by implication), but the image of an eye with wings brings to mind the ubiquity of the omniscient God, because the word deus was illustrated in the Hieroglyphica by an eye (fig. 84),[52] while the wings signify celeritas.[53] In this context the Ciceronian formula Quid tum assumes a fearful, eschatological meaning. Cicero used the phrase repeatedly as an expression of oratorical suspense, an exclamation ('What then') which filled a pause and aroused the

48. 'Avis nam ea pollet acumine visus et volatus celeritate', De Iside et Osiride 51 (Moralia, 371E), tr. Xylander, ed. cit., p. 212. 'Pingunt etiam hunc deum accipitris imagine nonnunquam, tum ob visus acumen, tum ob alarum pernicitatem', Calcagnini, De rebus Aegyptiacis, in Opera, p. 242.

49. Iconologia, s.v. 'ingegno'.

50. Hieroglyphica XXI, fol. 155ᵛ.

51. ibid. XIX, fol. 141ᵛ, s.v. 'ingenium velox', on the authority of Pindar, Nemean Odes iii, 80 f.

52. 'Oculo picto Deum intelligebant, quod ut oculus quicquid sibi propositum est intuetur, sic omnia Deus cognoscit ac videt', Horapollo, Hieroglyphica (Paris 1551), p. 222; cf. Hypnerotomachia, fols. c iʳ, p viᵛ, p viiʳ, q viiᵛ, etc., also Valeriano, Hieroglyphica XXXIII, fol. 234.

53. Valeriano, op. cit. XXI ('De accipitre'), fol. 155ᵛ. Is it possible that Virgil's numine afflatur (cf. above, page 175) contributed to the formation of Alberti's image? The eye of deus could be read hieroglyphically for numen; and in Raphael's Poetry, which bears the inscription numine afflatur, the afflatus is represented by wings. See also Ficino's reference, in Theologia Platonica II, x (Opera. p. 105), to the 'infinite eye' of the Orphics as a symbol of the divine mind: 'divina mens cum sit infinita, merito nominatur ab Orphicis ἄπειρον ὄμμα, id est, oculus infinitus'.

listener's expectation.[54] But if the *Quid tum* refers to the approach of the God, then the classical phrase of expectation expands into a threatening sense of the *Dies Irae*, the Day of Judgement which, as St Paul said in 1 Corinthians xv, 52, will come *in ictu oculi*,[55] 'in the twinkling of an eye'.

> *Quid sum miser tunc dicturus?*
> *Quem patronum rogaturus,*
> *Cum vix justus sit securus?*

Essential to the threatening effect of Alberti's hieroglyph is the incompatibility of the two components; an eye can focus clearly only from a steady point, its vision being blurred by rapid motion. But here the speed of the wings and the sharpness of vision are united in one supernatural act: *manens moveor*, Omnipresence.

It has long been thought that Alberti deliberately refrained from explaining this emblem anywhere in his writings, but a passage was recently found in a minor dialogue, *Anuli*, where he seems to break his silence: he discusses an image that he defines as *oculus alis aquilae insignis*;[56] yet the passage hides almost as much as it discloses. In describing the emblem Alberti omits the motto, and while giving a full explanation of the eye, hardly accounts for the wings at all.[57]

54. Cicero, *Tusculanae disputationes* II, xi, 26; but also Virgil, *Aeneid* IV, 543, *Eclogues* X, 38; Horace, *Satires* II, iii, 230; also Terence, *Eunuch* II, iii, 47, etc.

55. On the phrase *in ictu oculi* as applied to the Last Judgement by medieval writers, see Mâle, *L'art religieux du XIIIᵉ siècle en France* (1931), pp. 377 f.

56. *Opera inedita*, ed. H. Mancini (1890), pp. 228 f.; cf. R. Watkins, 'L. B. Alberti's Emblem, the Winged Eye, and his name Leo', *Mitteilungen des Kunsthistorischen Institutes in Florenz* IX (1960), pp. 256 ff. The manuscript (Bibliothèque Nationale, Cod. lat. 6702, fol. 148–58) gives the title as *Anuli, ex Intercenalibus Leonis B. Al.* The decisive passage, fol. 151ᵛ, begins: 'hoc in anulo corona inscripta est: quam mediam complet oculus alis aquilae insignis'.

57. Instead he seems to lay particular stress on the wreath that surrounds the emblem on his medal, explaining it as a symbol of joy and glory, although this cannot be essential to the argument since the wreath is absent from the otherwise identical emblem on the famous oval plaque that is presumed to be Alberti's self-portrait (formerly Gustave Dreyfus Collection, now National Gallery of Art, Washington, no. A278.1B).

The promising phrase with which the argument opens – 'these mysteries then need to be explained' (*explicanda igitur haec sunt mysteria*) – is half withdrawn in the next sentence: 'I shall speak only of one or two of these things so that you can recognize the rest by yourself'; and the same tantalizing manner of speech is resumed at the end: 'I prefer to be very short (*brevissimus*): for to give an exhaustive account of such a compact matter would be prolix; particularly as you yourself, in the measure of your wisdom, will be able, if you apply your mind to it, to perceive the meaning *plane et aperte*' – that is, without the last remnant of those mystical veils that the author declined to remove.

As an exercise in style, this commentary by Alberti is a perfect example of how the Renaissance thought that one should speak about mysteries: giving a baffling account, patently incomplete, so that the reader may be induced to figure out the concealed part for himself. Nevertheless, while leaving out a great deal, Alberti could not resist making the crucial point of his emblem clear: that omniscience in God and circumspection in man are represented by the same image: 'The ancients likened God to an eye seeing all and everything. Thus we are admonished . . . to conceive of God as ever present, seeing all our deeds and thoughts. At the same time we are also reminded that we must be vigilant and circumspect', *pervigiles circumspectosque esse oportere*.

It is worth recalling that Karl Giehlow, with his exceptional intuition of Renaissance hieroglyphs, understood the meaning of Alberti's cipher without having found the exactly relevant texts. He did not adduce the passage on the falcon's eye and wings in Plutarch, nor the *Quid tunc* or the *ictus oculi* of the *Dies Irae*, least of all the *Anuli*. Instead he quoted a tangential passage about hieroglyphs from Diodorus,[58] where the eye is associated with justice, and the wings of the falcon with speed; and from this text he inferred that Alberti 'on the basis of Diodorus interpreted the eye as *iustitiae servator*, the flight of the falcon as *res cito facta*, the whole therefore as the ever-present possibility of his being called before the judgement-seat of God. It conveys the symbolic warning always

58. *Bibliotheca historica* III, iv.

to remember "what then", and does not allude, as has been supposed, to Alberti's scientific accomplishments.'[59]

The case proves that the image has an inherent eloquence, that it speaks the universal language of the imagination,[60] but that, like the lovers' emblems in Politian, it was 'meant to be understood by the lovers only, and exercise the conjectures of other in vain'.[61] Perhaps the hope that Alberti entertained with regard to these images was not quite so ill founded as has been supposed. 'All over the world,' he thought, 'they would be easily understood by experienced men (*a peritis viris*), to whom alone the noblest subjects should be communicated.'[62]

On the whole this 'conceited' art has not met with much sympathy from experienced men. Mr E. M. Forster, for example, has said that if a work of art parades a mystifying element, it is to that extent not a work of art, 'not an immortal Muse but a Sphinx who dies as soon as her riddles are answered'.[63] Certainly there are symbols which fit this admirable description. They disturb us as long as we do not understand them, and bore us as soon as we do. The winged eyes and ears that flutter around an Allegory of Fame by Filarete, who associated them with the 'winged words' of Homer, are a good example of what Mr Forster means.[64] But Alberti's winged eye is a contrary instance. It shows that a great symbol is the reverse of a sphinx; it is more alive when its riddle is answered.

59. loc. cit. Giehlow quotes a gnostic seal discussed by Winckelmann, *Versuch einer Allegorie, besonders für die Kunst* (1766), pp. 4 f. (cf. also *Pierres de Stosch*, pp. 1 f.), which shows a combination of eye, wings, and arm. While it is doubtful whether Alberti knew this object, Winckelmann's wording suggests that he made use of Plutarch, *De Iside et Osiride* 51 (*Moralia* 371E), as quoted above, page 232 note 48.

60. It will be asked: why bother to find the exactly relevant texts if it is possible to grasp the correct meaning of an image without knowing them? An answer is given by the history of Giehlow's interpretation which, although essentially right, failed to gain universal acceptance. Historical texts are needed not so much for the discovery of a symbolic meaning as for its conclusive demonstration.

61. See above, page 164.

62. *De re aedificatoria* VIII, iv.

63. 'The Raison d'Être of Criticism in the Arts', in *Music and Criticism*, ed. R. French (1948), p. 26.

64. M. Lazzaroni and A. Muñoz, *Filarete* (1908), pl. xiii, 5.

AN OBSERVATION ON METHOD

UNLESS we allow for a certain ingredient of deliberate paradox, which qualified the imitation of antiquity by Renaissance humanists, we may misjudge altogether the atmosphere in which the pagan mysteries were revived. They were sponsored by men of letters who had learned from Plato that the deepest things are best spoken of in a tone of irony. 'Shall we, after the manner of Homer, pray the Muses to tell us how discord first arose? Shall we imagine them in solemn mockery, to play and jest with us as if we were children, and to address us in a lofty tragic vein, making believe to be in earnest?' (*Republic* 545–7). Lucian, Apuleius, even Plutarch had chattered of mysteries in a mocking tone. Their literary manner was admired and copied not only by professional stylists like Aldus, Erasmus, Aleander, and More – it was adopted also in the philosophical schools. *Serio ludere* was a Socratic maxim of Cusanus, Ficino, Pico, Calcagnini – not to mention Bocchi, who introduced the very phrase into the title of his *Symbolicae quaestiones*: 'quas serio ludebat'.[1]

It may also be remembered in this context that the *Golden Ass* of Apuleius was first published, in 1469, as a compendium of Platonic philosophy.[2] The preface by Giovanni Andrea de Bussi, who was a disciple of Cusanus, contained eulogies of Bessarion as a defender of

1. cf. Ficino, *In Parmenidem* (Prooemium), *Opera*, p. 1137: 'Pythagorae, Socratisque et Platonis mos erat, ubique divina mysteria figuris involucrisque obtegere, . . . iocari serio, et studiosissime ludere.' His commentary on Plato's 'nuptial number' (*Republic* 545D ff.) ends with the words: 'Nos autem una cum Platone musisque in re seria inextricabilique ludentibus satis confabulati sumus' (*Opera*, p. 1425). In Cusanus, *De ludo globi*, cf. *Opera* I (1514), fol. 159ᵛ, the idea of *serio ludere* was put into verse: 'Luditur hic ludus; sed non pueriliter, at sic / Lusit ut orbe novo sancta sophia deo . . . / Sic omnes lusere pii: Dionysius et qui / Increpuit magno mystica verba sono', presumably not by Cusanus himself but, as Fiorentino surmises (op. cit., p. 121), by de Bussi.

2. *Lucii Apuleii Platonici Madaurensis Philosophi Metamorphoseos Liber ac nonnulla alia opuscula eiusdem.* . . . Here quoted from the edition of 1500.

Plato, and of Cusanus as an explorer of Proclus's Theology. Bero-aldus's commentary on the *Golden Ass* resumed these reflections by quoting from Plato, Proclus, and Origen in order to explain the author's intention and design (*scriptoris intentio atque consilium*). 'And it appears that under that mystical cover, being deeply versed in Pythagorean and Platonic philosophy, he set forth the dogmas of both these masters, and conveyed the lessons of palingenesis and metempsychosis, that is, of regeneration and transmutation, through the disguise of that ludicrous story.'[3]

Serio ludere might also stand as a motto over a chapter which I have not attempted to write, and the omission of which may help to demonstrate the incompleteness of my observations on pagan mysteries: I have said nothing of the revival of ancient *grottesche*. With their sprawling ornaments, for which Giovanni da Udine had rediscovered the ancient stucco technique, Michelangelo intended to decorate the upper zone of the Medici Chapel. They were regarded by the Renaissance as the classical style for burial and mystery chambers. In their flimsy grace and inconsequence they gave rise to Raphael's paradox – religious *logge*. Addressing the devout in a foolish spirit, these calculated freaks represented to perfection what Pico della Mirandola had defined as the Orphic disguise: the art of interweaving the divine secrets with the fabric of fables, so that anyone reading those hymns 'would think they contained nothing but the sheerest tales and trifles', *nihil subesse credat praeter fabellas nugasque meracissimas*.

While the extravagance of mystical imagery is easiest to detect in this fantastical art, it is rarely absent from the more solemn Renaissance mythologies, those composed in a heroic, tragic, or sentimental style. A myth, it may be well to remember, was defined as 'a mendacious discourse figuring the truth'.[4] And whatever the

---

3. *Philippi Beroaldi in Commentarios Apuleianos praefatio* (1516), fol. a iiiᵛ. The alchemists, as shown in the mere titles of Michael Maier's works *Lusus serius* (1616) and *Jocus severus* (1617), were here again (cf. above, page 214) the heirs, or apes, of Neoplatonism.

4. Μΰθός· ἐστι λόγος ψευδής εἰκονίζων ἀλήθειαν: Theon, *Progymnasmata* III, quoted by Cumont, *Symbolisme funéraire*, p. 3. See also Macrobius, *Somnuim Scipionis* I, ii, 7, 'modus per figmentum vera referendi'.

merits of a robust common sense in the interpretation of images, it is fallacious, as Cumont observed, to trust 'probability in a region of ideas where the improbable is often the attested fact'.

There are historians, many of them admirable, who stress the importance of the commonplace in history. Their work is salutary and indispensable, because the commonplace is a relentless force. But in so far as their method is specially contrived to examine that particular subject, it is not suited to deal with the exceptional in history, the power of which should also perhaps not be underrated. In a perfect study, both aspects should be present; and it is one of the many weaknesses of this book that, except in one or two cases, it does not show how an adventurous proposition sinks to a platitude, and how genius is engulfed by complacency or inertia. For every one instance in which the interpretation of an image required a careful reading of Plotinus or Pico della Mirandola, I might have quoted several which can be resolved with the use of a common index. But inasmuch as we are forced to select, it would seem that to choose the exceptional for study is, in the long run, the lesser risk. An eminent iconographer who preferred the opposite course discovered that 'the symbolical creations of geniuses are unfortunately harder to nail down to a definite subject than the allegorical inventions of minor artists.' If this be so, there is something wrong with the manner of nailing down. A method that fits the small work but not the great has obviously started at the wrong end. In geometry, if I may use a remote comparison, it is possible to arrive at Euclidean parallels by reducing the curvature of a non-Euclidean space to zero, but it is impossible to arrive at a non-Euclidean space by starting out with Euclidean parallels. In the same way, it seems to be a lesson of history that the commonplace may be understood as a reduction of the exceptional, but that the exceptional cannot be understood by amplifying the commonplace. Both logically and causally the exceptional is crucial, because it introduces (however strange it may sound) the more comprehensive category. That this relation is irreversible should be an axiom in any study of art. In the present case it is offered as an apology for a book devoted to a manifest eccentricity.

APPENDIXES

APPENDIXES

APPENDIX I

CUSANUS IN ITALY

PICO DELLA MIRANDOLA's debt to Nicolaus Cusanus (cf. above, page 54)
poses an intricate historical problem. Despite Cusanus's great renown among
his Italian contemporaries, as shown by his inclusion in Vespasiano da
Bisticci's *Vite di uomini illustri* (ii, 16: 'Cardinale Cusano, Tedesco'), his
philosophical writings were difficult of access in Italy before the Milan
edition of 1502, although interest in them was not lacking. Filelfo, for
example, ordered a copy of the *Docta ignorantia* from Giovanni Andrea de
Bussi (letter from Milan, 1460, quoted in Fiorentino, *Risorgimento filosofico*,
pp. 119, 162 note 72); and Pomponius Laetus's teacher Pietro Odi da
Montopoli, who referred to Cusanus as 'magistrum meum omnibus
saeculis admirabilem' (Zabughin, *Giulio Pomponio Leto* I, pp. 15 f., 275 note
47), must surely have owned some of his works. Yet none of Cusanus's
philosophical writings appear among the manuscripts of the Laurentian
Library in Florence, the only Cusanus entries in Bandini's catalogue (I,
211, 213) being a few excerpts from his contributions to the Council of
Basle (Plut. 16, 11 f.). Nor is Cusanus ever quoted in Ficino's books;
Ficino included his name in a list of Platonic authors compiled for a German
correspondent, but without recalling any particular title: 'quaedam
speculationes Nicolai Cusii cardinalis', a fair sign that he knew them only
by hearsay (*Opera*, p. 899; Klibansky, *The Continuity of the Platonic Tradition*,
pp. 45 ff.). In the inventory of the manuscripts and books owned by Pico
(P. Kibre, *The Library of Pico della Mirandola*, 1936, pp. 119 ff.) the name of
Cusanus does not appear, which explains sufficiently why Pico does not
quote him. And yet Pico knew the relevance of Cusanus's doctrines to his
own philosophy so well that he planned, as he told the Inquisitors in Paris,
'to travel to Germany because of his great desire to see the library of the
late cardinal of Cusa', *cupiebat proficisci in Germaniam maxime studio visendae
bibliothecae olim cardinalis de Cusa* (L. Dorez and L. Thuasne, *Pic de la*

Mirandole en France, 1897, p. 159), although he did not ultimately undertake the journey. In Ferrara, Calcagnini's reference to the cosmology of Cusanus, at the conclusion of *Quod caelum stet, terra moveatur* (*Opera*, p. 395), which was written after 1500, is typical both of the quasi-legendary nature of the oral transmission, and of its relatively great accuracy:

I am told [*audio*] that in the last century Cusa, a man of great learning and penetrating intelligence, outstanding as a cardinal, but far more so in his erudition, held this view [that the earth moves]. Of his commentaries I could only wish that they had come into my hands: for he had a genius of such acumen that I believe he would have either spared me the present labour or supplied me with far weightier and better arguments for the proof of this proposition.

The passage supplies a welcome parallel to Pico's proposition *Contradictoria coincidunt in natura uniali* (see above, page 54), which seems to echo Cusanus, but appears among the *Conclusiones* introduced by Pico as new and entirely his own, *secundum opinionem propriam nova in philosophia dogmata inducentes* (*Opera*, p. 90, no. 15). Like Cusanus, but without knowing his demonstration in any detail, Pico had independently developed the proposition from his own study of Proclus and Dionysius the Areopagite. After the Milan edition of 1502, however, Cusanus's arguments were directly known to Pico's disciples, as shown by the quotations in Francesco Giorgio, *De harmonia mundi totius* II, ii, 1 (1525), fol. 203^v, and Gianfrancesco Pico della Mirandola, *Opera* (1601), pp. 488, 509, 568, 622, 685, 706, 715, 726, 732, 774, 796; which should dispose of the error, still occasionally heard, that Giordano Bruno was the first Italian philosopher to quote Cusanus at length. Gianfrancesco Pico died in 1533, that is fifteen years before Bruno was born.

PAGAN VESTIGES OF THE TRINITY

In his chapters on the *vestigia Trinitatis* (*De Trinitate* IX–XV; see above, pages 41 f.), Augustine explained that the Holy Trinity had left its mark on every part of creation, but that the three aspects of the deity that are co-essential in the creator become unequal and separable in created things: 'Aliud est itaque trinitas res ipsa, aliud imago trinitatis in re alia' (XV, xxiii, 43). What would have been Arianism if applied to the Holy Trinity itself was good Augustinianism if applied to its vestiges – a distinction of great importance to the Platonic theology of the Renaissance because it sanctioned the peculiar zeal with which Ficino, Pico della Mirandola, and other humanists searched for rudimentary trinities among the pagans. 'Dixerint isti quidem quod potuerunt, et id quidem adiuvante Deo,' wrote Ficino in an essay *De rationibus trinitatis*, with special reference to the foreknowledge of the Trinity supposedly shown by Orpheus, Plato, and Zoroaster.[1] Many such instances were collected by Gyraldus, who referred to Hermes Trismegistus and Orpheus as prophets of the Christian Trinity,[2] also to 'the famous oracle of Serapis' concerning the *mysterium trinitatis*[3] and to various Pythagorean and Platonic trinitarians.[4] See also Caelius Rhodiginus, *Antiquae lectiones* XII, ix; Agrippa of Nettesheim, *De occulta philosophia* III, viii ('Quid de divina trinitate veteres senserint philosophi'); Francesco Giorgio, *De harmonia mundi totius* I, iii, 2 (fol. 40ʳ), 'Quanto ordine a trino Deo per ternarium fiat in fabricata omnia progressus'; also I, i, 4 (fols. 5ᵛ f.), with reference to Augustine.

Some cursory notes on this vast subject will be grouped here under four headings: (i) The Shadow of Arianism, (ii) Hellenic Theology, (iii) Pagan Triads, (iv) Christian Apocrypha.

I – THE SHADOW OF ARIANISM

As was only natural, Platonic philosophers were particularly attracted by the three hypostases in Plotinus (*Enneads* V, i, 10, etc.) which they greeted as a vestige of the Trinity but with a characteristic mixture of enthusiasm

1. *In Epistolas divi Pauli* ii, *Opera*, p. 430.   2. *Opera* I, 309; II, 75, 77.
3. ibid. I, 197.   4. ibid. II, 673 f.

and caution. While praising the doctrine for its spiritual refinement, and for its unmistakable affinity to the Trinitarian dogma, Ficino, Pico, and their followers explained repeatedly that it would be an Arian error to identify the second hypostasis with Christ, although it was not wrong to call it 'son of God' or 'the Logos' (cf. Ficino, *In Parmenidem* lv, *In Timaeum* ix, *In sextam epistolam Platonis*; Pico, *Commento* I, iv; ed. Garin I, v; Rhodiginus, *Antiquae lectiones* IX, xvii, pp. 442 f.). The same distinction had been stressed by Gemistus Pletho in his treatise *On the Procession of the Holy Spirit*[5]: in it he candidly separated 'the view of the Church' from what he called 'the Hellenic theology'. Ficino added, however, that on the evidence of the sixth Platonic Letter (which he took to be genuine) it could be argued that Plato had fathomed the ultimate mystery of the Trinity in a less Arian sense than Plotinus and his disciples: 'Ac siquis unam trium ponat essentiam, Platonicis quidem multis videbitur adversari, Platoni tamen manifeste non repugnabit.'[6] Strange to say, this foible for Plato was shared by so intransigent a Dominican as St Antoninus of Florence, who not only accepted the doctrine of the 'vestiges of the Trinity' in its theological aspects (*Summa* IV, x, 7, § 6) but went out of his way to quote pagan witnesses, *testimonia Trinitatis in doctrinis ethnicorum*, among them Hermes Trismegistus, the Sibyls, and Plato: 'De verbo eterno seu filio dei multa dixit Plato . . . et satis clare' (ibid, IV, x, 7, § 4). Bessarion, on the contrary, although more committed to Plato than St Antoninus, insisted on a clear distinction: 'Plato vero multa certe de trinitate locutus est, sed longe aliter quam nostra religio doceat' (*In calumniatorem Platonis* II, v; also III, xv–xvii, on *vestigia Trinitatis*).

Much of that discussion was concerned with a triadic 'enigma' in Plato's second Letter (312E), introduced in the original as a calculated riddle (φραστέον δή σοι δι' αἰνιγμῶν, 312D). Ficino's exegetic zeal, naturally kindled by such a 'secret,'[7] was further increased by the observation that Plotinus

5. Appendix vii, in *Pléthon. Traité des lois*, ed. C. Alexandre (1858), pp. 300 ff.

6. *Opera*, p. 1533.

7. cf. Pico's extravagant plan: 'ex affectatis aenigmatum scirpis eruere secretae philosophiae sensus' (*De hominis dignitate*, ed. Garin, p. 162; also *Apologia*, *Opera*, p. 124). For the use of the word *scirpus* (a plaited rush) to designate the involutions of a riddle, see Politian, *Miscellanea* I, xxxix f.; after Gellius, *Noctes Atticae* XII, vi, 1. Pietro Crinito thought (*De honesta disciplina* IX, 'xiii) he had convinced Politian ('ingenue agnovit errorem', ibid.) that the reading of *scirpus* in Gellius was a corruption of *scrupus* (rough pebble); but although Badius referred to this view in his edition of Politian (*Opera* I, 1519, fol. 143ʳ: 'sunt qui scrupum pro scirpo dicendum censeant'), the emendation did not gain the wide approval that Crinito thought that it deserved: 'Neque visum est hoc loco eos nominare qui hac in re decepti sunt.'

had quoted that mystery in three different places (*Enneads* I, viii, 2; V, i, 8; VI, vii, 42), that Proclus had discussed it in the *Theologia Platonica* (II, viii f.; ed. Portus, pp. 103–6), and that Gemistus Pletho had proposed a 'Zoroastran' interpretation of it (cf. *In oracula magica Zoroastris*, ed. J. Opsopoeus, 1599, p. 50) which rested on a passage in Plutarch (*De Iside et Osiride* 46; *Moralia* 369E). Ficino followed Pletho in *De amore* II, iv (*Opera*, p. 1325), explicitly citing the Zoroastran trinity in connexion with the *mysterium in epistola ad Dionysium regem*.[8] However, in his extensive commentary on Plato's second Letter (*Opera*, p. 1531: 'Argumentum ad espistolam secundam quae est Platonis ad Dionysium Siciliae tyrannum') he fully exercised the gentle art of piloting these thoughts into a Christian haven: in Plato's 'enigma' (312E) he teased and twisted the words αἴτιον, περί, and ἕνεκα until they yielded a triad of causes – *causa efficiens, causa exemplaris, causa finalis* – which he had found in Proclus's commentary on the *Timaeus*;[9] and having learned, on the authority of Augustine and Thomas Aquinas, that a famous phrase of St Paul's in the Epistle to the Romans (xi, 36) – for which Ficino adopted the reading of Ambrose: 'quoniam ex ipso, et per ipsum, et in ipsum omnia' – may be referred to the Father, the Son, and the Holy Ghost,[10] he persuaded himself that the same phrase had already been used by Plato in the second Letter: 'Triplicem hunc ordinem causae penes Deum Plato noster regi Dionysio declaravit dum inquit, ex ipso, et per ipsum, et in ipsum omnia. Ex ipso efficientem, per ipsum exemplarem, in ipsum finalem causam nobis exprimens' (*In Epistolas divi Pauli* vii, *Opera*, p. 437). Pico repeated the statement in *De ente et uno* viii (ed. Garin, p. 426), but with a characteristic correction of *penes* into *post*: 'Omnia quae sunt post Deum habent causam efficientem, exemplarem, et finalem. Ab ipso enim,

8. Since it has been said that direct borrowings from Pletho are difficult to trace in Ficino, this unmistakable instance is perhaps worth stressing.

9. Proclus, *In Timaeum* IC–D (Diehl); cf. above, page 38 note 8. On the historical origins of Proclus's three causes (as against their legendary source in Plato's *Second Letter*, 312E) see W. Theiler, *Die Vorbereitung des Neuplatonismus* (1930), pp. 17–34, who points to a preparatory phase in Seneca, *Epistolae* lxv, where the Platonic *causa exemplaris* is added to the four Aristotelian causes. In this combination of five, Aristotle's 'material' and 'formal' causes sank down to the level of auxiliaries, leaving the other three ('efficient', 'exemplary', and 'final') in the position of primary causes, ἀρχικαὶ αἰτίαι in the words of Proclus (*Elements of Theology*, ed. Dodds, pp. 240 f., commentary on prop. 75).

10. cf. Ambrose, *Hexameron* I, v (*Patr. lat.* XIV, col. 151). The Vulgate reads: 'quoniam ex ipso, et per ipsum, et in ipso [!] sunt omnia', and so do Augustine (*Sermones de Scripturis* I, v) and Thomas Aquinas (*Super Epistolas Pauli* xi, 36), with trinitarian interpretation: 'ex Patre, per Filium, in Spiritu Sancto'.

per ipsum, et ad ipsum omnia.' A further variant (clearly dependent on Ficino, but avoiding Ambrose's *finis in ipsum*) was given by Francesco Giorgio, *De harmonia mundi totius* I, iii, 2, fol. 40ᵛ: 'Plato in Epistolis: "Omnia ab ipso proficiscuntur, et illum repetunt, atque in eo quiescunt."' In all of these versions, purporting to explain (with the help of Proclus) what Plato had meant in the second Letter, the Neoplatonic rhythm of *emanatio–raptio–remeatio* acquired a tantalizing biblical ring. A perfect English summary of these speculations may be found in Bishop Berkeley's *Siris* §§ 363–5, including the enigma from Plato's second Letter, 'which, being capable of diverse senses, I leave to be deciphered by the learned reader'. On 'a Trinity in the Godhead', Berkeley owns, 'some later Platonists of the Gentile world seem to have bewildered themselves (as many Christians have also done), while they pursued the hints derived from their predecessors with too much curiosity.'

II – HELLENIC THEOLOGY

Exactly to what extent Ficino and Pico were indebted in their triadic speculations to Pletho is difficult to determine because Pletho's great work, *The Laws*, in which he had planned to expound the cosmic and musical wisdom of the ancients as a means of reviving the old Hellenic virtues, was brutally mutilated by an intolerant cleric. That Pico was acquainted with Pletho's 'genealogy of the gods' is shown by a passage on Neptune in the *Commento*, where Pletho is quoted as *approbatissimo Platonico*.[11] For other quotations see B. Knös, 'Gémiste Pléthon et son souvenir', *Lettres d'humanité* IX (1950), pp. 97–184; cf. also M. V. Anastos, 'Pletho's Calendar and Liturgy', *Dumbarton Oaks Papers* IV (1948), pp. 289–99: 'Triadic division of the universe, and Pletho's use of Proclus.'

The anti-Christian policy imputed to Pletho by his adversaries, and still accepted by many historians,[12] seems to me disproved by at least five facts: (1) that he was among the Byzantine emissaries to the Council of 1438–9 for the reunion of the Greek and Roman Churches; (2) that he enjoyed the confidence of the Patriarch Joseph of Constantinople, who sought his advice during the Council; (3) that a contemporary chronicler of the Council, Syropoulos, quotes him as a forceful witness of orthodoxy; (4) that Cardinal Bessarion remained his devoted disciple, even when they differed on doctrine and policy; (5) that his presence in Florence inspired the sponsorship of

11. *Commento* II, xvi; ed. Garin II, xix, p. 510.

12. F. Masai, *Pléthon et le Platonisme de Mistra* (1956), pp. 321 f., with earlier literature, pp. 16 ff.

a distinctly Christian Platonism by the Medici.[13] To ascribe all these effects to Pletho's duplicity, assisted by the gullibility of his Christian admirers,[14] is a particularly flimsy way of begging the question, because Pletho was known as a boldly aggressive thinker who offended Scholarius by his outspokenness. Having explained, without a shadow of ambiguity, that the theology of Zoroaster and Plato rested on premises different from those of the Church, [15] he fearlessly praised the doctrines of those pagan founders as a precious philosophical and poetic heritage, administered in his school at Mistra as a secular sort of initiation, probably not more extravagant or sinister than the academic initiations in Rome which aroused clerical suspicion under Paul II because of their ritual paraphernalia.[16] Enthusiastically performed as ceremonious pageants, complete with calendar, liturgy, and a hierarchy of celebrants, these feasts were devoted to a spiritual communion with the ancients, on the pious and not unreasonable assumption (cf. Augustine, *Retractationes* I, xiii) that if the truths of Christianity were fundamental, they could not have been withheld completely from the sages of antiquity. The classic revival was thus bound up with utopian hopes for a universal creed that would transcend sectarian differences. *Una religio in rituum varietate* was the formula proposed for that doctrine by Cusanus (see *De pace seu concordantia fidei* § 1; also the earlier *Concordantia catholica*, written for the Council of Basle during the presidency of Cesarini).

In precisely what terms Pletho would have expressed such hopes we do not know,[17] except that he rested his system on 'common beliefs' (κοινὰ

13. cf. Ficino, *Opera*, p. 1537 (preface to Plotinus).

14. Masai, loc. cit.

15. See the texts published by Alexandre, op. cit., pp. 2, 300 ff.; cf. J. Bidez and F. Cumont, *Les mages hellénisés* I, pp. 158 ff., II, pp. 251 ff.

16. The similarity has often been noticed: see L. Mohler, *Kardinal Bessarion* (1923), p. 46. Although the connexion between the two academies was probably less intimate and certainly less conspiratorial than imagined by Masai – 'on se demande si l'Académie romaine n'était pas, en quelque sorte, une filiale de celle de Mistra' (op. cit., p. 343) – the historical links that prompted this remark did clearly exist and were openly affirmed: see Platina, *Vitae pontificum* ('Paulus II'), with important evidence of personal associations with Sigismondo Malatesta, whose enthusiasm for Pletho's doctrines induced him to transfer the body of the dead sage from Mistra to Rimini for burial in the Tempio Malatestiano; cf. also Platina's panegyric on Bessarion (*In laudem reverendissimi Cardinalis Niceni*), with reference to Pletho as 'doctissimum et quem omnes secundum a Platone vocant'. For Laetus's debt to Pletho's mythology, see B. Kieszkowski, *Studi sul Platonismo del Rinascimento in Italia* (1936), p. 45.

17. The fragments of the *Laws* are insufficient to answer that question. Their literary form was indubitably that of a Utopia, in which (not unlike what happens in More's *Utopia*) archaic customs are shown to be reasonable. Scholarius's destruction of the

δόγματα), whose strength he tested by their age.[18] In the presentation of Plato's thoughts, particularly on the One and the Many, he favoured a solid archaic order, intolerant of the dialectical mobility that led Dionysius the Areopagite or Cusanus to admit innumerable 'divine names' for one ineffable Deity. According to Pletho, divine invocations, if suited to the cosmic order established by God, could not exceed a finite number.[19] Hence his method for reaching fundamentals was regressive and positive, not dialectical. At the Council of Florence he sided with the intransigent Mark of Ephesus whose motto was Proverbs xxii, 28: 'Do not remove the ancient boundaries which your fathers set' (cf. Joseph Gill, *The Council of Florence*, 1959, p. 147). If Truth was at its purest in the beginning, and became defaced by stupid or ambitious innovators, then religious agreement might be achieved by carefully restoring the ancient creeds: for 'there is this difference between sages and sophists, that the sages always hold opinions that agree with older beliefs so that, even by their age, the true doctrines are superior to the false ..., whereas the sophists always aim for something new'.[20] Expounded with Pletho's caustic fervour, such reactionary precepts

---

entire framework (most noticeable in the last sentence where the writer is about to identify himself and his fictional community) reduces the whole argument to stark literal statements, which presumably suited Scholarius's purpose. The polemical remarks of George of Trebizond, too often quoted as authentic evidence (cf. below, note 52), are as suspect as Alexandre said (op. cit., p. xvi), although even he could not bring himself to dismiss them.

18. For the relevant passages see Masai, op. cit., pp. 115–30: 'Le consentement universel'. With the help of a Greek equivoque, admirably suited to his mystifying manner, Pletho associated the 'fundamentals of thought' (λογικαὶ ἀρχαί) with the 'study of antiquities' (ἀρχαιολογία): as if the logically 'first' and morally wisest must also be the oldest in time (preamble to the *Laws*, ed. Alexandre, p. 4). His low opinion of ancient Egypt (*Laws* III, xliii, ibid., pp. 252 ff.) is perhaps the only instance in which he found that the 'test of reason' can be in conflict with the 'test of age'. As a rule he expected them to agree, 'new' reasonings being by definition either shallow or sophistical or both. Hence his relentless attacks on Aristotle as a disenchanted innovator, impatient of the ancient wisdom preserved by Plato.

19. No doubt, he recognized that the 'One beyond Being', as defined in Plato's *Parmenides*, entails a plurality of adumbrations within the realm of being (cf. above, pages 218 ff.), but in specifying the modes of 'participation' he was rigidly intent on limiting their number so as to rule out dialectical contentions between them. Aloof to the temptations of the Infinite, and hence immune to 'negative theology', his thought was coloured by a touch of chauvinism, deliciously frank in *Laws* III, xliii (ed. Alexandre, p. 256), where he recommends his arguments not only for their truth, but more particularly because they represent a native tradition.

20. *Laws* I, ii (ibid., pp. 32 ff.). According to this criterion, contrary to what has been claimed, he could not have included Christ among the 'sophists' unless he had

must have added to the picturesque effect that he produced in Florence as a Platonic moralist imported from Sparta; and the romantic charm attached to his person may explain why the resonance of his thoughts outside the Council was so much greater than in its internal deliberations, where the conciliatory moves of Cesarini and Bessarion gradually gained the ascendancy.[21]

What the most recent historian of the Council has called 'the silent revolution effected at Florence' is unmistakably related to Cusanus's formula, *una religio in rituum varietate*: 'In the previous century, the popes had in practice made acceptance of the Latin rite synonymous with union. Florence distinguished between faith and liturgical rite, and effected union on the basis of identity of faith and diversity of rites, without ever discussing the almost, for that time, revolutionary principle that it was sanctioning by its action' (Gill, *Personalities of the Council of Florence*, 1964, pp. 291 f.). The technique of persuasion employed on the Greek side by Bessarion, and on the Latin by Cesarini (Cusanus's life-long protector and associate, to whom he dedicated the *De docta ignorantia*) was advocated in Cusanus's books; but although these are better preserved than the writings of Pletho, they occasionally meet with the same sort of historical incomprehension: 'Le cardinal de Cues poussa l'œcuménisme jusqu'aux confins de l'hérésie.'[22] In the postscript to the *Docta ignorantia* Cusanus told Cesarini that the final comprehension of 'that simplicity where contradictories are reconciled' was denied him until he was 'returning by sea from Greece', where he had gone in 1437 as envoy to John Palaeologus. The chief theme of the book, finished 12 February 1440, remained thus connected, in the author's own

---

denied any connexion between the Gospels and Old Testament prophecy. Of course, he found plenty of 'sophistry' in Christian theology, introduced by 'enthusiasts', 'hypocrites', and Aristotelians, not to speak of his vigorous campaign against privileged parasitical monks. Unfortunately, we know nothing of his views on Christian antiquities – except that he defended them at Florence against innovators. The logic of his system would seem to imply that all religions would agree in fundamental beliefs (κοινὰ δόγματα) if they were traced back sufficiently far, before they were adulterated by scholiasts. Although perfectly in tune with the mood of the 1430s, such a return to antiquity in religion comes close to the Protestant position, particularly in its disdain of the intervening scholiast.

21. In the Florentine debate Bessarion's change of sides from Pletho to Cesarini is philosophically much more interesting than the public battle between Pletho and Scholarius which merely brought out the elementary difference between Platonist and Aristotelian. Bessarion's defection, as it was called by the Byzantines, revealed a schism within the Platonic school: dialectic rose against archaism, both sanctioned by the example of Plato.   22. Masai, op.cit., p. 312 note 1.

mind, with the perilous diplomatic venture that got the Council of Florence under way (cf. above, page 228 note 33).

As a Christian Platonist, Cusanus was not frightened by polymorphic views of the deity; he had learned from Proclus to accept them as preparatory stages of initiation, necessarily imperfect but deserving respect.[23] For that tolerant outlook he sought support from the authority of Augustine: 'Sunt in unaquaque re trinitatis vestigia. Et haec est sententia Aurelii Augustini.'[24] The same thought occurs also in his popular tracts and sermons: 'In omni creato videmus trinum et unum deum.'[25]

If finally we turn to Fra Egidio da Viterbo, the future general of the Augustinian Order who was addressed after the death of Ficino as *Platonicorum maximus*,[26] we find that in his huge commentary on Peter Lombard (*In librum sententiarum ad mentem Platonis*, Cod. Vat. lat. 6325) he traced the 'vestiges of the Trinity' (fols. 45 f.) through Plato's dialogues and through a long series of pagan fables, thus producing a remarkable fusion of Augustine's *De Trinitate* and Proclus's *Theologia Platonica*.

III – PAGAN TRIADS

Once an imperfect foreshadowing of the Holy Trinity was admissible on the authority of Augustine and Proclus, the large number of triads that in fact appear in ancient ritual took on the colour of mysterious prophecies. A modern scholar (H. Usener, *Dreiheit, ein Versuch mythologischer Zahlenlehre*, 1903) counted more than 120 triadic groups in Greek myth and ritual, of which fifteen are in Hesiod alone; but the purpose of his study, the reverse of Neoplatonism, was to prove that the number was meaningless (pp. 348 f., 358 ff.): its frequency, he thought, survived from a time 'when the concept of number did not exceed three', the *trialis* (p. 360) having served originally as plural or as a term for a maximum. Renaissance speculation inclined to the opposite extreme: the prevalence of ritualistic triads was taken as proof of a trinitarian theology among the pagans, and attempts were made to harmonize all these picturesque trinities with each other, as partial aspects of a universal truth: 'He that understands profoundly and clearly how the unity of Venus is unfolded in the trinity of

23. *De docta ignorantia* I, xxv; *De pace* § 6.

24. *De docta ignorantia* I, xxiv; also II, vii, 'De trinitate universi', on which see R. Haubst, *Das Bild des Einen und Dreieinen Gottes in der Welt nach Nikolaus von Kues* (1952).

25. 'Ex sermone Sanctus, Sanctus, Sanctus', *Opera* II (1514), fol. 144ᵛ; also *De pace* § 8.

26. cf. Wind, 'The Revival of Origen', p. 417.

the Graces, and the unity of Necessity in the trinity of the Fates, and the unity of Saturn in the trinity of Jupiter, Neptune, and Pluto, knows the proper way of proceeding in Orphic theology' (Pico, *Conclusiones de modo intelligendi hymnos Orphei*, no. 8).[27]

In their enthusiasm for mystical triads Renaissance Neoplatonists accepted Iamblichus's view, *De vita pythagorica* xxviii, 152, that the tripod of Apollo was a trinitarian symbol, illustrating what Gyraldus called *ternionis numeri mysterium*.[28] That Diana shared in the same mystery seemed indicated by her byname Trivia and by the 'three faces' attributed to her in *Aeneid* IV, 511: 'tria virginis ora Dianae'; also Horace, *Carmina* III, xxii: 'ter vocata ... diva triformis'. The *Ovide moralisé* blandly called her a trinitarian goddess ('Dyane, c'est la déité / Qui regnoit en la Trinité'),[29] and she still appeared as such, with the inscription *Theologia*, on the Tomb of Sixtus IV, looking up towards the Christian heaven where three heads are surrounded by sun-rays. As pagan goddess of the moon she foreshadows the triple glory of the Christian sun.[30] On the triple-headed Hermes (*triceps Mercurius*) Gyraldus collected an impressive array of documents,[31] etc., etc.

27. Given this mirror-like multiplication of triads, it was possible to speak of Gods as reflected in Graces (Ficino, *Opera*, p. 890), and of Graces as reflected in Fates (Pico, *Commento* II, xxi; ed. Garin II, xxiv, pp. 516 f.). For visual illustration, see a medallic image of the three Fates assimilated to the three Graces (Hill, no. 860, a commemorative medal of Andrea Capelli): Clotho offering the gift of life, Lachesis nurturing it, Atropos returning it to its origin, the three thus enacting the Neoplatonic cycle of *emanatio–vivificatio–remeatio* (cf. above, page 37). Atropos stands in profile, like the 'returning' Grace in Raphael (fig. 19) and Valeriano (fig. 17). In Correggio's Camera di San Paolo, where images placed on opposite walls are connected crosswise through the design of the vault (a visual correspondence observed by Longhi, myself, and others, but denied by Panofsky, *The Iconography of Correggio's Camera di San Paolo*, 1961, p. 69 note 2), a remarkably pleasing group of Fates answers a picture of the Graces.

28. Gyraldus, *Opera* II, 655, quoted Iamblichus as his authority on the tripod, but he may also have remembered an incidental hint in Plutarch, *On the εἶ at Delphi* 2 (*Moralia* 385D). In the *Libellus de deorum imaginibus* (Cod. Vat. Reg. lat. 1290, fol. 1ᵛ, on which see H. Liebeschütz, *Fulgentius metaforalis*, 1926, p. 118, fig. 27), Apollo wears the tripod as a sort of crown: 'Iste super caput portabat tripodem aureum.' The unconventional headgear recalls some late-antique coins and gems which enjoyed a fairly wide circulation as amulets (Campbell Bonner, *Studies in Magical Amulets, chiefly Graeco-Egyptian*, 1950, pl. x, nos. 217–19A). Perhaps aware of the confusion, Perotti, *Cornucopiae*, s.v. 'tripus Apollinis', cites Aristophanes' humorous use of στέμματα (*Plutus* 39) to describe the seat of the Pythian oracle: 'per stemmata enim .. cortinam intelligit, quod vas id rotundum est, tres pedes habens ad coronae similitudinem'.

29. III, 635 f. (ed. M. de Boer, 1915).

30. L. T. Ettlinger, 'Pollaiuolo's Tomb of Pope Sixtus IV', *Journal of the Warburg and Courtauld Institutes* XVI (1953), p. 263.   31. *Opera* I, 302.

However, it was not the Greek pantheon alone that supplied Platonic theologians with triadic gods – their search extended to Egypt and Persia. Osiris, like Saturn, was supposed to have had three sons: Anubis, Macedon, Hercules Aegyptius.[32] If the 'Egyptian authority' for this triad was a bit shaky,[33] the Chaldean trinity of Ohrmazd–Mithra–Ahriman was solidly based on Plutarch, De Iside et Osiride 46 (Moralia 369E). Since Ficino, following Pletho, identified this exotic triad with the three Platonic hypostases,[34] Francesco Giorgio drew the natural conclusion by praising it as superexcelsae trinitatis vestigium,[35] an opinion accepted by Pontus de Tyard, Discours philosophiques (1587), fol. 301ᵛ, also by Franciscus Patricius, Zoroaster et eius cccxx oracula chaldaica (1591), fol. 6, etc.

Even the ancient Sabines were believed to have had an indigenous trinity – the thrice-named Dius Fidius of Ovid's Fasti: 'nomina terna fero' (VI, 213 ff.). A Roman relief with a Renaissance inscription endowed this notion with an air of archaeological authenticity: see Petrus Apianus, Inscriptiones sacrosanctae vetustatis (1534), p. 271.[36] Repeated in innumerable copies,[37] the image found its way into Alciati's Emblemata as 'Fidei symbolum',[38] which inspired a solemn digression by Claude Mignault in his commentary on Alciati, first published 1571: 'I understand that this may

32. See Lomazzo, Trattato della pittura (1584), p. 545.

33. The chief source was the forger Annius of Viterbo, Opera de antiquitatibus (1545), fol. 65ᵛ, 74ᵛ, etc. However, a few genuine Greek texts on Hercules Aegyptius are listed in Hopfner, Plutarch über Isis und Osiris II (1941), p. 185 note 5. On Cicero's remark in De natura deorum III, xvi, 42, see R. Reitzenstein, Poimandres (1904), pp. 164 f.

34. Theologia Platonica IV, i; De amore II, iv (Opera, pp. 130, 1325). Cf. Pletho, In oracula magica Zoroastris, ed. Opsopoeus, p. 50; also Traité des lois, ed. Alexandre, Appendix ii, p. 280; Bidez and Cumont, Les mages hellénisés II, pp. 253 f.

35. De harmonia mundi I, iii, 2, fol. 40ᵛ.

36. For a sceptical view, cf. Corpus inscriptionum latinarum VI, v, 4* b; W. Amelung, Die Skulpturen des Vatikanischen Museums I, 1903, pp. 225 f., no. 80a, pl. 25. As Roberto Weiss has recently shown ('A Note on the so-called Fidei Simulacrum', Journal of the Warburg and Courtauld Institutes XXIV, 1961, p. 128), the ancient relief and its apocryphal inscription were copied as early as 1478 (dated medal of Catelano Casati, Hill, no. 790), that is, well before Pico della Mirandola engaged in trinitarian speculations. The medallist responsible for this copy, 'Lysippus the Younger', had his chief clientèle in the Academy of Rome (cf. Hill, op. cit., p. 205), a circle in which Pomponius Laetus's edition of Varro, De lingua latina (1471), was treasured as a repository of classical learning: Dius Fidius appears in it, fol. 8ʳ. For Laetus's place in the Platonic tradition see above, page 239, also 245 note 16.

37. cf. P. L. Williams, 'Two Roman Reliefs in Renaissance Disguise', Journal of the Warburg and Courtauld Institutes IV (1941), pp. 52 ff.

38. No. 95 in the edition of 1542.

fittingly be referred to a prefiguration of the sacred Trinity by the ancient Sabines, among whom there existed, long before the advent of Christ the Saviour, an image of three faces whose triple name – Sanctus, Fidius, and Semipater – likewise represents beyond any doubt [*haud dubie*] the chief mystery of the Christian religion. Described by Ovid in the sixth book of the *Fasti*.'[39]

By including among the pagan trinities certain powers of Darkness, such as the Chaldean Ahriman, the Egyptian Anubis, or the classical Pluto, Renaissance Neoplatonists seemed to recognize that divine emanations could descend to Hades. Respect shown to the triple Hecate was not surprising, in view of her association with Diana.[40] More remarkable is that the triple-headed Cerberus was made to foreshadow the 'triple power of God'.[41] Yet, once Augustine's distinction was accepted between characteristics admissible in 'vestiges of the Trinity' and those belonging to the Holy

39. A genuine inscription, found in 1574 on the Isola Tiberina and now in the Vatican (cf. *Corpus inscriptionum latinarum* VI, i, no. 567), beginning SEMONI SANCO DEO FIDIO, was quoted by Scipione Sgambati (*Archivia Veteris Testamenti* I, 1703, p. 165; cf. I. A. Fabricius, *Codex pseudepigraphus Veteris Testamenti* I, 1722, p. 287) in support of another syncretic fantasy: on the assumption that the Janus of the Romans may be identical with the biblical Noah (a legend foisted on the humanist world by Annius of Viterbo's spurious *Antiquitates*, on which see above, note 33), Sgambati argued that Semo may have been meant for Noah's son Sem: 'Tenuis est quidem conjectura, sed uti in rebus antiquis, non contemnenda.' On verbal associations of Semo with Janus, cf. Gyraldus, *Opera* I, 20, s.v. 'Semones dei', with references to Livy and Augustine. Although rejected by Gyraldus as absurd and 'exotic' (ibid., 157), the equation of Janus with Noah remained popular in the sixteenth and seventeenth centuries: see Leone Ebreo, *Dialoghi d'amore* iii (tr. cit., p. 292); Egidio da Viterbo, *Historia viginti saeculorum* (MS cit., fol. 1ʳ: 'Noe: qui primo saeculo finem, sequenti initium faciens: duas se facies habentem sculpi iussit'); Sebastian Münster, *Cosmographia* II (1545), pp. 112 f.; Iacobus Laurus, *Antiquae urbis splendor* (1641), whose genealogical table of the founders of Rome refers to Janus as *quem cum Annio Viterbiensi Noem multi existimant*. A remarkable stone altar of uncertain date, in the Musée Épigraphique at Nîmes, combines an image of the classical Janus with scenes showing Noah's Ark afloat and Noah's sacrifice after the Flood. This may well be a humanist forgery, worthy of a place in Thomas Browne's *museum clausum* (cf. *Pseudodoxia epidemica* VI, vi: 'Janus whom Annius of Viterbo and the chorographers of Italy do make to be the same as Noah'). As Valeriano observed in the *Hieroglyphica* (fol. 228ʳ), the association of Janus with mythical navigation was encouraged by the symbols on the earliest known Roman coin, the *As*, celebrated in Ovid's *Fasti* I, 229 ff., which shows on one side a Janus-head, on the other a ship's prow.

40. Gyraldus, *Opera* II, 654, also Cartari, s.v. 'Diana triformis'; cf. Servius, *In Bucolica* VIII, 75.

41. Valeriano, *Hieroglyphica*, Curione's appendix, fol. 436ᵛ: 'triplex dei potestas'; also *Hypnerotomachia*, fol. p viiiᵛ.

Trinity itself, it followed that even infernal powers could reflect the divine.[42] As late as 1655 an English poem addressed to Pope Alexander VII reads a vestige of the Trinity into the Chigi coat-of-arms, 'Whose threefold scutchian from the Trinitie / Displayes three mightie powers *Heav'n Earth* and *Hell*.'[43]

The German humanist Conrad Celtes, having learned of the pagan trinities in Italy, chose a singularly pedantic and obvious way, but for that very reason instructive, of displaying his knowledge in a woodcut of 1507.[44] He adopted the traditional iconographic type of the Holy Trinity combined with the Deësis, but substituted pagan figures for the Christian (fig. 95). In the place of God the Father blessing Christ he introduced Jupiter hovering over his son Apollo, while the part of the Holy Ghost is transferred from the dove to the winged figure of Pegasus, whose hoof brings forth the fountain of Helicon – 'the spirit moving over the waters'. The Virgin Mary at Christ's side is replaced by the virgin-goddess Minerva, and the forerunner and announcer John the Baptist by the divine messenger Hermes. In the centre of the triads, Apollo playing the lyre is supplied with his trinitarian attribute, the tripod (specially inscribed with its name).[45] The

42. On the tradition of 'Satanic trinities', see G. J. Hoogewerff, 'Vultus trifrons: emblema diabolico, imagine improba della SS. Trinità', *Rendiconti della pontificia accademia romana di archeologia* XIX (1942–3); also R. Pettazzoni, 'The Pagan Origins of the Three-headed Representation of the Christian Trinity', *Journal of the Warburg and Courtauld Institutes* IX (1946), pp. 135–51. For a criticism of W. Kirfel, *Die dreiköpfige Gottheit* (1948), cf. Pettazzoni, *L'onniscienza di Dio* (1955) pp. 183, 189 f.

43. Cod. Barb. lat. 2181, fol. 48ᵛ, published by J. McG. Bottkol, 'The Holograph of Milton's Letter to Holstenius', *Publications of the Modern Language Association of America* LXVIII (1953), p. 619.

44. Tailpiece of Tritonius's *Melopoiae*, a book of songs composed for the scanning of Horace's meters but supplied by Celtes with didactic illustrations, the printing of which he supervised: 'ductu Chunradi Celtis feliciter impressae, 1507'.

45. The tripod recurs as a trinitarian emblem in an ambitious politico-Neoplatonic woodcut designed by Celtes in honour of Maximilian. In this fantastical piece of didactic pageantry, a complete system of the arts and sciences hovers, in the shape of an imperial eagle, round the tripod of Maximilian-Apollo, the base of the cumbersome structure being formed by the triadic Judgement of Paris (reproduced in A. Burkhard, *Hans Burgkmair d. Ä.*, pl. 9, no. 10; cf. above, page 197 note 23). The joint authorship of painter and poet is celebrated in the accompanying distich: 'Burgkmair hanc acquilam depinxerat arte Johannes / Et Celtis pul[c]hram texuit historiam.' On Celtes's pride as 'inventor' of such designs, see F. von Bezold, *Aus Mittelalter und Renaissance* pp. 82–152, 391–9, also H. Rupprich, *Der Briefwechsel des Konrad Celtis* (1934), no. 87, letter from Celtes to Schreyer of 24 March 1495: 'See to it that the figures are rendered by the painter in philosophic and poetic attitudes [corresponding to the inscriptions

nine Muses framing the scene correspond to the nine angelic choirs of the celestial hierarchy.

It is doubtful, however, whether Celtes's rough simplicity in reducing the agreement between Orphic and Christian theology to a rigid diagram would have pleased any Italian humanist. Far from hiding divine secrets, the choice of a familiar Christian pattern, filled in with equally familiar pagan figures, seemed to turn the mysteries inside out. Instead of inviting the spectator to seek for a hidden concordance, it provided him with a set of clear equations (Jupiter = God the Father; Apollo = Christ; Minerva = Mary; Hermes = St John; Pegasus = Dove of the Holy Spirit). Worst of all, from an Italian point of view, Celtes grouped the pagan figures in a conventional Christian composition: whereas the humanist artists of Italy strove to do the reverse, to resuscitate the pagan form in all its seemingly un-Christian splendour, while reading into it a secret meaning consistent with Christian theology. The patent ugliness of Celtes's design was thus due to the very cause that made it look unmysterious.

From this over-explicit woodcut, it is well to look back to the emblematic elegance of the *Hypnerotomachia* where a truly mysterious Graeco-Egyptian monument (explained fols. h iv^v–h v^v) is inscribed DIVINAE INFINITAEQUE TRINITATI UNIUS ESSENTIAE (fig. 94).

IV – CHRISTIAN APOCRYPHA

To appreciate the force with which Platonic theology fostered a search for 'vestiges of the Trinity', it is important to notice that the search was not confined to pagan subjects but inspired triadic innovations in Renaissance hagiography as well. The most remarkable of these was the so-called *trinubium Annae*, that is the belief that the biblical three Marys were daughters of St Anne by three different husbands – Joachim, Cleophas, Salomas. In pictures of the Holy Kin they are occasionally numbered I, II, and III, as for example in a woodcut illustrating the *Encomium trium Mariarum*, 1529.[46] Because of its poetic eccentricity the idea met with some opposition, not only from Luther, who rejected the entire cult of St Anne as a modern invention, but also from Agrippa of Nettesheim. Appalled by

---

proposed by Celtes] so that when I come to you I can pass judgement on what should be added or left out.'

46. cf. Wind, 'Sante Pagnini and Michelangelo', *Gazette des beaux-arts* XXVI (1944), pp. 218 ff.: 'The Genealogy of Christ in Renaissance Theology', fig. 7; also figs. 8 f. (paintings of the Holy Kin by Cranach: Staedelsches Institut, Frankfurt. no. 1398; Academy, Vienna, no. 542).

the imputation of three marriages to a saint who had immaculately conceived the Virgin, he wrote *De beatissimae Annae monogamia* (1534).[47]

Far more lasting in its effect was the cult, later sanctioned by the Counter-Reformation, of the Holy Family (Joseph–Mary–Christ) as a 'Trinity on earth'.[48] A variant that also remained popular was the triad of St Anne-Mary–Christ ('Heilige Anna Selbdritt'), which enjoyed a special humanist cult in the church of Sant' Agostino in Rome.[49] Since Savonarola had endorsed the doctrine of Trinitarian vestiges (*Triumphus Crucis* III, iii), it is not surprising that his disciple, Fra Bartolommeo, in his large altarpiece for the Sala del Gran Consiglio, Florence (now in San Marco), placed the triadic group of St Anne below a celestial image of the Holy Trinity shaped as a triple head, a form much used in the fifteenth and sixteenth centuries but condemned by a bull of Urban VIII in 1628.[50]

Orthodox fears that the proliferation of 'vestigial trinities' – *imagines Trinitatis in re alia* – might end by clouding the concept of the Trinity itself were confirmed by the apostasy of Servetus. While rejecting the Athanasian creed (*De trinitatis erroribus*, 1531), he accepted the Joachimite 'three reigns' on earth as *trinitatis oeconomia*.[51] It would be false, however, to read Servetus's attitude into the Platonic theology of the fifteenth century, and more particularly into Pletho's speculations on Plato and Zoroaster. The accusation made against Pletho by his enemy George of Trebizond, that he planned to establish a universal religion which would do away with Mohammed as

47. On the subject as a whole, see Beda Kleinschmidt, *Die heilige Anna* (1930), pp. 252 ff.; also Mâle, *L'art religieux de la fin du moyen âge en France*, p. 218. The confraternity of St Anne in Louvain, for which Quentin Massys painted a *Holy Kin* (now Brussels Museum, no. 299), clearly did not accept the *trinubium Annae*: in this painting the total number of husbands attending on St Anne and the three Marys is not six but four. The assignment of three of them to St Anne (Chastel, *The Age of Humanism*, p. 327, no. 150) goes against the symmetrical plan of the picture.

48. Cornelius a Lapide, *Commentaria in quattuor evangelia* (1660), p. 53, with quotation from Gerson; Usener, *Dreiheit*, pp. 45 f.; Mâle, *L'art religieux après le concile de Trente* (1932), pp. 312 f.

49. For a description of the cult, see Egidio da Viterbo, *Historia viginti saeculorum*, MS cit., fols. 197ᵛ–198ʳ. The Latin poems addressed to Andrea Sansovino's group of St Anne were collected in the famous *Coryciana* (1524).

50. Hoogewerff, 'Vultus trifrons', op. cit., pp. 216 ff. It is curious to note that St Antoninus of Florence, whose strictures were respected by Fra Angelico, denounced the three-headed image as *contra fidem . . . quod monstrum est in rerum natura* (*Summa moralis* III, viii, 4, § 11; cf. S. Orlandi, *Beato Angelico*, 1964, p. xi), but his veto, as Fra Bartolommeo's painting shows, did not prevail even within the walls of San Marco.

51. cf. D. Cantimori, *Italienische Haeretiker der Spätrenaissance*, tr. W. Kaegi (1949), pp. 40 f., 422.

well as with Christ,[52] was the sort of coarse polemical distortion that might have been used with equal fairness to discredit Cusanus's *De pace seu concordantia fidei*. In the Western Church it was only with the growth of the Reformation that the formula proposed by Cusanus – *una religio in rituum varietate* – was felt to entail intolerable risks. Pico's nephew, Gianfrancesco, was among the most emphatic recanters, explaining that his uncle's wish to refresh canonical doctrines from apocryphal sources was misguided. In his *Examen vanitatis doctrinae gentium et veritatis Christianae disciplinae* (Mirandola 1520), he explained that it was more useful to expose dissensions between pagan philosophers than to reconcile them with each other and with Christians, as the elder Pico had attempted: *utile magis, incerta reddere philosophorum dogmata quam conciliare, ut patruus volebat* (ibid. I, ii, fol. viiiʳ). Not without irony he wrote in the preface: 'Had I wanted to imitate my uncle Johannes Picus in these matters, and accepted a few of his dogmas, perhaps it would not have been above my faculties to achieve the effect that in several instances Aristotle would join hands with Plato', *ut cum Platone Aristoteles rediret in gratiam*. He thus recanted the youthful enthusiasm with which, in his letters to Baptista Mantuanus of 1494 (*Opera*, 1601, p. 835), he had praised the great Pico's *Concordia Platonis et Aristotelis*, of which he had inherited the unfinished manuscript. The renunciation of his early beliefs is not without grandeur: 'Am I superior to Augustine, who retracted and emended his published writings?' (*Examen vanitatis*, ed. cit., fol. cxiʳ; *Opera*, p. 658). By that time (1520) the growth of biblical philology and literalism had spread distrust of any search for hidden concordances. It was one of those distressing cases in which intolerance was bred by enlightenment.[53]

52. Georgius Trapezuntius, *Comparationes philosophorum Aristotelis et Platonis* III, xix; cf. Alexandre, op. cit., p. xvi note 1; Bidez and Cumont, op. cit. I, p. 162.

53. The dilemma was clearly expressed in a letter to Peregrino Morata by Celio Calcagnini who, on receiving a treatise on the reformed doctrine, in which he 'found nothing which may not be approved and defended', feared that the unlearned would 'instantly conceive that these things are to be stiffly maintained and observed: wherefore, in my opinion, the discussion of these points ought to be confined to the initiated, that so the seamless coat of our Lord may not be rent and torn' (tr. Thomas M'Crie, *History of the Progress and Suppression of the Reformation in Italy in the Sixteenth Century*, 1827, pp. 182 ff.).

BESSARION'S LETTER ON PALINGENESIS

ON the occasion of Pletho's death his sons received from Cardinal Bessarion a magnificent letter in praise of 'our common father and master', cast in the style of Pletho's mythology and accompanied by two epitaphs in elegiac verse, suggestive of a classical apotheosis.[1] Historians without an ear for the idiom have been driven to the strange conclusion that this most conscientious of Catholic prelates must have been as 'deceitful' a Christian as they suppose Pletho to have been, since the letter reveals a genuine sympathy with Pletho's cult of the 'theology according to Zoroaster and Plato' (see above, pages 245 ff.). Bessarion boldly imagined, for example, that Pletho's spirit would join the dance of the bacchic mystics in the Beyond; still worse, that while Pletho was on earth the soul of Plato had descended into his body – a proof (according to Masai, op. cit., pp. 307 ff.) that the Cardinal belonged to a private sect that subscribed to the pagan doctrine of transmigration. In fact, the grammatical form alone excludes any positive dogma from Bessarion's statement: 'If someone were to believe' (εἴ τις . . . ἀπεδέχετο) in the Pythagorean and Platonic doctrine of periodic return, 'he might not hesitate to append the proposition' (οὐκ ἂν ὤκνησε καὶ τοῦτο προσθεῖναι) that Plato had returned to the earth as Pletho. The jubilant tone of the letter, from which Bessarion pointedly banned any trace of condolence, recalls Pletho's festive rules for inciting the imagination, τὸ φανταστικόν (Laws III, xxiv, ed. Alexandre, pp. 150 ff.), of which he had left a splendid example in his exhortation to commune with the illustrious dead, τοῖς προαποιχομένοις συνοργίασον (ibid., pp. 196 ff.). Just as his twenty-seven Hymns, of nine verses each (ibid. III, xxxv), were based on Platonic numerology (Timaeus 35C), so he availed himself of Plato's myths of pre-existence and palingenesis to inspire a patriotic revival: the cultivation of archaisms was an essential part of his style. He also had cogent philosophical reasons for deprecating a concept of 'eternal life' that extends to the future but not to the past, a 'limping eternity', as he called it (Laws III, xliii; ed.

---

1. For the text see L. Mohler, Aus Bessarions Gelehrtenkreis (1942), pp. 468 f.; also Masai, op. cit., p. 307; Alexandre, op. cit., p. lxxxiv.

Alexandre, p. 260). That a positive doctrine of transmigration was contained in the Chaldean Oracles, from which he drew much of his inspiration, is as indisputable (cf. Lewy, *Chaldaean Oracles and Theurgy*, pp. 222 ff.) as the presence of the same belief in the writings of Pythagoreans and Platonists, not to mention Plato himself. For a Renaissance way of refining these doctrines without diminishing the authorities from which they issued, see Ficino, *Theologia Platonica* XVII, iii f., XVIII, x, *Opera*, pp. 391, 395, 420 (cf. Kristeller, *The Philosophy of Marsilio Ficino*, pp. 118, 361); also Beroaldus (*Commentarii Apuleiani*, 1516), Sepulveda (*Epistolae* V, lxxviii; ed. cit., pp. 234 f.). At least one of Pletho's own formulations (*Laws* III, xliii, ed. cit. p. 256), closely imitated in Bessarion's letter, would bear comparison with Thomas Browne, *Religio medici* I, vi: 'For as though there were a Metempsychosis, and the soul of one man passed into another, Opinions do find, after certain Revolutions, men and minds like those that first beget them. To see our selves again, we need not look for Plato's year: every man is not only himself ... there hath been some one since that parallels him, and is, as it were, his revived self.' For obvious reasons, palingenesis was a thought that fascinated the Renaissance: see above, page 116 note 11 (on Lorenzo de' Medici's motto *Le temps revient*, echoing Virgil's *redeunt Saturnia regna* and illustrated by a renascent tree, emblem also of René [*Renatus*] of Anjou).[2] Since the Church taught the second advent not only of Christ, but also of Enoch, Elijah, and Jeremiah, esoteric belief in periodic returns or restitutions, although a potential nuisance to the authorities, was not necessarily heterodox. Even Guillaume Postel, whose prophetic madness sought support from the cabbalistic notion of *gilgul* (see Secret, *Les kabbalistes chrétiens de la Renaissance*, p. 176), gave an almost sane account of what he meant by the 'circulation' of spiritual powers: 'Having full certainty from precedent in Holy Writ, which says that the spirit or the virtue or the perfect form of Elijah was present in St John the Baptist, ... I ascribe revolution or transmigration not to minds or spirits or souls, which have in themselves no quality by which they may be known except to their creator, ... but to diverse parts or degrees or distinctions of substance' within the Holy Spirit, 'of whom we are parts' (ibid., p. 183). He claimed that this was *literally* meant by Job xxxiii, 29: 'Ecce haec omnia operatur Deus tribus vicibus per singulos' – 'Voicy que Dieu le fort faict par trois fois avec

2. cf. the verbal association of 'renascence' and 'palingenesis' in Aldus's dedication of the *Iliad* (1504) to Jerome Aleander: 'cum enim renasci quodammodo videantur libri ... in aedibus nostris, licere mihi arbitror διὰ τὴν τοιαύτην παλιγγενεσίαν eos, cui libuerit, dedicare.'

chacun homme.'³ The same passage from Job was quoted by Agrippa of Nettesheim in a generous chapter on 'various opinions about the after-life', in which he presented many arguments for palingenesis (*De occulta philosophia* III, xli), but not without adding Augustine's maxim: 'Melius est dubitare de occultis quam litigare de incertis.' On the assumption that propositions about the return of the dead are necessarily uncertain, it was easy enough to combine Agrippa's ravenous appetite for an abundant variety of such propositions with a refusal to plead either for or against them. The tone of his *De vanitate scientiarum* is forecast in this industrious collection of spooks, culled from Hebrew, pagan, and Christian sources, some of them undeniably poetic.

3. On cabbalistic interpretations of Job xxxiii, 29, see G. Scholem, 'Seelenwanderung und Sympathie der Seelen in der jüdischen Mystik', *Eranos-Jahrbuch* XXIV (1956), pp. 73, 80, 83, 91.

APPENDIX 4

THE TRINITY OF SERAPIS

IN the great temple of Serapis at Alexandria the image of the Egypto-Hellenic god was attended by a triple-headed monster resembling Cerberus, but with this difference that the three heads of the beast were distinguished as wolf, lion, and dog. The most informative ancient text on this attribute (cf. Panofsky, *Hercules am Scheidewege*, pp. 1-35) is Macrobius, *Saturnalia* I, xx, where the three heads are explained as signifying the three parts of Time: facing left, the voracious wolf represents the vanished past; the hopefully sniffing dog looks to the right, anticipating the future; while the present, in the middle, is embodied in the majestic lion seen full-face. Petrarch's *Africa* III, 162 ff., gives a splendid description of the three heads, followed by a concise statement of the allegory: *fugientia tempora signant.*

Although it is more than doubtful whether Petrarch could have known the ancient invocation of the god as Helioserapis, he boldly transferred the animal attribute to Apollo, apparently on the authority of Macrobius who, in his belief that all the pagan gods are but aspects of the Sun, made Serapis into a solar deity like all the rest. Plutarch, in *De Iside et Osiride* 28 and 78 (*Moralia* 361F-362B; 382E-383A), preferred to accept the symbolic animal as a cousin of Cerberus, and Serapis himself as a variant of Pluto, that is as an Egyptian god of the after-life (cf. Gyraldus, *Opera* I, 197 ff., where the very considerable collection of texts concerning Serapis is subsumed under Pluto).

By the time Ripa published his *Iconologia* (1593), the mysterious attribute of Serapis had been refined to a moral hieroglyph. Still associated with the three parts of Time, it now signified that particular virtue which Aristotle called εὐβουλία (*Nicomachean Ethics* VI, ix, 1142B). Translated as *buon consiglio, Urteilskraft, consilium,* its English equivalent is 'good judgement', although *Good Counsel* has become its official title, at least in iconography. It consists in a sound practical instinct for the course of events, an almost indefinable hunch that anticipates the future by remembering the past and thus judges the present correctly. Since this ability is acquired only with age (Nestor being always quoted as its paragon), it is different from Prudence which, though rarely practised by the young, is not necessarily beyond their reach.[1] In iconography *Prudentia* may be seen with three human heads because this is the virtue of circumspection (fig. 91),[2] while *Consilium*, its more pragmatic counterpart, has the three animal heads of Serapis (fig. 90).[3]

A disturbing allegory ascribed to Titian (Panofsky, op. cit., fig. 1, now in the National Gallery, London) combines *Prudentia* with *Consilium* in a double trinity, arranged in two storeys, so that the human heads on the upper level correspond to the animal heads below. This is not, as might be thought, a pleonasm, since *Consilium* and *Prudentia* are not the same; but although the distinction may be logically clear, the aesthetic effect of the combination is coarsely repetitive. The literal symmetry between the six heads is indeed without parallel in Titian's *œuvre*. It would be tempting to associate this redundant exercise, performed in the bold manner of Titian's final period, with Cesare Vecelli's work in Belluno, the native city of Pierio Valeriano.[4] The ponderous inscription in antique letters is

1. On the distinction between *consilium* and *prudentia* see Thomas Aquinas, *Summa theologica* I, ii, q. 57, art. 6, with particular reference to Aristotle, *Nicomachean Ethics* 1142B. Although Dante simplified these arguments in *Convivio* IV, xxvii by introducing *consilium* as a mere sequel of *prudentia* ('dalla Prudenza vengono i buoni consigli'), he observed that *consilium* was the gift which Solomon asked of God (1 Kings iii, 5 ff.) when he was called to govern and felt too young. Dante adds that he that possesses *consilium* exudes that gift as the rose exudes her scent: which seems more like a grace than a virtue.

2. For the division of *prudentia* into three parts (*memoria–intelligentia–providentia*, corresponding to past, present, and future) the classical source is Cicero, *De inventione* II, liii, whose formula became a scholastic commonplace: see, for example, Albertus Magnus, *De prudentia* II, i–iv, 468–86 (*Opera omnia*, ed. B. Geyer, XXVIII, 1951, pp. 245–54); Thomas Aquinas, *Summa theologica* I, ii, q. 57, art. 6, no. 4; Dante, *Convivio* IV, xxvii.

3. Fig. 90 is a detail from a frieze by Quellinus the Elder in the Town Hall of Amsterdam, engraved by J. Vennekool for Jacob van Campen, *Afbeelding van't Stadt Huys van Amsterdam* (1661), pl. Q. On the particular council chamber for which the design was invented, see K. Fremantle, *The Baroque Town Hall of Amsterdam* (1959), p. 38 note 4, also p. 70. The iconography derives from Ripa, s.v. 'Consiglio'.

4. On 'the bold manner of Cesare Vecelli', Titian's most enterprising disciple in his old age, see Crowe and Cavalcaselle, *Titian* II (1881), pp. 435, 488, with reference to portraits named by tradition 'Pierio Valeriano' and 'Fra Urbano' and thus connected with the pioneers of hieroglyphics. According to Crowe and Cavalcaselle, Cesare's 'handling is rapid and bold, the pigments copious, the flesh tint deep in tone and relieved with dark shadow reminiscent of Schiavone and Tintoretto rather than Titian' – 'clearly a man of great skill ... enterprising yet on the whole a shallow disciple of a great master'. Is this the hand of the London allegory? If so, this would be a further reason for rejecting the theory that the man linked to the 'wolf' is a self-portrait of

conceived (again very unlike Titian) as a formal component in the design:
EX PRAETERITO / PRAESENS PRUDENTER AGIT / NI FUTURĀ ACTIONĒ
DETURPET. The three parts of the sentence are divided between the three
human heads, defining them clearly as Past, Present, and Future, which is
also shown by their ages and their animal attributes.

That such a triad of human heads associated with the three parts of Time
was meant to suggest a 'vestige of the Trinity', as defined by Augustine in
De Trinitate (see above, page 41), is rendered probable by two facts: (1)
Augustine himself quotes the three phases of Time as a 'vestige of the
Trinity' (X, xi, 17 ff.); (2) this particular part of his doctrine was familiar to
the Renaissance. A characteristic example is Gianfrancesco Pico della
Mirandola (Giovanni Pico's nephew), *De rerum praenotione* I, viii: 'quandam
etiam beatissimae Trinitatis imaginem .. . in anima ex praeteriti, praesentis
atque futuri temporis notitia praevestigabimus', with explicit reference to
consilium as defined by Aristotle (*Rhetoric* I, iii: συμβουλή, which is εὐβουλία
applied to rhetoric). In the *Hypnerotomachia*, whose large collection of triadic
images includes also the *signum triceps* of Serapis (fols. x viii^v–y ii^r), the Holy
Trinity is again traced in the three parts of Time (fol. h v^v). It follows that
in the allegory attributed to Titian the resemblance of the three human
heads to current representations of the divine Trinity is not accidental;
it is, in the language of Augustine, an *imago trinitatis in re alia*.

In a printer's mark designed by Holbein (P. Renouard, *Les marques
typographiques parisiennes*, 1928, no. 967) the hand of God, issuing from a
cloud, holds the triple-headed symbol of Serapis, a threatening apparition
of *Consilium* in the sky. Perhaps it is relevant to the design that in comparing the Bible with Plato, Avicenna, and Dionysius the Areopagite, Pico
found that *Consilium* is a true appellation of the supreme God who is hidden
in darkness (see below, Appendix 9). On a medal of Andrea Gritti by
Giovanni Zacchi, a figure of Fortuna supported by the three-headed symbol
of Serapis or *Consilium* bears the inscription DEI OPT MAX OPE (Habich,
Die Medaillen der italienischen Renaissance (1924), pl. lxxv, 5; see also above,

---

Titian, and that the two attached to the 'lion' and the 'dog' represent his heirs
(Panofsky, 'Titian's Allegory of Prudence: a Postscript', *Meaning in the Visual Arts*,
1957, pp. 165 ff.). As in Veronese's allegories (see below, page 275), the faces are designed as physiognomic types which, rendered in a realistic style, may produce an
illusion of portraiture. The illustrations of Valeriano's chapter *De tricipitio* (*Hieroglyphica* XXXII, fol. 229^r) are more closely related to the painting in London than
anything in the *Hypnerotomachia*. Valeriano excelled in the pettifogging art of making
commonplaces look abstruse.

p. 40 note 17). Of decisive importance in this context is the fact that the god Serapis was credited with an oracle that foreshadowed the Christian Trinity. Gyraldus, who referred to it as *oraculum quod celebre Serapidis fuit* (op. cit. I, 197), gave the text not only in the original Greek but translated it into his own inelegant Latin, which is nevertheless worth quoting:

> *Principio Deus est, tum Verbum, his Spiritus una est.*
> *Congenita haec tria sunt, cuncta haec tendentia in unum.*

He added to this the amusing sentence: 'I quote this to you so that you may see that Pluto' – whom he identified with Serapis – 'affirmed the mystery of the Trinity', *ut videas a Plutone Trinitatis mysterium assertum esse.*

Quite apart from its Augustinian development, the idea that triadic Time, attended by Prudence or Good Counsel, is a vestige of the Godhead recalls Plato's theory, *Timaeus* 37D-38B (resumed by Plotinus, *Enneads* I, v, 7; III, vii, 1 ff.), that the three parts of Time 'imitate Eternity', of which they provide a 'moving image' (εἰκὼ κινητόν τινα αἰῶνος). Hence Diogenes Laertius III, 106, was not, as has been supposed, ill-informed when he introduced triadic συμβουλία into his chapter on Plato.[5] In *Timaeus* 72A, the distinction of two forms of foresight in man, intellectual and animal, located in head and liver and reflecting each other 'as in a mirror' while they determine 'a future or a past or a present evil or good', might well have suggested the monstrous superposition of an anthropomorphic on a theriomorphic trinity in the Serapis allegory ascribed to Titian.

---

5. It should be noted that it was on the authority of Aristotle, who seems to have compiled a list of Plato's διαιρέσεις, that Diogenes Laertius ascribed this particular notion tó Plato (cf. III, 80 and 109). Aristotle adapted it to his own uses in *Rhetoric* 1358B ff., on which Cicero drew for the *De inventione* (I, v ff.; II, li). The classical concept of triadic *consilium* may well have inspired the medieval idea of a *Consilium Trinitatis*, pictured as the Holy Trinity 'taking counsel' before creating the world (see A. Heimann, 'Trinitas creator mundi', *Journal of the Warburg Institute* II, 1938, pp. 46 ff.). On the supreme cause as 'counselling cause', and the use of the word *consilium* as a 'divine name', see below, pages 276 ff.

APHRODITE'S SHELL

POLITIAN's assumption that Venus was carried over the sea on a shell ('sopra un nicchio', *Giostra* I, xcix, 8) is a poetic residue of a more primitive belief, that she was *born* from a shell: see Usener, 'Die Perle: Aus der Geschichte eines Bildes', in *Theologische Abhandlungen, Karl von Weiz-säcker gewidmet* (1892), pp. 201–13 (reprinted in *Vorträge und Aufsätze*, 1907, pp. 217–31), with demonstration how the shell was 'abgeschwächt zum Fahrzeug der Venus', for example in Lygdamus = Tibullus III, iii, 34: 'et faveas concha, Cypria, vecta tua'. In a Renaissance commentary on Tibullus (by Bernardinus Cyllaenius Veronensis, ed. 1520, fols. xxiv^r) this passage is taken as proof that the birth from the sea and the transportation on the shell are two separate events: 'qua [concha] mari devecta est in Cyprum, cum primum ex spumis genita est'. On the ancient iconography of Venus in the shell, and the use of that formula for aphrodisiac talismans, see L. Stephani, 'Erklärung einiger im südlichen Russland gefundener Kunstwerke', Supplement for the years 1870–71 of *Compte-rendu de la com-mission impériale archéologique*, St Pétersbourg (1874), pp. 11–176, with a stupendous array of ancient monuments and texts on the Birth of Venus; also Deonna, 'Aphrodite à la coquille', *Revue archéologique* VI (1917), particularly pp. 399 ff. on 'Aphrodite née d'une coquille'; M. Brickoff, 'Afrodite nella conchiglia', *Bollettino d'arte* IX (1929), pp. 563 ff.; A. Rumpf in *Die antiken Sarcophagreliefs* V, i (1939), pp. 36 ff.: 'Aphrodite in Muschel'; Erika Simon, *Die Geburt der Aphrodite* (1959), p. 42. Since the birth from the shell is mentioned by Plautus ('te ex concha natam esse', *Rudens* 704), it is not surprising that the primitive idea survives in elegant Roman wall paintings which show a luxurious Aphrodite stretched out in her shell like a living pearl (e.g. *Antiquités d'Herculanum*, ed. S. Maréchal, 1781, IV, 3; W. Helbig, *Wandgemälde Campaniens*, 1868, 307; A. Maiuri, *Roman Painting*, 1953, p. 7, from Pompeii). It was a mistake, however, to infer (as in Warburg, op. cit., p. 310, editor's note) that Botticelli's idea of placing Venus upright in the shell (fig. 39) had no ancient but only medieval pre-cedents. A Greco-Roman gem, which passed from Baron de Stosch's col-lection in Florence to the Berlin antiquarium, shows Venus in a huge scallop

shell (fig. 35), standing in the same posture as Botticelli's figure: see Furt-
wängler, *Beschreibung der geschnittenen Steine im Antiquarium* (1896), no.
2385: 'Aphrodite im Typus der mediceischen Statue in einer riesigen pecten-
Muschel stehend'; also H. B. Walter, *Catalogue of the Engraved Gems and
Cameos Greek Etruscan and Roman in the British Museum* (1926), no. 2810.
Winckelmann described the figure on the gem as an Anadyomene:
'Vénus sortant de la mer dans une coquille' (*Pierres gravées du feu Baron de
Stosch* II, no. 536). He associated the posture with Apelles (cf. *Geschichte der
Kunst des Altertums* I, iv, s.v. 'Mediceische Venus'), and so did Politian and
Botticelli when they added the celebrated motif of 'pressing the hair'
('premendo il crino', *Giostra* I, ci, 3); cf. Ovid, *Epistolae ex Ponto* IV, i, 30:
'aequoreo madidas quae premit imbre comas', annotated in Politian's copy
of Ovid (*Opera*, Parma 1477: Bodleian Library, Oxford, Auct. P. 2. 2, fol.
S iiᵛ) with a marginal note in his hand: 'Venus Apellis'.

From what is known of the frequent adaptation of large sculptural or
pictorial images to the diminutive scale of ancient gems, coins, and terra-
cottas, it would seem that conflations of a statuesque posture with an *Aphrodite
à la coquille* must have originated in the minor arts.[1] Since Botticelli's
draughtsmanship is related to goldsmith's work (cf. Warburg, op. cit., p.
53), it is perhaps not too fanciful to observe that his formal way of linking
figure and shell could well be imagined as a jewelled pendant. As a curiosity
it may be added that in Ovid's *Ars amatoria* (III, 223 f.) the posture of Apelles's Anadyomene is described with the same poetic phrase as in the *Epistolae
ex Ponto*, but instead of a painting the subject is a jewel, a rough stone turned
into a finely engraved gem:

> *Cum fieret, lapis asper erat: nunc, nobile signum,*
> *nuda Venus madidas exprimit imbre comas.*[2]

1. A late piece of Egyptian jewellery of exceptional grace (Dumbarton Oaks Collection, Washington, no. 184; *Handbook*, 1955, pl. 88, dated *c.* seventh century) shows
Venus standing upright in a shell and holding two strands of her hair symmetrically
with both hands – a classical type of posture for statues of Venus (listed in J. J. Bernouilli, *Aphrodite*, pp. 288 ff., who derives this type again from Apelles's Anadyomene
although the attitude looks rather like an adaptation of the Diadumenos to a *toilette de
Vénus*): it recurs, *with shell*, in a Graeco-Roman terracotta (Stephani, op. cit., pl. iii, no.
6; p. 83, no. 56; also pp. 103, 139, 176).

2. The inscription on a marble relief, by Antonio Lombardo, of a Venus Anadyomene wringing out her hair (Victoria and Albert Museum, London), quotes from
this distich only the pentameter, perhaps as a concealed tribute to the sculptor's art
and to the ready wit of a humanist beholder who would recognize and complete the
quotation: *cum fieret, lapis asper erat: nunc nobile signum.*

GAFURIUS ON THE HARMONY OF
THE SPHERES

In illustrating the music of the spheres (fig. 20) Gafurius placed the triads of the Graces and of Serapis at opposite ends of the great cosmic scale which he imagined in the shape of a serpent connecting heaven and earth. As in Julian's *Hymn to Helios* (*Orationes* IV, 146c–d, 148d), the three Graces dance in heaven under the guidance of Apollo, while he animates the spheres with music. The vase of flowers on Apollo's left probably signifies the νοῦς ὑλικός, associated by Macrobius with the celestial *crater* (*In Somnium Scipionis* I, xii) through which the divine spirit descends as far down as the φυτικόν, *id est, naturam plantandi et agendi corpora*. At the bottom of the scale, the trinity of Serapis hovers over the last and lowest of the musical emanations which is the realm of subterranean silence, as explained by Gafurius (*De harmonia musicorum instrumentorum*, 1518, fol. 93ᵛ), who identifies the animal with Cerberus, and the muse of nocturnal silence with the 'surda Thalia', adding that on the authority of Cicero things in the earth are silent because the earth is immobile (Macrobius, op. cit. I, xxii–II, i). On Serapis as a god of the underworld, Gafurius may have consulted Plutarch, *De Iside et Osiride* (as quoted above, page 259). In this realm of death, where the sheer passage of all-devouring Time has become a vacant copy of eternity, like prime matter in the definition of Plotinus, 'a ghost that never stays yet can never vanish' (*Enneads* III, vi, 7, tr. Dodds), the triple-headed monster, *fugientia tempora signans*, retains a shadowy vestige of the triadic dance that the Graces start under the direction of Apollo. The whole universe, from top to bottom, is thus permeated by the 'Pythian nomos', a triadic rhythm which Apollo himself is supposed to have initiated at Delphi when he battled against the python (see Warburg, *Die Erneuerung der heidnischen Antike*, pp. 283 f., 417–20).

It has been suggested that the great serpent in Gafurius's scheme, being placed below Apollo, might represent the vanquished python; yet it would be strange if this ferociously destructive beast, instead of lying dead at the victor's feet, were to assist him in harmonizing the universe. Supplied with three heads, leonine in the centre and wolf- or dog-like on either side, the animal is unquestionably the old *signum triceps*, the special Cerberus of Serapis, whom Petrarch identified with Apollo (see Appendix 4). It is therefore not unusual to find this dragon employed in the service of Apollo, occasionally even during his fight with the python, in which case the battle array is a bit confusing: the god mounted on a triple-headed apocalyptic serpent slays a supposedly evil dragon that looks no worse than his own conveyance (*Libellus de deorum imaginibus*, Cod. Reg. lat. 1290, fol. 1ᵛ; *Ovide moralisé*, MS. Thott. 399, fol. 21ᵛ, Royal Library, Copenhagen).

Gafurius's serpent is distinguished by a particularly engaging trait. While plunging head-downward into the universe, it curls the end of its tail into a loop on which Apollo ceremoniously sets his feet. A serpent's tail turning back on itself is an image of eternity or perfection (commonly illustrated by a serpent biting its own tail, but known also in the form of a circular loop on the serpent's back, as in the medal of Lorenzo di Pierfrancesco de' Medici, discussed below). Gafurius thus makes it diagrammatically clear that Time issues from Eternity, that the linear progression of the serpent depends on its attachment to the topmost sphere where its tail coils into a circle.

That the 'descent' of a spiritual force is compatible with its continuous presence in the 'supercelestial heaven' was a basic tenet of Neoplatonism. Plotinus illustrated this difficult doctrine, which was essential to his concept of emanation, by the descent of Hercules into Hades (*Odyssey* xi, 601 f.). Homer, he said, had admitted 'that the image of Hercules appeared in Hades while the hero was really with the gods, so that the poet affirms this double proposition: that Hercules is with the gods while he is in Hades' (*Enneads* I, i, 12). Pico della Mirandola extended the argument to Christ's descent into Limbo, in the most startling of his *Conclusiones in theologia*, no. 8, which it is not surprising to find among the articles that were condemned: 'Christ did not descend to Hell verily and in his real presence, as is supposed by Thomas and the common opinion, but only *quoad effectum*.' His chief reason for adhering to this unusual view, against the judgement of a papal commission (see *Apologia*, *Opera*, pp. 125-50), may be gathered from a simple proposition, remarkably short, *Conclusiones secundum Plotinum*, no. 2: 'Non tota descendit anima quum descendit.'

These words of Pico's apply exactly to the 'perfect' serpent on the medal of Lorenzo di Pierfrancesco de' Medici (fig. 21). Despite its round shape, this is a serpent that has 'descended': it rests visibly on a patch of earth. For that reason it does not bite its own tail; the head, stretched forward along the ground, remains outside the circle of perfection. Yet it is the circle that gives the animal such a peculiar splendour that those parts of it that creep on the ground look like a mere appendage of the heavenly portion. *Non tota descendit anima quum descendit.*

In combining elegance with ingenuity, the medal is suggestive of the taste and intelligence of the man for whom it was designed as a personal emblem – the same Lorenzo di Pierfrancesco who commissioned Botticelli to paint the *Primavera* and the *Birth of Venus* and to illustrate the *Divine Comedy.* Gafurius's serpent cannot equal the sheer felicity of this image; but it is fair to add that it was not meant to. The portion of the serpent outside the loop is here necessarily very much longer, being obliged to accommodate all the parts of the universe that lie between the topmost heaven and the centre of the earth. Yet the symbolic principle is the same, even though the intellectual baggage it is made to carry is disconcertingly manifold. Thus the curves connecting the stars with the Muses, and boldly intersected by the serpent's tail, are meant to be segments not only of circles but of three-dimensional spheres. What we are given here is a flat map (imperfect as flat maps of solid objects are) of a spherical universe whose centre is occupied by the serpent's leonine head, while the loop both marks and transcends the circumference.

The inscriptions distributed over this curious woodcut call also for some explanation. Those issuing from the images of the Muses signify the notes of an octave, listed in Greek, rising from *proslambanomene* to *mese*. Opposite to them, the corresponding Greek modes, beginning with the Hypodorian and ending with the Hypermixolydian, lead across to the astral signs. As a highly skilled theoretician and singer, Gafurius did not need to be told that the seven classical modes, which do not go beyond the Mixolydian, exhaust the variations obtainable from the diatonic scale. In adding the Hypermixolydian at the top, Gafurius was guided by Boethius, *De musica* IV, xvi f., who had argued, on the authority of Ptolemy, that this supernumerary mode was necessary *ut totus ordo impleatur.* Indeed, without it the sphere of the fixed stars would be without music, and the muse Urania, in her heavenly pride, would be as silent as the 'soundless Thalia' whose pitiful little bust, meticulously buried below the earth, defines the Beyond from which music rises in what Gafurius called 'the sigh of Proserpina' (see above, page 130).

The inscription at the top of the whole system explains that the spirit of Apollo descends into all the Muses, including the Muse of Silence because rests are essential to melody. *Mentis Apollineae vis has movet undique musas.* The verse comes from a poem, *Nomina musarum*, now relegated to the

Appendix Ausoniana, but the Renaissance believed it to be Virgil's, a counterpart to the more justly famous and genuine line, *Aeneid* VI, 727:

> *Mens agitat molem et magno se corpore miscet.*

A numerical refinement, which in such a finical scheme can hardly be dismissed as accidental, may be noticed in the flowers of Apollo's vase: there are six. Combined with the three Graces on the other side, they add up to nine, the number of the Muses. It follows that six of the musico-stellar spheres should be classed as sensuous, three as pure. Among the seven planetary modes, only the Dorian, associated with the sun and thus with Apollo, is pure. Placed in the centre of the planets it secures the symmetry of the other six by dividing them into two triads. The celestial sphere above the planets and the sphere of subterranean silence below them supply the two remaining pure modes that belong to the Graces. The fact that the Grace farthest removed and appearing to enter the dance from the Beyond is named Thalia, like the muse below the earth, confirms the correspondence. The sequence of spheres may then be read as follows:

Celestial Sphere				Sun				Subterranean Sphere
	Saturn	Jupiter	Mars		Venus	Mercury	Luna	
⑧	7	6	5	④	3	2	1	⓪
	Polyhymnia	Euterpe	Erato		Terpsichore	Calliope	Clio	
Urania				Melpomene				Thalia

In the order of the Muses, the triad Urania–Melpomene–Thalia would then emanate from the dance of the Graces, while the six intermediate Muses are 'planted' in Apollo's vase.[1] No doubt, the names of the three

1. A vase filled with flowers recurs as a Renaissance emblem for virtues or graces implanted in the soul; cf. Giovio, *Imprese*, ed. cit., p. 217 (Appendix by Lodovico Domenichi). On one of Andrea Riccio's reliefs for the Della Torre tomb in the Louvre (L. Planiscig, *Andrea Riccio*, 1927, fig. 495), a vase with plants is inscribed *virtus*, a motif elaborated by Vasari in his allegorical portrait of Lorenzo the Magnificent (*omnium virtutum vas*) in the Uffizi. See also A. [Ghisi] Scultore's engraving of *The Choice of Hercules* (Bartsch no. 26), where Virtue holds a vase filled with flowers. In the *Hypnerotomachia* (fol. c i^r) a vase serves as a hieroglyph for *animus* (also with twig = *animae clementia*, fol. p vi^v), suggested by Psyche's vase in Apuleius, perhaps also by a pun in Plato (*Gorgias* 493A), where the affective part of the soul (πιθανόν) is ironically

Graces and their current translations – Aglaia = *splendor*, Thalia = *viriditas*, Euphrosyne = *laetitia* (cf. Ficino, *De amore* V, ii) – were also taken into account: *laetitia* belonging to the celestial sphere, *splendor* to the Sun, *viriditas* to the subterranean seeds of music:

> *Germinat in primo nocturna silentia cantu,*
> *Quae terrae in gremio surda Thalia iacet.*[2]

---

called a jar (πίθος), interpreted seriously by Porphyry, *De antro nympharum* 30, who refers in this context to the Platonic *crater* (31); cf. above, page 265. On the vase as emblem in Seneca and Plutarch, see F. Husner, *Leib und Seele in der Sprache Senecas* (1924), pp. 77–84; 'Gefäss'.

2. Gafurius, *De harmonia musicorum instrumentorum* (1518), fol. 93ᵛ.

LOVE AND STRIFE IN THE 'JUDGEMENT OF PARIS'

AMONG Platonic interpretations of the Judgement of Paris (on which see above, pages 82, 197), the cosmic allegory devised by Sallustius (*Concerning the Gods and the Universe*, ed. A. D. Nock, 1926, § iv, p. 6) stands out by its pensive and haunting quality: 'They tell that at the banquet of the gods Strife threw a golden apple and the goddesses, vying with one another for its possession, were sent by Zeus to Paris to be judged; Paris thought Aphrodite beautiful, and gave her the apple. Here the banquet signifies the supramundane powers of the gods, and that is why they are together, the golden apple signifies the universe, which, as it is made of opposites, is rightly said to be thrown by Strife, and as the various gods give various gifts to the universe they are thought to vie with one another for the possession of the apple; further, the soul that lives in accordance with sense-perception (for that is Paris), seeing beauty alone and not the other powers in the universe, says that the apple is Aphrodite's.'

That the 'quarrel of the gods' is silenced for a brief moment by a mortal who sees 'beauty alone and not the other powers' is irresistibly suggested in Raphael's design of the *Judgement of Paris*, drawn freely from a Roman sarcophagus (Villa Medici, Rome; cf. Robert, *Die antiken Sarkophag-Reliefs* II, 11) and engraved by Marcantonio Raimondi (Bartsch XIV, no. 245). The presence of Oreads tending the springs of Mount Ida, and of River-gods and a Naiad on the banks of the Scamander (cf. Porphyry, *De antro nympharum* 10, 12; also Sallustius, op. cit., § iv, p. 8), locates the discord of the three goddesses in a world of flux – to which Pico assigned the apparition of Beauty 'because here begins contrariety' (cf. above, page 88). On the ancient sarcophagus, which survives only in a dilapidated state, the victorious Venus was attended by Mars,[1] the god of Strife, reconstructed as an ominous warrior by Bonasone in an important engraving that was

1. On the traditional interpretation of the armed figure next to Venus as Mars, see Zoega, Welcker, Gerhard, Jahn, Panofka, Matz, and others as quoted by Robert (op. cit., p. 17), who alone is dissatisfied with this view. He suggests, unconvincingly, that the warrior represents Paris after the Judgement.

probably meant to rival Marcantonio's (Bartsch XV, no. 112).[2] Raphael, by omitting Mars, concentrated the design on the supreme moment in which Beauty transfigures the world of the senses, and Paris necessarily succumbs to the spell because he is, as Sallustius put it, 'the soul that lives in accordance with sense perception'. In a woodcut by Burgkmair, invented for him by Conrad Celtes, the words *errando discitur philosophia* are inscribed over the Judgement of Paris while Concord and Discord attend the scene (see above, page 197 note 23; also page 252 note 45). Raphael's design interprets Paris's 'error' as an entranced and exclusive homage to beauty. While the hortatory moral gesture of Juno and the 'unveiling of truth' performed by Minerva invite Paris to look beyond sensibility, the perfection of Venus is 'palpable to sight' (*Phaedrus* 250D). The classic nostalgia that pervades the scene expresses Raphael's poetic subject: he celebrates Beauty as descended from the sky and made visible – with tragic effects – to a mortal. The theme is conceived as an epiphany, a mysterious communion between mortal and gods, where concord arises out of discord, but only for a fleeting moment.

For an intimation of the sequel we must turn to Bonasone's version of the Judgement of Paris. Despite a touch of archaeological flatness in the incidental parts of the engraving, his Mars is designed with extraordinary power as the figure dominating the composition. Indeed the character is so well conceived, in his insidious readiness to release disaster, looking back at Venus while going off to war, that one wonders whether Bonasone did not also have some sketch by Raphael to work on. In any case these two engravings, both inspired by the same ancient marble, represent the Judgement of Paris in contrasting moods, one centred in Venus, the other in Mars, as if to anatomize the two components in the mutual entailment of Love and Strife (see above, pages 94 ff.).

2. Bonasone's attempt to restore all the broken pieces of the sarcophagus betrayed him into archaeological rhetoric. The nymphs on the left have a vacant look. In the sky, the segment of the zodiac, forming in the original a sort of celestial gate through which Apollo drives the chariot of the sun, is mistaken for a flying veil. The same error occurs in Codex Coburgensis (on which see Robert, loc. cit.). Although the original is badly damaged, some fragments of the zodiacal sign of Pisces are recognizable on the remnants of the arch, a fact which did not escape Raphael, who expanded this puny little piece of evidence into the splendid zodiacal halo surrounding Apollo.

A CYCLE OF LOVE BY VERONESE

(NATIONAL GALLERY, LONDON)

UNTIL recently the four allegories by Veronese in the National Gallery (nos. 1324, 1326, 1325, 1318), which form a coherent cycle of Love, went under peculiar names:

        (1) Scorn (our fig. 43)
        (2) Happy Union (fig. 49)
        (3) Respect (fig. 46)
        (4) Unfaithfulness (fig. 47)

The second title, although the most trivial, is perhaps the least misleading: the scene is certainly one of concord and felicity. Peace is symbolized by the olive twig flamboyantly raised by the two lovers; the conjugal chain is held by Amor, and the dog indicates *fidelitas*. The girdle of Venus – emblem of *piacere honesto* (cf. Ripa, s.v.) – is worn by the goddess of Fortune (enthroned on a sphere, with cornucopia) who crowns the pair. Since a firm pedestal supports the sphere, the Good Fortune of the couple is steady.

That this desirable state was preceded by ordeals is shown by the picture of castigation (fig. 43). As Ripa put it (cf. above, page 147), 'la castità è nome di virtù detta dalla castigatione.' Amor, who has vanquished the prostrate man, makes him suffer the tortures of love. That the victim is in the throes of *voluptas* is indicated by his nakedness (all the other men in the cycle are dressed) and also by the emblems of Satyr and Pan's Flute that emerge from the architectural ruins in the background. While Amor is responsible for the lover's plight, he is also the force that chastens his passion: he uses his bow on him without touching the arrows. (For the symbolic distinction between bow and arrow, see above, page 78, with special reference to Titian; hence certainly known to Veronese.) The woman – the true cause of these tortures – is in the same plight as the man. Although she is attended by Chastity carrying the symbolic ermine, her general disarray characterizes her as passionate; and it is just this fatal combination of a passionate nature with chaste resolutions that causes the lover's agony. In plain words, this is a picture of courtship.

Courtship is followed by ceremonious concord, crowned by a *Fortuna amoris* (fig. 49). The partners, although jointly holding the emblem of peace, still retain some of their contrarious characters: the man's gesture in lifting the olive twig is more florid than the woman's, and while he wears a bracelet of pearls on his naked arm, her arm is covered to the wrist by the long sleeve of her courtly dress. Within Veronese's gallant style, this festively robed and jewelled woman, who modestly displays her flowing hair while invoking the blessing of the goddess, represents Chastity heightened into Beauty by love. In the formal splendour of her attire she should be compared to Botticelli's figure of Pulchritudo (fig. 30). The restraining Amor and the spirited dog (expressive of the temperaments of the wedded pair) look up with suspense at the crowning goddess who promises the good fortune of *piacere honesto*.

The pains of love, having been resolved in ceremonious concord, are compensated by the pleasures of love, represented in the third picture (fig. 46). Instead of the bow, used in the scene of chastisement, Amor now relies on his arrow; yet restraint is predominant even here. *The Continence of Scipio*, set into the vault as an ornament, is like a gloss on the man's gesture of awe (which is also echoed by an attendant, who holds him back by the arm). To illustrate the consummation of love Veronese reverted to a traditional formula, the device of suggesting an epiphany of Venus: the mortal lover, in elegant costume, is brought into the presence of a deified nude. The obvious disparity in this type of image appealed to the good humour of Florentine *cassone* painters who decorated the lid of many a fifteenth-century marriage chest with such an incongruous-looking pair (figs. 44-5). Raised by Titian to a somewhat tiresome show-piece (see above, page 143 note 7), the theme was twisted by Veronese into a conceit so audacious as to seem unprecedented; which is precisely what it is not. For its full effect the picture depends on being seen opposite to the ordeal of chastisement, of which it is the exact reversal: here a recumbent woman approached with awe, there a prostrate man causing indignation and dismay.

The final painting (fig. 47) is perhaps the most brilliantly contrived of the series. It represents the 'tripartite life', defined by Marsilio Ficino (*De triplici vita et fine triplici*) as a well-regulated strife between the contemplative, the active, and the pleasurable parts of the soul in which the dominant part is given to Pleasure. Committed to a mystical hedonism, an Epicurean refinement of Neoplatonic ecstasies, Ficino argued (against the Stoic view, cf. above, page 71) that meditation and action find both their incentive and their fruition in the *vita voluptaria* – provided that *voluptas* is understood as 'Voluptas Urania' who turns her back to the world, as she does in this painting. Seated on her throne, the goddess of supreme Delight fills the musical poet with divine meditations, while the man of heroic action, dressed in a cuirass, returns to her and grasps her hand. The Neoplatonic circuit of love – 'giving', 'receiving', and 'returning' – is here translated into a courtly pageant. The contemplative mood of the poet, while he receives his brief from the inspiring muse, is clearly directed towards heaven, but the steady outward glance of the martial courtier brings the movement back to its beginning in Pleasure.

The two *amoretti* in the left corner repeat the contrast in a jocose vignette: the winged putto plays on a musical instrument in a meditative mood that corresponds to the poet's, but his wingless brother, not equipped for flight, embraces the foot of the goddess, as if he were trying to hold it down, while glancing towards the man of action, whose well-shod legs are deliberately stressed. Judged in terms of spatial recession, the poet's figure is farthest removed, while the warrior, boldly foreshortened, seems to descend towards the spectator. An image of the tripartite life – contemplative, active, and given to delight – the circular dance signifies perfection: a strife of love dominated by joy, which Ficino defines as the *summum bonum*.

Veronese did not hesitate to endow Ficino's goddess of Supreme Pleasure with the attributes of a real *voluptas*: naked and jewelled, she is seated on silk covered with luxurious fig leaves. By these tokens alone, she might be the goddess of lust; but her celestial powers are revealed by her exalted station, her noble attendants, and the incontrovertible fact that she turns her back; not to mention the winged Cupid playing the spinet: *musicam docet amor*.

The sequence of the four paintings is then as follows:

(1) The Pains of Love
(2) The Concord of Love
(3) The Pleasures of Love
(4) The Perfection of Love,

forming a circle to be read clock-wise:

2

1   3

4

The title of the whole might be *Erotomachia*, since the cycle begins and ends with a 'strife of love'.

Although some of the actors in Veronese's allegories are so vividly characterized as persons that they seem to approach the condition of portraiture, it would be rash to assume, on the visual evidence alone, that any of them were actual portraits. In the context of allegory they represent *types of character* that correspond to the states of exaltation they are meant to illustrate. Viewed as types, the chivalrous lover in fig. 46, handsome and impetuous but impeccably tactful, or the soft musing poet in fig. 47, with some of the obesity of a coloratura tenor, or the elated bridegroom in fig. 49, who accepts his victory with a touch of vainglory, are as perfectly revealed in their physiognomic traits as they are in their costumes and coiffures. The realism of these faces is a pictorial contrivance adopted from pageantry: Veronese used it to superb effect in the allegorical decorations of the Villa Maser, where the features of men that cannot possibly be portraits (as in the Stanza della Lucerna and the Stanza del Cane) are individually as marked as in our cycle (see also our fig. 76).

On the interesting provenance of these paintings, possibly commissioned by Rudolph II, acquired by Christina of Sweden after the Sack of Prague, later in the Orléans Collection (where they seem to have got their absurd names, first listed in the catalogue of 1727), see Cecil Gould, *National Gallery Catalogue of the Sixteenth-Century Venetian School* (1959), pp. 149 ff. In the last picture, the piece of paper slipped by the goddess into the hand of the poet bears an inscription that is partly effaced. Gould reads the surviving letters as: *Ch. ./(?) mi. p(ossede) (?)*, which might be a phrase from a Petrarchan love-poem (cf. Trissino, Sonnet xxii, line 7, or the like). In that case it would be in style that this most mystifying of Veronese's paintings should have been called Unfaithfulness. According to Pico della Mirandola, it is the peculiar cunning of great mystical hymns that, deprived of their transcendental dimension, they suggest 'nothing but the sheerest tales and trifles' – *fabellas nugasque meracissimas.*

PORUS CONSILII FILIUS

NOTES ON THE ORPHIC 'COUNSELS OF NIGHT'

AN extreme instance of syncretic boldness, extreme even for a Renaissance Platonist, is the inscription on a medallic portrait of Christ by the Paduan master Giovanni dal Cavino (fig. 92).[1] It reads PORUS CONSILII FILIUS and is taken from a passage in Plato's *Symposium*, 203B, where Porus, the drunken god of Affluence, is introduced as 'son of Counsel'. Habich (*Die Medaillen der italienischen Renaissance*, p. 111) was rightly startled by this inauspicious appellation of Christ, yet the argument is to be found in Pico, *Commento* II, xviii (ed. Garin II, xxi, p. 513), *Di Poro e perchè sia detto figluolo del Consiglio:* 'Since Porus is the affluence of ideas that issue from the true God, he is called son of Counsel by Plato, who imitates the sacred writings of the Hebrews, where that God is called by the same name, whence Dionysius the Areopagite says that Jesus Christ is called angel of Counsel and also messenger of God, meaning by Counsel nothing other than the first Father, God. In imitation of which Avicenna also called the first cause "counselling cause". . . .'

Pico repeated the observation in *Conclusiones . . . de modo intelligendi hymnos Orphei*, no. 17 (*Opera*, p. 107): 'Ex eisdem dictis potest intelligi, cur in Symposio a Diotima Porus consilii filius, et Iesus in sacris literis angelus magni consilii nominetur.' The statement was preceded in the *Conclusiones* by two equally extravagant propositions (nos. 15 f.), suggesting that the supreme deity hidden in darkness, who is called *Night* by the Orphics and *Ensoph* by the Cabbalists, is identical with the 'first cause' of the universe, called 'counselling cause' because it is antecedent and superior to creation itself. At first glance it might seem self-contradictory that the abyss of *Ensoph* or the Orphic *Night*, which can be worshipped only in Silence, should be identified by Pico with the 'counselling cause': but he knew from Proclus's *Commentary on the Timaeus* (ed. Diehl, 96C, 146E) that the 'counsels

---

1. G. F. Hill, *The Medallic Portraits of Christ* (1920), fig. 35.

of Night' (Νυκτὸς ὑποθῆκαι) were the primeval sources of Orphic wisdom;[2] and according to Pico it was from the wealth of these nocturnal infusions that Porus, son of Counsel, was said to be drunk. In his audacious use of these Orphic metaphors – 'counsels of Night' causing inebriation – Pico may have remembered a cunning rule proposed by Dionysius the Areopagite: that in holy matters, which necessarily transcend the powers of human reason, incongruous symbols are the best.

As a figure of speech, the drunkenness of Porus would not have offended Christian allegorists who had learned from St Jerome that the drunken Noah, for example, was an image of 'Christ drunk with his passion' (*Breviarium in Psalmos* lxxx; cf. H. Lewy, *Sobria ebrietas*, 1929, p. 162 note 1). For the Neoplatonists, too, the bacchic frenzy was a sacred state of supernatural seizure (as shown above, pages 60 ff.). They distinguished between two kinds of drunkenness (cf. Ficino, *Opera*, p. 1399; Pico, *Opera*, p. 104, *de duplici ebriatione*): the one a vulgar, 'sublunar' excess, the other the divine madness that was known to St Paul as well as to Orpheus and Plotinus, and among the Jews to Moses and David. On the authority of the Cabbala Pico claimed that the words of the Psalmist *Inebriabor ab ubertate domus tuae* (Psalms lxiv, 5, Jerome's translation) meant the same divine state of disencumbered ecstasy as was vouchsafed by God to Moses (Numbers xii, 7 f.) because he was *in omni domo mea fidelissimus*; and Pico suggested that on that biblical evidence Moses was 'little inferior to that overflowing plenitude of ineffable intelligence by which God's angels get drunk with his nectar' (*De hominis dignitate*, ed. Garin, p. 120). What the Cabbalists had called 'the purest wine' (*Conclusiones cabalisticae*, no. 17) was associated by Pico with the ritual need, supposedly discovered by Orpheus, of pairing each raging Bacchus with a spiritual Muse (*Conclusiones de modo intelligendi hymnos Orphei*, no. 24);[3] and since the Greeks knew nine Muses, it was fortunate that nine Bacchuses were invoked in the Orphic Hymns. (Their names are given by Ficino, *Theologia Platonica* IV, i, conclusion; also by

2. *Orphicorum fragmenta*, nos. 160, 166; also nos. 164 f., 167. Did Plato perhaps indulge in one of his Orphic allusions when he used the phrase 'Nocturnal Council' (νυκτερινὸς σύλλογος, which somehow recalls Νυκτὸς ὑποθήκας) for the supreme consultative assembly of the *Laws* (968A; cf. *Critias* 120B–C)?

3. This particular Orphic conclusion of Pico's (no. 24): 'Non inebriabitur per aliquem Bacchum qui suae Musae prius copulatus non fuerit', should be compared with Ficino's proposition: 'Quapropter apud Orpheum singulis Musis praeest Bacchus aliquis, quo vires illarum divinae cognitionis nectare ebriae designantur' (*Opera*, p. 131).

Gyraldus, 'Syntagma de Musis', *Opera* I, 537 f.)[4] In *De hominis dignitate* (ed. cit., pp. 122 ff.) Pico managed to throw all these witnesses into one dithyrambic sentence, which only the 'initiates' were meant to understand:

Tum Musarum dux Bacchus in suis mysteriis . . . inebriabit nos ab ubertate domus Dei, in qua tota si uti Moses erimus fideles, accedens Sacratissima Theologia duplici furore nos animabit.

The same thought expressed in *Conclusiones cabalisticae* (no. 17) sounds almost sober in comparison:

Qui sciverit quid est vinum purissimum apud Cabalistas sciet cur dixerit David: 'Inebriabor ab ubertate domus tuae', et quam ebrietatem dixerit antiquus vates Musaeus esse felicitatem, et quid significent tot Bacchi apud Orpheum.

The *vates Musaeus*, here mentioned in lieu of Moses (cf. Eusebius, *Praeparatio evangelica* IX, xxvii; *Orphicorum fragmenta*, p. 14, no. 44), a substitution that aroused the mirth of Lobeck (*Aglaophamus*, p. 353 note a), is the Eleusinian priest of whom Plato had said, not without irony (*Republic* 363C–D) although Ficino took it seriously (*Opera* II, p. 1399), that he believed in an 'immortality of drunkenness' as 'the highest meed of virtue'. (For further documents on this Musaeus see I. A. Fabricius, *Bibliotheca graeca*, I, 1790, pp. 119–23.)

In the context of a bacchic theology, the drunken Porus of the *Symposium* had a particular distinction: his divine parentage was known. He was 'son of Counsel', *Consilii filius*, that is, descended from the supreme

4. The following table lists the nine Bacchoi and their Muses in the sequence given by Ficino and Gyraldus, preceded by the numbers of the relevant Orphic Hymns. In some editions and translations of the Hymns (e.g. Abel's or Thomas Taylor's) the first hymn, being a prelude, is left unnumbered, with the result that the numbers of the other hymns are one lower than here:

ORPHIC HYMNS	BACCHOI	MUSES
no. xlvi	Licnites	Thalia
no. liv	Silenus	Euterpe
no. l	Lysius	Erato
no. lii	Trietericus	Melpomene
no. xlv	Bassareus	Clio
no. xlviii	Sabazius	Terpsichore
no. liii	Amphietus	Polyhymnia
no. xlvii	Pericionius	Urania
no. xxx	Eribromus	Calliope

wisdom hidden in that darkness which Pico revered as 'the solitary cloud of the Father': *solitaria Patris caligo*, also *caligo quam deus inhabitat* (*De hominis dignitate*, ed. cit., p. 106; *De ente et uno* v, ed. cit., p. 412). Convinced that God's counsels are concealed from man, he regarded the impossibility of attributing positive features to the divine Father of Porus as an irreducible fact of true religion, the supreme deity being approachable only through the Cloud of Unknowing: *et posuit tenebras latibulum suum* (Psalms xvii, 12; quoted in *De ente et uno*, loc. cit.).

To think of supreme wisdom without cloud or abyss seemed to Pico a philosophical folly, of which even venerable Platonists were occasionally guilty. Proclus was misguided, he thought, in projecting the ultimate counsels of God onto so familiar a figure as the classical Saturn, instead of leaving them hidden in the Orphic Night.[5] As he put it in *Conclusiones de modo intelligendi hymnos Orphei*, no. 16: 'From the preceding conclusion [that the Orphic *Night* and the cabbalistic *Ensoph* are the same] it is possible to expound more correctly than did Proclus what Orpheus meant when he said that the world's maker consulted with *Night* on the making of the world.'

In Plutarch's *De Iside et Osiride* Pico detected the same fault as he had found in Proclus, and he bluntly denounced this elaborate attempt to sanction Egyptian cults by Platonic arguments as *magnum fomentum idolatriae* (*De ente et uno* v, ed. Garin, p. 416). Considering the sacerdotal unction with which other Platonists spoke of the secret wisdom of the Egyptians, it is surprising that phrases like *non ut putant Aegyptii* slip without hesitation from Pico's pen. Almost all the *Conclusiones secundum opinionem Chaldaeorum theologorum* (*Opera*, pp. 79 f.) are directed against the Egyptian religion because it failed to rise above the cosmic order of things to what Pico called *ordo fontalis unialiter superexaltatus* (*Conclusiones ... Chaldaeorum*, no. 1). Particularly emphatic is the fifth of these 'Chaldean' propositions: that ('contrary to what Amasis the Egyptian said') the supreme source of universal order is located *super omnem intellectualem hierarchiam in abysso primae unitatis et sub caligine primarum tenebrarum imparticipaliter abscondita*.

Were it not for his peculiar contempt for the ritual tangibility of Egyptian symbols (which may help to explain his lack of interest in the hieroglyphs

---

5. For Proclus's view of Saturn as 'counselling cause', see *Orphicorum fragmenta*, nos. 129, 155. According to Pico, Saturn 'counsels' Jupiter only on the administration of the world, whereas Saturn is 'counselled' by Night on its creation. See the use of *consiglio* in *Commento* II, xvii as against II, xviii (ed. Garin II, xx f., pp. 512 and 513), where the 'angelic mind' is identical with Saturn (cf. ibid., p. 511).

of Horapollo),[6] it would be difficult to understand why Pico ignored a famous and much debated Egyptian image that bears on 'divine counsels hidden in darkness'. The god Serapis, identified by Plutarch with the classical Hades or Pluto (*De Iside et Osiride* 28; *Moralia* 361F–362A), was equipped with a triadic attribute that was taken to signify *Consilium* (see above, Appendix 4, page 259). To imagine the god of the underworld as the highest god of secret wisdom not only satisfied the mystical postulate that the opposites should coincide, but the theory rested, surprisingly enough, on the authority of Plato. For etymological as well as philosophical reasons, both given in *Cratylus* 403A–404B, Plato defined Hades, the king of the dead, as the god of supreme intelligence residing in the Beyond, from whose wonderful converse no mortal visitor has ever chosen to return. Plutarch was so profoundly pleased with this transformation of the dreaded Pluto or Hades into a benign sovereign delighting his subjects with supercelestial discourse that he quoted it twice in *De Iside et Osiride*, 29 and 78 (*Moralia* 362D, 382E–383A), first ascribing the thought to Plato, then praising it as one of the sacred truths that the Egyptian priests withhold from the vulgar. 'When the souls are set free,' he says, 'this god becomes their leader and king' who satisfies their rapturous longing for 'that beauty which is for men unutterable and indescribable'. No doubt, this sociable picture of the Beyond was much too positive for Pico's taste, who would not accept a divine ecstasy devoid of gloom and solitariness. As an Averroist and Dionysian, he hoped to lose his personal identity *in abysso primae unitatis*, vanishing into the source of all being, not by 'participating' in its glory but by dissolving into that transcendent plenitude which was *super omnem intellectualem hierarchiam . . . sub caligine primarum tenebrarum imparticipaliter abscondita* (cf. also *De hominis dignitate*, as quoted above, page 65, on the ultimate goal of self-extinction 'qua omnes animi in una mente, quae est super omnem mentem, non concordent adeo sed ineffabili quodam modo unum penitus evadant').

For such a destructive hope of divine communion the idealized Pluto, Hades, or Serapis was as inadequate a symbol of God's hidden counsels as

6. So far as I can see, a letter to Giorgio Valla, in which he asks for a copy of Horapollo (cf. P. Kibre, *The Library of Pico della Mirandola*, p. 14), is the only indication that Pico concerned himself with this book, which does not appear in the inventory of his library (ibid., p. 119 ff.) nor seems to be quoted in his works: surely a significant omission in such a determined explorer of the occult tradition. His prejudice against Egypt may have been inspired by Pletho, who extolled the Chaldean mysteries at the expense of the Egyptian, describing the latter as degraded (*Laws* III, xliii; ed. Alexandre, pp. 252 ff.).

Proclus's substitution of Saturn for the Orphic Night. Pico's distrust of these static figments seems prophetic of the later history of Pluto. In Pierio Valeriano's *Hieroglyphica* this god still signifies *occulta consilia*, but for remarkably platitudinous reasons: Pluto is now an emblem of Secret Counsel 'because the subterranean worlds, of which Pluto is said to be the god, are hidden and concealed', *quod lateant absconditaque sint* (fol. 426ᵛ, appendix by Celio Agostino Curione). That the god of hidden things is supremely wise is irrelevant to this use of the image: it merely inculcates the common rule, observed by any whispering conspirator, that counsels and deliberations require secrecy: *consilia et cogitationes occultas esse debere*. See also Gyraldus's allegorical argument (*Opera* I, 162 quoted from Servius, *In Aeneidem* VIII, 636, and particularly appreciated by Ripa, s.v. 'Consiglio') that the god Consus, a special deity for dispensing good counsels, was worshipped by the Romans underground: *ut ostendatur tectum debere esse consilium*. Whether the purveyors of these trivialities were unaware of any mystical meaning behind them, or deliberately confined themselves to the worthless crust so as to hide the true marrow from the profane (cf. above, page 17), is of course a tantalizing question with such a motto as *occulta consilia*.

Fortunately, Giovanni dal Cavino's medal provides documentary proof that Pico's paradoxes about *Consilium* and *Porus* were still alive in the late sixteenth century, but their currency may not have been very wide since the medal is of Paduan origin, and by an artist belonging to an erudite élite.[7] Although Pico had gone from Padua to Florence, where his belief in ecstasy as self-extinction was reinforced by the study of Plotinus (φυγὴ μόνου πρὸς μόνον), it is certain that his radical opinions on that subject had been formed originally in the school of Padua, the old stronghold of Averroism. However limited in circulation, the late medal does therefore suggest that Padua remained hospitable to this particular strain in Pico's thought, and perhaps more so than either Florence or Rome.

7. A medal by Giovanni dal Cavino combines his own portrait with that of the Paduan scholar Alessandro Bassiano (National Gallery of Art, Washington, no. A1127.390A, formerly Dreyfus Collection). His other medals confirm that he moved in a circle of Paduan jurists, physicians, and poets. Among Paduan artists, Andrea Riccio must have been intimately associated with Cavino and Bassiano since he made them the executors of his will (L. Planiscig, *Andrea Riccio*, 1927, pp. 371, 373, 474).

INDEXES

INDEX OF SOURCES

I. TEXTS AND PASSAGES

INDEX OF SOURCES

Alexandre, C., *see* Index I, s.v. Pletho

Alföldi, A., *Die Kontorniaten*, 145

Allen, D. C., 'The Rehabilitation of Epicurus and his Theory of Pleasure in the Early Renaissance', 70

Allen, P. S., *see* Index I, s.v. Erasmus

Altheim, F., 'Maske und Totenkult', 165

Amelung, W., *Die Skulpturen des Vatikanischen Museums*, 250

Anagnine, E., *G. Pico della Mirandola, Sincretismo religioso-filosofico*, 22, 65

Anastos, M. V., 'Pletho's Calendar and Liturgy', 244

Angeleri, C., *see* Index I, s.v. Crinito

Armand, A., *Les médailleurs italiens*, 99

Babelon, E., *La gravure en pierres fines*, 116

Baeumker, C., *see* Index I, s.v. [Hermes Trismegistus]

Bailey, N., tr. *The Colloquies of Desiderius Erasmus*, 70 f.

Baltrušaitis, J., *Anamorphoses ou Perspectives curieuses*, 223

Bandini, A. M., *Catalogus codicum Latinorum Bibliothecae Mediceae Laurentianae*, 239

See also Index I, s.v. Manuscripts, Florence

Barb, A. A., 'Diva Matrix', 137

Barnes, J. H., *see* Index I, s.v. Leone Ebreo

Baron, H., 'Aulus Gellius in the Renaissance and a Manuscript from the School of Guarino', 98

'La rinascità dell'etica statale romana nell'umanesimo fiorentino del Quattrocento', 69

Leonardo Bruni, Humanistisch-philosophische Schriften, 2 f.

Barozzi, L., and R. Sabbadini, *Studi sul Panormita e sul Valla*, 138

Bartsch, A., *Le peintre-graveur*, 91, 96, 102, 105, 176, 268, 270 f.

Baumann, Hermann, *Das doppelte Geschlecht*, 204

Bayersdorfer, A., *see* F. von Reber

Béguin, S., 'A Lost Fresco of Niccolò dell'Abbate at Bologna in Honour of Julius III', 147

Bellori, P., *Admiranda romanarum antiquitatum*, 158

Benedetto, L. F., *Il 'Roman de la rose' e la letteratura italiana*, 145

Benz, E., *Adam, der Mythus vom Urmenschen*, 212

Berkeley, George, *Siris*, 221, 244

Bernouilli, J. J., *Aphrodite*, 132, 264

Berve, H., *Dion*, 3

Bezold, C., *see* F. Boll

Bezold, F. von, *Aus Mittelalter und Renaissance*, 181, 252

Bidez, J., 'À propos d'un fragment retrouvé de l'Aristote perdu', 1

Catalogue des manuscrits alchimiques grecs, 214

'La liturgie des mystères chez les Néoplatoniciens', 6

'Le philosophe Jamblique et son école', 6

'Notes sur les mystères néoplatoniciens', 6

'Proclus, Περὶ τῆς ἱερατικῆς τέχνης', 6

Vie de l'empereur Julien, 6

Vie de Porphyre, 5 f.

Bidez, J., and F. Cumont, *Les mages hellénisés*, 154, 245, 250, 255

Blasi, B., *Stradario Romano*, 178

Blau, J. L., *The Christian Interpretation of the Cabala in the Renaissance*, 21, 54, 226

* Titles in italics refer to books, titles in quotation marks to articles. Bibliographical details are given in the first entry of the footnotes.

GENERAL INDEX

Other Paperbacks from Oxford

*

PRAETERITA:
THE AUTOBIOGRAPHY OF JOHN RUSKIN

With an introduction by KENNETH CLARK

Praeterita is one of the most remarkable autobiographies of the nineteenth century. Written in the 1880s in the periods of calm between Ruskin's raging attacks of brain fever, it gives a fascinating account of his upbringing in a severely respectable Victorian household, his Continental travels, his friends and relations, and the development and refinement of his aesthetic tastes. In it Ruskin speaks only of 'what it gives me joy to remember . . . passing in total silence things which I have no pleasure in reviewing'. Thus he includes ecstatic descriptions of the Swiss Alps or a Turner painting, but omits all reference to his disastrous marriage. Ruskin had a magnificent command of language, and this unfinished, rather impressionistic account of his life is written in a vivid, fluent style which compels the reader's attention and admiration.

PAINTING AND EXPERIENCE IN FIFTEENTH-CENTURY ITALY

A Primer in the Social History of Pictorial Style

MICHAEL BAXANDALL

'It would be hard to think of a more valuable book to put into the hands of students of Renaissance painting to sharpen their observation, widen their outlook and stimulate their curiosity.' *Burlington Magazine*

This book is both an introduction to fifteenth-century Italian painting and a primer in how to read social history out of the style of pictures. It examines the commercial practice of the early Renaissance picture trade in contracts, letters, and accounts; and it explains how the visual skills and habits evolved in the daily life of any society enter into its painters' style. Renaissance painting is related for instance to experience of such activities as preaching, dancing, and gauging barfels. Sixteen concepts used by a contemporary critic of painting are defined and illustrated, and in this way a basic fifteenth-century equipment for looking at pictures is assembled.

THE FIRE AND THE SUN

Why Plato Banished the Artists

IRIS MURDOCH

In this book, based on her 1976 Romanes Lecture, the distinguished novelist and philosopher discusses Plato's views on art and examines sympathetically the reasons for his hostility towards it. She offers a coherent and fully argued account of Plato's theories of art and of beauty and of their metaphysical background, which shows also that Plato was aware of the dangers of his own artistry. The argument more widely concerns the place of art in life, and includes brief discussion of ideas of many other thinkers, including Kant, Tolstoy, Freud, and Kierkegaard. The book also comprises in an accessible form a general view of the development of Plato's thought.

'Iris Murdoch's book is a triumph of lucid and light-textured compression as well as of vividly illustrated relevance to our own world. Her laconic and primly mocking asides are delightful.' Kathleen Nott, *New Society*

'This little monograph is meant to set out Plato's views rather than to rebut them. But discreet as it is, Iris Murdoch's counter-attack is lucid and moving.' George Steiner, *Sunday Times*

THE MIND OF THE EUROPEAN
ROMANTICS

H. G. SCHENK

With a preface by ISAIAH BERLIN

'This enthusiastic and ambitious book is certain to be a standard work on European romanticism for many years to come' Anthony Levi

Dr Schenk provides a comprehensive study of the nineteenth-century Romantic movement – in literature, painting, music, philosophy, and religion – and a detailed interpretation of all its main issues: intellectual, emotional, social, historical. The initial revolt against eighteenth-century ideas is first seen in the larger context of history, and then particular themes are examined in pen portraits of individual Romantics – Schelling, Coleridge, Lamennais, and others. This is the first paperback edition of the book in the U.K.

ARTISTIC THEORY IN ITALY 1450–1600

ANTHONY BLUNT

This book seeks to broaden the comprehension of the student of Italian Renaissance painting by concentrating not on the works of art themselves, but on the various artistic theories which influenced them or were expressed by them. Taking Alberti's treatises as his starting-point, Anthony Blunt traces the development of artistic theory from Humanism to Mannerism. He discusses the writings of Leonardo, Savanarola, Michelangelo, and Vasari, examines the effect of The Council of Trent on religious art, and chronicles the successful struggle of the painters and sculptors themselves to elevate their status from craftsmen to creative artists.

THE ROMANTIC AGONY

Mario Praz

'*The Romantic Agony* is now a classic in a sense which places it among such books as have, in the depth of their insights, power to alter a reader's understanding of the history of his society, and perhaps of his own history.' Frank Kermode

In his remarkable study, Mario Praz has described the whole Romantic literature under one of its most characteristic aspects, that of erotic sensibility. This 'exceedingly learned, informative book' (*New Statesman*) is, in effect, an analysis of a mood in literature – one which, however transient, was widespread. Expressed in dreams of 'luxurious cruelties', 'fatal women', corpse-passions, and sinful agonies of delight, the mood – as seen in the influence of Byron and De Sade – had a major effect on poets and painters of the nineteenth century. And the affinities between them and their twentieth-century counterparts make Professor Praz's account of the Romantic–Decadents 'one of the indispensable guides', as Frank Kermode observes, 'to the study of our own literature and our own epoch'.

First published in 1933, *The Romantic Agony* was reissued in 1951 in a second edition containing much new material, and was further revised in 1970, when Frank Kermode's Foreword was also included for the first time. It has been translated from the Italian by Angus Davidson.

THE PRINCIPLES OF ART

R. G. COLLINGWOOD

This treatise on aesthetics is perhaps the most important of all R. G. Collingwood's books. It begins by showing that the word 'art' is used as a name not only for 'art proper', but also for certain things which are 'art falsely so called'. These are (a) craft or skill, (b) magic, and (c) amusement. Each of these, by confusion with art proper, generates a false aesthetic theory. In the course of attacking these theories the author criticizes the current psychological theories of art, offers a new theory of magic, and reinterprets Plato's so-called 'attack on art', showing that it has been entirely misunderstood. Art proper has two characteristics: it is imagination and expression. In explaining what these terms mean the author attacks the modern doctrine of 'sensa' and demands a return to Hume, whose most important contentions are neglected by his professed disciples today. Finally, important inferences are drawn concerning the position of art in human society.